OUT OF THE MUCK

OUT OF THE MUCK

A History of the Broward Sheriff's Office, 1915–2000

William P. Cahill

Robert M. Jarvis

CAROLINA ACADEMIC PRESS

Durham, North Carolina

Library of Congress Cataloging-in-Publication Data

Cahill, William P.
 Out of the muck : a history of the Broward Sheriff's Office, 1915-2000 /
William P. Cahill, Robert M. Jarvis.
  p. cm.
 Includes bibliographical references and index.
 ISBN 978-1-59460-584-0 (alk. paper)
 1. Broward County (Fla.) Sheriff's Dept.--History. 2. Sheriffs--Florida--
Broward County. I. Jarvis, Robert M., 1959- II. Title.
 HV8145.F6C33 2010
 363.28'209759350904--dc22

                                   2009048882

On the front cover: The Broward Sheriff's Department "Brahman bull" patch (1935). This insignia was used until 1959 and paid homage to the county's agricultural roots. (Courtesy of Jay Harris/Patch Me Thru)

On the back cover: The Broward Sheriff's Office "Pride in Service with Integrity" logo (2007). This mark was adopted after Alfred T. Lamberti was named interim sheriff. (Courtesy of the Broward Sheriff's Office)

CAROLINA ACADEMIC PRESS
700 Kent Street
Durham, North Carolina 27701
Telephone (919) 489-7486
Fax (919) 493-5668
www.cap-press.com

Printed in the United States of America

For Joan and Judith

We are soon forgotten, even those that for a moment seem big among us.

Arthur Brisbane
Fort Lauderdale Sentinel, May 18, 1923

CONTENTS

LIST OF ILLUSTRATIONS

FOREWORD

For most of American history, the county sheriff shaped the operation of the criminal justice system. To be sure, legislators made state law; prosecutors and state attorneys proffered charges; and judges and juries determined the guilt of defendants and dispensed punishment. But county sheriffs, particularly in more rural regions, have served as the key "gatekeepers" of the legal system. Until relatively recently, when municipal police departments began to supplant county sheriff's offices, the local sheriff, more than any other public official, determined which laws were to be rigidly enforced, which were to be selectively enforced, and which fell into abeyance.

Without law enforcers, the criminal law was inert. And without sheriffs to apprehend suspects, there were no defendants in most jurisdictions; hence, the work of prosecutors, judges, and jurors depended on the activities of local sheriffs. African-Americans were especially aware of the power of sheriffs. During the Reconstruction era, for example, violent battles over voting rights often hinged on the election of local sheriffs, who then either safeguarded minority rights or permitted the legal system to preserve racial discrimination, regardless of the letter of the law. Likewise, Southern sheriffs played central roles in lynchings during the late 19th and early 20th centuries, by being complicit in the violence or by using their authority to persuade lynch mobs to stand down.

Despite the enormous influence of county sheriffs, historians have largely overlooked these law enforcers. The legislative process and law formation have commanded great attention from legal scholars. Similarly, the operation of the courts, the judicial and social philosophies of judges, and even the means through which juries reach verdicts and make sentencing recommendations, have been analyzed in considerable depth. Although numerous studies of individual crimes and court cases have noted the important role of local sheriffs, these officials have received surprisingly little systematic attention from historians.

Thus, *Out of the Muck: A History of the Broward Sheriff's Office, 1915–2000* is a welcome addition and contributes to our understanding of the legal, political, and institutional histories of Broward County and of the state of Florida. William P. Cahill and Robert M. Jarvis offer encyclopedic coverage, including detailed biographical sketches of every Broward County sheriff and careful examinations of the elections and appointments that carried these men to office.

Written in the tradition of local history, the narrative is solidly grounded, using a wealth of government reports, legal records, newspaper clippings, and official correspondence. In addition, it tells an engaging story, complete with larger-than-life characters, vicious criminals, and strident reformers. Among others, Lucky Luciano, Al Capone, Geraldo Rivera, and the rap musicians *2 Live Crew* pass through its pages. *Out of the Muck* discusses corruption scandals, gambling syndicates, prostitution rings, and racial violence, focusing on the role of Broward County's sheriffs in either bringing the criminals to justice or participating in their illegal activities. Furthermore, in charting the history of the Broward County sheriff's office, the authors recount the history of South Florida, particularly the region's transformation from an underdeveloped backwater at the start of the 20th century to a major cosmopolitan population center by the close of the century.

Although Dr. Cahill and Professor Jarvis document the increasing modernization and professionalization of local law enforcement, they also explore the seamier side and the pressures that contributed to the successes, failures, and recurring corruption scandals in the Sheriff's Office. For instance, they identify the sheriffs who participated in racial violence and whose tenures were marred by scandal, such as the three sheriffs indicted while in office and the fourth who went directly from his post to prison. Again and again, the text suggests the ways in which partisan politics shaped the operations of the Sheriff's Office and therefore the criminal justice system in Broward County.

Even as they recount colorful tales about crime and punishment, and as they carefully describe changes in budgets, equipment, and personnel in the Sheriff's Office, the authors underscore the dangers inherent in a system in which the chief law enforcer, as an elected official, is yoked to partisan politics. In sum, *Out of the Muck* simultaneously tells a fascinating story of local development and provides an intriguing glimpse into the political and institutional battles that shaped law enforcement in South Florida. This is a book about Broward County, about Florida politics, and about the ways in which political and legal forces conflicted and collided.

Jeffrey S. Adler
Professor of History and Criminology
University of Florida

PREFACE

Of all the types of law enforcement officers in the United States, the one with the most storied pedigree is the sheriff. Although now popularly associated with either the lawless Old West of the 19th century or the racist Deep South of the 20th century, the office actually traces its roots to 10th century England, where each "shire" was headed by a local official known as a "reeve," whose duties included collecting taxes, keeping the peace, and serving writs.[1] In time, the unwieldy phrase "shire reeve" was shortened to "sheriff," and it is from this root that we get the word "shrievalty," which denotes the jurisdiction served by a particular sheriff.

Although sheriffs are still found in nearly all common law countries, there is considerable variation in their modern functions and responsibilities, which run the gamut from administrative (Australia, Canada, and Ireland) to ceremonial (England, India, and Wales) to judicial (Scotland). In the United States, however, the title is most often used to denote the chief law enforcement officer of a county (although in some counties the criminal law enforcement responsibilities of the sheriff's office—and sometimes even its jail keeping duties—have been taken over by other agencies). In addition, the United States is nearly alone in its practice of electing sheriffs.

The first American sheriffs appeared in Virginia in the 17th century. Like their English counterparts, they were local officials who collected taxes and enforced laws, but they also handled prisoners and ran the jails. Beginning in the 18th century, the practice of appointing sheriffs gradually fell into disfavor, and the position increasingly became an elected one. By the time of the Revolutionary War, the office was well-entrenched throughout the colonies, and has remained remarkably unchanged during the past 200 years.

Today, there are approximately 3,000 sheriffs in the United States, collectively employing some 150,000 deputies. With the exceptions of Alaska (which never has had sheriffs and instead uses state troopers) and Connecticut (where the office was abolished in 2000 following a series of scandals), sheriffs can be found in every state (although in Hawaii they are part of the department of public safety). In some jurisdictions, the office's formal name is "high sheriff," although this term now is almost never used in everyday conversation. By the same token, the words "under-sheriff" and "vice sheriff," which refer to a sheriff's second-in-command, also have fallen into disuse (normally being replaced by the more familiar "chief deputy").

In Florida, the office is referenced in the state constitution, which requires counties to elect a sheriff once every four years.[2] Because the constitution also es-tablishes the separate posts of property appraiser and tax collector, Florida's sher-iffs no longer perform the duties of these offices, but instead focus on arresting lawbreakers, operating jails, serving warrants, and assisting the local courts.[3]

Despite their importance in everyday life, most members of the public know very little about sheriffs. Indeed, when the average citizen thinks about sheriffs at all, he or she is more likely to think of a fictional sheriff—such as the wise Andrew J. "Andy" Taylor (*The Andy Griffith Show*), the befuddled J.W. Pepper (*Live and Let Die*), the buffoonish Rosco P. Coltrane (*The Dukes of Hazzard*), the foul-mouthed Buford T. Justice (*Smokey and the Bandit*), the scheming Elroy P. Lobo (*B.J. and the Bear*), or the fabled Sheriff of Nottingham (Robin Hood's arch nemesis)—than a real-life sheriff like Patrick F. Garrett, William B. "Bat" Masterson, or Buford H. Pusser (who many viewers know only though his on-screen portrayal by Joe Don Baker in the movie *Walking Tall*).

The public's lack of awareness is due, at least in part, to the absence of shrieval scholarship. Indeed, for many years, the only readily available work was a treatise aimed primarily at lawyers.[4] In the last ten years, however, this state of affairs has begun to change due to the appearance of a national sheriffs' his-tory[5] as well as two guides to Florida's sheriffs.[6] Still more books have appeared about individual sheriffs (many of them autobiographies) or specific depart-ments (including a series by the Turner Publishing Company of Paducah, Ken-tucky, that features a number of Florida titles).

The history of the Broward Sheriff's Office dates from 1915, when Aden W. Turner was overwhelmingly elected the county's first sheriff. In 1922, Turner was suspended by Governor Cary A. Hardee for failing to do enough to curb crime, a decision that was confirmed the next year by the Florida Senate. By and large, Turner's successors turned out to be even worse, with three of them— Paul C. Bryan, Walter R. Clark, and Allen B. Michell—being indicted while in office and a fourth—Kenneth C. "Ken" Jenne II—being sent to prison after pleading guilty to mail and tax fraud.

Curiously, despite its long and colorful history, no previous work has at-tempted to tell the story of the Broward Sheriff's Office. As such, we hereby offer this book. Its title (for those who may be wondering) reflects the historical facts that Broward County was partially formed out of the muck of a massive state dredging project and the Broward Sheriff's Office has had to repeatedly drag itself out of the muck of scandal.

Andy Griffith, in his role as the sheriff of the fictional town of Mayberry, North Carolina (c. 1965), and William B. "Bat" Masterson, sheriff of Ford County (Dodge City), Kansas (1878–80)

In preparing this work, we received help from many people, including Vickie Allan (Maryland State Archives), Larry Atwell (Broward County Library), Steve Belleme (Broward County Aviation Department), Aida Borras (Dade County Medical Examiner's Office), Denyse M. Cunningham (Broward County Historical Commission), Joyce R. Dewsbury (University of Florida Archives), Valerie A. Emhof (State Archives of Florida), Stacie A. Faulds (Greater Fort Lauderdale Convention & Visitors Bureau), Dolly J. Gibson (Broward County Supervisor of Elections' Office), F.J. "Jay" Harris (Patch Me Thru), Christopher B. Havern (United States Coast Guard), Jane Hidalgo (Broward County Sheriff's Office), Gertrude Laframboise (Rollins College), Broward County Historian Helen Landers, Lynne C. Martzall (Broward County Sheriff's Office), C. Allen Pylman (Utica Police Department), Merrilyn Rathbun (Fort Lauderdale Historical Society), Alechia E. Smith (Duke University), and Joe Williams (Broward County Sheriff's Office). We also wish to thank our publisher, Carolina Academic Press, for embracing our manuscript and supporting us at every turn.

William P. Cahill
Bluff City, Tennessee

Robert M. Jarvis
Fort Lauderdale, Florida
July 1, 2009

OUT OF THE MUCK

CHAPTER 1

THE SOUTHERN FRONTIER (PRIOR TO 1900)

It was 1890 and the frontier was gone! At least, so declared Robert P. Porter, the superintendent of the U.S. Census, who officially reported the closing of the American frontier in that year.[7] Undoubtedly, he was looking westward when he made his pronouncement, for the Wild West indeed had been settled. Railroads connected regions that earlier could be reached only through arduous travel, while forts and trading posts had grown into cities and towns. Had Porter's glance wandered in a southerly direction, however, he might have noticed that the entire region of South Florida was still an American frontier in every meaning of the word.

For most Americans, thinking about the Old West conjures up images of struggling pioneers facing myriad difficulties. During the 1800s, the Western frontier was a place of lynchings, outlaws, vigilantes, and general lawlessness. And the men who wore the badges, whose job it was to handle these problems, were often little different than the men they hunted (and who occasionally hunted them). Yet even a cursory look at South Florida in the 19th century makes it clear that all of these conditions were present not only in the "Wild West," but in the "Wild South" as well. And on this Southern frontier, many of the problems would continue well into the 20th century.

Perhaps the only element of frontier life that finished earlier in Florida than in the West was Indian attacks, for the third and last Seminole War (1855–58) occurred more than three decades before Wounded Knee (1890), the final conflict of the Indian wars in the West. By then, such hostilities had exerted a tremendous influence on the development of Florida, and would continue to do so for years to come.

Florida's Indian conflicts were unique in several ways. For one thing, these wars technically never came to an end, for the Seminoles never surrendered and no final peace treaty was ever signed (thereby giving the tribe a special place in Native American history). And the Second Seminole War (1835–42), known throughout the nation as the "Florida War," was longer and more ex-

3

Robert P. Porter (second from right, pointing),
U.S. Superintendent of the Census (1889–93)

pensive than any Indian war ever fought on the Western frontier, with 1,500 soldiers killed and a cost that exceeded $20 million.

Indian wars in the West resulted in such names as Crazy Horse, Geronimo, and Sitting Bull gaining widespread fame, although each of these valiant warriors ultimately found it necessary to yield to the overwhelming might of the U.S. Army. In contrast, Florida's most famous Indian leader, the Seminole chief Osceola, never gave up.

Seminole Indian Chief Osceola (1804–38)

In fact, his capture in October 1837 was viewed as a national disgrace, for Major General Thomas S. Jesup seized Osceola as he approached under a flag of truce. Of course, time has somewhat evened the score. While few remember Jesup, by the end of the 20th century Osceola's name graced "20 towns, three counties, two townships, one borough, two lakes, two mountains, a state park and a national forest."[8]

Although most people living in South Florida are unfamiliar with the details of the Indian wars that plagued the region in the 19th century, they are quite familiar with the tangible by-products of these conflicts. In 1838, volunteers from Tennessee toiled to create a road upon which troops could move through Florida's wilderness, and the result of their labors is the aptly-named "Military Trail." Similarly, Fort Lauderdale, Broward's best-known city, started as an actual military base erected by Major William Lauderdale during the Second Seminole War. The name "Fort Lauderdale" was chosen when the town was incorporated in March 1911, and periodic efforts to drop the word "Fort" have consistently failed. Likewise, Lake Worth, a prominent feature of the South Florida landscape, was named by Seminole War troops in honor of Brigadier General William J. Worth.

The West had "Custer's Last Stand," one of the best known incidents in American history, in which Major General George A. Custer and all of his troops lost their lives. While not as famous as the Battle of the Little Bighorn, a similar military disaster occurred in South Florida during the 19th century, one that came to be known as "Dade's Massacre."

In December 1835, at the start of the Second Seminole War, Major Francis L. Dade and the men under him were ambushed by Indians as they made their way from Tampa to Ocala. More than 100 soldiers were killed, including their commander. The following year, the Florida legislature dubbed a newly formed county in honor of Dade, and the territory that comprises Broward County today was originally part of a massive Dade County (which itself was carved out of a county named for President James Monroe).

The Indian Wars ended in Florida decades before they did in the American West, but in most other respects frontier life continued in South Florida long after the Western frontier closed. One of the principal factors in the settlement of the West was the coming of the railroad, which turned cowtowns into centers of commerce and was immortalized by the driving of the golden spike at Promontory Summit, Utah, in May 1869. In contrast, a railroad route connecting Fort Lauderdale and Miami to the rest of the country would not be built until nearly three decades later.

Without a railroad, South Florida remained a sparsely populated frontier even after many of the notoriously wild towns of the West had grown into thriving communities. By 1876, Dodge City, Kansas, had a population of 1,200 people, and five years later Tombstone, Arizona, held over 6,000 hardy souls. And when the Western frontier was declared non-existent in 1890, Wichita, Kansas, was a flourishing city with about 24,000 residents. Yet at the start of the 20th century, the entire area of present day Broward County had a population of slightly less than 200 people (of whom about 125 lived in Fort Lauderdale).

Monument honoring Major Francis L. Dade in Bushnell, Florida,
near the site of his death (erected 1922)

Another frontier staple was cowboys. Although these rough and ready men have come to be viewed as a Western phenomenon, South Florida had its own range riders. In fact, the open range was so much a part of Florida that it was not until 1949 that the state legislature passed a law forbidding cattle owners from letting their livestock roam free.[9]

Indeed, when the Western frontier became too tame, Frederic Remington, the American artist most closely associated with the Old West, turned to Florida for inspiration. In 1895, he traveled south instead of west, and the result was an illustrated article in *Harper's New Monthly Magazine* entitled "Cracker Cowboys of Florida." Describing his first encounter with two Florida cowboys who had come into town, Remington declared that "the only things they did which were conventional were to tie their ponies up by the head in brutal disregard, and then get drunk in about fifteen minutes."[10]

Where there are cowboys and herds roaming free, one should not be surprised to find cattle rustlers and range wars. And, in fact, both were common in Florida in the late 19th century, as Remington quickly discovered.

Downtown Fort Lauderdale (1900)

Frederic Remington's "Cracker Cowboys of Florida" (1895)

Frederic Remington's "Fighting Over a Stolen Herd" in Florida (1895)

In October 1881, the legendary "Gunfight at the O.K. Corral," which pitted the Clantons against the Earps, took place in Tombstone. By then, however, Florida had recorded an even bloodier feud, one that had occurred a decade earlier and resulted in twice as many deaths.

Like its Arizona counterpart, the Florida vendetta involved two families who, at least nominally, were on different sides of the law. In 1868, David W. Mizell was appointed sheriff of Orange County while his brother was made a judge. Two years later, a full-blown war was touched off when Sheriff Mizell was ambushed and killed by an unknown assailant. After Judge John R. Mizell took it upon himself to name a replacement for his late brother, the new sheriff immediately formed a posse—or, as the official history of the Orange County Sheriff's Office describes the group, "a vigilante mob."[11] Within a short period of time, at least seven members and associates of the Barber family turned up dead. The first two victims were summarily executed, while most of the others were listed as killed while trying to escape from the custody of the sheriff.

Years later, Judge Mizell, widely known as a "two-gun man,"[12] settled in the area that eventually became Broward County. When the town of Pompano was incorporated in June 1908, he was elected its first mayor. Mizell's reputation as a gunman, however, paled beside that of one of the quietest, most unassuming men in Broward County at the time—George T. Hinkle, who operated a grocery store on Northwest Fourth Street in Fort Lauderdale until his death in 1922.

David W. Mizell, sheriff of Orange County, Florida (1868–70)

Although he was never a law enforcement officer in Florida, Hinkle was perhaps the toughest sheriff who ever lived in Broward County. He had been a scout and an officer during the Indian Wars in the West, but it was as a Dodge City lawman that he would be best remembered. In November 1879, while working as a bartender, Hinkle handily defeated Bat Masterson, who was then at the height of his fame, in the race for county sheriff. Hinkle held this post for four years, and during his tenure built a well-deserved reputation as someone who could handle even the wildest cowboy or desperado.

One historian, comparing Florida's frontier lawlessness in the late 1800s to that of the American West, described South Florida as a place "where cattle wars, family feuds, rustling, assassinations, vigilantes, hangings, lynchings, cowtown duels, and fence-cuttings abounded."[13] From such accounts, the similarities between the Western frontier and Florida's frontier are unmistakable. But it is equally apparent that Florida was *not* the West but the South—and in many respects, the *deep* South. Even Remington alluded to this fact when, in comparing Western cowboys to cracker cowboys, he noted about the latter that "there is also a noticeable absence of negroes among them, as they still retain some *ante bellum* theories."[14]

What did this frontier mentality, coupled with a negative sentiment toward African-Americans, mean for South Florida law enforcement? It meant that during the 19th and early 20th centuries, many of the area's law enforcement officers would be harsh men, difficult to distinguish from the region's law-breakers—indeed, they would sometimes be one and the same. Just as in the Old West, where a man might be a gunslinger one year and the sheriff the next, so too some of the early law enforcement officers in Broward County would be, as described by one observer, thugs with badges.[15] It also meant that the term "redneck sheriff," which today is a caricature ridiculed in the popular media, became an accepted—and frightening—reality in South Florida.

It would be many years before the Broward Sheriff's Office would begin to change. Although there is no reason to believe that it was any worse than most other Southern sheriff's departments in the early 20th century, there is certainly substantial evidence (such as the removal of its first sheriff and the indictment of his two immediate successors) that suggests it was far from the best. And yet, despite being mired in scandals and corruption for much of its existence, by the end of the 20th century the Broward Sheriff's Office had evolved into a modern, professional law enforcement agency, "the largest fully accredited sheriff's office in the United States."[16]

CHAPTER 2

Frontier Justice (1900–15)

From the beginning, Western frontier towns were filled with vice, and cowboys, homesteaders, and sheepherders were all subject to its siren call whenever they visited. The same was true on the South Florida frontier.

But as the 20th century dawned, a spirit of change began to sweep through the country, leading Congress to enact far-reaching legislation designed to protect both consumers and workers. Most Americans applauded these initiatives, for they had come to view government as having a responsibility for improving their daily lives.

In certain instances, however, the reform movement was greeted with a colder welcome, such as when it pushed for laws aimed at eradicating drinking, gambling, and prostitution. Although local newspapers and the Sunday pulpits were uniform in their condemnation of these indulgences, the people of South Florida were ambivalent about them. In October 1913, for example, when the citizens of Dade County (which at the time included present-day Broward County) agreed to ban alcohol, the vote was surprisingly close, with 978 "for" and 863 "against" (a margin of 53%–47%).

Because of the public's conflicted attitude, the vice laws would prove to be a continuing headache for Broward's early lawmen. As a result, some turned a blind eye, others opted for selective enforcement, and a few went so far as to use their positions to promote the very activities they were hired to fight. Still, when it came time to report arrests, vice crimes consistently topped all others.

In addition to its criminal and social effects, vice affected the area's politics, and for a time even held up the creation of Broward County. As originally constituted, Dade County stretched from Stuart to the Upper Keys, taking in all of what later became Broward County. Because of its massive size and small number of law enforcement officers, Dade County operated in a very rough-and-tumble fashion. After the county seat was transferred from Miami to Juno in February 1889, for example, all of the governmental records had to be moved clandestinely, under cover of darkness, for fear of violence on the part of gun-toting Miamians. Likewise, when the Florida East Coast Railway bypassed Juno a decade later, causing Miami to again become the county seat in May 1899, the jail cells in Juno were put on a barge and towed back to Miami (with, according to some reports, prisoners still inside them).

Adding to Dade County's problems was a budding rivalry between its two major population centers—Lake Worth (to the north) and Miami (to the south). As the tensions increased, calls for a divorce grew steadily louder. Finally, in April 1909, the Florida Legislature put an end to the feud by creating Palm Beach County.

In the meantime, a population boom had begun in Fort Lauderdale, caused by the state's decision in 1906 to drain the Everglades. This massive reclamation effort, a favored project of Governor Napoleon B. Broward (who from 1888 to 1894, and again from 1897 to 1901, had been the sheriff of Duval County in Jacksonville), resulted in the creation of acres and acres of rich farmland and attracted thousands of settlers. By 1913, these new residents were ready for their own county, one that would extend from Fort Lauderdale south to Hallandale.

Although local public opinion strongly favored the idea of a new county, the legislation authorizing a referendum on the question required near-unanimous approval (due to the gerrymandering efforts of politicians who opposed any partition). Thus, in July 1913, despite 234 "yes" votes and only 89 "no" votes (a margin of 72%–28%), the proposal failed.

Three months later, Dade County faced its third showdown over the issue of prohibition. By narrow margins in 1907 and 1909, the county had voted to remain wet. Now, the outcome was reversed, with the winning edge supplied by the teetotalers of Dania, Fort Lauderdale, and Hallandale. Stunned by this outcome, the wets went to court, claiming that the election had failed to follow proper procedure, but lost.[17]

Unable to overturn the results of the prohibition election, the wets switched tactics and began trying to annul the partition election. Their reasoning is easy to understand—if Broward actually had become a separate county back in July, its votes in the October prohibition election would be thrown out and alcohol would still be legal in what was left of Dade County. When these efforts failed, the wets decided to join forces with the drys. Although their motives differed, both groups wanted a separate county, a goal they realized in 1915.

By now, Deerfield and Pompano (both of which were in Palm Beach County) had been added to the proposed county's area, bringing its population to 4,700. They joined the towns of Dania, Fort Lauderdale, and Hallandale, as well as the communities of Colohatchee, Davie, and Progresso. The original name chosen was "Everglades County," a term that was being used by the *Fort Lauderdale Sentinel* as late as January 1915. However, sentiment soon shifted in favor of the ultimate designation, "Broward County," in honor of Governor Broward, who had died in 1910 and without whom the area, quite literally, would not exist.

A map of northern Dade County (1900)

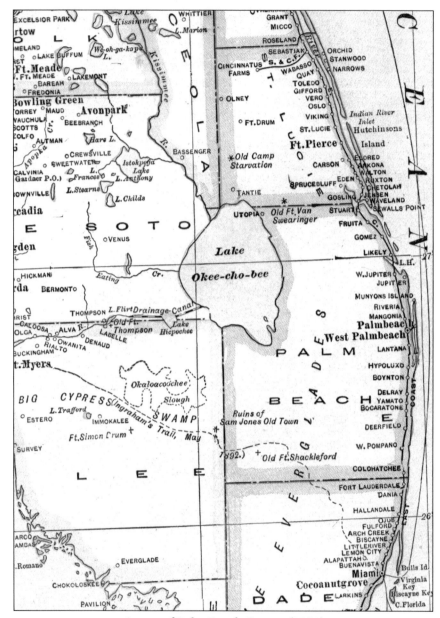

A map of Palm Beach County (1909)

On Friday, April 23, 1915, a headline in the *Fort Lauderdale Sentinel* announced that "Broward County is Assured." A week later, another proclaimed "Fort Lauderdale a County Seat," accompanied by the prediction that Broward

Florida Governor Napoleon B. Broward (standing, far right)
touring the Everglades (1906)

was "a county destined to become in the near future one of the best counties in the state."[18]

In addition to the creation of the county, two other events took place in 1915 that were to have a profound influence upon the area's development. The first was the inauguration of bus service between Fort Lauderdale and Miami.

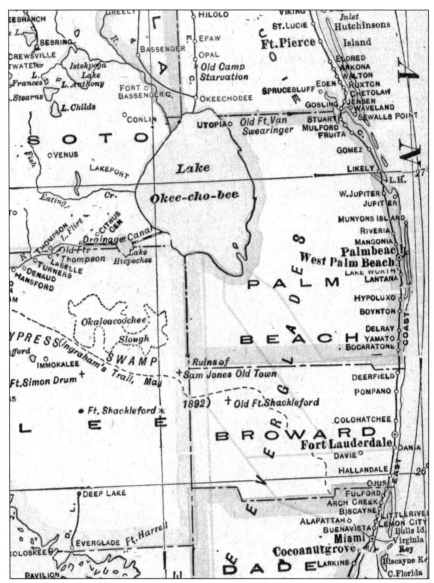

A map of Broward County (1915)

The White Star Auto Line began scheduling trips every two hours in what were described as its "new auto cars,"[19] which seated twelve people and had space in the rear for luggage. These vehicles traveled at thirty miles per hour and charged passengers three cents a mile.

A White Star Auto Line bus in the Everglades (1916)

The second significant advancement was the opening of the Dixie Highway, which connected Chicago to Miami. Following the roadway's dedication on Friday, October 8th, its entire length was traveled by a parade of intrepid motorists. Three weeks later, when this caravan of "Pathfinders" reached Fort Lauderdale, a reporter described Dixie as "one of the longest and most important [roads] in the United States."[20]

Not many years before, horses and stagecoaches had been the predominant modes of travel in Broward County. Now, the area was fully accessible by automobile and connected to Miami by bus as well as by rail. Moreover, it had abundant agricultural opportunities, a growing population, and a nascent tourism industry. The net result was that Broward was no longer a region of small frontier outposts but a community ready to take on the responsibilities of modern self-government. But first, the people would need to pick their leaders.

On Saturday, June 12, 1915, a primary was held to choose candidates for the county's various offices. As everyone knew, this was a *de facto* election, for Governor Park Trammell had promised to appoint the winners to their respective posts as soon as the county officially came into existence. In analyzing the results, the *Fort Lauderdale Sentinel* noted that "[v]ery little mud-slinging was indulged in and the losing candidates accepted defeat gracefully."[21] Among

"The Pathfinders" arriving in Dania (1915)

those chosen was a local businessman and farmer, Aden W. Turner, who was destined to have a long and colorful career as Broward's first sheriff.

Before Turner took office, the area that would become Broward County was not without law enforcement—but it was certainly stretched pretty thin, and the fact that the sheriff and county jail were in Miami only made things worse. The Dade County sheriff assigned deputies to the northern regions, of course, but their designated territories were huge. In 1910, for example, Deputy Kossie A. Goodbread was responsible for covering the area from Hallandale all the way up to the Palm Beach County line.

Prior to 1915, there were only three incorporated jurisdictions in the territory that would become Broward County: Dania (chartered in 1904), Pompano (1908), and Fort Lauderdale (1911). Each of these had its own town marshal, but law enforcement for the vast unincorporated areas was the responsibility of the Dade County sheriff. Soon after Fort Lauderdale was incorporated, the town council offered Deputy Goodbread the position of town marshal, and he gladly accepted. Not only was the patrol area much smaller, but the job came with a very attractive salary: $40 per month, plus $1 for each arrest and $10 for expenses.

Unfortunately, the lack of a local jail meant that when the marshal did make an arrest, he had to lock up the prisoner in a railroad boxcar. Then, using the one phone in town, he would have to call the Dade County sheriff in Miami to come and pick up the prisoner.

Park Trammell, governor of Florida (1913–17)

As the town's only paid employee, the marshal had a host of responsibilities in addition to law enforcement. He had to supervise the local roadwork, which was done by convicts leased from the state. He was both the tax assessor and the tax collector. He also was responsible for garbage collection, and the town council eventually ordered him to increase the frequency of trash pickups to twice a week. Undoubtedly, however, the least attractive duty facing Goodbread was making sure that the outhouses were cleaned regularly and their contents hauled away. Not surprisingly, the astute lawman always managed to keep at least one prisoner on hand to drive the town's "sanitary mule."[22]

Goodbread served as Fort Lauderdale's town marshal from March 1911 to April 1913. Like his contemporaries in early Broward law enforcement, he was a hard man. After meeting him in 1954, when he was eighty-three, an interviewer exclaimed: "This was a tough frontier village and a policeman's lot was not a happy one. The commercial fishermen were a wild lot, young and full of whiskey and violence. Goodbread carried a gun and a club, and used the club freely."[23]

But Goodbread at least had a boxcar in which to keep his prisoners — not every Broward lawman was so fortunate. When Dania was organized in November 1904, its town marshal was P.H. Hart. After making his first arrest, Hart had to chain his prisoner to a tree to await the Dade County sheriff's arrival from Miami. During the inevitable delay, the man got away.

In retrospect, there is perhaps an element of comedy in the escape of a suspect bound to a tree. However, the early history of law enforcement in Dania was marked by significant tragedy as well. One of Hart's successors, Town Marshal John Clifton, was shot and killed in March 1914 while handling a domestic dispute. In August 1915, his replacement, William L. Cox, was killed dealing with the same type of incident. These were the first and second law enforcement officers to die in the line of duty in the region that would become Broward County.

Traces of the frontier obviously still lingered in the area during the first decades of the 20th century, and the job of law enforcement attracted many of the same types of men as had policed the Western frontier a generation earlier. In order for a marshal or sheriff to survive, he had to be tough, whether the troublemakers were cowboys in Tombstone or fishermen in Fort Lauderdale. Many early law enforcement officers in Broward, including those in the Sheriff's Office, were products of a frontier atmosphere, coupled with a Deep South mentality, and this made them not only tough, but at times brutal and lawless as well.

Some also were on the take and a few even participated directly in criminal enterprises. Of Broward's first three elected sheriffs, one would be removed from office for allowing illegal activities to go unchecked; another would be arrested, along with his entire department, by federal prohibition agents; and the third would be suspended from office twice, condemned by J. Edgar Hoover, investigated by the Kefauver Organized Crime Commission, and indicted for gambling. During this same period, one chief deputy would be tried for first degree murder while another would be suspected of conducting a lynching.

William L. Cox, town marshal of Dania (1914–15)

Ultimately, none of these men would stand convicted of anything. Even when a deputy admitted he had beaten up a disabled war veteran who had cursed at him, he was quickly exonerated by a local jury, who accepted the officer's explanation that his honor required him to hit the fellow. These were different times, and the standards of acceptable behavior for law enforcement personnel obviously were not all that demanding.

Today, most of Broward County's early sheriffs and their deputies would be regarded as bigots, and the manner in which they dealt with the county's African-American citizens would be viewed as indefensible (as well as criminal). Their actions and attitudes reflected the mores of a very troubled period, an era in which a racially segregated Florida was home to many significant injustices. Many years earlier, U.S. Senator William H. Seward (R-N.Y.) had declared that "no man who spells Negro with two *gs* will ever be elected President of the United States,"[24] but that caveat did not apply to Florida's sheriffs, as is testified to by much of the correspondence that passed through the Broward Sheriff's Office during its first two decades.

The prejudices of this period were quite pronounced. The Ku Klux Klan was reborn in America in the same year that Broward County came into existence, and in the period from 1921 to 1926 it reached its greatest strength, claiming a national membership of five million. Although the Klan is best known for its hatred of African-Americans, it had more than enough venom to also inflict great harm on Catholics and Jews, as well as the occasional "un-American" foreigner.

Lynching was a "punishment" often employed by Klansmen and like-thinkers, particularly in the South. Although African-Americans were lynched with far greater frequency than any other group, they were not alone (more than 3,000 hangings took place between the 1880s and the 1960s). In August 1915, for example, Leo Frank, a 31-year-old Jewish pencil factory manager, was lynched in Marietta, Georgia, amidst a wave of anti-Semitic public sentiment, just four months after the legislation creating Broward County was passed. Lynch mobs did their dirty work in South Florida on a number of occasions during the 1920s and 1930s, and several made the news in Broward County (with at least one "succeeding" in the murder of its helpless victim).

In Miami, the Klan held annual open air ceremonies to induct new members and regularly drew large crowds. During one such spectacle in May 1923, Klansmen held a parade through the city's business district escorted by police officers on motorcycles. They then went across the causeway to Palm Island, where they initiated 150 new members. The ceremony began with the burning of a cross at least twenty feet high, which could be seen from a great distance. Spectators were not allowed on the island during the ceremony, but were able to observe the rituals from across the water. Thousands of people turned out to witness the goings on, leading to a major traffic jam that involved an estimated 2,500 cars.

Fifteen years later, the Klan was still making news in Miami. In May 1938, its members threatened two Filipino sailors (Pedro Acoba and Francaskio Rubia) who were serving aboard the U.S. Coast Guard cutter MOJAVE. The ship's commander, C.H. Abel, demanded action from local law enforcement officials and promised that if none was forthcoming, "I will take steps to see that they [Acoba and Rubia] get it [the protection they need]."[25]

Although the Klan never played a major role in Broward, its influence was felt and the prejudices it promoted were firmly established in the county. A piece in the *Fort Lauderdale Sentinel*, published in October 1915, insisted: "No one loves the memory of [Confederate president] Jefferson Davis more than we do."[26] As late as 1976, Klan activities in Broward made national headlines, when the planned participation of the United Klansmen of America caused the cancellation of a Memorial Day parade in Davie.

A Ku Klux Klan initiation ceremony in Miami (1922)

Klansmen marching in a Christmas parade in Miami (1925)

White superiority and the need for segregation of the races was dogma in South Florida, and various measures were employed to disenfranchise African-American voters. But while blacks received the brunt of discrimination in Broward, Catholics and Jews also suffered. Lynchings, public beatings, and "tar and featherings" were the methods typically employed by the Klan to get its message across. And although Broward vigilante mobs burned no crosses and wore no sheets, they were responsible for all of these activities in the county's first quarter century. More often than not, the sheriff and his deputies did little to discourage them.

Officially, Broward County had only one instance—in July 1935—of an African-American being lynched.[27] This was one of the sixty-one reported lynchings that took place in Florida from 1921 to 1946, the third highest number of any Southern state. However, lynchings were not the only way in which vigilantes murdered African-Americans who violated the norms imposed by segregation, or who were suspected of a crime. Many were shot while supposedly resisting arrest or trying to escape from a lawman or his posse. And in some cases, the barbarity of the event was such as to cause it to stand out.

One such example occurred in February 1922, when the sister of a Fort Lauderdale fireman was murdered. Upon learning of her death, he immediately went to Perry, Florida, where she had been slain, and joined in the search for her killer. When they captured the African-American man accused of the crime, they burned him at the stake.

Another common method used during this era to punish those who broke the segregation code was tarring and feathering. Although this cruel practice was employed with some regularity in Broward, perhaps the most dramatic example occurred in Miami in July 1921.

P.S. Irwin, the white archdeacon of St. Agnes Episcopal Church, a racially-mixed congregation, was attacked one evening at home by eight masked assailants. After gagging and handcuffing him, the men drove Irwin into the woods. Once there, they severely whipped him and then tarred and feathered him. Later, they dumped him out of a speeding car, naked except for the tar and feathers, with a sack tied over his head. According to the clergyman, "the men told me that I had been preaching social equality to the negroes ... and that this was the South where the people did not believe in that sort of thing and no person would be allowed to advocate it or preach it under threat of instant death."[28] He also was warned that unless he left Miami for good within forty-eight hours, he would be lynched, and that there were several other men who would be getting the same treatment he had received. An account of the incident in the *Miami Herald* noted that several weeks earlier, H.H. Higgs, an

African-American pastor at a Baptist church in Coconut Grove, had been kidnapped, whipped by a band of masked men, and ordered to leave town, which he did by boarding a ship bound for Nassau.

Newspapers during this period typically highlighted the race of their subjects. A September 1917 headline in the *Fort Lauderdale Sentinel*, for example, advised, "Arrests Negroes With Liquor." But perhaps even more unsettling was the occasional suggestion that it was not only acceptable to insult African-Americans, but that such taunts should be viewed with humor. A story in April 1913, appearing shortly after L.M. Bryan had been elected Fort Lauderdale's second town marshal, succeeding Kossie Goodbread, ran under the headline, "Marshal Bryan Kills a Coon." The item that followed explained, with feigned dismay, how Bryan had found it necessary to kill a "coon" in the city council's chambers. The paper went on to say:

> [W]e confess our heart was chilled as we contemplated that just a few hours before the life of a coon had paid for the folly of invading the Council Chamber. But when we were told it was a raccoon, we felt that we should change the name of the raccoon to prevent confusion in the future.... Think of coons being so plentiful that they not only invade the town but take possession of the Council Chamber.[29]

As noted before, African-Americans were not the only minority made to suffer. In Fort Lauderdale, prejudice against Catholics was so open and pronounced that a September 1915 editorial in the *St. Augustine Meteor* referred to it as "Ft. Lauderdale's Shame." The piece warned that:

> [T]he little burg on the edge of the Everglades bids fair to become infamous. The town harbors a nest of as short-sighted bigots as could be found anywhere in the world.... They voted their approval of religious discrimination at a public meeting.... They cast to the winds all principles of common decency, justice and fairness.[30]

Colonel George G. Mathews, the editor of the *Fort Lauderdale Sentinel*, responded to this attack by vigorously defending the anti-Catholic sentiments of his city's inhabitants. He claimed that Catholics were trying to take over the United States and repeat the Spanish Inquisition in America. He went on to say that the Catholic religion is "better suited to paganism than christianity. That is the reason that savage tribes take to your church...."[31] The following year, Mathews strongly endorsed Sidney J. Catts for governor of Florida. Catts, who was running on the Prohibition ticket and openly called for the oppression of African-Americans and Catholics, narrowly won.

Colonel George G. Mathews, editor of the Fort Lauderdale Sentinel (c. 1920)

The incident that brought so much negative attention to Fort Lauderdale in-volved Julia T. Murphy, who had been a public school teacher in Nebraska. After being offered a similar position in Fort Lauderdale, she was rejected when it was learned that she was a Catholic. At a public meeting held in August 1915 to review the matter, two of her supporters—architect F.W. Dames and Dr. D.T. Firor, pastor of the Lemon City Baptist Church—were hissed off the floor; the audience then voted 181–7 (a margin of 96%–4%) to confirm the school board's decision. For many years thereafter, no Catholic would be hired as a teacher in Fort Lauderdale.

This, then, was the Broward County that existed when Aden Turner be-came its first sheriff in October 1915.

A 1916 campaign poster for Florida gubernatorial candidate Sidney J. Catts (the second paragraph warns against "Catholic control of American politics")

CHAPTER 3

THE TURNER-BRYAN YEARS (1915–33)

The population of Broward County grew rapidly in the years following its creation, increasing from 4,700 in 1915 to 20,000 by the time of the 1930 census. A land boom in 1920 helped to raise the county's profile, but a devastating hurricane in September 1926 marked the start of various economic calamities that culminated in the Great Depression of 1929.

Throughout this period, the prohibition of alcohol played a profound role in daily life. Initially a matter of local legislation, in January 1920 the Eighteenth Amendment made the entire country dry, a status that did not change until ratification of the Twenty-First Amendment in December 1933. As a result, prohibition was in effect in Broward County for virtually the entire period in which its first two sheriffs, Aden W. Turner and Paul C. Bryan, were in office.[32]

Despite its teetotaler beginnings, resistance to prohibition was widespread in Broward, whose largest city soon earned the nickname "Fort Liquordale." In addition to local residents flouting the law by brewing "moonshine," the county's long coastline made it an ideal location for smugglers to land their boats. Accordingly, destroying stills and catching "rum runners" came to occupy much of the time of Broward's early lawmen.

Sheriff Aden W. Turner (1915–22)

In June 1915, two months after the legislation authorizing Broward County was enacted, a primary was held to choose its officers. This was, in actuality, the official election, because Governor Park Trammell had promised to appoint the men selected. The winner of the four-way race for sheriff was a local businessman named Aden Waterman Turner, who received 295 votes, which was more than the combined total of his opponents. After the results were announced, the *Fort Lauderdale Sentinel* claimed: "In the election of Mr. Turner

Aden W. Turner, sheriff of Broward County (1915–22 and 1929–33)

of Pompano as sheriff, we named one of the best men for the place. He does not drink [and] is a man of the very best habits."[33] The sheriff-elect did not share the paper's confidence, saying that "you have put the wrong man up this time, but I will promise you that I will do my full duty so far as I see it."[34] These discrepant views eventually would be held by many Broward County residents, sometimes simultaneously.

On Friday, October 1, 1915, Turner was sworn in as sheriff.[35] A native Floridian, he had been born on September 14, 1865, in Jacksonville, and had come south in 1905 to supply lumber to the Florida East Coast Railway. Impressed by the fertility of the region's soil, he settled in Pompano in 1907, becoming a farmer and road contractor. When the area incorporated in June 1908, Turner was named to the town council. Given his widespread popularity, it is not surprising that he won election as Broward's sheriff four times.

Turner had been in office for just over a month when, on Saturday, November 13, 1915, the county's first murder took place. Although they had been best friends, Jimmie Reed shot and killed Mack I. Smith during an argument over a cat. Blaming the crime on alcohol, the *Fort Lauderdale Sentinel* used it to promote the cause of prohibition: "Another question of too much whiskey; there should be none in the world. We stand for State-wide prohibition. This is the first murder we have had in the new county of Broward; but unless whiskey is done away with, it will not be the last."[36]

Prohibitionist sentiment was strong in Broward, and in August 1916 the county voted 421–170 to ban alcohol (a margin of 72%–28%). The dry votes were in the majority in all six precincts, ranging from Hallandale, which registered only a single wet vote, to Pompano, where the measure passed by just two votes. The biggest surprise was Fort Lauderdale, where the anti-prohibition forces had expected to win by fifty votes but ended up losing by more than 100. As Sheriff Turner and other law enforcement officials would learn, however, these results had little practical meaning.

Governor Trammell's appointment of the county's first officers in 1915 was only effective until the next regular election, which was scheduled for November 1916. In the June 1916 Democratic primary, Turner easily defeated his only opponent, C.L. Harper, by a tally of 440 votes to 181 votes (a margin of 71%–29%). When the Republicans subsequently declined to put up a candidate and the Socialist E.B. Steele was ruled ineligible (along with the rest of his party's slate) just days before the election,[37] Turner was automatically declared the winner. On Tuesday, January 2, 1917, he began his second term as Broward sheriff.

During this time, local newspapers began carrying an increasing number of stories about Turner arresting bootleggers, destroying stills, intercepting "booze boats," and organizing liquor raids. In May 1917, for example, the *Fort Lauderdale Sentinel* proclaimed "Bootlegger Gets Six Months and $100" and gushed, "Sheriff Turner has cut another bootlegger nick in his gun stock."[38] An August 1919 headline announced, "Sheriff Captured Three More Stills," with the accompanying story explaining that Turner was "determined to break up the booze business in this county."[39] In August 1920, under the caption "Moonshine Liquor User in Trouble," it was reported that "[t]he search for a moonshine still or two, located somewhere in the Everglades west of Davie is the almost daily occupation of Sheriff A. W. Turner now."[40]

Although destroying stills did take much of Turner's time, he also found himself facing off against smugglers, most of whom were using the island of Bimini in the Bahamas as their launching point. In this effort, Turner often worked with other law enforcement agencies. For example, when a ship called the CARRIE MAY was captured in January 1920, halfway between Fort Lauderdale and Pompano, the operation (which netted twenty-three cases of whiskey) was conducted by one of Turner's deputies and three federal officers. Likewise, the March 1921 seizure of an unnamed vessel that had sailed up the New River (so as to be able to land thirty-one cases of alcohol above the city) was carried out by Turner, two deputies, and two Fort Lauderdale police officers.

While enforcing the prohibition laws garnered Turner the most news coverage, it was just one aspect of his job. Another, less glamorous part was traffic enforcement, including making sure that vehicles were properly registered. In carrying out this duty, matters sometimes took a comical turn.

Automobile licenses in Broward ran from October 1st to September 30th, but virtually everywhere else in the country tags were good from January 1st to December 31st. Thus, while a Michigan tourist's plates stated they were valid until January 1, 1917, one of Sheriff Turner's deputies decided they had expired in Broward County on Sunday, October 1, 1916. When the officer insisted the motorist pay the county's $5 license fee, the ensuing protest was brought to the public's attention by the local press. Looking for a graceful way out, but not wanting to appear soft on scofflaws, Turner dropped the charges but warned that come early January, he and his men would be on the lookout for expired tags.

A more serious threat, and one the Sheriff's Office did little to stop (and sometimes seemed to encourage), involved extremism against those who expressed unpatriotic thoughts. In April 1917, shortly after Turner began his first full term in office, the United States entered World War I, setting off a wave of anti-German sentiment. This was especially true in Broward County.

In April 1918, R.G. Laycock upset his Davie neighbors by voicing his religious objections to the war (which he supported with Biblical quotations) and refusing to express hatred for the Kaiser (who was, in Laycock's view, one of God's creatures). The notion that God did not hate the Germans proved too much for the town's residents, who decided to end the theological impasse through collective action. A mob, which a local paper referred to as the "patriotic citizens of Davie," but who called themselves a "vigilance committee," went to Laycock's home on a Monday night at midnight and "reminded [him] that God made tar and feathers, therefore they are good clothes for a slacker."[41] The same story observed that no one from the Sheriff's Office was making any attempt to identify the culprits.

Two weeks later, a similar event took place, leading a local newspaper to remark, "Davie has again made herself a record for loyalty and successfully closed another German sewer."[42] Edward Rink, a Colohatchee farmer, had made several unpopular remarks while in Davie. He claimed he did not believe reports of a major British advance along the Western front and insisted that most of what was published in the newspapers were "damned lies,"[43] the Germans were no fools, America had no business joining the war, and Uncle Sam would never get him into the Army.

After being "politely told to keep his mouth shut"[44] and reminded that someone else had been tarred and feathered just a short time earlier for such utterances, Rink was told to get out of town. Before he could do so, however, "patience ceased to be a virtue [and] his jaw was made a target for Uncle Sam's fist; some missed it however and landed on his mouth, nose and eyes with good effect. The next time he opens his mouth it won't be in Davie."[45]

With his face badly smashed, the 44-year-old man was forced to walk all the way to Fort Lauderdale. He had tried to get passage on a boat, but his assailants decided it "would disgrace [the ship] to haul such a gink."[46]

This time, the Sheriff's Office took prompt action. As soon as Rink staggered into the city, he was arrested and locked up in the county jail. There, he was interrogated by Sheriff Turner. Although Rink claimed to be a Swedish immigrant and a naturalized citizen, Turner summoned a U.S. Secret Service agent and it was felt Rink had "good prospects of landing in a detention camp for the rest of the war if he don't [sic] have to face the firing squad."[47]

There would be other cases in which Turner exhibited a laissez-faire attitude toward lawbreakers. In May 1917, for example, a Dania farmer named N.C. Pike was arrested for assault, bootlegging, gambling, and highway robbery. He was convicted only of the second charge, with the others being held in abeyance. It subsequently was reported that on a "Saturday night he was accompanied to the depot by Sheriff Turner who bid him good bye, wishing him God speed."[48]

In addition to enforcing the law, operating the county jail, and providing a steady supply of labor to the convict camp, there were numerous administrative chores that occupied Turner's time, such as executing arrest warrants and serving subpoenas. This was not as burdensome as it might seem, for the Sheriff's Office worked on a fee-for-service basis, meaning that the more money it collected, the more Turner earned.

Occasionally, there would be a prisoner who needed to be brought back from another jurisdiction, and in the department's early days the sheriff himself often performed this duty. In October 1920, for example, Turner made a two-day journey to Valdosta, Georgia, to pick up a man named Edward Allen. According to Colohatchee resident Franz T. Herbert, Allen had asked to borrow Herbert's car to go to Miami but after being given the keys had headed north. To capture him, Turner sent telegrams to the towns Allen seemed most likely to pass through.

At times, Turner also attended to traffic duties. On a Saturday night in October 1920, for example, he personally cited half a dozen motorists for displaying only one license plate or having no visible tail light.

It is difficult to determine with any certainty the department's personnel roster during these early years. Not long after he took office, Turner apparently hired Alonzo P. "Lon" Gore to be his one regular deputy. Many reports of moonshine raids and other enforcement activities indicate that Gore was quite active in carrying out these duties. By 1918, he was living in the jail, so it is possible that running the county lockup was an additional part of his duties as "chief deputy" (whether this title was used at that time, however, is unclear). But after the early months of 1920, no newspaper reports include Gore and his place apparently was taken by A.H. Walker.

A 1916 newspaper story mentions a "Deputy Priest" being involved in traffic control, and it is possible that this was Raiford R. Priest, who had been hired in 1915 to supervise convicts working on the county's road crews. In January 1920, he and Gore accompanied Sheriff Turner on a raid. Oddly, the reporter who wrote about this incident referred to "Deputy Gore" but "Mr. Priest." A year later, in April 1921, when Priest took part in a raid with Sheriff Turner and Deputy Walker, he was called "Special Deputy Priest." A month later, he was called "Jailor Priest."

Regardless of what titles were used, Sheriff Turner had responsibility for a very large area with very few deputies to assist him. He therefore probably was heartened by a May 1921 headline in the *Miami Herald* that announced, "Mailmen Now Heavily Armed."

William H. Hays, who recently had been appointed U.S. Postmaster General by President Warren G. Harding (but who today is chiefly remembered for the Hays Code, which was used to censor movies), had ordered mail carriers to be armed as a precaution against robberies. As a result, South Florida post offices were provided with guns from the federal arsenal in Augusta, Georgia. The majority of postal employees were issued Colt .45 revolvers, which they were expected to wear in holsters that, thoughtfully, also had been provided.

Although most of the crimes Sheriff Turner handled were routine, some attracted significant public attention. In September 1919, for example, a newspaper headline shouted "Pompano School Teacher in Trouble." The story explained that Turner had arrested L.B. Winslow, a local school principal, for adultery, as well as the woman involved in the affair. Both pled guilty to fornication and were fined $30. The newspaper fretted that this left "the Pompano school without a principal and no doubt the board will find difficulty in securing one at this season of the year."[49]

Only a week later, a far more serious crime took place. It was, as one newspaper exclaimed, "A little of the old time 'Wild West.'"[50] The midnight White Star bus was stopped on Dixie Highway by two masked men, about midway between Fort Lauderdale and Dania. The robbers made the driver and four passengers line up outside the bus and took their valuables, worth about $200. Sheriff Turner was called in and quickly formed a posse, but the assailants were not caught.

What made this incident particularly embarrassing for the Sheriff's Office was the fact that Deputy Gore had gone to the scene to investigate an earlier stick-up by the pair. Although he spotted them, "by the time [his car] was turned around and started back the bandits had stopped the bus, relieved the passengers of their money and made their escape into the brush just as the officers came up to the place."[51]

One of the most dramatic stories during this period arose in January 1920. While the *Fort Lauderdale Sentinel* led with "Sheriff Turner Attacked by a Negro Desperado," the *Fort Lauderdale Herald* began "Sheriff Turner Narrowly Escapes Death at Hands of Desperate Negro."

The *Sentinel* wrote that "Sheriff A. W. Turner was badly butchered up last Sunday night by a negro, Jim Taylor, whom he attempted to arrest."[52] Then, in a remarkable bit of understatement, it indicated that, "Taylor is evidently a bad man."[53] The paper insisted it was difficult to understand why the attack had occurred, because the charge that had brought Turner to Taylor's doorstep was a relatively minor one: "On this occasion he was not accused of any serious offense, at least, not considered a grave offense among the negroes, so the sheriff was not expecting any resistance and was caught off his guard."[54] The reporter then explained that Taylor was wanted for running away with another man's wife.

The *Sentinel* noted that Sheriff Turner had taken Deputies Gore and Priest with him, stationing them around the house while he entered. Then, "whack! came a large knife or machete across his hands, breaking his left wrist and severely injuring his right hand. This caused the sheriff to drop his gun and light and the next blow struck him across the head, almost paralyzing him."[55] Turner's injuries were so serious "it took all [the deputies'] efforts for some time to stop the flow of blood and get the sheriff into the doctor's care."[56] In the meantime, Taylor escaped.

The *Herald* was in agreement with the *Sentinel* on two points: 1) Turner had been badly hurt, and, 2) Gore and Priest had been with him. In almost every other respect, it told a far different tale. For one thing, the *Herald* claimed that Taylor was being sought not for a minor crime, but for murder. It also stated that after the initial blows, Taylor picked up Turner's gun and "shot at the prostrate figure of the sheriff but missed."[57] The *Herald* further claimed that "as he went through the yard [Taylor] shot at Mr. Priest, the ball going through his coat and through his shirt but not touching his body."[58]

Despite the seriousness of his injuries, Turner recovered and later that year sought re-election. After handily defeating former Fort Lauderdale policeman Henry H. Marshall in the Democratic primary, 359 votes to 153 votes (a margin of 70%–30%), Turner faced truck farmer Quinten M. Gornto, the standard bearer of the Socialist Party, in the general election.

In "The Sting" (1973), a New York banker (played by Robert Shaw, left) is fleeced by two Chicago wiretappers (Robert Redford and Paul Newman)

Gornto, however, ran a decidedly low-key campaign, and when the ballots were counted Turner had captured 661 votes while Gornto had received just 116 (a margin of 85%–15%). It was a landslide for the well-liked sheriff, and Tuesday, January 4, 1921, marked the beginning of what promised to be his third successful term. But within little more than a year, Turner would find himself out of office.

In 1917, a new type of scam had come to Florida, one which was referred to as "wiretapping." It was an elaborate ruse, requiring a large gang to make it work, and, like most confidence games, depended on the avarice of the victim. Many years later, it would be showcased in the Oscar-winning movie *The Sting*, starring Paul Newman and Robert Redford.

The wiretappers would begin by renting a nice house, where they would set up a phony bookmaking operation. Next, a wintering tourist would be selected as the mark and lured to the site, having been enticed by the prospect of a good time. Once inside, the victim-to-be would see a whirlwind of gambling activity—humming telegraph machines, ringing telephones, and clerks scurrying about, posting odds, accepting bets, and paying off winners.

The mark would then be let in on a secret. This was no ordinary bookmaking operation, he was told, because these wiretappers could tap into the wires that reported the racetrack results, thereby learning which horses had won before anyone else knew. Then, it was claimed, they could place wagers with other bookmakers just before the betting closed. The intended victim was assured that the plan was foolproof—all it required was split-second timing. And to prove it, the guest was allowed to place a small bet, which naturally paid off.

Thus the trap was set. Having seen how easy it was to make a buck, the victim readily went along with the suggestion that he put up the money needed for a large bet, one that would net him a significant return on a sure thing. Often the tourist would have to wire back home to get enough cash to ensure a truly magnificent payoff. And once the bet was placed, the victim was told he had to wait only a short time before picking up the payoff, which supposedly was being held for him by the bookmakers who had been duped by the tourist and his newfound friends.

Somewhere along the way, however, the travel arrangements always seemed to go awry, and the mark would become separated from the gang member who was taking him to collect the money. Once he realized what had happened, the victim rarely wished to report the crime. It was not just the embarrassment of having been taken, but also the fact that gambling was illegal. In addition, the dupe could expect little sympathy for his loss, as he obviously had been more than willing to cheat others out of their money.

Wiretappers had been operating in South Florida for years by the time Sheriff Turner began his third term, and in May 1921 the *Miami Herald* ran a long exposé about the con. The details it reported had come to light largely as a result of several murders, including that of Willard Powell, a criminal better known as the "Waco Kid," who had been shot to death two months earlier while dining at the Hotel Ponce de Leon in St. Augustine, Florida. According to detectives, local wiretappers found many of their victims in Miami and brought them to Fort Lauderdale for fleecing. All told, it was estimated that victims were being cheated out of more than $2 million a year.

To avoid prosecution, the wiretappers relied on bribery and corruption, with as much as a quarter of their take being allocated to pay for "protection." Their activities resulted in a number of deaths, with at least five homicides being linked to a single band of wiretappers operating out of Miami. And while most victims quietly endured the swindle, for some the financial losses were too much to handle. One such unfortunate was Newton C. Blanchard, Jr., the son of the former governor of Louisiana, who killed himself after losing $50,000.

In Broward County, the first trial involving a wiretapping scam took place in early 1919, after a winter visitor from Philadelphia was cheated out of $25,000.

The Hotel Ponce de Leon in St. Augustine (c. 1925)

The gang that was to bring down Sheriff Turner, however, arrived in Fort Lauderdale in January 1922. Soon, they established a thriving operation in the Oliver House on North River Drive.

It was not long before their neighbors realized what was going on and appealed to Turner and the other local authorities to do something. When no action was taken, they took their concerns to the state capital, where they found a willing listener in Governor Cary A. Hardee.

On Friday, February 3, 1922, the *Fort Lauderdale Herald* reported: "Thirteen Wiretappers Caught Here—Raid Made by Governor's Agent Assisted by Local Sheriff's Office." It was, according to the story, "the biggest raid on wiretappers that has ever been pulled off in the State of Florida."[59]

Governor Hardee had sent Robert H. Shackelford, a deputy sheriff from Duval County, to Fort Lauderdale as his "special representative." Within ten days, Shackelford had gathered sufficient evidence in Fort Lauderdale, Miami, and West Palm Beach to take action.

Sheriff Turner had not been notified of Deputy Shackelford's arrival in Fort Lauderdale, and apparently knew little about his activities. Shackelford selected ten local businessmen and brought them to Turner's office, where they were sworn in as deputies. The group then went to the Oliver House and at 2:00 p.m. on Wednesday, February 1st, raided the place. There was no mention of Deputy Walker or any other regular deputy taking part in this action.

Fred B. Shippey, county judge of Broward County (1920–33)

After spending the weekend in jail, the accused appeared before County Judge Fred B. Shippey. Following two days of hearings, he ruled there was sufficient evidence to bring the twelve to trial (another man, who had been arrested with the wiretappers, was held as a witness). Bail for the defendants was set at $110,000, which was reportedly a state record. It was noted in the local press that "when the amount of the bonds was announced there was great applause. This peeved the attorneys for the defense, but the Judge was powerless to stop the cheering."[60]

Six of the men bonded out, but the other six sat in the county jail for seven weeks. When they finally appeared in circuit court, they "made strong endeavors to be agreeable to the court and handshaking and cheerful greetings was the order of the day."[61]

On Monday, March 27, 1922, all of the defendants entered guilty pleas and begged for mercy. Circuit Judge Edwin C. Davis, to the surprise of many, levied fines but did not impose any jail time. Instead, he announced that the sentences would be suspended pending good behavior. Not an unreasonable stipulation for probation, perhaps, but certainly easy enough for even the most dishonest to live up to, considering that all of the defendants left the county that very day.

Before they did so, however, they paid their fine, which came to a whopping $20,000, or twice what it had cost to build the courthouse in which their case had been heard. It has been claimed that the men cut a deal, and it is interesting to note that the fine was set at exactly the amount needed to construct the county's badly-needed first hospital.

Edwin C. Davis, circuit judge of Broward County (1921–23)

Regardless of its pedigree, the fine represented a substantial windfall for local officials. It also pleased the general public, who believed it would deter future scammers. And, as a local newspaper pointed out, "The result of the trial is felt to be a vindication of the citizens who took the matter into their own hands and helped to secure the arrest and conviction of the wiretappers after the failure of the authorities to take any steps in the matter."[62]

In the meantime, Sheriff Turner had lost his job. On Saturday, February 25th, just three weeks after the raid, Governor Hardee had suspended him for "non-feasance in office."[63] In other words, Turner was being punished for failing to take timely action against the wiretappers.

Throughout the county there was great sympathy for Turner, as almost no one believed he was connected to the wiretappers or had accepted a bribe from them. There was, in fact, an immediate effort by some of Broward's leading citizens to convince Hardee to reinstate Turner. But the governor was adamant, and made it clear he would do whatever was necessary to put an end to wiretapping in Florida, even it meant removing every one of the state's sheriffs.

Although he was out of office, Turner still had a chance to get his job back. Pursuant to the state constitution, the final say belonged to the Florida Senate, which could either remove him or reinstate him. But its decision was a long way off, for it was not scheduled to meet again until the spring of 1923. Until then, someone would have to step in and serve as Broward's sheriff.

Sheriff Paul C. Bryan (1922–29)

To fill the vacancy created by Sheriff Turner's suspension, Governor Hardee named, in the opinion of one local newspaper, "a young man of splendid qualifications for the office."[64] Ironically, the administration of the man being written about, Paul Calhoun Bryan, was destined to be plagued by two of the most serious scandals ever to occur in Broward County. One involved the mass arrest, on charges of corruption, of every officer in the Broward Sheriff's Office. The other arose from the trial of Bryan's long-time chief deputy on a charge of murder.

Bryan was born in Crescent City, Florida, on January 13, 1891, and moved with his family to Fort Lauderdale in 1900. From 1908 to 1910, he was a student at Rollins College in Winter Park. After returning home, he became an assistant postmaster, working under his sister Susan M. "Susie" Craig, one of the county's first female settlers.[65] Bryan left again to fight in World War I but was back in Fort Lauderdale by 1921.

Bryan began his tenure as sheriff on Monday, March 6, 1922. Although he had no law enforcement experience, by the end of his first year he was making arrests for killings and other serious crimes. Bryan also became quite familiar with the petty violations and vice matters that had kept Sheriff Turner busy.

Upon being appointed, Bryan made it clear that he planned to take an active role in the fight to save the morals of his fellow residents: "I shall co-operate with the governor in forcing wire-tappers and confidence men out of the county. I wish to serve notice upon anyone engaged in the liquor traffic in Broward county that I expect to enforce the letter of the law if it is within my power to do so."[66] Commenting on this statement, one newspaper wrote: "The purveyors of swamp juice and Wall street killings have had the glove thrown in their faces in true feudal style, and will now have to be extremely cautious or the spirit of the pigskin or the horsehide will prove an uncomfortable counterirritant to the spirit of the corn stalk and the bones."[67]

Bryan quickly proved good to his word, and one of his first arrests garnered a lot of attention. On Sunday, June 25, 1922, a baseball game was being played at Stranahan Park between a club from Fort Lauderdale and a club from Miami.[68] At the end of the second inning, Bryan stepped onto the field and arrested the

Fort Lauderdale baseball club (c. 1920)

entire Fort Lauderdale squad for failing to respect the Sabbath, a violation of the local "blue laws." For some reason, the Miami players were not cited and, in an even odder twist, the game then was allowed to continue (the home team ended up dropping the contest by a final score of 9–7).

When the case went to court later that week, the lawyers for the defense asked for a jury trial. Assisting them was Circuit Judge Will H. Price, who was a member of the Miami club and who had been present at the game. After hearing from both sides, the jury returned a "not guilty" verdict in less than ten minutes. Unlike Sheriff Bryan, it appears the jurors accepted the argument that the game was merely a friendly match (supporting this contention was the fact that no admission fee had been charged).

In August 1922, two armed men met, quarreled, and engaged in a shootout on Dixie Highway. The headline in the *Fort Lauderdale Herald* read, "Negro is Killed—Two Negro Farm Hands Meet and Shoot It Out Sunday Night." When Bryan arrived, he found one of the protagonists dead and the other seriously wounded.

Six months later, the *Herald* reported on another such incident. County Commissioner Daniel R. Johnson, who represented the Deerfield district, was shot to death on Dixie Highway by William L. Bracknell, the postmaster at Deerfield and a former county commissioner. Although the two men had been close friends, they had gotten into a dispute over an anonymous letter that accused Johnson of committing blackmail (and that Johnson was convinced had been written by Bracknell's wife). The killer, it was reported, "made no effort to escape, but left word for Sheriff Bryan to call at his home for him when he arrived."[69]

Bryan also found himself dealing with sex crimes. In April 1922, for example, Frederick L. Cook of Miami was charged with "transporting a woman for immoral purposes."[70] As it turned out, Cook had driven her in a stolen car.

In November 1922, the newspapers reported that a Dade County man named J.H. Jones had taken his wife and a 14-year-old girl for a ride. He then got them to share some liquor, after which he left his wife in the car and took the girl for a walk in the woods, where he attacked her. His wife came running when she heard screams but was knocked unconscious. Remarkably, Jones was acquitted after two trials.

In another case, Bryan investigated the alleged rape of an Indian girl by Floyd Williams of Fort Lauderdale. Despite the introduction of a great deal of evidence, in January 1923 a headline in the *Fort Lauderdale Herald* informed readers: "Jury Acquits Man of Charge of Assaulting Young Local Seminole Indian Woman." Inexplicably, one local newspaper blamed the crime on idleness. Its proposed solution? "Enforce the vagrancy law, we say."[71]

For the most part, however, the arrest reports filed by the Sheriff's Office during Bryan's tenure involved much more mundane offenses, such as: 1) driving without a license, reckless driving, or driving under the influence; 2) carrying a concealed weapon; 3) passing a bad check; 4) assault and battery; and, 5) petit larceny. Other common violations included beating a board bill and riding on a train without a ticket. Of course, some crimes—such as bastardy, fornication, and profanity—were products of the era's fussy morals.

As already pointed out, many arrests during this period were due to the prohibition laws, and one finds numerous cases involving the production, sale, or possession of alcohol. Gambling was another charge frequently written up by Bryan and his men, and the possibility that a new generation of wiretappers would emerge remained a constant worry. In December 1923, Governor Hardee wrote to Bryan to remind him that such criminals "are likely to return at any time, [and] I am calling upon the sheriffs of a great many counties of the State, especially where tourists come, for constant vigilance regarding them[.]"[72]

In a preview of things to come, Bryan also occasionally had to deal with drug-related offenses and their consequences. In a note to one prisoner's family, for example, the lawman wrote:

[Y]our brother is in very good shape and has not had any dope for about three weeks. If you desire to come and get him please let me know or do you wish me to turn him loose here. He says he never expects to take any more dope.[73]

There were times, however, when the department had to explain that no crime had taken place, at least in Broward County. In June 1925, for example, Bryan received a letter stating:

We have been advised by Sheriff [Henry R.] Chase of Miami that you recently arrested several men upon whom were found American Express Cheques issued to Joseph Zacharzowsky. The above checks were stolen from the person of Mr. Zacharzowsky in Miami sometime in February. We are desirous of obtaining the full particulars in connection with this arrest and we would thank you to write us and let us have the full particulars stating in detail just how the checks were recovered....

This company maintains a staff of special agents throughout the world whose duty it is to cooperate with the police authorities in apprehending crooks who make it a practice to prey upon tourists.

Thank you for your kind assistance in the recovery of the cheques and we congratulate you upon the arrest.[74]

In a gracious reply, Bryan suggested: "There must be some error in this as I have no record of such arrest and do [not] think any such parties were apprehended in Broward County or I would have known of same. I would suggest that you again communicate with Sheriff Chase of Miami as it is probable that these parties have been apprehended in some other county."[75]

When a violation did occur in Broward County, it normally carried a fine ranging between $5 and $100, with the alternative being imprisonment. For a sizeable number of offenses, however, incarceration was mandatory. In such instances, defendants typically received sentences ranging from thirty to sixty days.

One particularly notorious crime concerned breaking a labor contract, for which the penalty was two months in prison. With employees scarce due to the booming economy, minority rights non-existent, and the sheriff expected to look out for the interests of businessmen and farmers, such arrests were seen as a civic necessity.

Indeed, in May 1923 Governor Hardee wrote to Bryan to discuss "the effort in many sections of the State to recruit labor from Florida to other States. We have a stringent statute on this subject and the industries of Florida are sorely in need of all our labor."[76] Hardee then admonished Bryan to make certain "to arrest any violators of this law."[77]

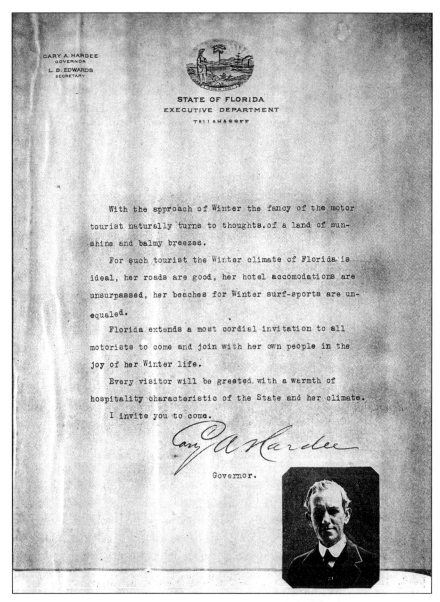

CARY A. HARDEE
GOVERNOR
L. B. EDWARDS
SECRETARY

STATE OF FLORIDA
EXECUTIVE DEPARTMENT
TALLAHASSEE

With the approach of Winter the fancy of the motor tourist naturally turns to thoughts of a land of sunshine and balmy breezes.

For such tourist the Winter climate of Florida is ideal, her roads are good, her hotel accomodations are unsurpassed, her beaches for Winter surf-sports are unequaled.

Florida extends a most cordial invitation to all motorists to come and join with her own people in the joy of her Winter life.

Every visitor will be greeted with a warmth of hospitality characteristic of the State and her climate.

I invite you to come.

Governor.

*A 1924 letter from Florida Governor Cary A. Hardee (inset)
inviting tourists to visit the state*

Hardee was not the only one to bend Bryan's ear about the labor situation. In May 1925, Bryan was told that employers in Fort Lauderdale were becoming concerned about "the scarcity and the prevailing high wages of common negro labor [and were demanding that the sheriff] compel idle negroes to engage in some sort of work or [else] leave the city."[78]

Yet another problem that Bryan was expected to deal with was the smuggling of illegal aliens (which was proving to be a problem all along Florida's coasts). In April 1923, twenty-three aliens landed on the beach in Deerfield. Upon coming ashore, they were arrested by Bryan and locked up in the county jail.

Although most of these men were from Czechoslovakia, a few hailed from Italy. After reaching Cuba, they had paid $140 to $200 each to be smuggled into the United States. Sailing in an open boat for seven days, they had subsisted on food that was virtually inedible. As a result, it was reported that they "were all ravenously hungry when given an opportunity to eat at the county jail."[79]

While in custody, the group put on a concert. The Friday night performance was attended by courthouse officials and invited guests and consisted of a musical play (fittingly, a tragedy) followed by a selection of native folk songs. The *Fort Lauderdale Herald* reported that one of the ballads (sung by a man named Guiseppe Lombardi, who had spent several years in the United States before returning to Italy to fight in World War I) particularly touched the audience and elicited a long round of applause. Nevertheless, most of the refugees soon were sent back to Cuba.

It was during Bryan's third year in office that the notorious Ashley gang finally was eliminated as a threat. From 1915 to 1924, the group had committed a long list of crimes throughout the Gold Coast, including hijackings, hold-ups, and train robberies. These activities had made them the most hunted outlaws in Florida's history.

In September 1924, in what turned out to be their final job, they robbed the Pompano Bank, making off with $20,000. By now, Robert C. Baker, the sheriff of Palm Beach County, was relentlessly pursuing the gang, although his absence at the decisive showdown later became a subject of much discussion and criticism.

Three of Baker's deputies, together with John R. Merritt, the sheriff of St. Lucie County, stopped John Ashley and his men at a roadblock. When the smoke cleared, the four gangsters were dead. The official story was that they had gone for their guns, but many people believed they had been executed while handcuffed. Among those killed was a teenager named Hanford Mobley, who two years earlier had escaped from the Broward County Jail.

Shortly before the shootout, Governor Hardee had written to Sheriff Bryan and made it clear he expected action. "The time has come when these desperadoes must be captured."[80] He then suggested, quite strongly, that Bryan meet

The members of Florida's notorious Ashley gang (clockwise from top):
John Ashley, Hanford Mobley, Clarence Middleton, Roy "Young" Matthews,
Ray "Shorty" Lynn, and (inset) Ashley with longtime girlfriend
Laura Upthegrove (1923)

with Sheriff Baker and devise a joint plan. Eight days later, having grown increasingly agitated, Hardee again wrote to Bryan and asked what steps were being taken to address the situation. The question, of course, soon became moot.

What makes Bryan's apparent lack of interest in pursuing these outlaws intriguing is not simply his indifference to Hardee's entreaties—he would demonstrate similar behavior on other occasions. Rather, what is so strange is that Bryan refused to play his best card.

Robert C. "Bob" Baker, sheriff of Palm Beach County (1920–23 and 1923–33)

Eight months into his term, Bryan had appointed William A. Hicks to be his chief deputy. For the next four years, "Big Bill" lived in the jail and virtu-

William A. "Big Bill" Hicks, chief deputy of Broward County (1922–26)

ally ran the Sheriff's Office for Bryan. And due to the department's growth, there was much to do, including overseeing several deputies and juggling large amounts of paperwork. Soon, almost all of the correspondence from the Sheriff's Office was coming from Hicks, who would either add his initials under Bryan's signature or close with "Sheriff Bryan (by William A. Hicks, D.S.)." Indeed, so dependent did Bryan become on Big Bill that it is difficult to see how anything got done without him.

After two years in office, Bryan faced an election that would determine whether he would continue to be Broward's sheriff. And as usual, the real challenge was not winning the general election, but coming in first in the Democratic primary. As the incumbent, this should have been easy for Bryan, but there was a problem.

When Sheriff Turner was suspended from office in 1922, he had to wait until the Florida Senate met the following year to ask for his job back. It finally took up the issue in May 1923 and quickly voted for removal.[81] Undaunted, Turner immediately turned his attention to the 1924 election.

Turner was justifiably optimistic about his chances in this contest. He had been a popular sheriff, many people remained troubled over how he had been treated, and his successor was a mere appointee with no law enforcement experience. In all respects, Turner was an impressive opponent.

Hicks, however, was a savvy politician with numerous connections. Among other things, he was one of the founders of the Fort Lauderdale Elks (serving

Dade County Jailer Wilbur W. Hendrickson, Sr. (far right)
at a family picnic (1913)

as the first "Exalted Ruler," or president, of Lodge 1517), was active in several civic organizations, and owned a significant amount of local real estate. Liking his job and wanting to keep it, Hicks called in numerous favors, and in the end Bryan beat Turner.

In addition to his campaign skills, Hicks was a seasoned lawman and, as it turned out, personally acquainted with John Ashley. In June 1915, Bob Ashley had tried to break his brother out of the Dade County Jail, where he was waiting to go on trial for murder. In the course of this unsuccessful attempt, Deputy Wilbur W. Hendrickson, Sr., the jailer, had been killed. To take his place, Sheriff Dan Hardie had hired Hicks.

Hicks and John Ashley got along well, and it was during one of their frequent conversations that Hicks suggested to Ashley that the outlaw dictate his life story to another prisoner, which Hicks would then edit and get published. According to a local newspaper, "Deputy Hicks declares the story, as far as the writers have proceeded with it, makes intensely interesting reading, and some of its chapters read like a tale of the Wild West in its wildest days."[82]

It appears that Hicks had a certain degree of admiration for Ashley, and it is possible that this was the reason why Bryan was so reluctant to become involved in his pursuit. For if anyone stood a good chance of capturing Ashley,

*"Big Bill" Hicks (far left) with Deputies J.P. Martins, S.L. Barfield,
E.G. Grimes, Byrne B. Baker, Jot Shiver, and Virgil Wright and
Sheriff Paul C. Bryan (1926)*

it was Hicks, a fact Governor Hardee alluded to when he suggested that "some man [be] put on the job in the way of detective service."[83] Before coming to Fort Lauderdale, Hicks had worked for the William J. Burns International Detective Agency and had run its Memphis office. Yet when the showdown with John Ashley took place, no one from the Broward Sheriff's Office was present.

There is one other interesting connection between Hicks and the Ashley gang. Years later, when Hicks himself was facing criminal charges, Joe Tracey, one of its members, stepped forward and offered to provide him with an alibi. At the time, Tracey was a prisoner in the state penitentiary.

On Tuesday, January 6, 1925, four months after John Ashley and his companions met their bloody end, Paul Bryan was sworn in for a four-year term. Things looked good for the Sheriff's Office, and some might even have been tempted to use the word "prosperous." Although the department's responsibilities were increasing as the county's population grew, this was matched by the hiring of more deputies—first five, then six, and then seven officers. The amount of paperwork also was increasing, but Hicks was on top of it, and in any event it meant more income.

Within a year, however, things started to change as an economic downturn began to take root. In August 1926, Hicks wrote to a friend up north, who had asked about the situation, and advised him that conditions were rotten. The situation got even worse on Saturday, September 18, 1926, when a monstrous hurricane struck. More than 400 people lost their lives, and both Fort Laud-

Hurricane damage to downtown Fort Lauderdale (1926)

erdale and Miami were devastated. Given the region's already shaky economy, this new blow threatened complete financial ruin.

The worst, however, was still to come for Hicks. In the days after the storm, he resisted the efforts of Fort Lauderdale Mayor John W. Tidball to declare martial law. Two weeks later, Bryan fired Hicks, presumably at Tidball's insistence.

The loss of his deputy's salary caused Hicks no great financial distress, but for the first time since he had moved to Fort Lauderdale he lacked an official position. Moreover, the Democratic primary—the key to being elected in Broward County—already had been held. Hicks therefore decided to run as a write-in candidate for a position most people were not even aware existed, and for which no one had bothered to file.

When the election results were printed in the local papers, readers learned that Hicks had been elected justice of the peace for the Third District. Hicks expressed gratitude to the eighteen friends who had written in his name on their ballots, claiming that their decision to do so had been "unsolicited and without my having been consulted."[84] It is doubtful anyone believed him.

The county commission was particularly skeptical, and refused to recognize Hicks's victory. Yet Hicks charged ahead. After opening an office, he began holding court sessions, convening coroner's inquests, and remanding prisoners to the care of his old boss.

Getting paid for these services, however, proved impossible. Although Hicks regularly submitted bills to the county commission, they just as regularly ignored them. Finally, Hicks took the commission to court but lost. Although he made plans to appeal to the Florida Supreme Court, a far bigger problem soon arose in his life.

Hicks, however, was not the only one with troubles. In April 1926, Philip F. Hambsch, the Federal Prohibition Administrator for Florida, had written a letter to Sheriff Bryan. It began by saying that "the general impression throughout the United States outside of Florida is that the State and City authorities in Florida are doing little or nothing towards enforcement of the National Prohibition Laws or the State Prohibition Laws."[85] Hambsch went on to ask Bryan for a monthly report on his arrests and seizures, so that Hambsch would "be in a position to tell the truth about Florida in regard to enforcement of the liquor laws...."[86]

Two days later, Bryan wrote back to Hambsch and was quite solicitous: "I am ready to cooperate with you and your forces at all times, and nothing would please me any better than to have the prohibition laws enforced one hundred per cent."[87] He then sought to defend himself, pointing out that in the past, federal prohibition officers had come into town without any advance warning and made minor arrests, thereby ruining major investigations being conducted by the Sheriff's Office. Still, Bryan assured Hambsch of his good intentions:

> I do not expect you to give me advance information and I do not want you to labor under such impression, but I do feel that if your agents would get acquainted with us and get a little closer together in a friendly way, that it would help to bring on better cooperation when the necessity arose.[88]

Apparently the prohibition officials took Bryan at his word, for they did not provide him with any advance information about the raids they were planning. And while they arranged for their agents to become better acquainted with the sheriff and his deputies, they did so in a rather novel way. As for Hambsch, he kept his promise to Bryan "to broadcast through the press the truth in regard to the work that you are doing."[89]

At 7:00 a.m. on Thursday, January 27, 1927, federal agents swooped down on Broward County to break up what they later described as one of the country's largest liquor conspiracies. According to one newspaper report, the operation involved "every prohibition enforcement agency of the United States government,"[90] including the U.S. Coast Guard (which assigned twelve men to the operation).

The raids were an enormous success, netting the expected number of bootleggers. But in a development that took everyone by surprise, they also led to the arrest of seven Fort Lauderdale police officers as well as the *entire* Broward Sheriff's Office: Sheriff Bryan, Chief Deputy Robert G. Kendall (Hicks's suc-

John W. Martin, governor of Florida (1925–29)

cessor), and Deputies Byrne B. Baker, E.G. Grimes, J.P. Martins, Glen Maugans, Jot Shiver, and Nathan Shiver.

According to published reports, the lawmen were brought to the local U.S. Coast Guard station, relieved of their weapons, but "not deprived of their badges of office."[91] At a preliminary hearing before U.S. Commissioner C.W. Russell, bail was set at $5,000 for Bryan and $2,000 for each of his deputies. Following the hearing, Bryan told the press, "I have in no way violated my oath of office nor have I been guilty of any conspiracy to violate the law. I have no fear of the outcome of any investigation of my acts in office and welcome the opportunity to have my case presented for a hearing."[92]

Despite the fact that he and his men were facing serious criminal charges, Bryan was not suspended by Governor John W. Martin, in stark contrast to how Governor Hardee had treated Sheriff Turner during the wiretappers case. But the scandal was enough to doom Bryan's chances of being re-elected in 1928.

Remarkably, several months after his arrest, Bryan found himself engulfed in a new crisis, and this time suspension was a very real possibility. Rather than alcohol, the vice that now threatened to sink Bryan was gambling.

Administration building at the Pompano Race Track (1926)

Under Florida law, betting on horses was illegal but racing them was not. So when Governor Martin approved the incorporation of the Pompano Race Track in 1925, there seemed little reason for its investors to be apprehensive. And when the track opened to great fanfare on Christmas Day 1926, it looked as though their high expectations were more than justified. It therefore came as a great shock when County Commissioner John M. Bryan went to court and convinced Circuit Judge Curtis E. Chillingworth to grant a temporary restraining order preventing the track from selling "investment certificates."

To get around the state's ban on betting, race tracks had turned to these legal fictions, which allowed gamblers to make a voluntary "contribution" toward the purse of a particular horse. If that horse ended up winning, its "investors" split the resulting "profits."[93]

Chillingworth's injunction meant that Pompano could not operate in this fashion. And with no other means of taking bets, the track was forced to close on Friday, January 7, 1927. Two months later, the Florida Supreme Court affirmed Chillingworth's ruling.[94]

In the interim, however, the track's owners had come up with a new way to take bets that did not depend on investment certificates, and therefore announced they were reopening. Bryan now found himself in a bind, for while he did not want to upset the track's many fans, he still had the bootlegging charges hanging over his head. Deciding to err on the side of caution, Bryan had his deputies arrest the track's owners. But when they appeared in court, Judge Shippey decided the men had done nothing wrong. In a telegram explaining this turn of events, Bryan advised Martin:

Curtis E. Chillingworth, circuit judge of Broward County (1923–27)

> I arrested race track officials. They were operating under different system. They were tried and acquitted before Judge Shippey. Judge Shippey holds present system not gambling. Feel I have done my duty but will await your instructions.[95]

Upon receiving Bryan's news, Martin became furious and immediately fired off a reply: "I shall expect you to break up the gambling at the Pompano race track this afternoon. If gambling continues there this afternoon, as much as I regret it, I am going to appoint a new sheriff for your county."[96]

By the time Bryan received Martin's telegram, some 2,000 patrons had gathered at the track. According to the *Miami Herald*, there were a few delays, which the spectators did not seem to mind at all, and the only deputy on hand was Robert Kendall. Soon, an announcement was made that the first race would be held at 3:15 p.m., after which the "money wagon" was brought out, signaling that bets were now being accepted. At 4:00 p.m., however, Bryan arrived and cancelled the remaining races, much to the crowd's disappointment.

Unbowed, the owners made plans to try again the following year. Once more, Martin wired Bryan and told him to stop them, explaining that "[i]f necessary, I will send state troops to Pompano to enforce [the ban]."[97] By return telegram, Bryan assured Martin that he was "in position to handle Pompano Race Track situation and will see that State laws are not violated."[98] Apparently mollified, Martin let the matter drop.

Just as things were beginning to get a little better for Sheriff Bryan, life got much worse for his former chief deputy. On Thursday, July 7, 1927, Big Bill Hicks was arrested for first degree murder, setting the stage for one of the most sensational trials in Broward County's history. And to this day, no one is sure whether Hicks was guilty or innocent—or even if there was a murder.

The story had begun in August 1925, when a mutilated, gunshot-riddled body was found floating in a canal. A coroner's inquest decided that the unidentified victim had been killed by an unknown assailant. The body was then buried, but later exhumed. Once again, identification proved impossible. After a second exhumation, however, it was decided the victim was Robert R. Barber, a missing local carpenter. The body was then buried a third time, after which nothing more happened until Hicks was arrested.

The case against the former lawman, while circumstantial, was straightforward. Eight months before he disappeared, Barber had been sentenced to the county jail for a minor offense. As warden, Hicks regularly used prisoners for his personal affairs and soon had Barber doing woodwork in several homes he was building.

Problems arose when Hicks allegedly refused to pay Barber, leading Barber to complain to his union. After this, the animosity between the two men escalated, and one month before he disappeared, Barber was charged with assaulting Hicks. And if these facts were not damning enough, two eyewitnesses—Wesley Corell and Steadman T. Gray—claimed to have seen Hicks murder Barber. Yet Hicks had a simple explanation for all these things—he was being framed.

Although such a claim is frequently put forward by criminal defendants, in Hicks's case it had a certain ring of truth to it. Indeed, the former lawman had managed to make many powerful enemies, including Mayor Tidball, who had wanted to impose martial law after the 1926 hurricane, and the county commission, which had refused to pay Hicks after he was elected a justice of the peace. Even the judge hearing the case disqualified himself because he was personally prejudiced against Hicks. And in a change of venue motion, Hicks's lawyers claimed that his unflinching enforcement of the prohibition laws had aroused so much hatred that Hicks could not get a fair trial anywhere in Broward County.

At the heart of his defense, however, was Hicks's insistence that Bryan and his deputies were angry because they believed Hicks had tipped off the federal prohibition agents, leading to their arrest. Now, he claimed, they were out for revenge.

Hicks's theory received a substantial boost when Glen Maugans, one of the deputies who had been arrested (and later resigned) admitted that he and the others had conspired to get Hicks for the raid. There also was testimony that a plan to kill Hicks had been discussed.

Even Corell and Gray, the two supposed eyewitnesses to the murder, turned out to be less than trustworthy, inasmuch as they had confessed to bootlegging and were testifying in the hope of receiving reduced sentences. Interestingly, Bryan had temporarily deputized both men twice—once in 1926 (for the hurricane) and again in 1927 (during the race track crisis).

Although the state's case had several holes, it still managed to convince a lot of observers. The prosecution scoffed at Hicks's claim that he had been a vigorous enforcer of the prohibition laws, introducing evidence that he had associated with bootleggers and taken kickbacks from speakeasies. It also sought to bolster Corell and Gray by calling to the stand Jot Shiver, who testified that in a conversation held six months after Barber's body was discovered, Hicks admitted to his fellow deputy that he had committed the crime. Inconveniently for the state, of course, was the fact that Shiver was one of the deputies who had been arrested in the federal prohibition raid.

During cross-examination, Shiver admitted he had not reported Hicks's confession to Sheriff Bryan. When asked why, Shiver claimed that he had been afraid of Hicks. This explanation raised quite a few eyebrows:

> Sheriff Bryan had a reputation for hiring the toughest men in the county as his deputies, and one of them had just testified under oath that he was afraid of another. If not for the stern warning of [Circuit] Judge [Lexie L.] Parks at the beginning of the trial, no doubt Shiver's statement that he was afraid of Hicks would have caused an outburst of laughter.[99]

On Sunday, September 11, 1927, the jury found Hicks guilty. The defense immediately moved for a new trial on sixty-seven separate grounds, including the fact that Joe Tracey, the former Ashley gang member, had come forward with an alibi for Hicks. Unimpressed, Parks sentenced Hicks to life at hard labor.

Hicks spent almost eighteen months in the state penitentiary at Raiford. During his time there, he received a serious injury from which he never fully recovered. But on Wednesday, February 13, 1929, his forty-fourth birthday, the Florida Supreme Court overturned his conviction.[100] At his second trial, which proceeded along the same lines as the first one, the jury deadlocked, resulting in a mistrial being declared on Saturday, November 23, 1929. While six jurors voted to convict, the other six believed Hicks.

In April 1930, a third trial was held. This time, evidence was introduced that cast doubt as to whether the body really was that of Barber. In addition, L.F. McLendon, a bootlegger, testified that at a gathering of law enforcement officials held shortly after the federal raid, he had offered to put up money for a fund to get Hicks. According to McLendon, Sheriff Bryan, three BSO deputies, and James B. Croft (Fort Lauderdale's assistant police chief) had been present when the offer was made.

Another new witness was L.H. Shealy, a liquor dealer who claimed he had kept quiet until now out of fear that he would "be taken for a ride"[101] if he told the truth. Among other things, Shealy said he had been shaken down for a contribution to help pay for Hicks's prosecution.

On Sunday, April 20, 1930, Hicks was acquitted. The following day, he visited the sheriff's department to pick up his belongings. When he was asked about his plans, he talked about renewing old friendships and spending as much time as possible in the open air and sunshine. In August, he registered to vote and paid his poll taxes, still claiming to be a justice of the peace. A short time later, however, he left Fort Lauderdale and returned to his hometown of Utica, New York.

While Hicks had been fighting to prove his innocence, his nemesis, Sheriff Bryan, had been having his own problems. First, in June 1928, he lost the Democratic primary for sheriff. Then, a few months later, he and seventeen co-defendants went on trial in federal court for conspiring to violate the National Prohibition Enforcement Act.

One of the star witnesses at the trial was Hicks, who was brought in from prison to testify against his former boss. From the stand, Hicks accused Bryan of protecting bootleggers, selling seized liquor, and taking bribes. Despite this damning testimony, the case ended in a mistrial, as did a second trial. Deciding that they would fare no better a third time, the prosecutors gave up, leaving Bryan in permanent legal limbo—not guilty, but not exonerated.

After his time as sheriff, Bryan remained in Broward County and opened a restaurant in Dania called Bryan's Cafe. He passed away in the Bay Pines Veterans Administration Hospital, near St. Petersburg, Florida, on July 16, 1942, at the age of fifty-one, just two days after his sister Susie, the former postmistress, died.[102] A double burial was held for the pair at Fort Lauderdale's Evergreen Cemetery.

Years later, Hugh Lester, a Fort Lauderdale attorney who knew Bryan, was asked if the lawman was responsible for the scandals that plagued his administration. He answered by saying, "He asked for it. He hired a bunch of thugs

Tombstone of Sheriff Paul Bryan (Evergreen Cemetery, Fort Lauderdale)

as deputies."[103] There appears to be at least some truth to this observation. In February 1928, a citizens committee in Oakland Park (which at the time was known as Floranada) complained about a local bootlegger's operations and asked Bryan to investigate. They claimed that no action was being taken by the city's officials, which was the reason they were writing to him. They stressed, however, that the investigation should be conducted by a trustworthy deputy who would not be tempted by a bribe.

As for Hicks, his guilt would be debated for decades. And after his many battles, it did not surprise anyone that he moved away from Fort Lauderdale. However, his problems with the Broward Sheriff's Office were not yet over, in large part because of his wife.

In June 1928, when Hicks was completing his ninth month in prison, Gertrude W. Hicks, who was living in Miami, made the papers. The headline in the *Miami Herald* read: "Life Ended as Miami Police Fail to Act," and the story that followed was quite critical of the local constabulary.

One evening, shortly after midnight, the cops were informed that a man named John A. Lynch planned to commit suicide in his hotel room. It was raining at the time, and the police chose not to investigate because warnings of this sort invariably proved false. But at 3:30 a.m., Lynch did kill himself.

It turned out that the 65-year-old victim recently had deserted his wife in Jacksonville and, on the night in question, had dined with Gertrude. After the pair had finished eating, she had driven him back to his hotel and then sought out the police. To top matters off, Lynch had made Gertrude the sole beneficiary of his estate, cutting out his entire family.

Hicks apparently did not bring Gertrude with him when he left Fort Lauderdale. As a result, the Broward Sheriff's Office dispatched several letters and telegrams seeking his arrest for desertion and non-support. In December 1930, for example, such a request was made to W.B. Cahoon, the sheriff of Duval County, Florida. Two weeks later, a letter was sent to J.A. Johnson, the sheriff of Polk County, Florida, advising that Hicks "is interested in and pays quite a bit of attention to a Miss Bailey at Lakeland. This lady is [a] librarian."[104] Soon after this, Frank Karel, the sheriff in Orange County, Florida, was contacted and told: "It is reported [Hicks] is living in Orlando with one Dolly Morgans, a decided blonde. He is supposed to be running liquor, drives a [C]adillac sedan."[105] In March 1931, Richard W. Thomas, the sheriff of Oneida County, New York, was given a weekend address for Hicks in Utica and asked to "[d]o what you can to locate this man."[106] And in December 1931, a telegram was sent to Thomas advising that Hicks "will spend Christmas Day in Utica [at] number Four Two Three Cooper Street. Arrest and notify me."[107]

According to some accounts, Hicks resumed his law enforcement career in Utica and eventually became the city's police chief. However, the department's files contain no mention of him.

Two years of imprisonment, coupled with the ordeal of three trials, eventually took their toll on the robust Hicks. In 1940, while living in Utica, he died of a heart attack at the age of fifty-five. Several months later, Gertrude married a man from Miami in a ceremony conducted at the Broward County Courthouse.

Sheriff Aden W. Turner (1929–33)

In June 1928, Paul Bryan sought the Democratic nomination for sheriff. Despite his upcoming trial on the federal prohibition charges, Bryan retained a fair amount of support around the county, and for a time it looked like he might actually win despite facing four challengers. But when the results were announced, Aden Turner had eked out a narrow victory, collecting 1,538 votes to Bryan's 1,415 votes (a margin of 32%–29%). The rest of the votes were divided among three other candidates.

Beating Bryan was a particularly sweet moment for Turner. Broward's first sheriff was still bitter about being ousted from office in 1922, and when he tried to regain his post in 1924, Bryan had blocked his path. But now Turner had a new challenger: Republican Fred M. Wertz, a candidate who actually had a chance to win the general election. Turner therefore was forced to keep on campaigning after his primary victory.

On Election Day, Turner collected 2,402 votes to Wertz's 1,986 votes (a margin of 55%–45%). Two months later, on Tuesday, January 8, 1929, Turner was sworn in as the sheriff of Broward County for the fourth time.

As one of his first acts, Turner hired a bookkeeper and three full-time deputies. Each deputy received a yearly salary of $1,800 (a 20% increase over the figure Bryan had offered a 1926 applicant). Sara H. Freeman, who, in addition to her bookkeeping duties, also acted as the jail's matron when needed (thereby becoming the department's first female officer), was paid the same amount. Turner's semi-annual financial reports to the state suggest these salaries remained steady until 1932, when the Sheriff's Office found itself in a deep financial crisis.

One of the new deputies was W.H. "Hobb" Campbell, who gave up his job as chief of the Dania Fire Department to accept Turner's offer. Another new appointee was jailer W.J. "Dad" Howell, who resigned in 1929 and was replaced by Arden D. Marshall.

The number of deputies increased by one each year, and in October 1930 Turner purchased six deputy badges at a cost of $2 each. In his order, Turner wrote that the shields were to read "Deputy Sheriff, Broward County ... [and in the middle I] [w]ould like the seal of the state to be substituted in place of [the] star."[108]

Although some deputies soon left, most stayed—by 1932, each of the department's officers had been on the job for at least two years. In addition to Campbell and Marshall, the force consisted of R.B. McDonald, C.J. Turner, and Virgil Wright.

C.J. Turner was listed on the payroll as "Fingerprint Department," but he was directly involved in law enforcement activities and helped capture a suspected bank robber from Texas. He also was Sheriff Turner's son and the first officer in the department's history to benefit from nepotism. He would not be the last.

While most of Broward County's early deputy sheriffs were tough, especially when it came to dealing with minorities, police brutality complaints were rare. But in August 1929, such a charge became the talk of the town.

Deputy Hobb Campbell had gone to see Emil M. Gertz to buy some chickens, but the two men had gotten into an argument after the farmer refused to extend credit to the lawman. Allegedly, this caused Campbell to attack Gertz, beat him up, and leave with several birds while Gertz sought medical attention. The incident probably would not have become public knowledge had Gertz not been a disabled war veteran, but once it did a firestorm erupted.

Campbell quickly resigned but then defended his actions by claiming that Gertz had called him a liar (among other things). Campbell also denied hitting Gertz more than twice. Two days later, Sheriff Turner reinstated Campbell after deciding he had been provoked. This infuriated officials at the Hollywood American Legion Post, who accused Campbell of assault and battery and issued the following warning:

> When the sheriff of the county contends that one of his deputies was justified in beating up a helpless, gassed, mentally sick war veteran irrespective of provocation who had already given his all for his country, and our investigating committee finds that the brutal attack was unwarranted we wish to let the Sheriff know that the matter is not yet ended.[109]

Several days later, an arrest warrant was sworn out against Campbell. At the preliminary hearing, Gertz testified that the deputy had knocked him into a pile of washtubs, chased him into a swamp, threatened him with a gun, struck him a second time, and torn the shirt off his back. Campbell admitted hitting Gertz twice but insisted the farmer had called him vile names.

Although Campbell was bound over for trial, Sheriff Turner refused to suspend him. Four days later, Campbell resigned for a second time. In announcing his decision, Campbell explained he had received several attractive business offers. J.A. "Gus" Roberts, a former deputy sheriff in Columbia County, Florida, was hired to take Campbell's place.

While waiting for the trial to begin, Turner vigorously defended Campbell. In addition to describing him as one of the most efficient and fearless deputies he had ever had, he claimed that the "[r]ecor[d] will show that convictions have been found in nearly every case of arrest he has made."[110]

Campbell also sought to influence public opinion. In a letter to the *Fort Lauderdale Daily News*, he denied he had been forced to resign, repeated his provocation defense, and for the first time said Gertz had started the fight. The names he was called, Campbell assured readers, "would make any man, do, no doubt, the same thing, or even worse, in the defense of his honor."[111]

On Thursday, November 7, 1929, Campbell's trial got underway. Coincidentally, the court had just accepted a "no contest" plea from J.P.A. Hertlein, Fort Lauderdale's police chief, in a case stemming from an altercation with two local youths. Campbell fared better on his assault charges. After a mere fifteen minutes of deliberation, the jury acquitted him. Sheriff Turner promptly rehired Campbell.

Meanwhile, illegal alcohol continued to be readily available throughout the county. Occasionally, there would be a push to curtail it, but these efforts generally were short-lived and relatively ineffective. At times, however, the sheriff was forced to take action. When a gas station owner and his wife were shot by two inebriated men, for example, Turner, under pressure from the governor, announced a major anti-drinking initiative.

Gambling was another problem that persisted, even after the crackdown at the Pompano race track. Every so often Turner's men would conduct gambling raids, and on one occasion Deputies Albert Jones and Gus Roberts arrested nine men at a casino outside Hollywood. But for the most part, such enterprises operated with impunity.

By March 1930, violations of the vice laws had become so open in Broward that the Fort Lauderdale Woman's Christian Temperance Union publicly denounced the lawlessness. In particular, they complained bitterly about "the prevalence of slot machines, gambling and bootlegging."[112] Upset by the situation, Governor Doyle E. Carlton sent Turner a list of people who were known to be engaged in such activities in Broward County. Turner promised "that any violators will be brought to justice."[113]

Because of the state's increasing financial problems, a host of additional responsibilities began to fall to Turner and his men, such as enforcement of the wildlife laws. As a result, a harbor raid became big news in March 1932.

Deputy Virgil Wright had arrested eight fishermen for illegal harvesting near the Port Everglades inlet. In addition to their boats and nets, Wright confiscated 2,000 pounds of mackerel and other game fish. At the court hearing that followed, numerous sport fishermen, concerned about the threat such activities posed to the county's tourist trade (as well as their own livelihoods), demanded that the lawbreakers be given stiff penalties.[114]

Even more dramatic, however, was the blasting of a 40-foot gap in the West Dixie Highway in October 1929. The explosion, which could be heard for several miles, released a torrent of water. Two hours later, six masked and heavily-armed men held a guard at gunpoint while they cut a hole in the Middle River Drainage District dike.

The perpetrators were thought to be farmers whose lands had flooded when the normal flow of water to the New River was blocked (a condition that now was entering its third week). Fearing attacks, Turner had assigned special deputies to the roads and dams that were preventing the flood waters from draining but had ordered these officers not to use their firearms.

The destruction of West Dixie Highway and the Middle River dike afforded some relief to the western farmers, but at the expense of flooding the lands of the county's eastern farmers, who were wealthier and had more political clout.

Doyle E. Carlton, governor of Florida (1929–33)

Despite being at home sick in bed, Turner took charge of the situation, his main goal being to prevent further violence. Meanwhile, the county commission indicated it planned to do nothing for the time being and refused to let the drainage district intervene.

Fed up, the eastern farmers sent a telegram to Governor Carlton. In part, it read as follows:

> Appeal has been made to the sheriff for adequate protection, to investigate and apprehend participants in this lawless mob.
>
> He refuses to perform his duty and take necessary steps. We therefore appeal to you, as our governor, to take all immediate measures to protect us and to compel law enforcement in Broward county.[115]

In the meantime, administrators at the drainage district "made official demand upon Turner, as high sheriff of Broward county, to investigate these crimes"[116] and to apprehend the guilty parties. If he failed to do so, they promised to "seek redress to higher powers."[117]

In an attempt to restore order (and prevent further damage to his political reputation), Turner announced that he and his deputies were actively gathering evidence and would soon bring the guilty to justice. And, in fact, only a short time later six western farmers were arrested and charged with dynamiting the highway and damaging the drainage dike. The trial of these men took place on Friday, January 24, 1930. After hearing the state's evidence and deciding it failed to prove anything, Judge Shippey ordered the jury to acquit them.

It was around this time that newspapers began using the word "detective" in describing some of the investigations being conducted. Under the headline "Sheriff Wars on Robbers," for example, a reporter recounted how a "band of Negro robbers" had been broken up by "[s]pecial detectives and deputies from the office of the sheriff,"[118] who trailed the criminals to Miami, where they were arrested.

As before, humorous incidents sometimes found their way into the news. A thief, dubbed the "pants burglar" by the press, had been pilfering clothing all over Fort Lauderdale. When he broke into the home of Deputy McDonald and made off with his trousers, the red-faced lawman attempted to downplay the event, claiming that his pockets contained only a nickel and a slot-machine slug. Apparently, no one thought to ask McDonald what he was doing with the latter item.

Another story reported that "Sheriff A. W. Turner had eighty sacks of choice liquor stored in the courthouse here. 'Had' is right. He hasn't got it now."[119] The article then explained that the robbers had made off with 480 quarts, estimated to be worth $2,500. Adding insult to injury, during their getaway they had driven their car across the courthouse lawn, destroying the flower beds.

It is hard to say whether Turner personally supported prohibition, although in public he always expressed strong anti-alcohol sentiments. Of course, doing so was good politics. To further burnish his teetotaler credentials, Turner sometimes held "teasing parties" at which confiscated liquor would be poured into the streets (thereby teasing the wets). While these events normally generated favorable newspaper coverage, on one occasion some ashes fell from Turner's pipe. When they reached the alcohol-saturated ground, they ignited a fire that quickly spread to the drainage trap in the courthouse garage. Luckily, Deputy Campbell (the former Dania fire chief) was able to put out the blaze before Turner suffered further embarrassment.

There were still more off-beat stories that came to the public's attention. When federal agent Lucian A. Spencer discovered that Lonnie Buck, a 25-year-old Creek Indian, was living on the Seminole Indian reservation near Dania with Lena Huff, a 15-year-old girl, he had Turner arrest Buck. After several days in the county jail, Buck reluctantly agreed to marry Huff, and later that afternoon a ceremony was performed at the county courthouse with Deputy Howell and BSO bookkeeper Sara Freeman serving as witnesses. According to one newspaper account, "The bride was neat but gaudy, in a wedding gown of approximately 75 yards of calico of various colors, predominantly bright red … [while the] groom wore the conventional green shirt and a pair of grey trousers."[120]

Buck was not the only unhappy inhabitant of the Broward jail, for another cell soon held "Doc" St. Clair, a self-proclaimed voodooist. He ended up doing time for selling, for the princely sum of $12, a magic powder he promised would give buyers the ability to commit crimes without being caught and attract members of the opposite sex. When John H. Brooks, a Pompano man, complained that the powder had failed to live up to its advertising, St. Clair was arrested. According to a local newspaper, the authorities had been "seeking St. Clair for a long time … for 'quack' doctoring."[121]

In March 1930, Alphonse G. "Al" Capone, the notorious Chicago gangster, was released from the Eastern State penitentiary in Gratersford, Pennsylvania, after serving ten months on a weapons charge. When he mentioned that he was thinking of moving to Dade County's Palm Island (into a house he had purchased in 1928), Governor Carlton immediately sent telegrams to all of the state's sheriffs advising: "It is reported that Al Capone is on his way to Florida. Arrest promptly if he comes your way and escort him to [the] state border with instructions not to return. He cannot remain in Florida."[122] Three days later, however, U.S. District Judge Halsted L. Ritter (who in 1936 would be removed from the bench for accepting free meals and lodging) issued an injunction preventing Carlton's instructions from being carried out.

Capone reached Miami on Easter Sunday 1930 and told reporters that he was looking forward to "a rest which I think I deserve."[123] Local reaction was both quick and furious. The Dade County grand jury denounced the mobster and "indorse[d], command[ed] and urge[d] all legitimate efforts to exterminate from this community what clearly appears to be a cancerous growth of organized crime,"[124] while government officials repeatedly had Capone arrested on spurious charges, a tactic his attorney, Vincent C. Giblin, labeled harassment.

Although Capone was unwelcome in Miami, Broward was a different story. Mayor J. Dewey Hawkins, for example, said that

> [i]f Al Capone desires to live in Florida, he can come to Oakland Park. If he obeys the laws and respects the rights of other residents of this community he can remain as long as he likes.
>
> Our city offers many attractions to prospective residents….
>
> While I do not approve of Capone's actions as reported in newspapers and magazines, his past does not concern me. I have known hundreds of so-called "undesirables" who later became useful citizens. Oakland Park is a city of opportunity.[125]

Al Capone's estate on Palm Island (1930)

Halsted L. Ritter, U.S. District Judge for the
Southern District of Florida (1929–36)

Al Capone (right) arriving in Miami (1930)

As tempting as Hawkins's invitation might have been, Capone wanted to build a mansion a little further north, on a quiet and isolated finger of land extending out from Boca Raton into the Hillsboro Canal. To do so, he took an option on fifty acres of land, but when officials balked at the idea he abandoned the plan. In 1952, five years after his death, a canal was cut through this peninsula, creating "Capone Island" in Broward County.

In the meantime, Capone's associates had begun causing serious problems for Sheriff Turner. After a string of burglaries baffled Dania's cops, Turner assigned Deputy Hobb Campbell to investigate. Together with Dania night patrolman Horace Mathews, Campbell began going on stakeouts. Finally, at dawn one morning, the pair noticed a car driving around the city's business district before stopping at a fruit store on Dixie Highway. When the store was broken into, Campbell and Mathews sprang into action and arrested three men and a woman. Although the charges against one of the men and the woman were dropped, Dan Collins (also known as Blowser Walsh, Dapper Dan, John Leeger, and the Kinkaid Kid) and A. Pond (sometimes called Roy Rogers) were unable to make bail and were remanded to the Broward County Jail to await trial.

Al Capone's attorney Vincent C. Giblin (1897–1965)

At some point in their stay, Deputy Arden Marshall decided to move the two prisoners to the jail's third floor, where they could be guarded more closely. During this transfer, six hacksaw blades were found in Pond's possession. From that point on, extra efforts were made to prevent an escape.

Three days later, Sheriff Turner received an unsigned note. Written on stationery from the Savoy Hotel in Miami, it warned: "Spring Dan Collins and A. Pond before Saturday night or take [the] consequences."[126] In a press conference, Turner exclaimed, "Let there be no doubts—when Saturday night has passed, Dan Collins, Blowser Walsh or whatever his name is, and Pond will still be in my custody up there in jail."[127]

The next day, Turner received another anonymous message. Although he claimed not to mind the threats, the sheriff expressed annoyance at the fact they were being sent postage due. "Why don't they come up here and do something instead of bombarding me with all these letters and telegrams?"[128] he asked. "Why not a little more action and less talk?"[129]

Nevertheless, Turner ordered his deputies to take extra target practice. "We have one of the latest things in machine guns," he explained, "a Thompson submachine gun capable of firing 250 shots per minute, and what is more, we have an expert machine gun wielder and plenty of ammunition to go along with it."[130] The expert was Deputy Albert Jones, who had been trained in the use of machine guns in Illinois. This precaution turned out to be unnecessary, however, and Collins and Pond remained in jail until their trial two months later, at which time they were acquitted.

Apart from these moments of high drama, the work of the Sheriff's Office was fairly routine. In November 1931, for example, Benjamin A. Tolbert, the Dean of Students at the University of Florida, sent Turner a directory of current undergraduates

> to enable you to help us detect people who are posing as students ... and thereby attempting to work some kind of crooked game. We have letters from various parts of the state informing us that young men posing as University students have cashed worthless checks and, in many ways, have imposed on people who desire to help worthy students. This list may enable you to detect such imposters.[131]

Indeed, a review of Turner's correspondence during this time reveals he often was bogged down in minutiae, much of which involved other law enforcement agencies. In April 1929, for example, Turner wrote to J.C. Sheffield, the head of the U.S. Immigration Service's local office, to complain about the failure of one of Sheffield's agents to comply with Florida's vehicle registration law. "It is very embarrassing to me to have your man driving over the county with an old license tag as I have instructions from the Governor to enforce this law in every case."[132] Turner also sarcastically inquired whether "any distinction [is] to be made between your department and any ordinary citizen who violates this law."[133]

In fact, Turner was under strict orders to enforce the state's tag laws, and one month earlier had promised Governor Carlton that no exceptions would be made:

> In reply to your letter of March 5th, with regard to enforcement of the Motor Vehicle Law [I] will say that I am very much in favor of the stand you have taken in this matter and am doing all in my power to cooperate with you in bringing any and all violators to justice.
> I am always ready to do my duty when ever called upon in enforcing the laws of our state.[134]

Even touchier was having to deal with the ire of the St. Lucie County Commission, which in October 1931 accused Turner and his men of regularly helping to dump vagrants from South Florida in their territory. Being completely accurate, Turner found it hard to respond to this charge.

The "Hobo Special," as it was called, was the coordinated movement of "undesirables" from Miami to points north, carried out by the various police departments and sheriff's offices along the way. Cops in Miami would round up vagrants and other petty offenders and transport them to the Dade County line. There, Turner's men would pick them up and deliver them to the northern boundary of their county, where Palm Beach deputies would take over, moving them further along. During one two-week period, it was reported that the Broward Sheriff's Office had transported more than 100 vagrants "in an effort to eliminate the large number of petty offenses that have been perpetrated [by such persons]."[135]

At times, it must have seemed to Turner that there was no end to the petty problems he had to handle. In February 1929, for example, L.M. Hatton, Jr., the sheriff of Hillsborough County, Florida, wrote to Turner to request a $2.55 refund following the arrest of a suspect named Porter Brown. Although Hatton had asked Turner to take Brown into custody, "we did not mention any thing about [his] car or his personal belongings."[136] As such, Hatton disclaimed responsibility for the cost of impounding Brown's automobile, saying, "We do not feel that this item should be charged to us as we are not interested in any of the ... defendant's personal effects."[137]

Another letter, from the Florida Attorney General's Office, informed Turner that in the June 1932 Democratic primary for sheriff he would have to refrain from giving away pencils and blotters bearing campaign messages. Although the monetary value of such items was indisputably "slight," Turner was warned that distributing them would constitute "a violation of the corrupt practice act."[138] At the same time, Turner was being pestered by the Miami Broadcasting Company to buy campaign spots on its radio station WQAM, which, its advertising director claimed, "is heard clearly night and day throughout all of Broward County ... and ... will be a powerful medium in determining who is to be successful in the coming primaries."[139]

Yet despite many daily frustrations, Turner appears to have retained his basic decency. In July 1929, for example, he sent a letter to a sheriff in Georgia asking him to try to recover the $4.50 an employer owed a man who was being held in the Broward County Jail. Likewise, in February 1930, he took the time to help a woman get back twenty-one chickens that had been confiscated by the department (the surviving records do not indicate the reason for the birds' seizure).[140]

One of Turner's most pressing concerns during his fourth term was his department's fiscal health. Times were tough, budgets were lean, and conditions kept getting worse. But compared to municipal police departments, the Broward Sheriff's Office was a bit better off because it operated on a commission basis.

Ernest Amos, comptroller of Florida (1917–33)

The nature of this system can be most readily understood by examining a letter Turner sent to Ernest Amos, the state comptroller, in January 1930, reporting on the previous year. According to Turner's calculations, the department had total net receipts of $5,623.46, and "[a]s the statutes show a Sheriff is entitled to a net income of $5,000.00 and sixty per cent of the next $3,000.00 or any fraction thereof, I have given the county commissioners a check for $249.38."[141] In other words, Turner had earned $5,374.08 in 1929, a figure that was to drop dramatically in each of the next three years.

As sheriff, Turner needed to keep the department's costs under control, because every extra dollar spent literally came out of his pocket. In addition to the salaries of his regular deputies and bookkeeper, Turner had to pay his special deputies and bailiffs. In a typical month, fifteen to twenty such auxiliary personnel were on the payroll, although few made more than $10.

Wages, however, were just one part of the equation. There also were fees to be paid to other sheriffs for making arrests, the cost of picking up and transporting prisoners, oil and gas (as well as general maintenance) for the department's cars, and food for the jail's inhabitants. From 1930 to 1932, the expenses of the Sheriff's Office averaged $15,200 a year.

Income was derived primarily from the county, which paid for various services. In addition, small amounts came from attorneys (for serving papers) and other sheriffs (for making arrests).

Between 1930 and 1932, the department collected roughly $18,500 a year; after expenses, Turner was left with an annual average of $3,300. Much of this amount was attributable to the relatively large "profit" he made feeding prisoners. In 1929–30, Turner charged the county sixty-five cents a day for each prisoner. In 1931–32, this figure stayed the same for the first 3,000 prisoner-days but then dropped to fifty cents.

In May 1932, Turner wrote to the U.S. Marshal's Office in Miami and explained that the daily cost to feed a federal prisoner named John W. Brazier would be ninety cents because "[t]his man's diet requires special care in selecting and preparing his food."[142] In a July 1932 letter to the U.S. Marshal's Office in Jacksonville, Turner, apparently referring to Brazier, declined to offer the federal government any discounts because "[s]ome of your prisoners in the past have required a special diet [which] necessitated the purchasing of extra food from the regular list bought for county prisoners."[143]

As small as these amounts seem, the sheriff's food bills were even smaller. From 1930 to 1932, Turner's grocery and meat costs averaged $1,450 per year, while the fees generated for food services averaged $4,630. The difference ($3,180) accounted for nearly all of Turner's net income during this period.

In his financial report for 1931, Turner listed $1,479.29 in unpaid county fees. He also recorded an expense that had never before appeared: "interest on money borrowed to make payroll."[144]

In 1932, at the height of the Great Depression, matters became downright desperate. Many Broward residents were unable to pay their taxes, and in August nearly two-thirds of the county's property roll was put up for auction to pay back taxes.

A short time earlier, Turner had written to Florida Attorney General Cary D. Landis explaining that the county owed him more than $3,000 and asking what he could do about it. According to the distraught lawman, "[i]t is impossible for me to run my office and furnish the people the protection they need without money, and the only way I can get the money is from the county. I have tried every way possible to get the commissioners to raise enough money to pay me."[145]

In spite of these difficulties, Turner wanted to remain sheriff and in June 1932 sought the Democratic nomination. Although he was one of two favorites in a field of eight candidates,[146] he lost in the first round and therefore spent the last six months of his term as a lame duck.

Cary D. Landis, attorney general of Florida (1931–38)

By this time, the county owed him $4,000, and in early July a headline in the *Fort Lauderdale Daily News* informed readers: "Sheriff Threatens to Shut Down County Jail." In the article that followed, it was reported that Turner planned to close the jail, and set all the prisoners free, if he was not paid by Monday, August 1st. In a letter to Governor Carlton, Turner explained: "Feeling that I have exhausted my credit to carry the county and spending money out of my own pocket to feed prisoners and run the office I feel that I am justified in taking this action."[147]

Uncertain what would happen, the Broward courts began dispensing rapid— and very questionable—justice. The grand jury was hastily reconvened and the following week a special court session was held. After five days, twelve defendants had been tried, and not one of them had been acquitted, leading the *Fort Lauderdale Daily News* to declare, "Circuit Court Juries Go on 'Guilty' Spree." The sentences, which ranged from nine months to twenty years, were all to be served in the state prison.

Just as matters were about to come to a head, Judge Ritter stepped in and warned Turner that if he tried to close the jail he would be arrested on federal charges. This caused Turner to back down, and a short time later the county paid Turner some of the money it owed him.

Nevertheless, the situation remained tense. In late August 1932, it was reported that "[n]o expense fees, no arrests—is Sheriff A. W. Turner's policy from now on."[148] Nevertheless, the county continued to fall behind—by the end of the year, it owed Turner almost $7,000. To economize, Turner let Deputy McDonald go in July 1932 and reduced the salaries of his remaining officers by 40%.

When he asked the county commissioners why they were having so much trouble paying him, Turner was told there was no money left in the Fine and Forfeiture Fund. In 1922, the wiretappers case had pumped $20,000 into this account, so where had it gone? The answer, laid out in a November 1931 editorial in the *Fort Lauderdale Daily News,* was quite ironic: Big Bill Hicks's three murder trials had cost the county more than $30,000, thereby draining the fund and resulting in taxpayers having to "contribute a special millage to go into the fine and forfeiture fund."[149] At least Turner could take solace in the fact that one of the few fees he *had* been able to collect from the county was the $39.38 it had cost to "carr[y] Bill Hicks to Dade County for trial."[150]

In January 1933, Turner left office after nearly eleven years of service. As the first man to hold the post of Broward County sheriff, he had established most of the department's guidelines and procedures, and many of his policies would remain in place for years to come. Although still quite popular when he departed, his record was a decidedly mixed one, particularly on minority rights.

Turner's views on race relations are perhaps best captured by a letter he wrote in September 1930 regarding a proposed Fort Lauderdale hotel and golf course aimed at African-Americans. Saying he had "given careful consideration" to the idea, Turner expressed support for the project on the condition that

> such a development would be entirely surrounded by water, and no property owned by white people would be located within such water boundary.... My firm belief is that the white citizenry of this county would heartily welcome a colored development such as you propose, excluded and isolated as it would be, from all property holdings of the white race.[151]

Ever the pragmatist, Turner also noted that the project "would add considerabl[y] to the value of the taxable property of the county and furnish employment to quite a number of the local people."[152]

While serving as sheriff, Turner appears to have had a used car dealership, and a 1929 Fort Lauderdale occupational license application was mailed to him at his "Auto Boneyard." After turning in his badge, Turner again became a farmer, but in 1937 his health began to decline. He died at his home in Fort Lauderdale on December 13, 1940, at the age of seventy-five.[153]

Sheriff Aden Turner during his final term in office (c. 1930)

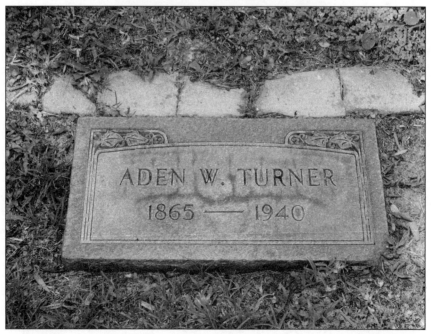

Tombstone of Sheriff Aden Turner (Evergreen Cemetery, Fort Lauderdale)

CHAPTER 4

The Clark-Lee Years (1933–50)

In the 1932 Democratic primary, most people expected Sheriff Aden Turner to win, but when the votes were counted Jerome R. Barnes, a 40-year-old county commissioner from Hollywood, and Walter R. Clark, a 27-year-old butcher with no political experience, stood atop the crowded field. Turner, who had come in third, immediately endorsed Clark and in a newspaper ad said, "I wish to announce to my friends that I will support Walter R. Clark in the second Primary, because I have every reason to believe that he is a man of unquestionable character and I feel that he would make Broward County a good Sheriff."[154] With this backing, Clark easily beat Barnes in the run-off, 2,408 votes to 1,633 votes (a margin of 60%–40%), and in November recorded a similar victory over Republican Joseph P. Moe, 3,065 votes to 2,077 votes (a margin of 60%–40%).

Except for a brief interruption in 1942–43, Clark would be Broward's top law enforcement officer for the next seventeen years. He remains the county's longest-serving sheriff, having been elected five times, and his record seems almost certain to stand forever.

Clark's durability, however, pales in comparison to his dishonesty. Suspended by two different governors, grilled by a U.S. Senate committee investigating organized crime, and indicted and placed on trial for gambling offenses, Clark is the very embodiment of law enforcement run amok. And yet, for much of his tenure, he wielded enormous influence, not just in Broward, but in the halls of power in both Tallahassee and Washington. Indeed, there even was a time when Clark counted President Harry S. Truman among his friends.

Sheriff Walter R. Clark (1933–42)

Walter Reid Clark was born December 11, 1904, on a farm along the New River. His parents were poor and eventually moved to the Lake Okeechobee area, where recently drained land had been opened for settlement. The family's situation became desperate in September 1917, when Clark's father James died

Walter R. Clark, sheriff of Broward County
(1933–1942 and 1943–50)

from a rattlesnake bite, leaving his widow with four boys between the ages of seven and twelve. Several months later, Annie Clark moved them to a home in the center of Fort Lauderdale, and Walter, as the oldest son, left school to help support his siblings. He was hired by a local butcher and began to learn a trade.

While meeting at the White House, President Harry S. Truman and
Fort Lauderdale businessman Harold A. "Hal" Keats sent their regards to
Sheriff Walter Clark (1948)

In October 1919, Clark nearly lost his hand in an industrial accident. According to a news item in the *Fort Lauderdale Sentinel*, "Walter was grinding sausage at Lasher's Market and while pushing down the meat got his fingers caught in the grinder. He had sufficient presence of mind to immediately turn off the electric current."[155] Despite suffering severe cuts, Clark recovered from the mishap.

During these years, Clark became known for being scrupulously honest, and this reputation would prove a major plus when he decided to seek office. In contrast, Bert Lasher, Clark's first boss, was a crook. Accused of dealing in stolen automobiles and found guilty of grand larceny, Lasher fled to the Bahamas after the Florida Supreme Court upheld his conviction.[156] Eventually tiring of being a fugitive, he returned to the state to serve a three-year prison sentence.

Clark faced a number of hurdles when he entered the Democratic primary for sheriff in 1932. He was young, had no law enforcement experience, and was a political neophyte. But Clark had several things going for him. He was personable, well-liked, a leader in his church, and a Sunday school teacher.

And as an "honest butcher," he could count on the votes of numerous struggling housewives, who had relied on him for years for a fair shake.

Clark also had name recognition. In March 1931, during Fort Lauderdale's River Revelry festival (where he had been crowned king), he had claimed to be the first white baby born in Broward. While this was pure fiction, it propelled him into the public eye and allowed Clark to bill himself as the "pioneer candidate."

Walter Clark and Margaret Oliver, king and queen
of Fort Lauderdale's 1931 River Revelry festival

Robert L. "Bob" Clark, chief deputy of Broward County (1933–42 and 1943–50)

After defeating Barnes in the Democratic run-off, Clark managed to turn his political inexperience into an advantage in the general election. Running as an outsider against Moe, he styled himself a man of the people rather than a member of the "old crowd." His newspaper ads insisted that if he was elected, he would "enter upon his duties without any political promises."[157] They also described Clark as having been a successful businessman for fifteen years. The public, eager for an honest sheriff who was beholden to no one, enthusiastically embraced Clark's candidacy.

After taking office on Tuesday, January 2, 1933, Clark announced his list of appointments. For chief deputy, Clark chose his brother, Robert L. "Bob" Clark, whose previous work experience consisted of jobs as a deliveryman and soda jerk. Once again, nepotism had found its way into the Broward Sheriff's Office.

Surprisingly, Clark then reappointed several deputies. This was a significant step forward for the department. In the past, sheriffs always had cleaned house, leading to a loss of institutional memory and a steep learning curve. Clark's decision to forego this practice recognized the significant benefits to be gained by having a cadre of career lawmen.

*Broward County Commissioner Henry J. Driggers (left) and
Sheriff Walter Clark after a day of hunting (c. 1940)*

Arden Marshall was rehired as the warden of the Broward County Jail. Marshall had been on the job since 1929 and by all accounts had performed his duties well. Clark also retained Deputy Virgil Wright, whose patrol area was the county's northern territory, and bookkeeper Sara Freeman, whose services proved crucial as the office continued to suffer from a lack of funds. Clark completed his personnel roster by bringing on a new officer, C. "Dick" Goodrich, as a deputy-at-large.

During Clark's first year in office, the Twenty-First Amendment repealed prohibition, and a short time later Broward voted to become a wet county. As a result, the Sheriff's Office suddenly found itself relieved of what had been a major preoccupation. Nevertheless, alcohol-related arrests did not disappear completely. In September 1934, for example, Clark's deputies conducted a series of raids designed to curtail the sale of moonshine. Clark also cooperated with federal authorities and occasionally helped them take into custody local residents accused of selling "liquor to Indians."[158]

Throughout his many years in office, Clark was well-liked in the white community, which regarded him as generous and kind. One reason for this was his unrelenting efforts to find work for his unemployed constituents. When this proved impossible, he often reached into his own pocket to provide gifts or make loans.

Clark's reputation was quite different in the African-American community, which viewed him as the stereotypical Southern sheriff. Clark insisted, for example, that blacks stand up as he entered a room, and in 1944, when a man named John Wooten failed to do so, he was arrested for vagrancy and died later that night in his jail cell. Clark brushed off the incident by saying that Wooten had fallen "out of his bunk and hit his head."[159]

Clark further abused African Americans by rounding up poor blacks every year at harvest time and charging them with vagrancy. The prisoners then would be given a choice of paying a $35 fine (which they could not afford) or working it off by picking fruits and vegetables. After the crops were in, the farmers would pay Clark for each prisoner's work (thereby erasing the fine), an amount far below the going rate. In addition to providing the Sheriff's Office with money, this scheme endeared Clark to landowners. The fact that Florida law prohibited such arrangements did not deter Clark in the least.

African-Americans were not alone in their suffering. In January 1934, the famed British aviatrix Amy J. Mollison (the first woman to fly solo from England to Australia) spent three hours in the county jail waiting for friends to arrive with the $70 needed to pay her fine. Mollison claimed that when two deputies tried to stop her car, she fled because they were too "harsh and discourteous"[160] to be officers. In England, she said, "[p]olice don't act like gangsters."[161] When the pair finally caught her, Mollison hit one and then tried to escape on foot. Bob Clark denied any wrongdoing and insisted he had shown Mollison his badge.

The Sheriff's Office conducted two major criminal investigations during Clark's first years in office, and both involved African-Americans. On Saturday, May 13, 1933, Robert M. Darsey, the white owner of a fish market in Pompano, was beaten and robbed of $75. He died the next day. Immediately after the crime, Deputy Virgil Wright rounded up more than twenty suspects. Within twenty-four hours, only four remained in custody—Isiah Chambers, Charlie Davis, Jack Williamson, and Walter Woodward.

When rumors began circulating that a lynch mob was heading to the courthouse, Clark wisely moved the prisoners to the Dade County Jail (a tactic that was frequently used, at least when the sheriff wanted to keep someone alive). Soon, the mob, which by now had grown to fifty, besieged the courthouse but left when it became clear the men were not inside.

In the meantime, confessions were obtained from all four defendants, who were charged with first degree murder. While Davis, Williamson, and Woodward quickly agreed to plead guilty, Chambers chose to go to trial. After less than thirty minutes of deliberation, the jury brought back a guilty verdict and refused to recommend leniency.

African-Americans picking crops on a Broward farm (c. 1935)

British aviatrix Amy J. Mollison (1930)

Broward County deputy's badge (c. 1935)

Sheriff Walter Clark with (from left to right) Walter Woodward,
Jack Williamson, Charlie Davis, and Isiah Chambers (1933)

George W. Tedder, Sr., circuit judge of Broward County (1929–55)

On Saturday, June 17, 1933, Circuit Judge George W. Tedder, Sr. sentenced the quartet to the electric chair, the first time in Broward's history that the death penalty was imposed. He then commended Clark and his deputies for their professionalism in solving the case.

For the next nine years, however, the quality of their work would be the subject of intense debate. At issue was whether the confessions had been coerced. Throughout the ensuing appeals, the lawmen denied using brutal tactics to obtain the statements, but the evidence, including the defendants' physical scars, told a different story. According to the Florida Supreme Court:

> On the issue joined in this case, the evidence is in hopeless conflict. The defendants in their behalf testified that they were brutally treated and put through all sorts and kinds of third degree methods for about a week before the confessions were secured and on the last night before they confessed, they were not permitted to sleep but were threatened, whipped, and tortured all night. The confessions were secured about 6 o'clock the following morning. As to the charges of having been whipped, tortured, and ill treated, their testimony is not corroborated.

It is corroborated as [to] the fact of having been kept up all night and questioned the night before the confessions were secured.

The evidence of defendants as to torture and cruel treatment is flatly denied by the sheriff, the jailer, and other witnesses. The latter testimony is corroborated by that of several prisoners who were in jail with [the] defendants at the time, a telephone workman who was working about the jail, the State's Attorney, who took the confessions, and other witnesses. All of the questioning took place in the jail.[162]

Monday, August 7, 1933, was set as execution day. The condemned men had remained in the Broward County Jail for several weeks after their sentencing, but as the fateful date drew near they were transferred to death row at Raiford State Prison. They were still in the county lockup when an editorial in the *Fort Lauderdale Daily News* boasted: "A quadruple electrocution will be unprecedented in the annals of state history, and it is believed that very few such electrocutions are on record in modern penal history in the country."[163] Under a sub-headline announcing, "To Set New Record," it was reported that the executions would surpass the "record of three electrocutions in the state's death chair on the same day."[164]

In fact, however, an appeal to the Florida Supreme Court resulted in a stay of the executions.[165] Indeed, the dispute would reach all the way to the U.S. Supreme Court (a first for a Broward County case), where in February 1940 the confessions were ruled inadmissible.[166] Besides its practical effect (at their new trials, the men received directed verdicts of not guilty), the ruling, coincidentally issued on Lincoln's birthday, was long on symbolism.

As the legal proceedings ground slowly forward, many of Broward's white residents began to feel that justice was being thwarted. Frustrated by the initial stays of execution, they grew increasingly angry as the appeals mounted. Finally, their rage boiled over.

On Tuesday, July 16, 1935, Marion Jones, a 30-year-old white woman, allegedly was attacked by a black man at her home on Davie Road. She fought him off, and she was *not* raped (although a rumor to the contrary later circulated freely). The assailant ran away and for a time managed to elude law enforcement. Three days later, an African-American tenant farmer named Rubin Stacey was captured near Deerfield. Jones identified him as her attacker, as did her young son, and Stacey's shoes matched prints found in Jones's yard. Stacey was locked up in the county jail and news of his capture spread quickly throughout the area.[167]

In the official version of what happened next, Clark learned that a mob was planning to march to the courthouse, grab Stacey, and lynch him. He therefore ordered two of his regular deputies (Bob Clark and Virgil Wright) and three spe-

Spectators observing the lifeless body of Rubin Stacey (1935)

cial deputies to drive Stacey to the Dade County Jail. Avoiding several roadblocks that had been set up to stop them, the six men began the long trip to Miami.

As they made their way south, they found themselves being pursued by the crowd, who soon managed to force the deputies' car off the road. Fearing for their lives and badly outnumbered, the lawmen decided to temporarily surrender Stacey to the growing throng.

Having gotten their hands on him, the horde drove Stacey to a tree near Jones's home. There, they used a wire to hang him, after which he was shot repeatedly. By the time the deputies managed to reach the scene, Stacey was dead.

Upon learning what had happened, Clark immediately ordered the body cut down and taken to the mortuary. It would be several hours before this could be accomplished, however, due to the fact that people were now driving to the site to view the ghastly display for themselves. According to the *Fort Lauderdale Daily News*, more than 1,000 spectators turned out, with some bringing their children with them. There also were reports of souvenir hunting, with the more ghoulish taking pieces of the wire, bark from the tree, and items from the mutilated body.

David Sholtz, governor of Florida (1933–37)

At the coroner's inquest that followed, the deputies were found to be blameless and Stacey's death was attributed to the actions of "a person or persons unknown."[168] But Governor David Sholtz ordered local prosecutors to conduct a full investigation, which led to a grand jury hearing.

A front page editorial in the *Fort Lauderdale Daily News* summed up public opinion fairly well. It supported the inquiry and condemned the lynching, but only in half-hearted terms, and suggested that the incident was the understandable by-product of the public's frustration with Darsey's killers, who, it was said, were using legal technicalities to avoid punishment. And while the editorial denounced Stacey's death as a violation of law and order, it left no doubt that the right man had been punished, observing that "[t]he execution here yesterday wiped out a menace to society."[169]

The grand jury called twenty-nine witnesses over a two day period, after which it concurred with the conclusion reached at the coroner's inquest. According to the deputies, 100 men in fifty cars had run them off the road and taken Stacey, and it had been some time before they had been able to get their vehicle restarted. They also claimed that based on a hunch, they had hurried to where they thought Stacey was being taken, thereby explaining how they were able to get to the scene so soon after the hanging.

Oddly enough, none of the deputies recognized any of the vigilantes, nor could they identify any of their automobiles. Apparently, all of those who had participated in the hastily-organized chase had had the foresight to hide their faces and cover their license plates.

The foregoing, representing the official version of Rubin Stacey's death, now was supported by both the findings of the coroner's inquest and the grand jury's investigation. But there also was an unofficial version, which was repeated throughout the county in hushed tones. And it was both more believable and much more sinister.

In this alternative telling of the story, the deputies never lost their prisoner to an anonymous mob. Instead, Stacey had been driven to a clearing in the sheriff's car. After getting out, he was led, handcuffed, to a tall pine tree by Bob Clark. The chief deputy then went to Jones's house and tore down her wire clothesline. After walking back, Clark looked at Stacey, yelled, "You black son of a bitch,"[170] and then strung the frightened man up while fifteen to twenty white people, who had gathered upon hearing there was going to be a lynching, watched.

As Stacey swung back and forth, Bob Clark told the onlookers that if they wanted to see a lynching they had to be part of it. He then passed around his handgun and ordered the crowd to shoot. While many of the bullets missed, seventeen found their mark. A woman who had been present (and who, along with her husband, had shot at the body) later explained that Clark intended to silence the witnesses by making them culpable. And indeed, the coroner's report expressed uncertainty as to whether Stacey had died from asphyxiation or a bullet wound.

Former Municipal Court Judge G. Harold Martin later noted that he and most whites believed the unofficial version. "That was no doubt planned.... Maybe not by the sheriff, but his deputies were a party to it. Bob Clark was unscrupulous."[171]

Although Rubin Stacey's hanging usually is referred to as Broward County's only lynching, this is largely a matter of semantics. In a 1992 interview in the *Miami Herald*, Louis Benton, the son of George Benton, Broward's first black funeral home owner, pointed out that "[y]ou didn't have to hang a man to lynch him. You could get a man in the back of a car and tell him to get out and run for his life. And bang, bang. That was it. They'd say he was escaping...."[172]

Trial by gunfire came to be an accepted part of life in Broward County in the 1930s, and the disfigured bodies of murdered black men almost always wound up at the Benton funeral home. As Louis Benton noted, "Usually my father and his crew would go get them. Or sometimes they'd bring them by themselves, usually in a police car."[173]

Two months after Stacey was lynched, another prisoner in Bob Clark's custody died a violent death, but this time there were no accusations of foul play. The chief deputy had gone to the home of John G. Flanders, a beer salesman, shortly after midnight and arrested him for embezzling $700. Not wanting to leave the house in his pajamas, he asked Clark for permission to change. "I told him to go and get dressed," Clark explained, "and he stepped into a bathroom. A minute or so later he came out and said he had taken poison."[174] Flanders then asked to speak to his wife, and spent the next few minutes calmly discussing their insurance policies. When it became clear he really had taken poison, Clark rushed Flanders to the hospital, where he was pronounced dead.

In the meantime, Walter Clark's popularity kept soaring. In the 1936 Democratic primary campaign, he ran on his record and spoke about adopting modern crime fighting techniques to make the department more efficient. His opponent in the primary was Brack Cantrell, the owner of a local car dealership. Cantrell likewise favored efficiency, but also promised that if he was elected he would not hire any of his relatives. Cantrell's effort to make nepotism a campaign issue fizzled, however, and Clark won the primary handily, 3,486 votes to 1,634 votes (a margin of 68%–32%). In the November general election, Clark again beat Republican Joseph P. Moe, this time trouncing his 1932 rival. The final tally showed Clark with 4,862 votes to Moe's 1,367 votes (a margin of 78%–22%).

Early in the campaign, Clark endorsed Frederick P. Cone for governor. When Cone captured the statehouse, Clark had an important new ally, especially because Cone was not the sort of man to forget his friends. As a result, after he was sworn in on Tuesday, January 5, 1937, Clark found himself spending increasing amounts of time on political affairs, thereby leaving day-to-day matters to Bob Clark.

Broward County benefited handsomely from its sheriff's newfound clout. Road construction increased, the Tenth Street Causeway (now Sunrise Boulevard) was built (linking Federal Highway and State Road A1A), and the massive Pompano State Farmers Market (the biggest in the United States) was erected. In 1940, Clark convinced Cone to relocate the Florida State Road Department's regional headquarters from Miami to Fort Lauderdale, giving the local economy an enormous boost.

In March 1937, in a further bit of politicking, Clark was elected president of the Florida Sheriffs Association. At the organization's annual convention in Clearwater, Clark and "[lawmen] from forty counties listened to an array of speakers who included the state attorney general, Jerry Carter and a colleague on the railroad commission, the commissioner of agriculture, four state senators, two state representatives, the state comptroller, and Secretary of State Robert Gray."[175]

Inauguration of Florida Governor Fred P. Cone
(standing to the right of the microphone) (1937)

The Pompano State Farmers Market (c. 1940)

Governor Fred Cone (second from left) and his wife Mildred at Sheriff Walter Clark's wedding (Clark's bride Odelle Pitts is at the far right) (1937)

Besides enhancing Clark's personal reputation, these accomplishments caused a profound shift in public thinking. Suddenly, the Broward sheriff was recognized as the county's most powerful elected official. This perception would have important future consequences.

In July 1937, Clark, having divorced his first wife (Avis), married Odelle Pitts, a striking brunette, in a lavish ceremony in Jacksonville. The guest list, headed by Governor Cone, left no doubt regarding Clark's standing in the state.

Back in Broward, however, the newspapers were starting to publish stories about the amount of gambling that was taking place. The hard economic times had made betting more popular than ever among the locals, and in June 1935 the Florida Legislature had taken the extraordinary step of legalizing slot machines in a desperate effort to increase tax revenues. Although the statute's legitimacy was immediately questioned,[176] Clark allowed the machines to operate while the legal issues were worked out.[177] In his view, gambling created jobs, attracted tourists (who otherwise would go elsewhere), and provided the government with the funds it needed to operate. Many people agreed with this assessment.

A "temporarily legal" slot machine in Fort Lauderdale (1937)

Ironically, the upswing in both legal and illegal gambling brought a new generation of wiretappers to Broward County. Although it had only been thirteen years since Sheriff Turner had been driven from office by such swindlers, a newspaper editorial noted that, "Confidence men have been thick in south Florida this winter."[178] After finding it "strange that ancient gags, hoary with age, still catch suckers year after year," the piece quoted a recently-arrested wiretapper, who explained:

> The man we get is a crook himself. He is willing to take unfair advantage of somebody else. He is willing to enter a crooked dice game. He is willing to use illegal information about horse races. He is greedy. We do not consider it robbing him. It is merely a case of matching wits—and usually we are smarter than the people who try to beat us at our own games.[179]

In November 1936, Florida's voters decided to end the state's experiment with legalized slot machines. As a result, no new devices could be installed, and the existing ones would become illegal when their licenses expired on

Gangster Jacob "Jake" Lansky (at right, holding cigar box) entertaining servicemen at his Hallandale casino (1943)

Thursday, September 30, 1937.[180] In reporting the election results, one local newspaper said, "Florida showed nearly as much opposition to the slot machines as to the Republican candidates in Tuesday's general election."[181] Missing from this comment was the fact that it would be up to local (rather than state) officials to enforce the ban, and as far as Sheriff Clark was concerned, other matters were more important. Once again, most of his constituents seemed to agree.

With the authorities turning a blind eye, gambling of all types (but particularly bingo, bookmaking, craps, and roulette) flourished in Broward. And before long, the profits being generated by these enterprises caught the attention of organized crime figures.

In December 1936, brothers Jacob "Jake" Lansky and Meyer Lansky opened a gambling parlor in Hallandale. Similar ventures bankrolled by Al Capone, the Purple Gang from Detroit, and Charles "Lucky" Luciano and Frank Costello of New York soon followed. Overnight, the county became home to a number of high-end gambling clubs, which featured first-class restaurants and elaborate floor shows.

The list of shareholders in these establishments read like a "Who's Who" of the underworld, and even Albert Anastasia, the Mafia's "Lord High Executioner," had a piece of the action. Despite this fact, not a single mob hit took place in Broward, due to an agreement that the county was off-limits to killings. No one, it seemed, wanted to mess up a good thing.

In January 1937, however, *Real Detective Magazine* ran a story entitled "Exposing Florida's 'Fountain of Loot.'" After describing the county's gambling

The Hollywood (Florida) Country Club (c. 1925)

operations in detail, it claimed that "Broward is wide open as a barn door at milking time. Officials wink and turn their sun-tanned heads."[182]

The heart of the piece was a detailed reconstruction of a robbery that had taken place at the Hollywood Country Club. While the amount of money stolen was large ($18,000), what made the tale particularly intriguing was the role of the cops.

Prior to the heist, the casino manager had been visited every Saturday night by A.M. Wittkamp, the Hollywood chief of police. "What happened at these conferences was never revealed, except that the club's gaming privileges were never threatened."[183]

After the heist, the five robbers escaped in an old car with a shattered cylinder gasket, which significantly limited its speed. Although three Hollywood police officers were sitting outside the casino "in a 1936 model Hudson Patrol car, specially geared to make 110 miles an hour,"[184] they did not pursue the men. The plot then thickened:

> By sheer coincidence probably, insurance investigators from Chicago discovered that the Buick Sedan used by the bandits had been picked up by Hollywood police five days before the robbery, as a stolen machine from Titusville, Fla., some 200 miles up the coast. The car had been in the police garage until [shortly before the robbery], according to the young mechanic in charge, who was not a policeman. A parking attendant at the club and a cook, who happened to be sneaking a cigarette … established the identity of the car.[185]

In addition to the odd getaway car and the lack of a chase, the story noted that the insurance company had only grudgingly paid the $18,000 claim, the young mechanic was later found badly beaten in an alley (he had been worked over by men with blackjacks), and both the parking attendant and the cook were fired from their jobs two days after the robbery.

Although the article gained national attention, in South Florida it was hard to find. According to the *Fort Lauderdale Daily News*, all of the copies "disappeared from newsstands as if by magic. Where they went, who bought [up] this issue, has not been revealed, but it became almost impossible for anyone to obtain a copy."[186] As a result, the newspaper arranged to publish excerpts.

Hoping to contain the situation, Governor Cone ordered Sheriff Clark to "stop gambling in Broward County, if there's any gambling there."[187] This peculiar wording was intentional—after a quick investigation, Clark could deny that gambling was taking place and Cone could say that there was no problem that needed addressing.

Incensed by this subterfuge, the Fort Lauderdale Ministerial Association sent Cone affidavits identifying the county's gambling houses. According to Reverend James W. Marlin, the group's president, "the Governor has asked for proof that gambling does exist in the county and we are giving it to him. We are confident that ... he will take immediate action to effect the clean-up that is so badly needed and to wipe out this blot."[188]

When Cone failed to respond to the affidavits, the clergymen turned to the courts and succeeded in getting the issue before a Broward grand jury. After studying the matter, however, it declined to issue any indictments and echoed the sheriff's line that there was "no evidence of gambling"[189] in the county. Like most of the public, it appears the jurors were more worried about putting food on their tables than about the influence of organized crime.

Broward's attitude towards gambling during this period is perhaps best captured by the following story. On Sunday, February 28, 1937, Jack Bell, a sports reporter for the *Miami Daily News*, was visiting the casino at the Hollywood Country Club, where "smartly dressed people watched the dice cubes tumble or the roulette wheels spin."[190] There was fun and excitement in the air, but

> [t]hen Edgar Hoover, the Gee-est of the G-men, walked into the room....
>
> In an instant every eye was on the trim figure in the doorway. Every player stopped; every croupier stood immovable.... Only the roulette wheels moved, spinning endlessly, silently.
>
> Mr. Hoover, realizing what had happened, quickly stepped back out of the room. But even after he had gone, no one made a move to-

J. Edgar Hoover, director of the Federal Bureau of Investigation (1935–72)

ward the tables. In two minutes after his departure every player had quitted the gaming room, leaving only the croupiers and the dealers alone with their toys.

Why did it happen? Perhaps 'twas instinctive reaction caused by the realization that what they were doing was against the law.[191]

Despite the hard economic times, the county's population continued growing, forcing Sheriff Clark to increase his staff. A.M. Wittkamp, the police chief who had looked out for the casino at the Hollywood Country Club, was hired and given patrol responsibilities in south Broward. Clark also bolstered the department's crime-solving capabilities, adding Roy May, who had been a detective in New York, and Gene Ryan, who was put in charge of criminal investigations.

In April 1938, a chain gang being supervised by Deputy Ed Hansen discovered $150,000 in stolen jewels while cleaning up a graveyard near Hollywood. Although this find was hailed by both the FBI and the press, within weeks it was overshadowed by an even more sensational story.

Sheriff Walter Clark (center) and Chief Deputy Bob Clark (far right) with (from left to right) Deputies Lloyd Miller, Earl Sharp, and Roy May (c. 1940)

Sheriff Walter Clark (left), flanked by two FBI agents, examining a portion of the jewels discovered by Deputy Ed Hansen's chain gang (1938)

According to the *Fort Lauderdale Daily News*, Clark and his men had arrested "20 persons, including a white woman and man, and 18 Negroes,"[192] for being communist sympathizers. For proof, deputies pointed to a letter that had been written to one of the suspects (Willie R. Davis) that referred to him as "comrade." Another letter "was said to have been from a white woman in New York, furnishing [Davis with the] addresses of two other white women he met at a [communist] convention there...."[193] As a result, the entire group was charged with vagrancy.

Clark's actions unleashed protests from individuals and organizations all over the country. The National Negro Congress was particularly vocal in its criticism and threatened to take the matter all the way to the U.S. Supreme Court. Clark also was condemned by several labor unions (the president of the Broward Building Trades Council, however, praised him).

Locally, a circular distributed throughout Fort Lauderdale suggested that the raid had been conducted on behalf of a handful of "big planters" in Broward who wanted to maintain the "old terror system"[194] for keeping black workers powerless. "[T]hese people are represented by the brutal Deputy Sheriff [Bob] Clark," it insisted, "who terrorizes the Negro people into working on the plantation for slave wages."[195]

Notwithstanding the mounting pressure, Walter Clark stood his ground and made it clear that the case would not be dropped. He also threatened more raids on communist meetings "which [a]re [held] behind closed doors and [a]re attended by both white and colored people."[196] Two weeks later, however, all of the defendants were released when Judge Tedder found that the evidence "was not sufficient."[197]

In the 1940 Democratic primary, Clark faced two opponents—Brack Cantrell, whom he had defeated in the 1936 primary, and R.B. McDonald, who had been a deputy under Sheriff Turner. Although his opponents accused him of failing to enforce the gambling laws, Clark ignored the issue and instead reminded voters that he had repeatedly used his political influence in Tallahassee for their benefit.

Clark's strategy was a solid one. When the results were announced, he had carried every precinct in the county, piling up more votes than his two opponents combined. So overwhelming was Clark's primary victory that the Republicans did not bother to field a candidate against him in the general election. This was true even though Clark was obviously soft on vice. Then again, so was much of the public, particularly those who had figured out a way to make money from all the bootlegging, gambling, and prostitution that was taking place.

Clark's third term began on Tuesday, January 7, 1941, as the war in Europe dragged on. While the United States remained officially neutral, there was considerable fear that foreign spies were operating on American soil. The large number of German tourists visiting the country helped feed this concern, although given the fighting their vacation choices obviously were limited. Still, many of the sightseers seemed to end up chartering Florida fishing boats, and some locals argued that the real purpose of these outings was to gather naval intelligence.

Clark responded by forming the "Broward County Bureau of Investigation," a covert organization that was to look into suspicious activity and report back to the Sheriff's Office. To fill its ranks, Clark recruited retired lawmen and military officers, as well as other trusted individuals, and swore them to secrecy.

During its brief existence, the BCBI submitted numerous reports, some of which led to arrests. But the FBI, concerned about the organization's legality—one agent later referred to it as a "sort of vigilante society"[198]—pressured Clark to shut it down, and the group was disbanded.

In the meantime, federal and state officials began to take a hard look at Clark's failure to eradicate gambling. On Wednesday, January 10, 1940, in an appearance before the Committee on Appropriations of the U.S. House of Representatives, J. Edgar Hoover testified that corruption and inefficiency permeated law enforcement agencies in both Broward County and Dade County. The FBI director also claimed that his agency's South Florida investigations had been hindered by local officers. Hoover leveled his most serious complaint against Clark, whom he accused of allowing "a notorious gambling casino in Broward County, known as 'The Farm,' to operate in violation of the law, but with full knowledge of the sheriff."[199] Shortly after this hearing, the Broward State Attorney's Office began making plans to break up the county's gambling establishments.

In addition to giving Clark a third term, the 1940 general election put a new occupant in the governor's mansion. Spessard L. Holland had been a no-nonsense lawyer, prosecutor, judge, and state senator, and he quickly set his sights on Clark.

During his first year in office, Holland ordered Clark and Dade Sheriff D.C. Coleman to close down the gambling operations in their jurisdictions, warning them that special state investigators would be tracking their progress. These agents subsequently prepared a blistering report about Clark. As a result, on Wednesday, July 15, 1942, Holland ordered Clark to appear in Tallahassee. The summons also advised the lawman that he could bring along his attorney as well as witnesses to testify on his behalf.

Following a hearing on Monday, July 20, 1942, Holland announced he had suspended Clark for allowing "open gambling and illegal bookmaking"[200] to go

Florida Governor Spessard L. Holland (right) being sworn into office (1941)

unchecked in Broward County. Strangely, however, Holland did not name an interim sheriff, nor did he immediately relieve Clark of his duties.

Returning to Broward, Clark took charge of a posse engaged in what the *Fort Lauderdale Daily News* dubbed "the greatest manhunt ever witnessed in South Florida."[201] The search had started when a report was received that the "two-gun killer"[202] of four people in Miami—including a six-year-old boy—had been spotted on the outskirts of Dania. A band of 500 men was organized, including American Legionnaires, armed volunteers, deputies representing three counties, police from a dozen cities, soldiers, and state highway patrolmen. Despite its intensity, the search was hindered by the roughness of the terrain. Shoulder-high sawgrass bottoms, heavy growths of scrub palmetto, and thick, jungle-like hammocks allowed the fugitive to elude his pursuers, who called off their chase after three days. Overseeing this operation would be Clark's last act as a law enforcement official for some time.

After the hearing in Tallahassee, Christopher L. Chancey, Clark's lawyer, boasted that in the next general election Clark would win re-election easily. Upon hearing this, Governor Holland retorted, "[i]f Clark is re-elected you are still going to have a different sheriff down there."[203] Most people took this to mean that Holland would refuse to commission Clark and would name a substitute.

As a ploy, Clark submitted his resignation to Holland, which was rejected. Had it been accepted, Broward would have been forced to hold a special election, which Clark undoubtedly would have won. Clark then announced that when the Florida Senate convened in April 1943, he would seek reinstatement.

Sheriff Edward T. Lee (1942–43)

Three days after Clark's hearing, Edward Tullis "Eddie" Lee was named Broward's new sheriff. Handsome and rugged, a local newspaper described the 31-year-old Lee as "[o]ne of the burliest men in this area, standing six foot four and one-half inches tall and weighing 245 pounds."[204] This was a marked contrast to Clark, who was broad shouldered but short in stature.

Lee was born in Brooklet, Georgia, on December 31, 1910. When he was seven years old, his family moved to Jacksonville, Florida. After leaving high school, he went to work for a construction company, but then enlisted in the U.S. Coast Guard. Assigned to Fort Lauderdale, Lee played on the Guard's baseball team, where his hitting prowess made him a fan favorite.

When his four-year hitch was up, Lee left the service and signed on as a catcher with the semi-professional Fort Lauderdale Tarpons. By the time he was selected Broward's sheriff (due in part to the intercession of his father-in-law, Fort Lauderdale City Commissioner Claude L. Nichols), Lee had been with the Florida Power and Light company for eight years, having worked himself up from lineman to chief district dispatcher.

Because of a dispute with the county's bonding firm (which for a time insisted on auditing Clark's books), Lee's installation as sheriff did not take place until Saturday, August 1, 1942. His appointment elicited very favorable comments from the local press, and a front page editorial predicted that "a force of skilled investigators will be taken on as deputies and the courthouse office developed into this area's law enforcement focal point."[205] This, the writer continued, was in keeping with the new sheriff's view "that his office should function as an efficient police agency with his aides selected on the basis of previous meritorious law enforcement records—and not from the ranks of the political faithful."[206]

One of the men named by Lee as a deputy was Frank Tuppen, who in 1948 would run unsuccessfully for sheriff. Another appointee was R. Dwight Johnston. Ed Hansen, the former supervisor of county prisoners, roads, and shops, was made jailer, replacing Deputy Arden Marshall. Three days after Lee took office, the county commission abolished the position of county road patrolman, which for many years had been held by Virgil Wright. Lee then fired Wright.

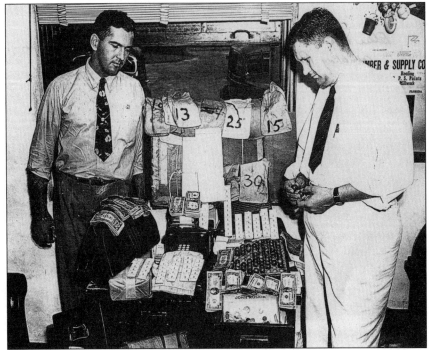

*Deputy R. Dwight Johnston and Sheriff Edward T. "Eddie" Lee (right)
with items seized during a gambling raid (1942)*

When he first received word of his appointment, Lee stated that "[a]s far as I am concerned, gambling is out. The laws are going to be enforced to the limit as long as I am in office."[207] To make good on his promise, Lee instructed his deputies to stop giving warnings and start making arrests. "Law violators have had sufficient warning both personally and through the newspapers, and it's time they realized we meant business."[208]

During his first month in office, Lee conducted a highly-publicized crackdown on gambling. With Deputy Tuppen, he arrested a Hollywood man for taking bets on horse races. Two weeks later, Lee and Tuppen burst into a bolita establishment in Hallandale, where they nabbed five people counting the day's take. Two days later, Lee, along with Tuppen and Deputy Johnston, raided a gaming room in Oakland Park, capturing eight suspects. Three days later, Lee and Johnston, assisted by a highway patrolman, seized a truck carrying fifteen slot machines.

A few days after assuming office, Lee conducted the first of what became monthly summits at which he compared notes with representatives of the Deer-

Sheriff Eddie Lee (left) reviewing plans for protecting Broward's beaches from a possible Nazi invasion (1942)

field, Fort Lauderdale, and Hallandale police departments. This coordinated approach to the vice problem marked a turning point in inter-agency cooperation. In addition to bootlegging and gambling, the meetings focused on prostitution and venereal disease, which had become major problems since the start of the war. The state recently had opened six detention centers to isolate infected prostitutes, and Lee quickly arrested a Fort Lauderdale streetwalker named Maude Pierce for vagrancy. After booking her, he told reporters, "We mean to rid this city of all vice and make it one of the cleanest cities in the state."[209]

In the meantime, Walter Clark prepared to take his case to the Florida Senate. In a series of scathing editorials, the *Fort Lauderdale Daily News* strongly opposed Clark's return, continually stressing that it was the mob that was trying to put him back in office. Nevertheless, on Tuesday, June 1, 1943, he was reinstated with back pay.

Lee took the news calmly, saying simply, "I feel that I've executed my duties here to the best of my ability."[210] FBI officials were more effusive, describing the former ballplayer as the "best sheriff Broward County ever had."[211]

Tombstone of Sheriff Eddie Lee (Evergreen Cemetery, Fort Lauderdale)

Asked about his plans, Lee indicated he might go back to FPL or rejoin the Coast Guard but ended up accepting an offer from Eastern Air Lines in Miami, where he served as director of security and later became president of its credit union. On February 17, 1969, he died at his home in South Miami at the age of fifty-eight.[212]

Sheriff Walter R. Clark (1943–50)

On Monday, June 7, 1943, Walter Clark resumed his duties as Broward County's sheriff. After complimenting Lee on the job he had done, Clark reappointed his brother Bob as chief deputy and rehired Arden Marshall.

Throughout his suspension, Clark had retained strong local support, and his popularity only seemed to grow during his first year back in office. As a result, no Democrat opposed him in the 1944 primary and no Republican bothered to run against him in the general election. Thus, on Tuesday, January 2, 1945, Clark was sworn in for a fourth term.

To Clark, his continuing success at the polls represented a clear endorsement of his liberal attitude towards illegal games of chance, but he was wrong. During the dark days of the Depression, Broward's residents had accepted gambling as a necessary evil. After World War II, however, as prosperity returned, the public's attitude changed. This was particularly true of the county's newcomers. Now, illegal gambling was seen as a hindrance to legitimate business

A 1946 group photo of the Broward Sheriff's Office includes (from left to right) bookkeeper Sara H. Freeman; Deputies Earl Sharp, Arden D. Marshall, A.M. Wittkamp, Gene Ryan, and Lloyd Miller; Chief Deputy Bob Clark; Sheriff Walter Clark; Deputies Roy May, Harry Cook, Claude A. Tindall, and Virgil Wright; and an unidentified secretary

and the old argument that it was needed to attract tourists found few supporters.

Clark, however, remained firm in his belief that gambling was beneficial. As a result, Broward's casinos, gambling parlors, and nightclubs again began to flourish. Bolita (Spanish for "little ball"), a Cuban lottery game that had first appeared in Florida in the 1880s, also became a fixture, particularly in Fort Lauderdale's African-American community.

Not only did Clark not deter gambling, his department often seemed to go out of its way to help it. Chief Deputy Bob Clark, for example, had opened an armored truck business (reputedly the county's first), and each night his vehicles would pick up money from the casinos. Because no records were kept as the vans made their rounds, no paper trail existed to indict the guilty. As for Walter Clark, he was paid $2,000 a year to deputize the guards who manned the trucks.

In fact, Clark and his men received myriad payoffs. The records of the Colonial Inn in Hallandale, for example, listed $40,000 in annual payments to "charities," a euphemism in criminal circles for protection money paid to law enforcement officials. Of course, when asked about such payments, Frank Erickson, one of the owners of the club, said, "I never had no protection from no place."[213]

The notorious Colonial Inn in Hallandale (c. 1940)

Although Clark spent considerable time looking out for himself, he did not forget about his constituents. When heavy rainfall combined with two hurricanes to produce the Flood of 1947, causing catastrophic damage in Davie, Clark and his deputies worked tirelessly to help the victims. Clark also played a pivotal role in convincing the federal government to part with the Fort Lauderdale Naval Air Station, which in 1948 reopened as Broward County International Airport.

Clark even occasionally attended to his actual duties, placing special emphasis on improving inter-agency relations. In April 1948, Chief Philip A. Thompson of the Hollywood Police Department thanked Clark for his help during a recent wave of burglaries, praising the efforts of Deputies May, Ryan, and Wittkamp. A short time later, in June 1948, Clark decided that it would be beneficial for the Sheriff's Office to utilize the Fort Lauderdale Police Department's radio dispatch service. With the county short on funds, Clark personally advanced the money needed to pay for connecting his patrol cars to that system.

As the 1948 election approached, Clark, although still popular, faced growing resentment over his failure to enforce the gambling laws. Making matters worse, the State Attorney's Office had decided the time had come to use the courts to close down the county's gambling establishments.

Things really got difficult for Clark, however, when, three weeks before the Democratic primary, Robert H. Gore, Sr., the editor of the *Fort Lauderdale Daily News*, started running a series of articles on the county's "bolita racket."

Aerial view of the Town of Davie after the Flood of 1947

Broward County International Airport (1959)

Newspaper editor Robert H. Gore, Sr. (1886–1972)

According to Gore, organized crime was making $500,000 a year from the game and Clark was doing nothing to stop it.

One editorial began, "No matter what the sheriff's office tells you, the most vicious form of gambling—bolita—flourishes throughout Broward county."[214] It continued by noting that racketeers were "reap[ing] rich rewards each week at the expense of the negroes and the rewards are rich enough to 'buy the protection' they need to keep in business year after year."[215] The piece closed by saying that "[b]olita is nothing more than daylight robbery of these negroes and it's about time the sheriff's office did something to close up these houses!"[216]

Not surprisingly, Clark's opponents in the Democratic primary—Joseph C. Mackey and Frank Tuppen—made gambling their main issue. The contest soon took an ugly turn, with the challengers receiving anonymous telephone threats and vandals targeting their campaign materials. In addition, allegations were made that non-resident casino and racetrack employees were being registered to vote. As a result, both Mackey and Tuppen dispatched their supporters to polling places to look for fraud.

In his stump speech, Mackey, a Fort Lauderdale city commissioner, lashed out at Clark's political machine, condemned his do-nothing attitude toward illegal gambling, and promised that if he was elected he would put an end to gambling in Broward and "run out the gangsters and hoodlums."[217] Tuppen likewise promised strict enforcement of the law, pointed to his experience as a probation officer, and reminded voters he had served as a deputy under Sheriff Eddie Lee. Tuppen also proposed to modernize the Sheriff's Office. Holding up the FBI as a model, he called for better records, the establishment of an identification division, and placing deputies on call twenty-four hours a day, seven days a week.

To deal with these attacks, Clark reverted to his past strategy of denying that there was a problem. As far as he was concerned, mobsters did not "dare come into Broward county [because] they know they'd be picked up 'in 20 minutes.'"[218] Instead, he claimed, they went to Dade County (and, in particular, to Miami Beach).

Ignoring the gambling issue altogether, Clark's ads stressed that he was benevolent, competent, and efficient. They pointed out that Broward's crime rate was low compared to similar-sized counties, claimed that Clark was considered trustworthy by both the FBI and the U.S. Secret Service, and argued that "[d]oing good, helping his fellow man and his native county, is perhaps Walter Clark's best known quality.... He gave physically, financially, spiritually to recent flood victims.... He has never refused a just plea for aid."[219]

Although outrageous, these statements proved effective. On primary day, Clark received more votes than Mackey and Tuppen put together, and in November he beat Republican George J. Burckel by a tally of 11,100 votes to 5,594 votes (a margin of 66%–34%). And so, on Tuesday, January 4, 1949, Clark was sworn in yet again. Soon, however, his career, as well as his life, would be over.

The effort to curtail illegal gambling had continued to build up speed, and both Dade County and Palm Beach County had joined the fight. Yet even as grand juries began meeting and judges started issuing injunctions, Clark declined to act. Finally, Florida Attorney General Richard W. Ervin, Jr. ordered Clark to close down the local bookmakers. Clark did so but left other types of gambling alone. When Ervin subsequently told him to move against slot machines, Clark again went no further than required. As a result, the county's fifty illegal casinos continued to operate.

By now, however, the constant drumbeat in the *Fort Lauderdale Daily News* had begun to take a toll. On Tuesday, February 21, 1950, Gore penned his strongest attack yet, openly challenging Governor Fuller Warren to suspend Clark. Warren's response was a letter to all of the state's sheriffs ordering them "to use the full power of your office to enforce strictly all laws, particularly the

Richard W. Ervin, Jr., attorney general of Florida (1949–64)

laws against gambling."[220] Clark, apparently finally realizing how precarious his hold on power had become, reacted to this edict by immediately cracking down on gambling.

Even as Clark scrambled to shore up his position, Senator C. Estes Kefauver (D-Tenn.), the chairman of the newly-formed U.S. Senate Special Committee to Investigate Crime in Interstate Commerce, began making plans to hold national hearings. By the time the committee finished its work in 1951, it had met in fourteen cities and heard from nearly 800 witnesses.

Appearing before the committee during a closed session, Clark denied any knowledge of gambling or organized crime in Broward County, but added that if betting establishments existed, it was because the people enjoyed them. Clark also was questioned about receiving campaign contributions from gamblers and gangsters as well as his income and investments. His answers, particularly those relating to his personal finances, were evasive and incomplete.

In July 1950, the committee returned to Florida for public hearings. Clark sweated profusely as he was grilled about specific gambling locales and how often he had raided them. By the time he finished, Clark had answered "I don't know,"

Fuller Warren, governor of Florida (1949–53)

U.S. Senator C. Estes Kefauver signing autographs in Miami (1952)

"I don't remember," or "I forget" to twenty-six questions, causing the audience to erupt repeatedly in loud laughter. Similar derision greeted Clark's insistence that he had been powerless to act because no citizen had ever filed a complaint.

Clark continued to give evasive answers when the subject of slot machines came up. Kefauver then began an aggressive inquiry into Clark's wealth and ultimately got the lawman to admit what the committee already knew: namely, that his $7,500-a-year salary as sheriff represented only a tiny fraction of his income. Instead, the bulk of Clark's earnings were derived from his one-third ownership of a company that ran bolita games and owned slot machines.[221]

Clark's admission proved to be the final straw. According to the *Fort Lauderdale Daily News*,

> [t]he sheriff of Broward County stands revealed before the people today as a man unfit to any longer wear the badge.... [T]he sheriff of Broward county not only didn't enforce the law, but was an active partner in a gambling concern that was engaged in breaking the law.... He, and his chief deputy, should resign before an outraged public opinion demands ouster action from Gov. Fuller Warren.[222]

Even as his career was crumbling before his eyes, Clark's racial prejudice remained intact. When asked by the committee to explain bolita, Clark replied, "I never exactly understood [it]. Bolita is a game that niggers play."[223]

Events now moved quickly. Governor Warren summoned Clark to Tallahassee for a hearing, which was held on Friday, July 21, 1950. Warren began by asking Clark if he had testified before the committee. Clark responded, "I did."[224] Before he could say anything else, attorney Christopher Chancey (who had represented Clark during his 1942 suspension hearing before Governor Holland), jumped up and began presenting a laundry list of reasons why Clark could not (or should not) be suspended.

According to Chancey, Warren did not have the authority to suspend Clark for past abuses, the newspapers were out to get Clark, and it was not the sheriff's responsibility to go looking for gambling operations. When Chancey finally finished speaking eighty minutes later, Warren rose from his chair and said, "An order suspending Sheriff Clark will be made. The hearing is adjourned."[225] He then walked out of the room without further comment. Although a successor was not named for several days, Clark was finished.

Warren soon took similar action against other lawmen. During the next four months, he suspended the sheriffs of Dade, Okaloosa, Polk, and Volusia counties for allowing gamblers to operate in their respective jurisdictions.

Clark, however, had bigger problems. On Thursday, August 17, 1950, a grand jury returned three indictments against Bob and Walter Clark. The first charged the brothers with possessing and renting thirteen slot machines (thirteen counts), the second accused them of storing the devices in a warehouse they owned (one count), and the third alleged they had run bolita games (two counts).

The fourteen counts arising from the owning and storing of slot machines were misdemeanors, while the two bolita counts were felonies. If convicted on all of the counts, Clark and his brother faced twenty-seven years in prison.

Both men surrendered voluntarily and were released after posting bonds. In December 1950, they stood trial on the slot machine charges and were acquitted in under an hour. A month later, the bolita charges were dropped.

By now, Clark was suffering from leukemia. As a result, his supporters began mounting a campaign to have him reinstated as sheriff on humanitarian grounds. And indeed, most people believed the Florida Senate would do so when it met in April 1951. The *Fort Lauderdale Daily News* warned against such a move, however, and fretted that Clark's "illness is being used as a political football in a game to win control of the sheriff's office."[226] What most concerned the paper was the thought that if Walter Clark was reinstated, his brother Bob would end up running the department.

The Florida Senate was scheduled to consider Clark's suspension on Wednesday, April 11, 1951. On that same day it would decide the fate of several other sheriffs, including Dade County's James A. "Jimmy" Sullivan. Like Clark, Sullivan had testified before the Kefauver Committee and then been suspended by Governor Warren.

Sullivan's removal was considered to be a certainty, but just before the hearing he was given his job back. Although the Florida Supreme Court was largely to blame for this shocking turn of events,[227] the *Fort Lauderdale Daily News* instead lambasted Warren, who it accused of being "on the side of the crooks, the gangsters, the cheats and the racketeers and everybody else who makes a profit out of lax and shabby enforcement of our laws."[228] The paper then called for the impeachment of the "sorriest"[229] governor in state history.

Meanwhile, the Senate took up Clark's case and voted to remove him. Two weeks later, on Thursday, April 26, 1951, Clark died at the age of forty-six at Johns Hopkins Hospital in Baltimore, where he had spent his final month.[230] At his side was Bob Clark, who shortly would be indicted for tax evasion (for failing to declare his gambling-related income), wage an unsuccessful fight for his brother's old job, and die of a heart attack at the age of fifty-two.

Walter Clark's legacy remains a subject of considerable debate. Regarded by some as generous and kind, he was reviled by others as a bigot and a crook. Either way, his death clearly marked the end of an era. What remained to be seen was what would replace it.

James A. "Jimmy" Sullivan, sheriff of Dade County (1945–50 and 1951–52)

Tombstone of Sheriff Walter Clark (Evergreen Cemetery, Fort Lauderdale)

CHAPTER 5

THE HALL-LLOYD YEARS (1950–61)

The 1950s proved to be a time of great change for the Broward Sheriff's Office. The budget grew, education and training requirements were stiffened, the number of officers continued to increase, and, in a radical break with the past, African-Americans were hired as deputies for the first time.

Other developments were less positive. The department's internal politics became a matter of increasing concern, and in 1956 the "political purge" made its first appearance. From then on, sheriffs would regularly carry out mass firings to rid their ranks of both real and perceived political enemies.

But before any of this could take place, there was the matter of the vacancy created by the suspension of Walter Clark. Initially, Governor Fuller Warren's "county committee" proposed holding a special election, but it dropped the idea after lawyers pointed out that such a contest would violate state law. In the meantime, Circuit Judge Chillingworth, acting at the request of County Judge Boyd H. Anderson, Sr., signed an order naming Deputy Wittkamp "elisor."[231]

With the plan to hold a special election stillborn, State Senator George W. Leaird (D-Hollywood) put forth the name of Amos H. Hall, the former vice mayor of Hollywood. On Monday, July 24, 1950, Fuller accepted Leaird's suggestion and named Hall sheriff.

Sheriff Amos H. Hall (1950–57)

Amos Harris Hall was born in Morganfield, Kentucky, on November 14, 1914, but in 1925 his family moved to Hollywood, Florida. In 1933, the future sheriff briefly attended Duke University, where he made the swim team, and during World War II he served as a flight officer in the Pacific theater. From 1947 to 1949, Hall sat on the Hollywood city commission and served as vice mayor. But he declined to seek re-election, choosing instead to devote his energies to his insurance and real estate businesses. For a short time in 1940, Hall was as-

121

Boyd H. Anderson, Sr., county judge of Broward County (1933–68)

George W. Leaird, Florida state senator (1947–53)

Amos H. Hall, sheriff of Broward County (1950–57)

sociated with Chief Deputy Bob Clark in a bowling alley venture, but by the time he was named sheriff he had no ties to the Clark family.

Upon being appointed, Hall pledged to Governor Warren that he would stamp out illegal gambling in Broward County. As he explained to the press, "My office will act on every tip received. It will cooperate fully with every other law enforcement agency and with every facility in the county. I intend to enforce the law to the fullest extent."[232] Of course, there was one minor matter that the new sheriff had to take care of first: he had to get rid of his holdings in a jai alai fronton that Miami Beach newspaperman John D. Montgomery was planning to build in Fort Lauderdale. Explained a sheepish Hall:

> I agreed last May to buy [ten shares of] the stock at $1,000 a share. At that time I had no idea that I would be sheriff. Now, to prevent embarrassment, I'm going to sell the stock.[233]

Having gotten himself on the right side of the law, Hall next sought to clean up the department. He began by firing several deputies, including Bob Clark. Those not dismissed were told, in no uncertain terms, that they now were on probation and would have to prove themselves. In addition to Wittkamp, who was promoted to chief deputy, Hall kept on Earl Sharp, Claude A. Tindall, Virgil Wright, jailers Clarence B. Lewis and James Welch, and, not surprisingly, Sara Freeman, the department's longtime bookkeeper.

Hall made it clear to the survivors that if they wanted to keep their jobs, they would have to make sure that no illegal gambling occurred anywhere in the county. Speaking to reporters, the new sheriff said, "[i]f they fail to do the job, then they are out."[234]

To replenish the department's forces, Hall hired three new deputies: Kermit Ehly, Clyde Hudson, Jr., and Vincent Mrazeh. Later, Frank G. Tiller and W.E. "Woody" Tindall, the brother of Deputy Claude Tindall, would be added, along with Wayne D. Pittman, an identification expert formerly with the Dade County Sheriff's Office.

That Hall meant what he said about eliminating illegal gambling became apparent in August 1950, when the local American Legion post was forced to cancel its bingo operations. Hall initially had exempted from his crackdown games run by charities, but changed his mind after receiving complaints from the public. Now, he declared, "bingo ... [will] not be tolerated."[235]

In a letter to the county's police chiefs, Hall went still farther, informing his fellow lawmen that in addition to bingo, pinball machines that awarded free games to winners were forbidden. The press hailed this tough stance and proclaimed, "Hall's latest order ban[s] the last vestiges of illegal gambling in the county which has operated on a 'wide open' basis for many years."[236]

On the day after Hall's letter was made public, Governor Warren announced that he had written to all of Florida's sheriffs to demand that they vigorously enforce the state's gambling laws. In the future, Warren warned, he would suspend without a hearing any sheriff who failed to investigate complaints or shut his eyes to what was common knowledge in his community. "A sheriff or constable is not a mere process server. He cannot discharge his duty to enforce the gambling laws by remaining passive until someone swears out [an arrest] warrant or [a] search warrant."[237] This statement, of course, was a direct repudiation of the excuse for inaction that Walter Clark had given at the Kefauver hearings.

During Hall's first month on the job, the Sheriff's Office raided Club Boheme, a Hallandale gambling establishment suspected of making payoffs to Bob and Walter Clark, but deputies found it clean as "a pin—with not even one dice, card or chip"[238] in evidence. Two weeks later, a Broward County grand jury returned gambling indictments against twenty-two individuals, including four high profile members of the mob: Vincent "Jimmy Blue Eyes" Alo (an associate of Frank Costello), William H. "Lefty Clark" Bishoff, and Jake and Meyer Lansky.

Broward deputies with an illegal still (c. 1955)

In addition to wanting to work with local police departments, Hall also sought to cooperate with the Dade County Sheriff's Office. Hall's counterpart was Thomas J. Kelly, and the two men had much in common, starting with the fact that they both had just replaced sheriffs linked to illegal gambling. In November 1950, the pair met and agreed to help each other in the war on crime. Commenting on the meeting, a local paper crowed, "For the first time in years, the Florida 'Gold Coast' faces a winter season without openly throwing out the red carpet to gamblers and their clientele."[239]

Gambling, however, was not the only issue facing Hall and his deputies. Illegal liquor also was on their list, and from time to time moonshine raids were conducted. On one particularly notable occasion, Deputies Tindall, Wittkamp, and Wright, assisted by the police chiefs of Oakland Park and Pompano Beach, seized a 10-foot-high still that had been hidden in the palmetto groves between Federal Highway and the Intracoastal Waterway, just north of Fort Lauderdale. After being tipped off to its existence, Wright had gone on a 24-hour stakeout to discover who was behind its operation and ended up arresting a man named Malcolm Randall. Randall, however, insisted "that he had been setting opossum traps ... and knew nothing of the still."[240]

Although vice crimes were at the center of Hall's crime-busting efforts, arrests continued to be made for other violations, including, as it turned out, cattle rustling. Livestock was still being raised in Broward, and in April 1951 Hall's deputies caught a number of rustlers in Davie and Oakland Park. The subsequent conviction of these criminals greatly reduced the problem.

Hall was not in office long before he had to begin campaigning for a full term as sheriff. In the May 1952 Democratic primary, Hall faced three challengers, with his strongest opponent being Bob Clark. The other candidates—County Commissioner Tony Salvino and car salesman Justice A. Lloyd—were given little chance to win, but their presence in the contest kept Hall from winning a clear majority and forced him to beat Clark in a run-off. In a post-primary editorial, a local newspaper wrote: "[Hall] has done a splendid job in office and well deserves the support and confidence the voters extended to him yesterday."[241]

In the general election, Hall squared off against Republican Andy Phillips. A former deputy sheriff from Detroit, Michigan, Phillips had been in law enforcement for twenty-seven years and therefore sought to make an issue out of Hall's lack of experience. But the argument failed to connect with the public, and Hall captured 18,055 votes to Phillips's 13,623 votes (a margin of 57%–43%).

The public's faith in Hall soon was shaken, however, by a bizarre story. Under the headline "Deputy Reported Rebelling Against Sheriff," the *Fort Lauderdale Daily News* informed readers that Woody Tindall, one of Hall's criminal investigators, had been absent for days on end and was refusing to speak to the rest of the squad. The source of the trouble was Tindall's insistence that the investigators be relocated from the ground floor of the courthouse to the former residence of the night jailer on the fourth floor.

While Hall was out of town, Tindall had the jail's trustees move the investigators' furniture to the fourth floor. Upon learning what had happened, Hall ordered everything returned to the first floor. After meeting with Tindall (who threatened to quit over the issue), Hall changed his mind, but then changed it again when the other investigators protested. In the end, Hall claimed that the fourth floor put the deputies "too far out of touch with the general office routine."[242]

Of far greater consequence, however, was Hall's decision in August 1950 to hire James Primous, Jr. to be the agency's first African-American deputy, following black protests over segregation (an especially sore point was the county's whites-only beaches). Primous was both educated (having received a music scholarship from Bethune-Cookman College) and a veteran (having enlisted in the U.S. Army in 1942), and as such was an ideal trailblazer. Although he was forced out of the department in 1958 after a more conservative sheriff took over, he returned in 1962 (following yet another sheriff change) and then remained until his retirement in 1973.

African-American BSO deputies (c. 1960)

It is difficult today, if not impossible, to appreciate how significant—and unpopular—a step Hall was taking by hiring Primous. In the 1950s, most of unincorporated Broward County was still heavily rural and populated by white residents who were unabashedly racist. For them, pinning a deputy's badge on an African-American was tantamount to turning the world upside down.

Just how opposed Hall's constituents were to the idea of a black lawman can be seen in an incident that occurred seven years *after* Primous's appointment. Ozie Hankerson, an African-American Fort Lauderdale police officer, arrested Robert H. Bolden, Jr., a white man, for speeding. Incensed by this action, Bolden sued Hankerson, fellow officer John Burns, Police Chief J. Lester Holt, Assistant City Attorney Robert J. O'Toole, Municipal Court Judge John W. Douglass, and the City of Fort Lauderdale.

According to Bolden, because of Hankerson's actions he had "suffered great mental anguish, has become a general object of ridicule by being arrested by a Negro, is jeered at and scorned by his friends and relatives, and otherwise been the subject of obnoxious notoriety."[243] Bolden accused Burns of congratulating Hankerson "in a gleeful, willful, wanton and malicious manner" and Douglass of "joining in the mirth and celebrative festivities … over the arrest and humiliation of the plaintiff."[244] As for Holt, O'Toole, and the city, Bolden claimed they were all derelict in enforcing the state's segregation laws.

Very early in his BSO career, Primous was targeted for murder. Under the headline "Negro Deputy Attacked, Felled by Four Bullets," it was reported that the 39-year-old officer was ambushed as he was coming home from work. Although struck several times, Primous managed to get off one shot at his fleeing assailant before collapsing. Investigators quickly discovered that the motive was not race—the perpetrator also was black—but revenge. Lewis Floyd, the would-be assassin, had been cited by Primous five days earlier for carrying a concealed weapon. He had resisted arrest and during the ensuing scuffle had shot at Primous's car. Commenting on the situation, Deputy Claude Tindall called Floyd a "gun lover who has given the department trouble for a long time."[245] Yet another source of friction was Primous's decision to charge Floyd's wife Hattie with moonshining. Like her husband, she too had put up a fight when Primous tried to take her in.

In November 1952, Sheriff Hall announced another change—the shortening of the work week. Up until now, all deputies, with the exception of those in the civil department, had been required to work seven days a week. In the future, they would be working six, a move that required Hall to hire three more men.

In fact, there would be many new faces during Hall's tenure. When he took over, the Sheriff's Office had twelve employees. By the time he left, the number had grown to sixty. In 1950, five deputies, including Frank Tiller, were expected to cover the county's vast unincorporated territory. In an interview, Tiller explained that whenever there was a fight in one of the area's many bars, "I'd just tell the bartender to hit 'em over the head and wait until I got there. What else could I do?"[246] Recognizing the problem, Hall greatly increased the number of patrol deputies.

Hall also authorized the formation of a traffic division (to enforce driving rules and investigate accidents) and created a squad of motorcycle deputies. The latter move represented quite a change from earlier years, when it was felt that such officers tended to scare off tourists.[247]

After relying for years on the Fort Lauderdale Police Department, in 1954 the Sheriff's Office finally got its own radio dispatch system. This move was long overdue and much needed. In 1956, for example, the road patrol accounted for more than 42,000 man-hours and logged 463,000 miles. In addition to assisting 3,332 motorists, it made nearly 2,000 arrests and issued 2,808 citations and 2,612 warnings.

Sheriff Amos Hall with road patrol deputies (c. 1955)

Sheriff Amos Hall with members of the motorcycle squad (c. 1955)

By this time, Hall was widely respected, and in August 1955 Governor T. LeRoy Collins appointed him to the newly-formed Florida Sheriff's Bureau, one of five sheriffs so honored. The FSB, an early forerunner of the Florida

Sheriff Amos Hall (standing, far left) and local legislators look on as Florida Governor T. LeRoy Collins (seated) signs a bill authorizing creation of an African-American beach in Broward County (1955)

Department of Law Enforcement, remained in existence until 1967, when it was merged with the State Board of Health's Narcotics Bureau to form the Bureau of Law Enforcement.

It was at this point, with another electoral contest on the horizon, that Hall announced that he would not be seeking re-election but instead planned to return to the private sector. This made him the first Broward sheriff to voluntarily leave office and, with no major scandal or legal difficulties hanging over his head, the public was stunned. When pressed for an explanation, Hall replied, "I've just had enough of it," adding "I'd sooner dig ditches than run again."[248] A subsequent newspaper editorial neatly summed up his tenure:

> The present sheriff, Amos Hall, while under sharp criticism at times, nevertheless made a great many improvements in the office and can unquestionably be rated as one of this county's better sheriffs. He did an excellent job of keeping the county free of organized gambling, but the constant stress and strain of trying to do a good job under the

*Deputy Claude Tindall (center) at the controls of an airboat, with Sheriff
Walter Clark (left) and Chief Deputy Bob Clark (c. 1950)*

most difficult circumstances finally forced Sheriff Hall to call it quits
after seven years and not seek re-election.[249]

After taking himself out of the race, Hall quickly endorsed his chief deputy,
Claude Tindall, as a man who would "make a fine sheriff."[250] Hall then paid Tindall a high compliment, saying that he had been in charge of the department
for some time. In February 1956, the 45-year-old Tindall formally declared
his candidacy.

Tindall had joined the Sheriff's Office in 1945 and had been the head of its
criminal investigation division since 1950, but the political neophyte soon
faced a formidable field of challengers as automobile dealer Vance M. "Buzz"
Currin, County Commissioner Tony Salvino, Fort Lauderdale police chief
Roland R. Kelley, and former BSO deputy Frank Tuppen all threw their hats
into the ring. In a preview of his campaign, Kelley promised to bring the Sheriff's Office "up to the standards of a metropolitan police agency."[251]

From the start, all five men poured enormous amounts of money into their
primary campaigns, and for a time it appeared that Kelley, who was spending
the most (although both Salvino and Tuppen eventually surpassed him), would
win. Yet as a local reporter noted, the financial disclosure forms being filed by

the candidates did not accurately reflect their campaign finances. After reviewing them, he wrote, "I've been present when $50 bills were stuffed into the fists of certain candidates ... [but] ... I've yet to see the donor's name come up in the contribution column."[252]

On the eve of the primaries, the *Fort Lauderdale Daily News* urged the public to think carefully about the race and make an informed decision because of what it said were the high stakes involved:

> Probably the most important and certainly one of the most interesting is the race for Sheriff which has five candidates on the Democratic side and two on the Republican.
>
> Since the Sheriff's job is the top law enforcement job in the county, and since the responsibilities connected with the position are becoming heavier each year, it goes without saying that voters should give considerable thought to filling this job with a well-qualified person.
>
> In the old days here in Broward County experience in law enforcement was not a prime requisite for this position. Today, however, we firmly believe experience in the law enforcement field is a primary qualification for the job and should rate high on the list of qualities voters expect a candidate for Sheriff to possess.
>
> Considering all the factors in this race The Daily News believes Roland R. Kelley is the best qualified man in the race.[253]

Much of the public apparently agreed with these sentiments, for when all the ballots were counted Kelley was first, followed closely by Tindall. With neither man having gained a clear majority, a run-off would be necessary.

On the Republican side, car salesman Justice Lloyd easily beat the only other candidate, furniture dealer (and retired lawyer) Ernest C. Murray, 2,490 votes to 2,113 votes (a margin of 54%–46%). Their contest had been written off early; one observer, calling it inconsequential, claimed that in the general election the two Republican candidates "don't appear to have a snowball's chance of ever succeeding."[254]

In the Democratic run-off, Kelley's credentials made him a strong candidate. He had joined the Fort Lauderdale Police Department in 1938, had been a captain in the U.S. Army in World War II, and until his recent resignation to run for sheriff had been Fort Lauderdale's police chief for nearly ten years. He also was a graduate of the FBI Academy and during the Korean War had been asked by that agency to serve as a special agent in Birmingham, Alabama. Although granted a one-year leave of absence to do so, he was recalled by Fort Lauderdale officials after just four months when they realized their department could not function without him. Getting Kelley released from his FBI commitment had taken the special approval of J. Edgar Hoover.

Tindall, however, was no pushover. As a young man he had been one of Florida's last real cowboys, riding the range when it was still unfenced, making cattle drives, and helping to found the Davie rodeo (which in 1970 named its arena in his honor). Turning to law enforcement, he had started as a range detective (he later claimed he had never lost a cattle rustling case in court) and then was hired by his father Young Tindall, the sheriff of Osceola County. Shortly after joining the Broward Sheriff's Office, Tindall had helped curb a wave of cattle thefts that had swept through the southwestern portion of the county. By the time of his retirement, the former cowpuncher had earned the governor's medal for outstanding achievement in law enforcement and had been employed by the sheriffs of five different Florida counties.

In the 1956 race, Tindall pointed with pride to his leadership of the criminal investigation division, which had grown to twenty staffers and was clearing 70% of its cases at a time when the national average was 35%. In its first five years, the division had closed fifty-eight murders (out of sixty), sixty-two manslaughters (out of sixty-three), and forty-nine rapes (out of fifty-four), leading one reporter to say that Tindall "doesn't have to take a back seat to anybody when it comes to solving major crimes."[255]

Despite these impressive statistics, as the run-off approached it appeared that Kelley would prevail. Not only had he amassed more votes in the primary, he also had the all-important backing of the *Fort Lauderdale Daily News*. And when Frank Tuppen, who had come in third, threw his support behind Kelley on the day before the run-off, Tindall's candidacy seemed doomed. According to a local newspaper, "Frank Tuppen tossed a well-timed bombshell into the sheriff's nomination race today when he came out with a blanket endorsement of Roland R. Kelley.... [T]here was jubilance in the Kelley camp and dejection in that of Claude A. Tindall.... Tuppen's endorsement was viewed in Kelley quarters as a factor that could conceivably cinch the election for their man."[256]

When they woke up the next day, however, voters found a more complicated picture. Under a headline that read, "Tuppen Stand: He Is and Isn't Kelley Backer," the *Fort Lauderdale Daily News* reported that "Frank Tuppen said today that his personal backing of Roland R. Kelley for sheriff in the Democratic runoff primary should not be construed as an endorsement of the candidate."[257] Twenty-four hours earlier, Tuppen had said "he was strictly in back of Kelley" because "I am certain he can run a good clean county," but now he explained that while he intended to vote for Kelley, "I'm not endorsing him."[258] In a blistering editorial, Tuppen was excoriated: "Tuppen's definition of the word [endorsement] is rather peculiar, and ... it seem[s] to have changed overnight."259

In the end, Tuppen's waffling was of little consequence — in a huge upset, Tindall beat Kelley 14,162 votes to 10,988 votes (a margin of 56%–44%). In a speech thanking his supporters, Tindall described his victory as a public vote of confidence "on the way the sheriff's office is run."260 And it may well have been just that, given that the Hall years had been relatively problem-free and unclouded by the types of scandals that had plagued previous administrations.

Indeed, only a short time before the general election, a Broward grand jury, after considering self-professed bolita operator Norman O. Woodward's claim that deputies had been paid off, cleared the Sheriff's Office of any wrongdoing. In its report, the panel stated that "[a]fter a thorough investigation, the Grand Jury finds that neither the sheriff nor any member of his department has been engaged in any illegal [activity] or misconduct in office."261 The jury also had looked into allegations of profiteering at the county jail, but found that the sale of luxury goods to the inmates not only was not wrong, but actually gave "added comfort to prisoners."262

The good news from the grand jury was tempered, however, by the breakup of Hall's 20-year marriage, which the press reported on in detail. Alleging mental cruelty, Hall claimed that his wife Gladys had exhibited "an unreasonable, almost insane jealousy which caused many embarrassing incidents."263 He also revealed that she had falsely accused him of "consorting with other women when he [was] away from home attending to official duties"264 and had been unwilling to live within his means. According to Hall, his wife's behaviors had greatly upset him and caused severe injury to his nervous system, leaving him no choice but to seek a divorce.

While Hall dealt with his marital problems, his chief deputy was busy courting the county's voters. Touting his experience, Tindall claimed that his arrest and conviction record had earned him the respect of business and civic leaders throughout the state. In 1950, his appointment as chief criminal investigator had made him the head of the largest unit in the Broward Sheriff's Office. And in 1955, he had received a citation from the Florida Peace Officers' Association calling him one of the two most outstanding law enforcement officers in the entire state. Tindall also repeatedly told audiences that he was not a politician and had made promises to no one.

Opposing Tindall in the 1956 general election was the Republican nominee Justice Lloyd, who, after running and losing as a Democrat in 1952, had switched parties. After duly pledging to enforce fully all laws without prejudice or favoritism,265 Lloyd spent most of his time attacking Hall and

Tindall. In particular, he stressed that under Hall the Sheriff's Office had been investigated by two different grand juries. Although no charges had been brought as a result of these inquiries, as far as Lloyd was concerned this merely meant that the jurors had not been provided with the proper evidence. Thus, Lloyd explained, Hall was leaving office without having been exonerated.

Lloyd also charged that Hall and Tindall were lax in the performance of their duties and claimed that both men were often absent from their offices for extended periods, failed to properly supervise their subordinates, and allowed warrants to pile up on desks instead of being served. To top matters off, Lloyd even revived talk of a connection between Hall and the corrupt Clark brothers.

Not to be outdone, Tindall's supporters made much out of the fact that Lloyd had switched parties and had been fired from his patrolman's job with the Fort Lauderdale Police Department in November 1929, just ten months after joining the force. To the first charge, Lloyd insisted that he had been a "Republican all of my life,"[266] despite having run as a Democrat in the 1952 primaries. As for the second charge, Lloyd claimed that he had been with the department for three-and-a-half years and had resigned in good standing: "I was not fired. Someone has bungled up the records to suit themselves."[267]

These tactics made the race both bitter and nasty, and by Election Day the outcome was impossible to forecast. Nor were matters much clearer after Election Day. Although 56,250 ballots had been cast, Lloyd had won by just ninety-four votes (28,172 to 28,078, a margin of 50.1% to 49.9%). While Tindall had run well among African-American and rural voters, Lloyd had found support in the residential areas east of Federal Highway.

A recount was immediately demanded by Joseph B. Lawrie, Tindall's campaign manager, but in the end Lloyd was declared the victor. Anticipating that the recount would not change the outcome, Tindall issued a statement saying, "For the betterment of the county, I hope that every one of my friends will co-operate with the new sheriff. If I can be of any assistance to him, I will be available at all times."[268] And with that, the Democrats' hold on the most powerful office in Broward County was suddenly over after forty-two years.

As for Hall, his life continued to be turbulent, marked by another divorce and various business reversals. On September 2, 1966, Betty, his third wife, discovered him on the floor of their Plantation home, where he had fallen after taking a fatal overdose of sleeping pills. The former lawman,

Tombstone of Sheriff Amos Hall (Lauderdale Memorial Park Cemetery, Fort Lauderdale) (due to an engraving error, Hall's death date is misidentified)

who today almost certainly would be diagnosed as bi-polar, was just fifty-one years old.[269]

Sheriff Justice A. Lloyd (1957–61)

In addition to being the first Republican sheriff in Broward County's history,[270] Justice Acquilla "Quill" Lloyd stood out in at least two other ways. First, he was far older than any of his predecessors. Born on November 26, 1894, the roly-poly sheriff was sixty-two at the time of his swearing in (Amos Hall, in contrast, had been just thirty-five). Second, Lloyd, who hailed from Spencer County, Indiana, had not arrived in Florida until 1925, by which time he was thirty-one and had been married for eight years. All of Broward's previous sheriffs, of course, either had been born in Florida or had moved to the state as youngsters.

Lloyd grew up in the small town of Richland, Indiana, and as a young man turned to farming, eventually becoming known as the "Corn King of the Ohio River Valley." When he moved to Fort Lauderdale, he went to work for a tire company and later became a firefighter and police officer. In-between these stints he sold automobiles and farmed.

From the very beginning, Lloyd's administration was marred by conflict and controversy. As soon as he was elected, Lloyd announced that there would be major changes in the department's personnel. First to go would be Claude

Justice A. "Quill" Lloyd, sheriff of Broward County (1957–61)

Tindall, whom Lloyd had just narrowly beaten in the election. According to the sheriff-elect, "I just can't use him."[271] Others to be fired included Wayne Pittman, the chief jailer, and William E. Bates, the captain of the road patrol, as well as a number of deputies who had campaigned for Tindall.

Several weeks after the election, a notice was posted on the department's bulletin board. On it readers found the names of those Lloyd was willing to let stay after he was sworn in. Although Lloyd had promised that there would be no wholesale firings, there were twenty-seven names missing from the list, nearly one-third of the entire staff.

In addition to Bates, Pittman, and Tindall, virtually all of the top brass were shown the door, as were a number of Bates's road patrol officers, Pittman's lieutenants at the jail, and Tindall's head deputies in the criminal division. Three key figures spared the ax were A.M. Wittkamp, the head of the civil section, Thomas D. Nunn, the chief of the identification bureau, and Sara Freeman, who by now had been head bookkeeper for nearly three decades.

Upon learning of Lloyd's plans, Hall was furious. "We still have a good reputation outside of Broward County in spite of what appears to be our reputation here. Many of our men can get jobs anywhere in the state and I plan to help them all I can."[272] Hall also predicted that the firings would have unintended consequences, for even those allowed to stay were likely to seek employment elsewhere.

Some insiders suggested that Lloyd was planning to hire the top members of the Fort Lauderdale Police Department's detective bureau, an agency Lloyd held in high regard. But when this suggestion was run by two officers in that unit—Captain Robert W. Johnston and Detective Sergeant O.J. Franza—the pair made it clear that they were not interested. As far as they were concerned, there was "no future"[273] in a job with Lloyd because, unlike the city's police force, the Sheriff's Office did not enjoy civil service protection.

The enmity that was to become a hallmark of Lloyd's tenure was perhaps most clearly foretold in an event that took place just a few weeks before he was scheduled to take office. To familiarize himself with his new responsibilities, Lloyd decided to take a tour of the county jail. While being shown around, he ran into Wayne Pittman, the soon-to-be ex-head jailer, who demanded to know if Lloyd had obtained permission for his visit. Caught off-guard by Pittman's insolence, Lloyd finally replied that "he'd been invited by Hall to inspect the place anytime he felt so disposed."[274] Upon hearing this, Pittman turned around and stormed off.

After taking office on Tuesday, January 8, 1957, Lloyd got off to a good start by naming Ben W. Grigsby as his chief criminal investigator. The new appointee was a 31-year-old former FBI agent who had been working in the criminal investigation division for several months. A graduate of the University of Oklahoma law school, Grigsby had joined the FBI almost immediately after completing his legal studies and had been with the bureau for five years (the last four while stationed in Fort Lauderdale) before moving over to the Sheriff's Office. Described by those who had worked with him as "a cop's cop,"[275] Grigsby was highly regarded by law enforcement personnel throughout Broward County.

Although Grigsby's selection was universally applauded, Lloyd's next decision brought a storm of protest from the local media and led one newspaper to claim that "[a] curtain of secrecy settled around activities in the Broward County sheriff's office within hours after J. A. Lloyd assumed his sheriff duties at midnight yesterday."[276]

In an effort to stop leaks, Lloyd had decided to forbid his deputies from speaking to the press. As a result, reporters now would have to get their information from Lloyd or his designated representative. Moreover, the department's complaint sheets and radio logs would no longer be made available. In defending his new policy, Lloyd claimed that premature news stories had interfered with past investigations, a situation he was determined to correct. Yet when reporters questioned Grigsby, the chief investigator admitted he could not think of a single in-

Quentin V. Long, assistant state attorney of Broward County (1955–59)

stance in which a story had impeded work on a case. Nevertheless, he expressed support for Lloyd's decision, saying that it was worth trying "this way for a while."[277]

As things turned out, the experiment lasted just two days. Claiming he had never intended to black out the news or withhold information from the press, Lloyd rescinded his edict. He also announced that the press would have access to the names of those arrested and a list of such individuals would be available to reporters day and night. These rules remained in place for two years, until Lloyd once again changed his mind and directed that all information "was to be cleared through Grigsby."[278]

Shortly after making peace with the press, Lloyd became involved in a battle with Assistant State Attorney Quentin V. Long over the need for a citizens crime commission. As a result of a proposal by its local bar association, Dade County had created such a body in 1948, and after a lengthy investigation Long had persuaded a grand jury to recommend that a similar entity be set up in Broward County.

Although he had been in office for less than a month, Lloyd decided that he had to protect his turf. Thus, after denouncing the grand jury's suggestion as a "slap in the face to all law enforcement agencies,"[279] Lloyd attempted to steal its thunder by announcing the creation of his own crime commission and naming eighteen prominent individuals to sit on the voluntary panel (which was dubbed "The Citizens Committee on Law Enforcement"). When asked about this development, Daniel P. Sullivan, the director of Dade's crime commission, replied, "I have never heard of a citizen's crime commission appointed by a public official. Most crime commissions divorce themselves from public officials. It's very novel, to say the least."[280]

Lloyd also sought to undermine the grand jury's ability to conduct independent investigations. When he was asked to deputize its two inspectors (Lionel Grant and Dominic Vitale, both former Fort Lauderdale police officers), Lloyd refused on the ground that the Sheriff's Office already had enough qualified detectives. Likewise, he rejected the grand jury's request for funds to carry out its work, even though Sheriff Hall had found $3,200 in his budgets for such appropriations. Refusing to be bullied, Long announced plans to ask the Florida Attorney General's Office to give Grant and Vitale full police powers throughout the county.

In the meantime, the two investigators coordinated a sweeping series of raids in which, according to a local newspaper, "Broward County's bookmaking racket was struck a crippling blow"[281] and six top-ranking bookies were arrested. Immediately, however, the Sheriff's Office sought to paint a different picture of what had transpired, with Ben Grigsby claiming that the raids had been premature and had ruined a long-range crackdown planned by Lloyd. Not surprisingly, Long disagreed and held the raids out as an example of the value of the grand jury's investigative function. "The raids Saturday prove there's crime here,"[282] said the prosecutor. "A commission, working with law enforcement agencies, could help to combat it."[283]

Within days, however, Emerson Allsworth, the Broward County solicitor, acting on complaints from the Sheriff's Office and several local police chiefs, called on the grand jury to investigate Grant and Vitale for perjury. Allsworth also announced plans to look into their conduct himself. Ben Grigsby added that he was prepared to testify that by pushing for the raids when they did, Grant and Vitale had "loused up work we had been doing toward trapping the large bookmakers in the county."[284]

Grigsby further alleged that the pair had provided inaccurate information while seeking two search warrants. According to Grigsby, in the first case a confidant could not have telephoned bets into a home at the time stated by Grant and Vitale because the house's phone line had been disconnected two months earlier. In the second case, Grigsby claimed that the man whose name

Emerson Allsworth, solicitor of Broward County (1955–59)

appeared in the application had died eighteen months before the events cited by Grant and Vitale took place.

After listening to Grigsby and several other officials, the grand jury concluded that Grant and Vitale were innocent and commended them "for their tireless and conscientious work,"[285] which had resulted in the arrest of 112 people during the ten months of their employment. Accepting these compliments, Grant and Vitale accused Grigsby of harboring personal animosity toward them. They also claimed that when he had complained that their raids would interfere with his efforts, they had asked Grigsby when he would be ready, to which "[h]e was unable to give any definite time."[286]

To further prove that action had been necessary, Grant and Vitale pointed out that despite working on its investigation for three months, the Sheriff's Office had refused to seek any search warrants. They then derisively added, "[t]he Tropical Race Track season is over, Hialeah is well into its meeting and this prompts us to ask: When do we strike? The last week of Gulfstream?"[287]

Despite being lauded by the grand jury, Grant and Vitale found themselves out on the street. With Lloyd still unwilling to underwrite the grand jury's

Customers placing bets at Hialeah Racetrack (c. 1955)

work, there simply "wasn't any money with which to pay them their $100-a-week salaries."[288]

In the meantime, two of Lloyd's deputies (Ronny Albaugh and Patrick J. Blackmore) were under investigation for allegedly roughing up two African-American bartenders—Caleb Yates, Jr. and his brother Eddie—at the Piccolo Tavern in Fort Lauderdale in an attempt to learn what they knew about Grant and Vitale. Ben Grigsby claimed that the Sheriff's Office was being framed and called for an investigation by the FBI. A day later, Long announced that no charges would be filed against the officers, after which Grigsby dropped his threat to involve the FBI. In a statement to the press, Grigsby defended the department and said, "I'm convinced there was no illegal action taken by the deputies."[289]

The hard feelings between Lloyd and Long had burst into public view within a month of Lloyd taking office. While speaking at a meeting in favor of his advisory crime commission, Lloyd admitted that he was trying "to throw a check into Mr. Quentin Long's crime commission."[290] Lloyd then revealed that the real basis for his dislike of the prosecutor stemmed from Long's promise, "We'll have Quill Lloyd impeached in 90 days."[291] Lloyd also claimed that when he confronted Long about his boast, Long had "giggled."[292]

A few weeks later, Long announced that he was abandoning his effort to start an independent crime commission because surveys had made it clear there was insufficient community interest. The prosecutor insisted, however, that he was not upset by this development. "The decision was up to the people to make and they made it. It was not my purpose to try and sell anyone on a commission."[293]

Although Lloyd had been elected on an anti-gambling platform, it did not take much time for questions to arise regarding his commitment to stamping out the problem. In April 1957, for example, the *Fort Lauderdale Daily News* claimed that

> there's bolita rampant from Hallandale to Deerfield Beach.
>
> Miami interests control some of it, but since the change in administration in the sheriff's office [from Hall to Lloyd], locals have moved in pretty good.
>
> Not content with gambling alone, the racket boys are said once again to be finding the bawdy house business a profitable venture.[294]

Only days after this piece appeared, Ben Grigsby announced that he and Deputy Patrick Blackmore had arrested bolita kingpin Robert L. Smith. While on their way to the Sunset Tavern in Hallandale with search warrants, the pair had passed Smith on the road. "He got scared, stopped the car, started throwing books and pads out the window and jumped out,"[295] Grigsby explained. "That's when we arrested him."[296] Three weeks later, the same two officers reported the arrest of Holmes H. "Ham" Morris, a major bolita operator in Dania. According to Grigsby, Morris had been under surveillance for "quite some time."[297]

Some observers, however, viewed these raids as little more than show, meant to bolster Lloyd's anti-gambling image without doing any real damage to the county's illegal enterprises. Moreover, there were those who claimed that Lloyd was using his office to protect certain gamblers.

In March 1957, four deputies raided a trailer located just west of Pompano Beach. As one of the officers counted the money, another scooped up the cards from the table. Then a .38 caliber snub-nosed revolver was discovered. It was at this point that Lloyd drove up and ordered the deputies to put everything back. When it was explained that one of the suspects had been carrying a concealed weapon, the deputy was told to give that back, too.

Sheriff Quill Lloyd (right) taking a suspect into custody (c. 1960)

When this story later hit the papers, the State Attorney's Office launched an investigation.

Remarkably, this was not the only troubling incident making news. After five men were arrested on gambling charges in June 1957, Lloyd sought out Assistant County Solicitor Thomas M. Coker, Jr. and asked him to allow the men to sign guilty pleas, pay a $25 fine, and keep the $285 that had been confiscated. When confronted by reporters, Lloyd initially denied having had any such conversation, but after being informed that Coker had confirmed the story Lloyd switched gears and said, "I think I did talk to Coker, but I don't recall what was said."[298]

Commenting on Lloyd's actions, one reporter wrote that he had "never heard such gobbledygook before in my life as when Quill Lloyd tried to explain just what happened in [these] two recent gambling raids."[299] The sheriff had been getting himself in hot water throughout his first six months in office, the newsman said, in part because of his hiring of applicants with criminal records, and now Lloyd's credibility had suffered another serious blow.

Still, some progress was being made against crime. For example, in what deputies later described as "one of the most hectic nights in a long time,"[300] officers arrested fifty-five individuals during a seven-hour stretch on a Friday night in August 1957. Thirteen of those taken into custody were accused of gambling (at a house in Pompano), eleven were charged with vagrancy for sleeping in their cars outside a restaurant, and thirty-one were cited on a variety of charges, including public drunkenness and traffic violations.

Ten days later, the department suffered its first duty-related death when a tragic accident took place:

> Deputy [Arthur] Fillebrown had been on the job for only three weeks and was on road patrol alone for the first time [on Monday, August 26, 1957]. The [24-year-old] rookie deputy responded to a call of an overturned truck in a canal at Bailey Road and State Road 7. Running with his lights and siren [on], his marked unit collided with a passenger train at the Prospect Road crossing, which at the time was not equipped with warning lights or other safety signals[, and] died instantly.[301]

In September 1957, a series of raids resulted in "the largest number of White men ever arrested at one time in this county on bolita charges."[302] When six of the defendants (including William Green, a former deputy road patrolman) were subsequently convicted, the same paper claimed it was "the largest and most important bolita case ever tried in Broward County."[303] To get close to the men, Deputy Frank J. Blackmore had pretended to take a bribe. According to County Solicitor Emerson Allsworth, Blackmore had "lived a hellish life for a year to make these cases."[304]

Ironically, a short time later another Broward law enforcement officer also claimed that he had taken bribes as part of an attempted string operation. However, in this case, Patrick J. Young, a Hallandale police sergeant, was fired and then arrested for his activities. He insisted that he had been trying to trap two sheriff's deputies in a bribery scheme and claimed that his boss, Chief D.W. Baxter, had authorized his efforts. When Baxter refused to corroborate his story, Young had a ready explanation: the two men had had a disagreement over an unrelated matter and Baxter now was out "to get me one way or the other."[305] As for the confession he had given, Young claimed that the grilling he had been put through had left him so upset that he would have pled guilty to "anything less than murder."[306]

The charge that Lloyd was not doing enough to fight gambling in the county was leveled not only by Long and the newspapers, but occasionally by other law enforcement officials as well. In October 1957, for example, Lester Holt, Fort

Lauderdale's police chief, accused Lloyd of refusing to cooperate with his department in its anti-gambling efforts despite repeated requests. Lloyd told reporters he would not discuss this "or anything else."[307]

The very next day, newspaper headlines informed readers that "Sheriff's Agents Nab City Negroes." It was reported that vice squad deputies had conducted a series of raids in Fort Lauderdale and had arrested fifteen African-Americans on gambling and moonshine charges—an action that had "the appearance of being the sheriff's retaliation to Holt's charges against him."[308] Although Ben Grigsby claimed that this was the most arrests ever made by the Sheriff's Office in Fort Lauderdale on a single night, the chief criminal investigator seemed to distance himself from the operation. For one thing, the former FBI agent, who usually took a leading role in such raids, had declined to participate this time because "the vice squad boys know what to do."[309] When reporters asked Grigsby whether the increase in BSO's law enforcement activity had anything to do with the charges made by Holt, he answered by saying, "Please don't quote me because I don't want to get into a fight over this thing. I'm just doing my job."[310]

The effort to stamp out illegal gambling took on new urgency in June 1958 when Governor LeRoy Collins ordered Florida's sheriffs to go after the major figures in the bolita racket. Collins called bolita the most corrupting influence on public officials in Florida and said that "it is a physical impossibility for bolita to flourish unless the racketeers have not only the acquiescence but also the active help of the authorities...."[311] The governor also let it be known that if the sheriffs were unable to handle the problem, a state agency might be created to do so.

Even before Collins's call for more effective action, bolita prosecutions often resulted in untoward pressure on witnesses—from both sides of the law. Thus, for example, Hardy Hill, a former Deerfield Beach police officer who had been forced to resign after it was discovered that he was serving as a "bagman" in Delray Beach, fled the state to avoid threatened reprisals for testifying against his crime bosses. Conversely, R.S. "Buck" Forester complained that Ben Grigsby had told him he better "get out of the county" unless he decided to "go along"[312] with the government's case (which ended in a mistrial).

By now, Lloyd was under attack from both newspaper reporters and local officials, who often took issue with his decisions, as well as from Long, who, it was hinted, was still looking to remove him from office. Strangely enough, however, the man who would pose the greatest threat to Lloyd's career turned out to be neither a journalist nor a government agent but an ex-felon who had served four years in a federal penitentiary for moonshining. In May 1957, when Lloyd had been sheriff for only four months, Claude H. Anderson, Sr., a bail bondsman, announced that he planned to stand for sheriff in the 1960 elections. Although Anderson never presented a serious threat to Lloyd at the polls, he proved to be a perpetual thorn in the lawman's side.

Shortly after revealing his future candidacy, Anderson had James Gunn, his chief criminal bondsman, contact Florida Insurance Commissioner J. Edwin Larson and assert that Lloyd was being "wined and dined"[313] by rival bondsman Floyd E. Mincey, who at one time had worked for Anderson. County Solicitor Emerson Allsworth, against whom Gunn leveled the same charges, replied that "[t]he feud between these two bonding agencies has reached a ridiculous point,"[314] and added that he hoped Larson would conduct a thorough investigation so that the allegations could be laid to rest. Lloyd simply said, "I don't know how anybody could have made up such a story."[315]

On the following day, Gunn filed an affidavit detailing the role that Deputy Preston Olivet allegedly had played in the affair. According to Gunn, Olivet, who was the head desk clerk in the sheriff's booking office, was being constantly entertained by Mincey "for the purpose of obtaining favors and phone calls."[316] On numerous occasions, Gunn claimed, Olivert had told Mincey in advance when gambling raids would be conducted and had called Mincey when the arrests were made so that the bondsman could hustle down to the jail and get new business:

> [E]very morning when Olivet comes to work, his first duty is to check the arrests made the night before, and at that time he has been seen by fellow deputies walking out of his office to a pay phone booth.
>
> Shortly after these phone calls are made, Mincey appears at the sheriff's booking desk with a list of names of the arrests made the night previous…. Mincey then selects the best prospects for bonding.[317]

After a month-long investigation, Larson announced a series of charges, but they were all against Anderson, who was ordered to explain why his bondsman's license should not be revoked. Among the allegations was one that Anderson had proposed paying Deputy John G. Lang $150 to arrest Mincey and rough him up a bit and another that he had offered Deputy Roy Longbottom $1,000 if he could make a felony case against Mincey by planting bolita tickets or illegal liquor in his car.

Anderson claimed that the whole thing was a frame-up, the result of his disclosure of corruption by county officers, who now were trying to hide their tracks. Declaring that the charges were "a pack of lies," Anderson promised to conduct "open warfare" on the Sheriff's Office, "barring no holds from now on."[318] For their part, newspapers ran banner headlines repeating Anderson's vow "to blow the lid off 'the Court House crowd.'"[319] At the same time, the bondsman reaffirmed his electoral intentions. "I'm going to run for sheriff if there's breath in my body, and I hope [J. A.] Lloyd will have the guts to run for re-election."[320]

A few days later, however, Anderson's plans suffered two serious setbacks. The first was his indictment by a grand jury on a charge of attempted bribery of a deputy sheriff, one of the five allegations made by Larson. (Anderson eventually beat this rap.)

Second, a charge raised by Anderson against former Sheriff Hall fell apart. The bondsman had claimed that in October 1956, in order to protect a $1,000 bond that had been issued by Mincey, Hall had sent Ben Grigsby to Houston to bring back a fugitive named Bobby Ray Clenny even though no warrant had been issued. For this service, the county had been charged $499.95 in fees by the Sheriff's Office. It turned out, however, that a warrant had been issued, but Anderson had missed it because he "did not request a search of all the records against [Clenny, who had been arrested numerous times]."[321]

Despite these developments, Anderson continued to level accusations at the Sheriff's Office, which Lloyd shrugged off by saying, "He's just grabbing at straws. The roof is still on the Court House and I'm sure it's going to stay on."[322] And, in fact, two new accusations from Anderson were quite petty. For one thing, he now claimed that Mincey had been allowed to plug a lamp into a wall socket at the Sheriff's Office while taking pictures of prisoners for whom he provided bonds. Anderson claimed that because "the taxpayers pay the electricity bill, I think that makes the sheriff guilty of maintaining an office for Mincey."[323] Lloyd responded by saying, "[t]his charge is so immaterial it's pitiful."[324]

Anderson's other attack concerned food. The bondsman claimed that after he alerted the public that deputies were accepting free meals from Mincey, they had begun eating in the jail instead. Because the county only paid the sheriff $1.25 a day per prisoner for food, Anderson said the chief jailer had been cutting down on the prisoners' portions so that the deputies could dine well. Lloyd dismissed this charge, too, saying that "[d]eputies occasionally eat in the jail when they can't get out of the building, but it is not a practice with this department to feed its employees."[325]

In August 1957, Anderson appeared at a two-day hearing conducted by Larson (Dania's city hall was borrowed for the occasion). When it was over, Larson stripped Anderson of his bail bondsman's license, saying, "It has been clearly demonstrated to me that the state, without faltering in the least, has proved beyond any doubt in my mind that you, Claude H. Anderson, are not worthy of the trust the state has imposed in you."[326] Lloyd, however, had little time to enjoy his nemesis's loss of livelihood, for by now a Broward grand jury was investigating him.

The panel called numerous witnesses, including both Claude Anderson and Ben Grigsby. Yet when its final report was issued in September 1957, readers found in it no mention of the Sheriff's Office, a fact that was widely viewed as exonerating both Lloyd and the department. As for Anderson's accusations,

J. Edwin Larson, insurance commissioner of Florida (1941–65)

they were dismissed as groundless. Commenting on these developments, one reporter noted, "It's no secret that the Grand Jury probe rocked Lloyd a little bit. The office has been under fire for employing ex-convicts and the sheriff's interference in gambling raids made by his deputies."[327]

Although he had lost his license and his testimony had been repudiated, Anderson remained on the offensive. Within days of the grand jury report becoming public, he filed a petition in circuit court to void Lloyd's election and have him removed for campaign irregularities. Specifically, the former bondsman claimed that Lloyd had failed to report a $200 contribution that had been made by Anderson himself. This charge would prove very problematic for the sheriff, because he had previously publicly acknowledged receiving a contribution from Anderson that was not recorded. Lloyd insisted, however, that this was merely "an oversight,"[328] and that the $200 had been included in the total figures he had reported.

One month later, Anderson's complaint received a boost when Florida Attorney General Richard Ervin asked the court to look into whether Lloyd had knowingly violated the state election code. Emboldened by this unexpected show of support, Anderson soon filed a second petition asking to have Lloyd removed for seven additional campaign violations. Once again, Ervin sided with Anderson and urged the court to "decide whether Lloyd's alleged failures were done intentionally."[329]

Even as the case against him was picking up speed, Lloyd was feted in January 1958 at a testimonial dinner and dance held at the Galt Ocean Mile Hotel in Fort Lauderdale. In the days leading up to the event, a department spokeswoman urged the public to hurry up and reserve their seats, for 500 tickets already had been sold and "very few [are] left."[330] At the dinner, a feisty Lloyd made a speech and was presented with an expensive gold watch—the next day, the *Fort Lauderdale News* ran a large picture of the sheriff displaying the gift under a headline that read, "He's Got Time on His Hands."

Five weeks later, a court hearing was scheduled to sort out "all [of the] pending motions"[331] against Lloyd. It was expected that the defense would be costly, and stories circulated in the courthouse that deputies had been assessed $25 each as a contribution toward Lloyd's legal expenses, with approximately $1,000 being raised. Department heads in the Sheriff's Office vigorously denied that any employee had been forced to contribute and insisted that all of the donations had been voluntary. At the same time, Republican officials in Broward pledged their financial support for Lloyd and insisted that the accusations were just "a move by the Democrats to try to get Claude Tindall into the Sheriff's seat."[332]

In his answer to the charges against him, Lloyd raised three defenses. First, he questioned Anderson's right to bring the suit, inasmuch as he was not a qualified elector because his civil rights had not been restored following his federal felony conviction for moonshining. Second, he insisted that he had been unable to fully understand the state election laws, but had tried his best to comply with them. (This would not be the last time a Broward sheriff would claim ignorance of the law as an excuse for breaking it.) Third, Lloyd argued that the circuit court lacked jurisdiction to hear the case because even if the charges were true, they were misdemeanors and not felonies.

Remarkably, Anderson now launched another lawsuit against Lloyd. Claiming that his civil rights had been fully restored in 1953 by Charley E. Johns (who had become the state's acting chief executive upon the death of Governor Daniel T. McCarty), Anderson sued Lloyd for defamation and sought $750,000 for having been "damaged socially, economically and politically."[333] Still later, Anderson filed a second libel suit for an additional $815,000 in damages.

In July 1958, the action to void Lloyd's election went to trial, even as his attorneys continued to argue that the proceeding was an illegal attempt to remove him from office contrary to the provisions of the state constitution. From the bench, Circuit Judge Lamar Warren made it clear that the question of whether Lloyd had knowingly broken the law "is the most important phase of the case and may be the only phase."[334] On the stand, Lloyd acknowledged that he made mistakes but vehemently denied that he had done so knowingly, saying that "nobody ever explained the election laws to me."[335]

In October 1958, Warren ruled that while Lloyd had violated the state's election laws, he had not done so "knowingly, willfully or intentionally."[336] Although Anderson protested this decision, in time he let the matter go, explaining that he had made his point. In April 1959, the ex-bondsman also dismissed his two libel suits against Lloyd, saying that he was going to be a candidate for sheriff in 1960 and "I don't want it to be construed as a personal fight between Lloyd and me."[337] This statement seemed almost comical, given that the two men had been publicly feuding ever since Lloyd's election.

By the late 1950s, no one could mistake Broward County for the frontier region it had been only fifty years earlier. But much of the unincorporated land in the county was still rural and some criminal activities appeared to be vestiges of an earlier era. There were, for example, the moonshiners, who usually built their stills in undeveloped areas. In June 1957, Lloyd personally led a raiding party through a cypress jungle west of Deerfield Beach. After walking three quarters of a mile through dense undergrowth, they destroyed a 4,000-gallon still. The still, said to be the best one ever built in Broward County, was well hidden among the trees south of Homburg Road and west of State Road 7, with the nearest house being more than a mile away. Ben Grigsby, one of the raiders, commented that the moonshine made at this site "was the cleanest and the clearest"[338] he had ever seen.

Another throwback to earlier times was what was referred to as "beanfield piracy," which involved the stealing of local farm laborers to work outside Broward County. Migrant workers were being offered better wages to work in the fields of farmers in Lake County, and buses were being sent to pick them up and bring them north. When several angry Broward farmers complained to Lloyd, the lawman sprang into action. Although he had no legal authority to prohibit the workers from leaving the county, Lloyd instructed his patrolmen to begin "surprise roadblock checks."[339] Soon, at specific checkpoints manned by deputies, all migrant labor buses were being stopped and the credentials of their drivers (who usually were gang bosses) were being closely examined, a harassment technique that proved very effective.

In addition to the moonshiners and the beanfield pirates, Broward deputies occasionally faced yet another scourge usually associated with bygone times— cattle rustlers. In January 1958, four people wound up in the county jail after stealing eight cows from McArthur's Dairy Farm and selling them to a Dade County meat packing company. Seven months later, Lloyd's officers investi-

A Florida cattle herd (c. 1950)

gated another cattle rustling case, this time at a pasture on Oakland Park Boulevard half a mile west of the Turnpike. And in February 1960, a gang of thieves struck several times at Sunset Farms, near Taft Street and Davie Road, cutting through barbed wire to gain access to the herd. A $500 reward was offered for their capture.

While his men did battle with the cattle thieves, Lloyd had to handle another frontier problem—vigilantes. Over time, many men in the county's unincorporated areas had been given volunteer deputy cards, and now a number of them were trying to exercise their authority. Some were carrying guns and identifying themselves as sheriff's deputies, and one man even was soliciting donations for a "protective organization."[340] Lloyd's solution was to rescind the cards and withdraw his support for all volunteer police groups.

Reacting to a recent effort to organize a vigilante group in West Hollywood, Lloyd observed that "[t]he volunteers are going too far too fast."[341] And while he acknowledged that he would still have to use individual volunteers to help patrol the unincorporated areas, he promised that "[w]e will cut them down in size and take only two or three from each section and pick the best."[342] Moreover, he emphasized that "[t]hese men will work under the sheriff's office and with a regular man."[343]

The quaintness of these problems stood in marked contrast to the more modern difficulties faced by the department. In July 1958, for example, deputies were forced to impound all of the vehicles of the Great Checker Taxi Cab Fleet, which operated under the names Checker Cab, City Cab, Diamond Cab, and Yellow Cab, to satisfy a $3,498 judgment. As a result, Fort Lauderdale was left with only forty-two cabs for its 85,000 residents.

Lloyd also found his time taken up with con men and swindlers, including the notorious Williamson gang. Although often described as gypsies, the group's members had blond hair and blue eyes and used a variety of English, Irish, and Scottish names. Because they were constantly on the move and had an uncanny knack for staying one step ahead of law enforcement, the clan ultimately became known as "The Travelers" (the name also was applied to two other clans who operated in the same fashion and were related to the Williamsons).

In January 1958, the Williamsons set up headquarters in Dania and for several weeks engaged in fraudulent activities throughout the county. In addition to selling bogus merchandise, they performed phony roof cleaning jobs with the elderly as their preferred target. When word finally got out (many victims initially refused to file reports out of embarrassment), Lloyd's deputies began searching the county's trailer camps only to discover that the Williamsons already had moved on.

During the next several decades, the gang would return to Broward County again and again, arriving in shiny new pickup trucks, luxury automobiles, and motor homes. As before, they painted houses, paved driveways, and sealed roofs with inferior materials that washed off in days, altered checks so as to be able to cash them for higher amounts, burglarized homes they had just finished working on, and committed "diversion thefts," in which several members would fake an illness or stage a fight in a store while the rest of the gang stole cash and merchandise.

Like his predecessors, Lloyd also had to contend with public morals crimes, including those involving alcohol and gambling. But other morality offenses rarely rated a look. Profanity, for example, was technically illegal, but led to few arrests. There were exceptions, of course, but these usually involved a thin-skinned officer.

In July 1957, for example, a female deputy named Kathryn G. Bittoni made headlines when she slapped the cuffs on Foche Corbin, a Fort Lauderdale housewife. According to Corbin, she had gone grocery shopping with her two daughters (ages three and thirteen) and her 15-year-old niece. While on her way home, her car had stalled near her house. Leaving the two teenagers to watch the vehicle, Corbin walked the rest of the way with her younger daughter. When she later returned, she saw Bittoni arguing with the girls and demanded to know "what the hell is going on here."[344] Bittoni explained that she had observed the teenagers operating the car and had issued them citations for driving without a license.

Corbin took the girls home but told Bittoni that she planned to go down to headquarters and file a complaint. When Corbin subsequently arrived at the courthouse with her children in tow, Bittoni was waiting for her and had her arrested for using profanity and obstructing justice.

A year later, Bittoni's actions in another case led to even more fireworks. Bittoni had gone to the West Hollywood home of Glen Gavel, a 10-year-old boy, to question him about some vandalism at a bowling alley. After entering the house without either an invitation or a warrant, Bittoni ran into John Gavel, Glen's 16-year-old brother, who asked her what she was doing. Then, swearing at her, he told her to get out. Bittoni soon came back with another officer and arrested the teen, charging him with assault (for pushing her) and abusive language. Juvenile Court Judge Dorr S. Davis subsequently found the teen not guilty but lectured him regarding his choice of words.

In the meantime, Vincent F. Gavel, John's father, feeling that his son had been mistreated, filed a complaint with the U.S. Attorney's Office in Miami. "They seem to think they can treat you that way if you live in West Hollywood," the elder Gavel explained, before adding, "Somebody has got to stop it. It might as well be me."[345] Not to be outdone, Emerson Allsworth, the county solicitor, announced that he was looking into whether Broward's deputies were respecting the due process of law.

No matter where he turned, Lloyd found himself in hot water—an awkward position for a man who had run on a promise to clean up the Sheriff's Office. In fact, Lloyd seemed to suffer almost daily embarrassment:

- Waking up one morning, Lloyd was greeted with a newspaper headline that read, "Ex-Partner of Sheriff Awaits Trial," followed by a story that explained that Dan C. Brasel, one of his former business associates, had been arraigned for issuing a worthless $100 check. Lloyd claimed to have "severed all connections"[346] to the Nun Construction Company in which the two men had been partners but admitted he was still responsible for its unpaid bills.
- Four months after Lloyd hired Thaddeus Desmond to work in the criminal investigation division, Desmond was taken into custody in Miami Beach for exposing himself to two young women. As if this was not bad enough, it also was reported that Desmond had been arrested twice before on similar charges.
- Seeking to clamp down on juvenile delinquency, Lloyd's men padlocked the West Hollywood Community Center, a popular venue for teenage dances.

When Lloyd claimed that the department had been forced to act because the events attracted a "rowdy Miami element,"[347] his words (which were widely interpreted as a slur against African-Americans) ignited a firestorm of protest.

- While assisting a fraternal organization, Deputy John Hovey arrested George H. Peterson. An hour later, Peterson's nephew Don Reeves, who happened to be a Fort Lauderdale police officer, showed up and demanded to know why his uncle was sitting in the Broward County Jail. After much confusion, it turned out that Lloyd had agreed to help the American Legion initiate new members by "locking them up." Unfortunately, instead of arresting County Commissioner George H. Peterson, Hovey had gone to the house of a different George H. Peterson. A red-faced Ben Grigsby promised that "an 'apology' will be made to the 'wrong' Peterson."[348]

Lloyd also left himself open to criticism for some of his personnel decisions. Firing a third of the department's staff when he had taken office certainly had stirred up a storm. Things got even worse when it came to the public's attention that many of the replacements had criminal records. Yet when he was questioned about the matter, Lloyd did little to calm the waters—his response was that "it takes a crook to catch a crook."[349] But crooks were not the only ones finding work with Lloyd, for he also was hiring his former auto dealership employees, or, as one commentator put it, "Lloyd's making deputies out of his ex-car salesmen."[350]

Lloyd had been in office for only a short time when a local newspaper complained, "He [has] hired ex-convicts—Negroes convicted on bolita. He [has] hired White officers that other police departments wouldn't have on the staff."[351] With rumors circulating of widespread dissatisfaction among the office's employees, Lloyd decided to fire a number of deputies. One of those let go—John Lang, a Fort Lauderdale motorcycle officer whom Lloyd called disgruntled—countered, "[w]e had a right to be. Lloyd took away all the benefits Hall built up for his men."[352] Among these were bonuses for overtime work and sick leave pay. Lloyd, however, claimed to be surprised by Lang's outburst and "pointed out that ... he had added $25 a month to the salary of motorcycle patrolmen."[353]

Despite the constant barrage of criticism, Lloyd managed to institute a number of improvements in the operations of the Sheriff's Office, including the establishment of branch offices in the county's north (at Pompano Beach) and south (at West Hollywood) ends. These offices, it was felt, would provide citizens in the outlying areas with a more convenient way to make complaints, pay fines, and seek information.

Broward deputies checking out the equipment
in their new patrol wagon (1958)

Initially, each outpost had one deputy on duty during daylight hours, with the expectation that there later would be 24-hour coverage. The officer was given a direct telephone line to the Sheriff's Office for handling emergency situations and within a year both sub-stations were fully operational. As a result, when patrol deputies made arrests they now typically brought their prisoners to one of these locations. A Sheriff's Office wagon would then drive to the sub-stations and transport the detainees to the county jail.

On weekdays, this vehicle was available for runs to the state prison at Raiford, but on weekends it was kept in the county because of increased demand. The sheriff sometimes rode along, and on one such occasion a group of prisoners became unruly. Turning to Deputy Leo Spitler, Lloyd calmly advised, "[i]f they ever give you too much trouble, just swerve the wagon and knock their heads together. That'll settle them down."[354]

A second major change was Lloyd's abandonment of the county road patrol, which he replaced with a "security patrol" that operated in an entirely different fashion. Instead of the two-seat automobiles previously used, uniformed officers now drove three-seat station wagons. In addition to lights, radios, and sirens, the vehicles were outfitted with an impressive array of live-saving equipment, including axes, backboards, crowbars, first aid kits, three different kinds of fire extinguishers, and three oxygen tanks.

Other special features included steel mesh screens behind the driver's seat (to protect officers from prisoners) and no passenger window cranks or door handles (to prevent escapes). One patrolman and one auxiliary deputy were to man each wagon during the two night shifts, while a single officer would be used during the day. By Lloyd's third year in office, he had expanded the patrol force from eighteen to twenty-eight men, and all were trained in first aid and emergency firefighting. These officers covered Broward's unincorporated regions, which at the time made up roughly half the county.

A third change caused a great deal of friction between the Sheriff's Office and the local police departments. In September 1958, Lloyd decided to take over the investigation of all major crimes throughout the county, regardless of whether they occurred in the cities or in the unincorporated areas. Many of the county's police chiefs already were upset with Lloyd for failing to cooperate with their departments and for not attending meetings of the police chiefs association or the tri-county intelligence group. Now the relations between the Sheriff's Office and the local departments became even more strained.

In a letter to the chiefs, Lloyd explained that by major crimes he meant all "homicides, rapes, kidnappings and thefts involving more than $5,000."[355] He also requested that his office be notified immediately whenever one of these felonies was committed so that a cooperative investigation could be initiated. In closing, Lloyd said that he was not to blame for the changes:

> [I have] been advised by Jack Madigan, attorney for the Florida Sheriffs' Assn., that it is the responsibility of the sheriff to see that all felonies are investigated regardless of whether they occur within a municipality or unincorporated area....
>
> [I am] simply acting in accordance with the [state] law ... [which] for the past three years ... ha[s] not been followed.[356]

In July 1959, Lloyd unveiled a waterway patrol to enforce the state's new motor boat and water safety law on the canals and rivers in the unincorporated areas. This legislation covered a host of violations (such as operating a vessel in a reckless manner or while intoxicated) and included rules relating to water skiing. To make the new unit functional, Lloyd purchased a 17-foot boat, powered by two 35-horsepower outboard motors, and equipped it with diving gear, firefighting apparatus, and grappling hooks, as well as a two-way radio. A trailer also was purchased so that the boat could be transported throughout the county to respond to drownings and other emergencies. Deputy William Spitler became the first officer assigned to the unit.

Lloyd initially ran into some resistance from the county, which balked at his request for $10,000 for the water unit. Commissioners suggested that the money could be saved if the sheriff asked the city harbor patrols to also watch the waterways in the unincorporated areas, deputizing the municipal officers so that they would be authorized to do so. Lloyd responded that he did not want his office represented by law enforcement personnel under someone else's command. Moreover, he pointed out that he already had purchased the boat and trailer and that the only reason he needed money was because he had paid for certain items (such as a new courthouse elevator) that should have come out of the county's budget in the first place.

Other changes and innovations made by Lloyd during his time in office included:

- Calling on the county's bartenders and barmaids to take an active role in preventing intoxicated individuals from driving, an initiative that was years ahead of its time.
- Expanding the communications department to cover all municipalities, the entire unincorporated area, and the volunteer fire departments.
- Increasing the size of the Sheriff's Office to 122 employees before the end of his third year.
- Placing the Sheriff's Office on a firm financial footing. When Lloyd took over, there had been no money available to meet expenses, there was no food for the prisoners, and the department's equipment was in run-down condition. This situation actually forced Lloyd to borrow money to meet his early payrolls.
- Establishing periodic roadblocks at various points throughout the unincorporated areas of the county to "remove unlicensed and unfit drivers from behind the wheel."[357]
- Spending many hours on the road in his personal car to get a better handle on the department's operations. Indeed, officers on patrol frequently heard messages from "455," which was Lloyd's number.

It also was during Lloyd's tenure that an incident occurred that foreshadowed the eventual creation of the department's aviation unit. In April 1960, while detectives were investigating a series of thefts at construction sites throughout the county, they got a break when a trio of men was spotted loading a pickup truck with material from a storage shed at the North Broward Hospital. A watchman named Ross Williams chased them in his car and the thieves abandoned their vehicle on Powerline Road and ran into a palmetto thicket. It was during the search for these men that Deputy Robert Quinney "took to the air in a light plane"[358] to try to locate the fugitives, a technique that later became routine in such cases.

The biggest change during Lloyd's tenure, however, was one which was not initiated by the sheriff's department, and it came during his first year in office. Scrapping the antiquated fee system, which at the time was being used in forty-seven counties, including Broward (where it had been in effect since the county's formation in 1915), the state legislature ordered county commissions to begin paying their sheriffs a fixed salary and cover their operating costs. Reporting on this change, a local newspaper claimed that Lloyd now was "a happy man."[359] Not only would he be receiving an annual salary of $10,500,[360] but he never again would have to borrow money to meet his payroll.

As will be recalled,[361] under the fee system the sheriff had been expected to defray his expenses by charging for his services. In 1956, for example, Broward County had paid Sheriff Hall $87,536 for investigations, at the rate of $6 per day for each deputy assigned to a case. The bookkeeping problems and assorted abuses which the fee system invited could be seen clearly in the details revealed in a subsequent audit, which found (among other things) $30 being charged for five deputies to look into the disappearance of a lost French poodle and $24 for four officers to investigate the death of a manatee. To make matters worse, the time of two of these deputies simultaneously showed up in bills for running the county's jail. The fee system also allowed sheriffs to improperly reward loyal employees while charging off the expense to the county. During his final month in office, for example, Sheriff Hall had approved $39,000 in bonuses even though salaries for the period totaled just $23,000.

The abolition of the fee system, however, did nothing to help Lloyd with his existing debts. Upon taking office five months earlier, he had borrowed $20,000 to repair the department's equipment, buy tires for its patrol cars, and pay overdue salaries. A short time later, $10,000 in investigation costs were disallowed by state auditors, who felt the charges were for routine work and therefore not reimbursable. As a result, Lloyd was forced to borrow another $10,000. The county commission then balked at his request for $2,478, which he had spent on a station wagon to transport prisoners, because he had failed to put the purchase out for bids. In desperation, Lloyd wailed, "[w]e are finding ourselves with our backs to the wall."[362]

Lloyd, however, was not the only one with financial problems—because the Florida Legislature had ordered counties to immediately begin funding their sheriffs, the commissioners had no time to adjust their budget and suddenly faced the prospect of having to come up with an extra $100,000. In addition, some people predicted that under the new no-fee system, there would be a sharp increase in spite arrests and collection lawsuits.

Following negotiations, the county commission agreed to spend $804,000 on the Sheriff's Office during the 1957–58 fiscal year. Information collected by the State Comptroller's Office, however, soon had people questioning the reasonableness of this amount. According to the study, Broward ranked sixth in population among Florida counties but its Sheriff's Office was the second most expensive in the state. The press immediately blamed Lloyd and pointed out that during his first year in office the department's expenses had nearly doubled, going from $382,000 in 1957 to $754,000 in 1958.

To defend himself, Lloyd released his own report. In it, readers found three arguments: 1) the department's expenses were not out of line when compared to other police agencies; 2) the actual amount of money spent in 1957 was $641,000, a figure that covered only the first nine months of the year given that the fiscal year began on October 1st; and, 3) the department was paying bills that sheriffs in other counties did not have to worry about.

According to Lloyd, many county commissions were picking up the cost of road patrols. "Duval County has more than 100 automobiles which were purchased and are maintained by the County Commission for the sheriff's road patrol," he explained, adding that "the patrolmen's uniforms, salaries and insurance [also] are paid by the commissioners."[363] To underscore his point, Lloyd claimed that if the expenses of the Duval sheriff's office and road patrol were combined, they "would far exceed that of Broward."[364]

Lloyd also insisted that the expenses of the Sheriff's Office had increased significantly when the voters decided to do away with the county's constables and justices of the peace. In this regard, he appears to have been on fairly firm ground.

For the 1959–60 fiscal year, Lloyd sought a 29% boost in funding, with expenditures scheduled to reach $1 million for the first time in the department's history. Most of this money, Lloyd explained, was needed for pay upgrades, so as to ensure that the county received top-notch law enforcement around the clock. In accord with state law, Lloyd's salary also was going up, to $12,500.

In addition to asking for more money, Lloyd lobbied incessantly to shift expenses to other governmental units. One such proposal met with stiff resistance from the Broward County League of Municipalities.

In September 1959, Lloyd notified city leaders that they would have to start paying the cost of caring for mentally ill patients awaiting competency hearings. Because there was no other place to put such persons, they were taken to the county jail, a fact that Judge Boyd Anderson decried as "no more right, or humane ... than it would be to place the physically sick in jail."[365] Anderson found the situation particularly troubling given that, "In every other county in this state comparable in population to Broward, no mentally ill or disturbed person is ever placed in jail."[366]

Upon receiving such individuals, Lloyd typically sent them to the Miami Retreat, a secure psychiatric facility, where they remained until their cases could be heard. But having paid for 384 such referrals during the previous year, at a cost of $17 per day (state law allowed incarcerations to last for up to two months), Lloyd claimed he could no longer afford the expense. From now on, he expected cities to pay whenever one of their indigent residents was confined.

As the calendar turned to 1960, it was obvious that Lloyd was planning to seek re-election. But his bid to remain in power got off to a bad start when Ben Grigsby rang in the New Year by resigning as chief criminal investigator. His replacement was Jack H. Harris, a three-year deputy who had been one of the used car salesmen Lloyd had hired upon taking office. When Lloyd named Harris to take Grigsby's place, the charge that the sheriff was hiring unqualified personnel was revived. The rest of the month only got worse.

A short time earlier, Lloyd had purchased six new station wagons for the road patrol. When they were delivered in January 1960, each had Lloyd's name emblazoned in large gold letters on their sides. After Lloyd was criticized for grandstanding, Captain Howard V. Spangler, the newly-appointed head of the road patrol, tried to deflect the criticism by claiming that the signs had been his idea and had been done without Lloyd's knowledge. Asked to explain his thinking, Spangler replied, "A lot of people in the county might not know who the Sheriff is."[367] When it was pointed out that such advertising could come in handy during an election year, the beleaguered officer said, "I didn't think of that."[368]

As it turned out, name recognition was not something Lloyd had to worry about, for he was beginning to show up in the local papers with increasing frequency. Unfortunately for his election prospects, many of these reports presented the sheriff and his administration in a less-than-flattering light.

In January 1960, for example, Lloyd fired two deputies—Kenneth LeRoy and Irving Willis—after they were accused of police brutality. According to the grand jury, the pair had beaten William E. Griffin, an 18-year-old man, with their flashlights after stopping him for a minor traffic violation. When the officers subsequently were placed on trial, the jury heard from Griffin and his wife Jeanine (who also claimed to have been beaten). Another witness was Gertrude Wilson, the woman at whose home the incident had taken place; she described the officers as "downright brutal."[369] In an attempt to make a favorable impression, the defense brought in eight teenagers from Driftwood Acres who were members of a club that LeRoy helped mentor.

Stripper Syra Marty (c. 1955)

The trial got off to a raucous start. Pictures of Griffin, taken at the time of his arrest and showing the extent of his injuries, were missing. As the prosecution considered them essential to its case, it complained to Court of Record Judge O. Edgar Williams, Jr., claiming that the Sheriff's Office had been uncooperative when asked to help find them. Within minutes of this protest, the photos were located in Lloyd's private files and handed over. Despite this flap, the jury acquitted both LeRoy and Willis.

Just when it seemed that nothing else could go wrong, Lloyd's reputation took a serious hit when one of his men was accused of having authorized a stag show. Of course, such performances were common during this period and normally attracted little official notice. Even when an arrest was made, the strippers generally were viewed with sympathy. In April 1957, for example, Syra Marty, a statuesque blonde (and former Miss Switzerland) was arraigned on a lewd performance charge after dancing at The Torch Club in Fort Lauderdale. Not only was adjudication withheld by Court of Crimes Judge Thomas F. Tomkins, Jr., but her hearing date was pushed up to accommodate her touring schedule, which included nightclub bookings in New York and Paris. Despite this gentle treatment, an incensed Marty told the press, "There's not a bump and grind in my act. I have done my dance all over the world, and nobody ever told me before that it was wrong."[370]

Eyebrows were raised in January 1960, however, when it was reported that a stag show featuring nude women, obscene movies, and illegal sales of alcohol had been conducted by the Oakland Park Lions Club, whose president was a Sheriff's Office road patrol sergeant named John Barnhill. The smoker, held in a recently-built warehouse, had attracted an audience of 600 enthusiastic men, and while the club denied that anything improper had occurred, photographs taken during the evening proved otherwise. Although Barnhill insisted that he had not known what the show was going to be like and had left as soon as he realized what was going on because he "didn't want to have anything to do with anything like that,"[371] Lloyd suspended him for three days.

The scandal quickly spawned three separate investigations — one by the Sheriff's Office, another by the Oakland Park police, and a third by the County Solicitor's Office. In addition, the national headquarters of the Lions Club threatened to revoke the local chapter's charter. Several weeks later, five of the club's members were arrested on conspiracy charges. A Florida Lions official described the furor over the gathering as a political attack orchestrated by Lloyd's enemies, whom he declined to name.

Although Lloyd hoped that suspending Barnhill would bring the affair to a quick end, the matter dragged on for months, during which time Oakland Park Judge Al Skaf found the five Lions Club members guilty of staging an obscene exhibition and fined them each $250.

For its part, the U.S. Bureau of Internal Revenue demanded payment of both the federal cabaret tax (a 20% levy on drink sales) and the federal ticket tax (a 20% charge on admissions), in addition to whatever federal income taxes might be due. Likewise, the Florida State Beverage Department began its own tax collection effort while looking into criminal charges (due to the organizers' failure to obtain a liquor license).

In addition to the stories about eponymous patrol cars, police brutality, and pornography, January 1960 brought news that Governor LeRoy Collins was considering starting his own investigation into the Sheriff's Office. Having recently suspended the sheriffs of Duval and Manatee counties for countenancing bolita games, Collins now was interested in Lloyd's anti-gambling efforts. Lloyd reacted quickly and in mid-February local newspapers reported on a major bolita raid. "Five carloads of law enforcement officers,"[372] led by a deputy sheriff, made a lightning raid on a Dania poolroom known as The Past Time Club, arresting five men on gambling charges. One month later, the department's vice squad conducted a series of additional bolita raids, and over a period of several weeks made what one observer termed "an amazing number of arrests."[373]

But as the campaign season got underway, Lloyd's streak of bad publicity continued. In March 1960, reports circulated that the sheriff had been seen driving around on a Sunday afternoon in a county-owned wagon, plastering "Re-elect Lloyd" posters on poles and trees on State Road 7, just south of Margate. Howard Spangler, the chief of the road patrol, flatly denied the charge. "I can guarantee none of our vehicles were used for putting up campaign signs," he told reporters, and promised that "[a]s long as I am here they will only be used for police work."[374]

When asked about the matter, however, Lloyd admitted that he and Deputy Lacy Aaron had used a department wagon for political purposes and explained that he had not bothered to inform Spangler. While making this admission, Lloyd came off as both unapologetic and arrogant: "The wagon was purchased to be used for county business ... [and] ... I think it is the business of the county voters to re-elect me as sheriff."[375] For good measure, Lloyd added that he also had used a department stepladder to put up the signs.

Not surprisingly, many people were upset by this news, including Governor Collins, who said that while the matter "does not justify suspension ... protest of the people should be most urgently made and felt [in the upcoming primary]."[376] Lloyd's political opponents also were quick to seize on the issue, with one commenting, "If I found a man had used taxpayers equipment for political purposes he'd be looking for a job," and another saying he considered Lloyd's actions to be in "bad taste."[377]

Several days later, Lloyd suffered through still more unfavorable press. According to the newspapers, Lloyd had ordered his deputies to contribute money to his campaign and to change their registrations from Democratic to Republican so that they could vote for him in the primary. The sheriff angrily dismissed these charges as "a bunch of bull" and said that "[t]here's too much talk going around anyway."[378] When pressed, Lloyd admitted that some deputies had given money to his campaign but called these contributions "purely voluntary."[379] He also claimed that the deputies who had changed their registrations had done so of their own accord. And while he acknowledged it was possible that some officers may have taken it upon themselves to go out and solicit contributions for his campaign, he viewed this as "just protecting their jobs."[380]

Although Lloyd's own failings obviously led to most of these blunders, the last-minute appearance of a strong Republican rival contributed to his public relations difficulties. Lloyd had not been expecting any opposition in his party's May primary and therefore had focused all of his attention on winning the general election in November. But just before the filing deadline, Allen B. Michell, a former Philadelphia police captain, jumped into the Republican contest. Caught by surprise, Lloyd had to quickly adjust his strategy and as a result got a late start in a race he had not anticipated running. Complicating matters was the fact that Michell was a real threat. Sporting serious credentials and positioning himself as an outsider, Michell promised to "modernize the Sheriff's Department with qualified law enforcement personnel."[381]

On the Democratic side, a field of six candidates vied for their party's nomination, and about the only thing they agreed on was that they could all do a better job than Quill Lloyd. Claude Tindall, whom Lloyd had beaten by a paper-thin margin in the 1956 election, was back, promising "honest, efficient and economic administration of the sheriff's office."[382] Another hopeful, Lou Slone, emphasized his twenty-two years in law enforcement and claimed that the personnel of the Sheriff's Office needed pruning. Tony Salvino, the former county commissioner, promised to cut the department budget's by 25%.

Claude Anderson, who had announced his candidacy three years before everyone else and then tormented Lloyd in court, spent much of his time accusing Lloyd of corruption and said that in contrast to the present officeholder, he would be the people's sheriff and not the "Racket Man's Sheriff."[383] And in a reference to his earlier battles with Lloyd, Anderson promised that if he were elected, "[a]ny officer caught giving a bail bondsman a tip will be fired on the spot."[384]

As the campaign for the Democratic nomination got underway, a 25-page mimeographed booklet mysteriously appeared and caused quite a furor. Aimed squarely at Claude Tindall, it impugned his character and raised questions about his sobriety. It also claimed that the leading Democratic candidate once had beaten his wife so severely that her recovery had required eight weeks in a hospital. The pamphlet's publisher was listed as "The Broward County Decency Committee," but there was no record of such an organization anywhere in the county. All of Tindall's Democratic rivals denied having anything to do with its libelous statements, and the assailed candidate, calling the document a "pack of outright lies and slander,"[385] indicated that he planned to ignore it.

When the Republican primary was held on Tuesday, May 3rd, Michell garnered 6,480 votes to Lloyd's 5,794 votes (a margin of 53%–47%). In the Democratic race, Claude Tindall came close to capturing the nomination but failed to win the necessary 50%. As a result, he had to face Tony Salvino, who had come in a distant second, in a run-off. In this second contest, Tindall prevailed easily, 25,003 votes to 15,687 votes (a margin of 61%–39%).

Despite his defeat, Lloyd was not yet ready to give up his office. Soon after the primary results were tallied, a rumor began circulating that Lloyd was considering a write-in campaign for the November general election. On Tuesday,

Group photo of Broward deputies (1960)

May 24th, Lloyd confirmed that he indeed would be campaigning as a write-in candidate, and it quickly became clear that he expected the unqualified support of the department's personnel.

Lloyd explained that deputies received their pay from him and therefore he deserved their help in his attempt to remain in office. He also let it be known that there could be no neutral officers—all of them would have to be "for me or against me."[386] Already shaken up by four recent forced resignations, staffers found themselves in a very difficult situation—as a local newspaper reported, "[t]ight-lipped deputy sheriffs were walking a political tightrope" and there was "little question but that deputies who fail to support the sheriff in his write-in campaign face the ax, which may be disguised under the [excuse] of shortage of payroll funds in the budget."[387] As a result, many officers once again began wearing the "Re-elect Lloyd" lapel buttons they recently had taken off.

On Wednesday, June 1st, BSO employees were summoned to a "loyalty meeting" at which veiled threats were made against those who did not plan to assist their boss in his effort to hold on to his job. Lloyd asked that any deputy who planned to support one of his opponents say so. "Now is the time to make it known how you feel."[388] Not a single officer spoke up. Of course, their silence might have been influenced by Lloyd's admission that the reason Deputy Harvey Rogers, a six-year veteran of the department, had been fired was because he was "not loyal."[389]

In a scathing report on the meeting, the *Fort Lauderdale News* claimed that the sheriff had "dug back to the grave to explain his political defeat and set the stage for a desperate write-in campaign."[390] This remark was a reference to the fact that in blaming the press for his primary loss, Lloyd had singled out reporter Douglas McQuarrie.

Lloyd and McQuarrie had gotten into an argument in a bar three years earlier, during which the lawman had grabbed the journalist "by the head and belt."[391] The sheriff also acknowledged going to see Jack W. Gore, McQuarrie's boss, the day after the altercation and telling Gore that McQuarrie was a "no good [S.O.B.] that's going to get me in trouble."[392]

The problem with blaming McQuarrie for Lloyd's election defeat, the *News* pointed out, was that he had been dead for more than a year. It also was reported that "[t]he cajoling sheriff, who broke down and wept at one time during his 'family talk' to his employees, blamed his defeat on The News, 'three hours of rain,' and 'overconfidence of my supporters.'"[393] Never once did Lloyd take personal responsibility for his loss.

The day after the loyalty meeting, it was announced that Governor Collins was considering investigating the event because Lloyd clearly had violated a number of election laws. All it would take to trigger such a probe was "a single formal complaint,"[394] according to a spokesman for the governor, who added that those with the greatest right to act were the sheriff's two opponents in the November election. Claude Tindall, the Democratic candidate, told reporters that he "wouldn't bother to protest to the governor,"[395] and said he had only contempt for Lloyd's campaign efforts. His Republican counterpart, Allen Michell, suggested that the most appropriate person would be one of the deputies Lloyd had fired.

One week later, a formal complaint was filed with the governor. It came from Harvey Rogers, the former deputy who, until his firing, had been the department's fourth most senior officer. Claiming that he had been fired because "I was too jubilant over Tindall's ... victory in the May runoff primary," Rogers explained that he had been born and raised in Broward County and had known Tindall for years, but "[j]ust because I congratulate him on an election victory I lose my job."[396] To add insult to injury, Chief Civil Deputy Frank Ghiotto had notified Rogers that he was being let go while Rogers was recuperating from surgery at Broward General Hospital.

Remarkably, despite his earlier entreaties, Collins refused to act on Rogers's request. According to James F. Southerland, the governor's administrative assistant, "[i]n the absence of a merit system or civil service system, the employees of a sheriff serve at his pleasure and may be employed or discharged at his discretion."[397] In other words, Lloyd now had official permission to fire any deputy he suspected of disloyalty.

At the same time that he was working on his write-in campaign, Lloyd requested a 26.5% budget increase for the upcoming fiscal year, which was slated to begin on Saturday, October 1, 1960. The additional money, Lloyd told the county commission, was needed to pay for more equipment and personnel. From $809,246 in 1957–58, the Sheriff's Office budget had risen to $1 million in 1959–60. Now, Lloyd was presenting the commission with a budget totaling $1,265,250, of which 57% was earmarked for salaries.

One week after Collins declined to investigate Lloyd, Broward's top lawman faced a new challenge. Deputy Thomas W. Castle, who had been let go on the day after the June loyalty meeting, accused Lloyd of assault and battery. According to the former officer, who also was considering filing a lawsuit for false arrest, he had come to the courthouse to ask for money for an operation he needed due to a job-related injury. When he met the sheriff outside the building, Castle was told by Lloyd to "stop bothering us."[398] Then, according to the ex-deputy:

> A few more words were exchanged. I tried to show him that I thought my request for help on my operation was reasonable. Then, he started using every profane word in the book and shoved me.
>
> I never offered any resistance or swore back. I threw my arms up to defend myself and then he grabbed me by the belt and hauled me into the booking desk.[399]

Lloyd agreed that he "may have told [Castle] to get the hell on out of here,"[400] but claimed he had used no other profanity. And while he admitted shoving Castle, Lloyd insisted that the man had assumed "a menacing pose,"[401] which is why he had arrested him for disorderly conduct.

When Castle went to the Sheriff's Office complaint desk to file charges against Lloyd, he was referred (on the advice of the County Solicitor's Office) to the Fort Lauderdale Police Department. A municipal judge subsequently signed an arrest warrant, after which it was announced that Lloyd would be asked to turn himself in when he got back from a weekend at the Florida Sheriffs' Boy Ranch in Live Oak. Lloyd's arrest was expected to be especially embarrassing inasmuch as it would occur while the Florida Sheriffs Association was meeting at the Galt Ocean Mile Hotel in Fort Lauderdale.

Lloyd refused to say whether he would honor the warrant if it were served and there was some question as to whether a sheriff could be arrested by a city police officer. Lester Holt, Fort Lauderdale's police chief, said that he believed his officers had the authority to arrest Lloyd but wanted to wait until the validity of Castle's complaint could be verified. A Fort Lauderdale detective was assigned to look into the matter; at the same time, the County Solicitor's Office was scrutinizing Lloyd's disorderly conduct charge. It eventually was reported that investigators from both agencies felt that everyone would be better off if all of the charges were dropped.

On the day that the Florida Sheriffs Association's convention opened, City Judge Raymond A. Doumar dismissed the case against Lloyd after Acting City Prosecutor Ronald Sladon said that Castle's charges did not give him "sufficient grounds"[402] to proceed. One week later, County Solicitor Thomas Coker announced that the case against Castle also was being dismissed because "[i]t would not hold up in court."[403]

Although the negative publicity generated by this affair hurt Lloyd's write-in campaign, the facts actually were much more complicated than most of the public realized. In his thirty months on the force, Castle had been suspended twice before being fired, and the injuries that gave rise to his request for financial assistance had occurred while he had been drunk on the job. According to the former officer, however, he had been "keeping tabs" on a woman at the request of an investigator in the County Solicitor's Office and in doing so:

> I had to take three drinks of Benedictine while I was with her in order to conduct my investigation. But I was given a mickey. I called the substation in West Hollywood (where [I] was stationed) and they sent a man to help me. But instead of taking me to a hospital as I asked, they treated me like a common drunk and put me on a table in the back room of the substation.
>
> I rolled off the table in my sleep, landing on my right elbow.... [404]

In July 1960, Lloyd's prospects briefly brightened. As part of an effort to confiscate Cuban assets (due to Washington's deteriorating relationship with Fidel Castro), two planes belonging to Q Airways ("the Air Gate of Havana") were seized by Broward County deputies at Fort Lauderdale-Hollywood International Airport. As a result, Lloyd received favorable coverage from television station WTVJ (the region's CBS affiliate, broadcasting on channel 4). But within just a few weeks, the news began to sour once more when it was revealed that Lloyd had authorized installation of a department two-way radio in the car of WTVJ cameraman Roy Chevereton and had even assigned him a call number so that he could be contacted on important cases.

At first, Chief Civil Deputy Frank Ghiotto claimed that the radio was "only an old monitoring set, not [a] two-way."[405] After this turned out to be incorrect, a new explanation was offered: the radio was needed because

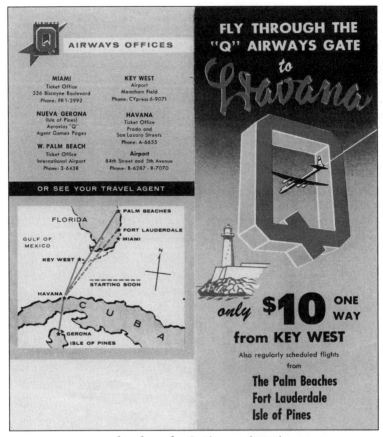

A brochure for Q Airways (1958)

Chevereton had to be "on 24 hours call"[406] to take pictures for court cases. When reporters pointed out that the department already employed several photographers, the Sheriff's Office reiterated that the radio was of very little value because it was "old and obsolete."[407] The problem with this claim was that the same model was in use in a number of the department's vehicles. Asked to clarify matters, Ghiotto replied: "You're trying to make a big issue out of nothing. If we didn't think this was all right, we wouldn't do it."[408] However, doing the right thing apparently was not as much an ethical judgment as a political one, for everyone agreed that by providing the radio Lloyd was increasing his chances of receiving positive publicity as the November election drew closer.

In August, both the State Attorney's Office and the County Solicitor's Office began new investigations after a former deputy named Victor H. Osborne

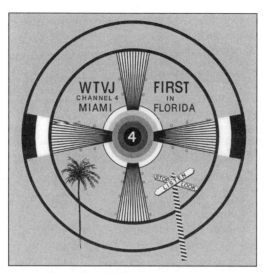

WTVJ Channel 4 (Miami) test pattern (c. 1960)

accused the Sheriff's Office of covering up certain illegal activities. According to Osborne, who had been let go in May 1960, he had gone to a North Broward shopping center just before Christmas 1959 to help investigate several break-ins. When he arrived, a regular deputy and an auxiliary deputy were in the process of robbing a sporting goods store, and told him "this is a good way to do our Christmas shopping."[409] The pair then loaded their loot into an unmarked patrol car and drove off.

Claiming to have been "dumbfounded" by what he had witnessed, Osborne initially "didn't say anything."[410] But three days later, he told the department and the two burglars were fired. However, no report was submitted to the County Solicitor's Office and Osborne was told to forget the matter. When they eventually learned what had happened, County Solicitor Thomas Coker and State Attorney Phil O'Connell decided to conduct a joint investigation, although they acknowledged that filing criminal charges might be difficult because the case was more than eight months old.

Lloyd defended himself by insisting that no crime had occurred and that Osborne had been dismissed "after a psychiatric check-up"[411] showed that he was unstable. Following several days of examination, Coker and Assistant State Attorney Curtin R. Coleman announced that while it appeared that Osborne's accusations were true, "we have been unable to obtain proof of all the necessary elements on which an information or indictment could properly be based."[412] Nevertheless, they criticized the sheriff for deciding on his own not to file any charges.

Although Lloyd had escaped with only a mild slap on the wrist, Osborne's troubles were just beginning. He had accurately predicted that the sheriff would "try to make me out as a screwball,"[413] and now the public was about to learn why, in what one newspaper called "a weird tale with all the trimmings of a dime novel plot."[414]

Shortly after Osborne made his allegations, his wife Elaine told him that she had come to believe that twelve years earlier she had killed her cousin Rita Buchard while the two were sharing a house in Pawtucket, Rhode Island. Seeking to reassure his distraught spouse, Osborne, while on duty and in uniform, went to Miami to speak to Linda Weiss, one of Elaine's childhood friends. In the course of his trip, the Miami police, having doubts about Osborne's identity, detained him and contacted the Broward Sheriff's Office. Several days later, Osborne was fired. (In the meantime, the authorities ruled out Elaine as a possible suspect in Buchard's murder. Although Buchard had been killed in 1948 in the woods near her home, Elaine had been only eight years old. Moreover, the murderer—who was described as a "sex maniac"[415] and remained at large—had stabbed Buchard forty-seven times, a feat that would have been difficult for a child to perform.)

Two weeks after it was announced that no charges would be filed concerning the Christmas thefts, Osborne was arrested for driving on State Road 7 without a license. Booked into the county jail, he remained in custody for eight hours before finally being released on a $36 bond. To many observers, this was a clear-cut case of retaliation, but Lloyd maintained that his former deputy had *wanted* to be arrested and had deliberately left home without his license. He "insisted on being arrested," the sheriff explained, adding that "he was hungry and wanted to eat."[416] Lloyd then noted, "I told him that he did not have to be arrested everytime he got hungry. I said all he has to do is get in touch with me and I'll feed him if he needs a meal."[417]

A number of other incidents found their way into the newspapers in the months leading up to the general election. When Lloyd hired two new deputies, for example, one of them turned out to be his son Alva, who previously had been a used car salesman. But because his primary duty would be "supervis[ing] maintenance of the sheriff's rolling stock,"[418] this bit of nepotism was largely overlooked.

Another blunder that made headlines occurred when Lloyd's men aided Steingrimur Hermannsson, an Icelandic government official who happened to be the son of the country's former prime minister. Hermannsson was involved in a nasty divorce with his wife Sarah, who had temporary custody of the couple's three children. When the Broward Juvenile Court was asked to investigate their living conditions, counselors reported that the kids were "in good health and well cared for."[419]

With his hopes of gaining legal custody based on maternal neglect dashed, Hermannsson procured an Icelandic court order awarding him custody. Armed with this piece of paper, which the U.S. Department of State later called worthless, he went to Sarah's home in Pompano Beach while she was at work. As Deputy Ted F. Zeuch watched for any trouble, Hermannsson grabbed Ellen, age 4, and Neil, age 2 (for some reason, the third child, John, age 9, was not covered by the Icelandic court order). Admitting that his department had "slipped up," Lloyd claimed that Hermannsson's attorney John Dye had "pull[ed] the wool over our eyes."[420]

Hard on the heels of this mistake, Lloyd suffered an even bigger blow when Ernest Murray, who had lost to Lloyd in the 1956 Republican primary but now was the chairman of the Broward County Republican Executive Committee, declared that "in announcing he is a write-in candidate, [Lloyd] has left the ranks of the Republican party and cannot be supported by loyal Republicans."[421]

Lloyd's campaign problems deepened during an appearance at the West Broward Republican Club in West Hollywood, where two uniformed deputies (Captain William Spitler and Safety Education Officer Paul Radcliff) screened a 30-minute color film about the Broward Sheriff's Office. Questions immediately began to be asked about the movie, including its purpose, who had paid for it, and who owned it. Lloyd answered that the film was an educational tool, that he had personally paid half of its $600 cost "[b]ecause we didn't have enough money in the fund," and that it "belongs to me, mostly."[422]

Upon hearing Lloyd's responses, Allen Michell pointedly asked, "What fund is he talking about? The department's expense fund, or the campaign fund?"[423] The Republican nominee also assailed Lloyd's motives, demanding to know why the sheriff had used any of his own money to make the picture, which "if truly educational, could have been paid for by the public."[424]

Because there had been no audit of the Sheriff's Office during the previous two years, there was no way to know whether taxpayers had in fact paid for a campaign tool. It was, however, discovered that the $300 Lloyd had paid out of his own pocket had gone to Roy Chevereton, the WTVJ cameraman whose car had been equipped with a BSO radio.

Two weeks before the November election, the Sheriff's Office announced a change in patrol operations that would "provide better coverage for the heavily populated unincorporated areas."[425] Beginning on Tuesday, November 1st, a five-zone system would replace the four zones that had been used for the past eighteen months. It was claimed that this would allow patrol officers to answer calls faster (because they would be traveling shorter distances) and permit rescuers to reach those in need sooner. "Naturally, I don't want to say how many men are to be assigned to any one zone or where the boundaries of the zones are,"[426] remarked John Berger, the road patrol's captain. "But we do want the people to know that the expansion to five zones will be a distinct advantage to them."[427]

In the days just prior to the election, an attempt was made to smear Allen Michell's reputation. A two-page background "report" was circulated containing, it was said, facts supplied by confidential informants. Both Claude Tindall and Quill Lloyd denied any responsibility for the report, which mocked Michell's law enforcement experience and described him as someone who had merely taken fingerprints and otherwise "did nothing but stand around[,] smile and smoke a cigar."[428] When reached by reporters, Murray Bookbinder, the personnel director of the Philadelphia Police Department, squashed this claim, explaining that Michell had taken a competitive exam prior to being promoted to captain and had won various awards while on the force. Bookbinder also noted that Michell had been commended for arresting a notorious criminal who had shot a policeman and terrorized the city's pawn shops.

When the ballots were counted, Michell had 54,414 votes to Tindall's 48,361 votes (a margin of 53%–47%), while Lloyd's total barely registered. Two weeks later, Claude Anderson, who had lost in the Democratic primary in May, was arrested in a grocery store in Dahlonega, Georgia, when he tried to buy a pack of cigarettes using a fake $20 bill. Embarrassed by the charge, Anderson protested that he was innocent and said that unlike past occasions, this time he was *not* guilty.

Following the election, Lloyd used his remaining time in office to settle old scores. In a particularly notable case, he demoted Joe Pierce, a criminal investigator, to road patrolman because Pierce had refused to actively campaign for him. When questioned about the reassignment, Lloyd denied that politics had played any role in the decision. Pierce, he said, simply "makes a better road patrolman."[429]

Even after he left office, Lloyd continued to be a controversial figure. Less than two months after his successor was sworn in, Lloyd was sued by an elderly man named Vincent Bedack who claimed that in September 1960, he had been roughed up by two of Lloyd's deputies (Jesse Crum and J. Harlan Munn) while being served with papers for non-payment of an insurance premium.

Tombstone of Sheriff Quill Lloyd (Lauderdale Memorial
Gardens Cemetery, Fort Lauderdale)

Lloyd also faced the possibility of being sued by Broward County after a state audit discovered he had exceeded his budget by more than $8,000. Among other things, the report said that Lloyd had overpaid himself, bought gold-plated badges for his deputies, and purchased vehicles without competitive bids. It also pointed out that the film Lloyd had made during the campaign focused almost entirely on him and therefore was "useless"[430] to the department.

Lloyd angrily denounced the auditor's findings and said that "[w]hen I went into office I had more money in the bank than I had when I left."[431] There was, however, one disallowed item for which he was willing to take responsibility—a $496 charge for nursing services provided by Hollywood Memorial Hospital to a deputy who had been injured while directing traffic at a supermarket. The former sheriff claimed that it was only later that he learned that the deputy had been off-duty, earning extra money, at the time of his injury. Nevertheless, Lloyd defended the payment by explaining, "I only did what any decent human being would have done."[432]

Lloyd died on May 11, 1978, at the age of eighty-three, at the South Florida State Hospital in Pembroke Pines.[433]

CHAPTER 6

THE MICHELL-WALKER YEARS (1961–69)

At the start of the new decade, Broward's voters had chosen a new sheriff, but his eight years in office would prove even more turbulent than those of his predecessor. During his first term as the county's top lawman, Allen B. Michell would be investigated by a grand jury and discover that sixty-one of his deputies were not bonded and therefore had been making illegal arrests. In his second term, Michell would be suspended from office, thereby becoming the third Broward sheriff to suffer such a fate. Although he eventually would be reinstated, the ongoing political drama would spell the end of his law enforcement career and leave the department bruised and the public disillusioned.

Sheriff Allen B. Michell (1961–66)

Allen Brandt Michell was born in Charleston, South Carolina, on April 18, 1903, and moved to Philadelphia in 1928. Two years later, he joined the Philadelphia Bureau of Police. Initially hired as a civilian identification expert, he advanced rapidly through the ranks and by 1940 was one of the department's top detectives as well as an instructor at the Philadelphia Police Academy.

A reservist in the U.S. Army, Michell was called to active duty in 1941 and made an assistant chief in the Military Police Corps. Sent overseas in 1943, he served as the assistant superintendent of police as well as the superintendent of prisons for occupied lands. After being promoted to colonel in 1945, Michell oversaw the closing of Nazi concentration camps in Austria and Germany.

Following the war, Michell returned to the Philadelphia Police Department and in 1953 made captain. In 1955, he left the force and later became an industrial security inspector for the U.S. Army. In 1958, Michell and his wife Florence moved to Florida, and in 1959 he retired from the U.S. Army Reserve (although a subsequent promotion elevated him to the rank of brigadier general).

Allen B. Michell, sheriff of Broward County (1961–66 and 1966–69)

Just days before becoming sheriff, Michell announced the names of his top appointees. Captain John Berger, the head of the road patrol, and Frank Ghiotto, the chief of the civil division, were both retained, but Chief Deputy A.M. Wittkamp was let go. Nine other employees received similar news. According to Michell, these firings were needed to make the department a "more efficient organization."[434]

Jack Harris, the chief criminal investigator, also was out, replaced by John N. "Bud" Mehl. A 30-year law enforcement veteran, Mehl had been a lieutenant with the Parkersburg Police Department in West Virginia and had served as a deputy under Sheriff Lloyd for four years. In announcing the change, Michell said that Mehl's record made it clear "he was the best man"[435] for the job. Mehl responded by promising that changes would be forthcoming, but said they would take time, explaining, "Right now we're in the process of setting everything up."[436]

Ralph J. Paul, a former Ohio sheriff, was given the job of administrative assistant, while Leo Hart, Michell's campaign manager, became an unpaid advisor to the department. Michell also hired two lawyers—one for the civil division (John D. Kruse) and the other for the criminal division (former County Solicitor Emerson Allsworth). Although previous sheriffs had found it sufficient to have one lawyer serve both branches, Michell explained, somewhat redundantly, that "[s]eparation of the civil and criminal divisions of the sheriff's department with separate attorneys is a new innovation."[437]

Michell made it clear that all of these appointments were being "made on a temporary basis pending a study of each department as to their efficiency, economy and workload."[438] To emphasize the point, he added that any of the provisional hirees could be gone within a month or two. "If they do not come up to my expectations," he said, "none of them will be there."[439]

On Tuesday, January 3, 1961, Michell was sworn in as sheriff. Later that day, he called a meeting of the department's 150 employees and told them that he was committed to clearing out the dead wood. "Anyone not helping to make this office a better one will have to step aside for there are many who will."[440] Michell also made it clear just how much he disliked the agency's longstanding practice of hiring husbands and wives, which sent a chill down the spines of such couples. (Ironically, Michell later married his executive secretary but kept her on the payroll.)

Michell then added to the angst by announcing that everyone would be required to fill out a detailed four-page application form. The information gathered through this effort, he explained, would be used to make new duty assignments and, depending on what was learned, could lead to more firings.

Four weeks after taking office, Michell sacked Frank Ghiotto, his chief civil deputy, and replaced him with Ralph Paul, his administrative assistant, who was put in charge of a new section that was responsible for auditing, bookkeeping, communications, licenses and permits, personnel, purchasing, records, and a number of other clerical functions. At the same time, Henry Dusenbery, a former Dania police chief, was hired and assigned to the complaint desk at the courthouse. Michell noted that these moves were part of his plan to surround himself with qualified men who were able to "get in step with my administration."[441] Those who could not, he added, "will have to step aside, because I know plenty who can keep my stride."[442]

One month later, three experienced lawmen were hired to fill vacancies in the understaffed criminal division. J. Edgar Bayreuther and Edward Conner were retired detectives from New York City, while Daniel Smith had been a member of the Indiana State Police before becoming the sheriff of Marion County in Indianapolis.

From the beginning, Michell sought to project an active image when it came to fighting crime. Within weeks of being sworn in as sheriff, he launched an assault on illegal gambling. One of his first targets was Carl Hoffman, a 70-year-old Hollywood bookmaker whose home was raided by deputies. After forcing their way in, the officers spent an hour answering Hoffman's phone and managed to take thirty horse racing bets. The astonished bookie was quoted as saying, "nothing like this has ever happened to me in the 25 years I have lived here."[443]

A short time later, the Sheriff's Office announced that anyone seeking a gun permit would face a rigorous screening procedure. According to Michell, only applicants with a legitimate reason for having a weapon would be granted a license, and anyone wanting a gun to satisfy their ego would be turned away. He also called for stricter gun control legislation to make it more difficult for criminals to arm themselves.

In March 1961, the Fort Lauderdale Police Department confronted the city's first Spring Break riot. The three-hour confrontation had been touched off by a lone prankster who blocked traffic by lying in the middle of Atlantic Boulevard near East Las Olas Boulevard. The stunt quickly escalated, and soon 15,000 people were running wild. With matters hopelessly out of control, firefighters were summoned and restored order by turning water cannons on the crowd.

In the view of many observers, the leading cause of the melee was Michell's order "to keep Jade Beach closed to collegians, [the] first year such a move has been made on the unlighted section of beach off A1A, long a trysting spot for students."[444] Yet when asked whether he felt any responsibility for what had happened,

> Michell said Jade Beach is plastered with "No Trespassing" signs as it is his sworn duty to see that the law is enforced.
>
> The sheriff said a solution would be for city officials to grant students the right to use Ft. Lauderdale's lighted beach for carousing and beer drinking.[445]

Within weeks of the riot, Michell once again was receiving favorable press coverage for his continuing efforts to curtail illegal gambling. The vice squad, led by Deputies Jack Brophy and Joe Pierce, was aggressively pursuing those suspected of being involved in such activities, and during Michell's first four months in office it recorded seventy-five arrests. And while bolita continued to be a major revenue source for Broward's gangsters (one estimate put the annual income from such games at $6 million), Chief Intelligence Deputy James Spears claimed that the raids were taking a toll on these illegal profits. Chief Assistant County Solicitor Douglas S. Lambeth added his own praise, telling reporters that "the vice activities of the sheriff's office have been greater in the past 30 days than they have in the past six months."[446]

Minnesota State University senior George "Buddy" Dalluge (hanging from the light pole) at the 1961 Spring Break riot on Fort Lauderdale beach

But the picture was not entirely rosy for Michell—according to persistent rumors, various gambling syndicates were moving their operations into Broward, something the sheriff vehemently denied. Pointing to the recent flurry of raids, Michell argued that the "[a]ctivities of our vice squad and others throughout the county are keeping all gambling activities to a complete minimum."[447] With his next breath, however, Michell seemed to contradict himself, saying that while it was true that northern gamblers were coming to Broward, "[w]e know they are here and are keeping a close watch on them."[448] And then, in an even odder comment, he defended the new arrivals by observing, "[t]he county accepts their taxes and there is no reason they shouldn't be treated as any other resident as long as they keep their noses clean."[449]

Michell's mention of taxes appears to have been intentional, for when he went in front of the county commission and presented his budget for the up-coming fiscal year, he asked for a 25% increase and suggested that the money come from new taxes — an idea H. Vivian Saxon, the commission's chairman, found frightening: "If we don't hold the line on taxes, we're going to be run out of the county."[450] Michell replied by saying that "[c]rime goes up during a re-cession. It would be false economy to curtail law enforcement."[451]

In defending his request for $1.3 million, Michell described the agency's equipment as "bedraggled"[452] and ticked off a long list of specific problems: fif-teen staff positions were vacant; the radios were aging and a new transmitter was needed (the current one had been borrowed from the civil defense corps); none of the seventeen criminal investigators had a desk at which to work; while the rest of the government had calculators, the Sheriff's Office was still doing its bookkeeping by hand; at night, one deputy had to guard 200 prisoners at the county jail, a ratio that was going to get much worse when the current renova-tions were completed and the facility's size doubled; and the department's seven patrol cars, which in 1961 were reported to have logged 1.8 million miles and responded to 6,000 calls for assistance, were unable to adequately cover the county's roadways (which had grown to more than 700 miles).

Michell also wanted money to keep the West Hollywood sub-station open around the clock. This proposal encountered fierce resistance, with County Commissioner Frank C. Adler saying, "We've not reached the point where we need 24-hour service. That's what you get when you live in the city."[453]

Wanting to send a message to Michell, but fearing a showdown with the state if they went too far, the commissioners opted for cuts totaling $75,000. At the same time, they urged the sheriff to consider further reductions, warn-ing him that if he failed to heed their advice he would have to answer to the voters at election time. They also pointed out that the department had not used all of its currently-appropriated funds and recently had returned $25,000 that had been earmarked for salaries.

In subsequent meetings, the commissioners pared another $98,000 from Michell's original request, resulting in a budget for 1961–62 of $1.15 million (which was still $85,000 more than the previous year's budget). In a separate appropriation, Michell was given $15,000 to buy new equipment and meet emergencies during the remaining three months of the current fiscal year.

Shortly after the budget passed, Michell announced a major personnel shakeup, which he blamed on the need to economize. The head of the road pa-trol, Captain John Berger, was promoted to commander of the enforcement de-partment, which oversaw the road patrol, the criminal investigation division, and the special investigation division. Chief Criminal Investigator Bud Mehl was demoted to lieutenant and now found himself reporting to Berger. In a final move, Criminal Investigator James Spears was made Michell's administrative aide.

Although the budget cuts had prevented the West Hollywood sub-station from operating at night, it remained open during the day. And, the sheriff added, the change in command structure would mean even better protection for the county's south area. "With one man assigning units, there will be no overlapping of duties."[454]

In August 1961, Michell hired seven new employees. Three of them were detailed to the criminal records division, for Michell intended to make its services available twenty-four hours a day (up from eight). The other four employees were to be trained as jailers to help handle the coming expansion of the Broward County Jail. Further hiring would have to be postponed until the start of the new fiscal year, Michell said, because $40,000 in bills left by Sheriff Lloyd had put him in a bind.

As Michell grappled with his budget problems, Palm Beach County Sheriff Martin M. Kellenberger fought to stay out of jail and keep his job. Accused of lying about illegal gambling to a grand jury, Kellenberger, who like Michell was a Republican in a heavily-Democratic county, was arrested and then suspended by Governor C. Farris Bryant. Although cleared of the charges and given his job back in August 1962 (by which time the county had run through three interim sheriffs), Kellenberger's ordeal left no doubt that gamblers were firmly entrenched in Palm Beach. In an effort to salvage some civic pride, Phil O'Connell, the state attorney, claimed "they have been operating in other places for 20 years too, including Broward."[455] As it happened, by this time the state already had begun looking into the Broward Sheriff's Office, prompted in part by reports that deputies were taking payoffs from gamblers.

Asked to comment on the inquiry, Michell expressed optimism. "I welcome the presence in Broward County of the state investigating team because the Gold Coast of Florida is the area most vulnerable to an attempted invasion by racketeers."[456] One day later, James W. "Jimmy" Kynes, Jr., the governor's chief administrative aide, announced that Bryant planned to undertake his own investigation, saying, "We have under scrutiny all the reports, and are taking notes of the situation in Broward."[457] Jose A. Gonzalez, Jr., the assistant state attorney handling the state's inquiry, then promised that while his examination would be "broad and exhaustive,"[458] it would not duplicate Bryant's probe.

In the meantime, press reports indicated that a Broward deputy had been subpoenaed by the Florida Attorney General's Office to give a deposition regarding local vice matters. The *Fort Lauderdale News*, which had staunchly supported Michell during the 1960 election, now declared that an examina-

James W. "Jimmy" Kynes, Jr., chief administrative aide
(1961–64) to Florida Governor C. Farris Bryant

tion was needed to determine if "something was decidedly amiss in the county's top law enforcement organization."[459] In an editorial, it advised:

> Our own investigation has clearly revealed that an unhealthy situation does exist in the Sheriff's office. It is readily apparent to those close to this situation that a nasty power struggle has been taking place in Sheriff Allen B. Michell's organization and that individuals who stand for anything but solid and honest law enforcement have been wielding power and making decisions in places where they should have no influence whatsoever.[460]

In fact, Michell *was* having personnel problems. Friction between the sheriff and his former campaign manager, Leo Hart, had gotten so bad that Michell had advised deputies to ignore any order issued by Hart. Michell also had a falling out with James Spears, another one of his top aides, after a veterans' post Spears belonged to (and once had headed) was raided by state agents who had been alerted to on-going gambling and liquor violations.

Although Spears insisted the incident had been politically motivated, Michell suspended him for nine days before deciding that Spears had played no role in the matter and therefore "was in the clear."[461] But when Spears subsequently claimed that "poker games are held nightly at some other private clubs in full view of many government officials," an angry Michell told him to "go out and prove it."[462]

In addition to his differences with Hart and Spears, Michell told the press that he was having other personnel problems. In particular, he said, he had been forced to put certain vice squad deputies "in isolation"[463] because questions had been raised about their conduct.

Within weeks of the announcement of the dual investigations, rumors began to circulate that the sheriff would be resigning. "I have never offered to resign my post as sheriff of this county,"[464] Michell replied. "I'll admit that with all the rumors and false charges I've been tempted at times to give it all up," but "I certainly have no intention of resigning now."[465]

In October 1961, James Spears was indicted on charges of running a gambling house, causing Michell to fire the deputy he had promoted only a few months earlier. (The charges were dropped the following year due to a faulty search warrant.) Soon, Michell lost one of his top investigators when Jack Brophy resigned after five years with the department. His departure only added to the questions surrounding Michell's willingness to go after gamblers.

Shortly after taking office, Michell had received a report from Brophy about a bolita operator who, upon being arrested, had angrily complained, "we have paid you people to operate here."[466] The man then named a deputy and another individual (who had ties to Michell) and said he had given them $2,500 in exchange for assurances that his business would be protected. Declining to take any action, Michell filed Brophy's report away.

During the ensuing state investigation, a grand jury repeatedly called Brophy to testify (in fact, he ended up appearing more often than any other witness). In Michell's first six months in office, Brophy had spearheaded many of the vice squad's gambling raids, but when that unit was reorganized as the sheriff's "special squad," new investigators were brought in and Brophy was reassigned to routine criminal cases. Interestingly, these changes had occurred at just about the time that Brophy had submitted his report concerning alleged payoffs.

For awhile, however, things seemed to be looking up for Michell. In June 1962, for example, he was able to announce improved patrol car coverage for the unincorporated areas. Six days later, newspapers gushed over Road Patrol Corporal George Murdock, who, while trying to capture a four-foot-long alligator in Hollywood, had sustained a severe bite to his hand. Immediately

thereafter, a call came in reporting that a double airboat accident had just occurred near Andytown (in the Everglades) that required urgent assistance. Ignoring his own wounds, Murdock raced to the scene and remained there for
more than three hours before finally going to Hollywood Memorial Hospital.
Dave Paget, an ambulance driver, explained, with a mixture of amazement
and awe, that while attending to the airboat victims Murdock had stopped
every so often so that emergency workers could "chang[e] the bandages on his
hand ... when they got soaked up with blood."[467]

During the following month, deputies Robert Mitchell and Cecil Stewart
solved a case that had been perplexing lawmen throughout the state. As a result of their investigation, a gang that had committed armed robberies in at least
seven different Florida counties was captured and put behind bars. And in
early September 1962, Michell himself was lauded as a hero when he cornered
John J. Bellomy, an escaped federal convict, after a chase that, as one local
newspaper put it, had "started in a hail of bullets."[468]

But the good news came to an abrupt end a few days later when a headline
in the *Fort Lauderdale News* proclaimed, "County Bolita Wide Open," and then
added, "Newsmen Find It, But Sheriff Can't." The article that followed informed readers:

> A $10,000 a week bolita operation has been flourishing under the
> noses of Broward County Sheriff Allen B. Michell and his "special
> squad" for almost five months now.
>
> The operation, obviously backed by big-time Dade County gam-
> blers, has been running out in the open without any sign of interfer-
> ence by the county police.
>
> I have, in fact, heard a tape recording of a bolita peddler saying
> "The county is paid off."
>
> ....
>
> I have seen the green and white cars of the Broward County sher-
> iff's office cruise amiably by the house which is the center of the op-
> eration—while the bolita number was being thrown.
>
> I have seen these squad cars slow down in front of the house, giv-
> ing the impression they were there to prevent interference, not crime.[469]

The story went on to describe how the paper's staff had been able to uncover
the operation, which raised the question why "neither [Michell] nor his deputies
were able to [do likewise]."[470]

On the following day, another headline announced, "Deputy Sheriffs Tied
to Bolita Loot." According to the paper, payoffs were being given to deputies
to allow the illegal gambling to continue. The piece also described a raid on a

gambling site that had lasted a mere five minutes, gathered no evidence, and resulted in no arrests. "We knew they were coming,"[471] one of the bookies explained. Most telling of all, Fred Burrall, the reporter who wrote the story, claimed that just before it was published, he had asked the sheriff whether gambling was taking place and "Michell told me he knew nothing about a large-scale operation in Broward County."[472]

Michell responded to the exposé by saying, "We have now and probably will always have bolita going on here. But I can assure you it is on a minimum scale and far from being part of the operation of a combine or syndicate."[473] Michell also lashed out at the paper—by refusing to reveal the names of the allegedly crooked deputies, he claimed, it was hampering his ability to take corrective action. As for allowing gamblers to operate openly, he explained that he was not interested in the buyer of bolita tickets (or as he put it, the "little man"), but wanted the game's "sellers and bankers."[474] The department's policy, the sheriff said, was to keep gambling operations under surveillance until "we get evidence to get the big boys."[475] In defending his approach, Michell graphically remarked, "[i]t's true that if you get the man on the bottom the guys at the top will fall, but if we arrested all the buyers we'd have to put a fence around colored town."[476]

Of course, most of the department's time was taken up with more mundane matters, and here progress could be seen. In December 1962, for example, the county commission approved Michell's request for $20,000 to build a vehicle service center on a parcel of county-owned land at First Avenue and Southeast Sixth Street. Up until then, the Sheriff's Office had used credit cards at commercial establishments. With its own depot, the department could buy gas at wholesale prices and keep routine maintenance chores in-house. As a result, Michell predicted "the garage will pay for itself in a short span of time."[477]

At the start of 1963, Michell divided the county into three criminal investigation zones, a move the sheriff was certain would improve law enforcement services. "I've appointed my three best men to take over the sectors,"[478] he said. "I feel if they work in smaller areas they will become better acquainted with the people in the sectors and increase the overall efficiency of the department."[479] Lieutenant Charles W. Alderton remained in charge of the 21-man criminal investigation division, while the special squad, under Sergeant Andy Murcia, continued to work the entire county. The three detectives responsible for the new sectors (James DeCoursey—South, Ray Reardon—Central, and Cecil Stewart—North) were each given the rank of sergeant and had their wages boosted to $418 per month.

In another important development, Michell announced a new deputy pay schedule. The plan, which Michell referred to as "a modified civil service,"[480] provided raises on a five-year basis. "All patrolmen are now given $395 base pay," the sheriff explained, but "[t]his plan will give them raises from $418 two years after it is put into effect up to $460 after five years of service."[481] Although not binding on future sheriffs, Michell felt sure his successors would adhere to it. "These people haven't had a raise since the year one, as near as I can figure out," he claimed, "and they certainly deserve one."[482] The sheriff also thought he deserved more pay, but his request for a salary increase to $15,000 was rebuffed by the state legislature.

As the calendar turned to 1964, Michell began looking ahead to November. But within a week, a serious threat to his re-election chances emerged. After refusing to sign a surety bond for a deputy, a county commissioner contacted the county attorney and explained that there had been a problem with the date. Nor was this an isolated incident—according to the commissioner, lots of bonds with retroactive dates were being approved, including some for periods commencing prior to the commissioner's election.

A grand jury was convened to look into the matter, and during its deliberations it heard from Paul G. Messenger and Walter E. Ramsdell, two former deputies. Ramsdell, who had been a road patrol sergeant, testified that in March 1963 Michell had ordered him to sign a bond application with an effective date of Tuesday, January 3, 1961, which was the day Michell had taken office. Ramsdell also claimed that when he began asking questions, he was fired for "saying things detrimental to the department."[483]

Further investigation revealed that sixty-one officers did not possess proper bonds, as state law required.[484] But it was only in the spring of 1963, when Court of Record Judge Douglas Lambeth dismissed a gambling case because one of the deputies lacked a valid bond, that Michell finally addressed the issue.

Despite this evidence, the grand jury ended its two-day session by exonerating Michell. Finding that he had not set out to do anything wrong and had believed that bonds could simply roll over, the panel said "there has been a good faith effort on the part of the Broward County Sheriff's office to comply with the requirements of the law as it pertains to deputy sheriff's bonds."[485] Eleven months later, Assistant Florida Attorney General John A. Madigan, Jr., in response to a request made by Senator A.J. Ryan, Jr. (D-Dania Beach), issued an advisory opinion that agreed with this assessment but said that the better practice would be for "a deputy sheriff [to] either be rebonded or [obtain] a signed extension of the bond … at the beginning of each new administration whether the cause be from death, resignation, removal or reelection of the principal."[486]

In March 1964, Michell was confronted once more with questions about whether bolita games were taking place in Broward. His answer was that although gambling was now minimal in the county, and not nearly as bad as in Dade, "It's like a disease. It can be controlled, but never entirely curbed."[487] Moreover, according to the sheriff, bolita was affecting only the African-American community, where, if one wanted to, "you could get hundreds of possession arrests."[488] But such arrests would solve nothing, he insisted, because what was really needed was to concentrate on the kingpins. Michell also reminded everyone that an all-out war on bolita was impossible because the vice squad consisted of only two men and "[t]hey've got more than bolita to worry about, you want to remember. There're moonshine stills, prostitution, and dope—just to name a few."[489]

Although the county's top cop had just declared his jurisdiction relatively free of the numbers racket, the *Fort Lauderdale News* begged to differ. Bolita, it claimed, "is so wide open in Broward County one would think it's legal.... [B]ig time bolita kingpins run a conservatively estimated $10,000-a-week business here—apparently without fear."[490] Reporters and photographers had been able to follow the gambling slips from the street sellers all the way to the top of the bolita racket, so why, they asked, could the Sheriff's Office not do likewise?

Back in 1962, Michell had criticized the paper for not providing him with the evidence it had gathered. This time, the *News* defended itself by saying it had tried in 1963 to give the sheriff information about a gambling operation in Plantation but had been told to "[q]uit playing cops and robbers and leave the police work to us."[491]

The paper's allegations caused both the County Solicitor's Office and the State Attorney's Office to begin investigations. Within days, the sheriff's vice squad, bolstered by half a dozen other deputies, carried out a series of bolita raids. When asked about their timing, Michell said that no inferences should be drawn: "We do it every weekend, and we've been doing it for the past several weeks."[492]

Nevertheless, Michell was called on the carpet by the State Attorney's Office, special investigators from Tallahassee (who had been dispatched by Attorney General Richard Ervin), and local prosecutors. But when the meeting took place, the group merely asked Michell to make a thorough investigation of gambling in the county, offering to assist him in any way possible. For his part, Michell promised to "cooperate 100 per cent"[493] and pointed out that he had already assigned a substantial force of deputies to the matter.

In the May 1964 Republican primary, Michell's only challenger was William N. Horgan, a one-time BSO deputy who Michell had fired in 1962. Michell raised nearly twice as much money as Horgan ($1,525.20 to $815.79) and beat his former employee easily, 11,412 votes to 3,593 votes (a margin of 76%–24%).

In the four-way race for the Democratic nomination, the top two finishers were Richard A. Basinger and former Sheriff Quill Lloyd. In a run-off election held three weeks later, Basinger beat Lloyd by a tally of 27,314 votes to 20,403 votes (a margin of 57%–43%). Promising to support Basinger in the upcoming general election, Lloyd—who had returned to being a Democrat—stated, "[w]e should all work together now to bring the sheriff's position back into the Democratic camp."[494]

In the meantime, Michell submitted his proposed budget for the 1964–65 fiscal year. Again unwilling to raise taxes, the commissioners cut $100,000 from Michell's $1.4 million request after noting that recent annexations and incorporations had reduced the sheriff's responsibilities. Michell responded that this was not true, claiming that the workloads of the civil and criminal divisions had remained the same and pointing out that the road patrol still had to drive through the cities to get to the unincorporated areas.

As the general election drew nearer, Michell reminded voters that because of him, deputies now had to meet specific education and training standards. Not only did applicants have to be high school graduates, but they also had to take a 13-week training course at the Dade County Sheriff's Police Academy. (Although the Fort Lauderdale Police Department ran a similar school, Michell questioned its capabilities.) In July 1964, when six new graduates were hired, Michell proudly announced that one out of every three patrolmen now were academy alumni. He also promised that when the next class completed its studies in August, two earlier graduates would be moved up from the road patrol to the detective division.

In a further effort to improve officer quality, Michell instituted a nine-week on-the-job training course, taught primarily by judges and lawyers, to keep both patrolmen and criminal investigators abreast of new developments. Michell also required all road deputies to take classes in riot control techniques, which covered such subjects as mob psychology, proper unit formations, and how to use tear gas and wield a baton. Michell invited local police departments to send their officers to these classes so that if a riot did break out, personnel from different jurisdictions would be able to work together.

A month before the election, Broward deputies, accompanied by reporters and photographers, threw one of Michell's opponents out of his own campaign headquarters. Ed Armstrong, a write-in candidate who had been using his Hollywood feed store as his base of operations, had fallen $915 behind on his rent. When his landlord sought to have him evicted, Michell was more than happy to have his officers execute the warrant, saying, "Armstrong is always accusing the sheriff's department of never doing anything. Well, now we're doing something."[495]

Broward deputies practicing riot control techniques (1986)

While Armstrong presented no threat at the polls, Basinger did, and he took every opportunity to attack Michell's record and claim that the sheriff was allowing illegal gambling to flourish. Basinger also reminded the public that while Michell said he could not hire more deputies, over the past three years he had returned to the county $247,000 in unspent funds. And, of course, Basinger repeatedly brought up the sixty-one deputies who had not been bonded. In the end, however, Michell narrowly squeaked by Basinger, beating him by a tally of 66,716 votes to 63,165 votes (a margin of 51%–49%).

Michell took his second oath of office on Tuesday, January 5, 1965, and for a short time received positive press coverage. In May 1965, for example, deputies apprehended the "River Rats," a burglary ring made up of two dozen boys who ranged in age from thirteen to sixteen and were responsible for fifty break-ins. They also regularly shook down other teenagers for money.

Once again, however, the good news did not last as critics renewed their charge that the Sheriff's Office was not doing enough to crack down on the bolita operators. Lieutenant Cecil Stewart, the head of the vice squad, defended the department's record and eventually claimed that the gamblers were "making it difficult for us to catch them … they've changed their signals and we can't catch them like we used to."[496]

Matters finally came to a head on Monday, March 7, 1966, when a grand jury indicted Michell on three misdemeanor charges (malfeasance, misfeasance, and nonfeasance) for " 'knowingly, willfully or corruptly' allowing gam-

W. Haydon Burns, governor of Florida (1965–67)

bling in Broward."[497] To clear his name, Michell asked Governor W. Haydon Burns to suspend him, which Burns did.

After asking Civil Division Chief James W. Knight, Sr. "to take charge of the office pending appointment of a replacement,"[498] Burns offered the $14,500-a-year job to Fort Lauderdale Police Chief Lester Holt, who declined to "elaborate on the reasons he rejected it."[499] Burns also briefly considered former FBI agent Richard Hunter but steadfastly refused entreaties from Richard Basinger (who, of course, had narrowly lost to Michell in the 1964 general election).

Finally, acting on the recommendation of "a nonpolitical citizens committee with representatives from all parts of Broward County,"[500] Burns picked local insurance broker Thomas J. "Tom" Walker to be the county's interim sheriff.[501] Before allowing him to take over, however, Burns—a Democrat filling a position held by a Republican—extracted two concessions. First, Walker agreed to step down if Michell was acquitted. Second, Walker promised that he would not run in 1968 if Michell was found guilty.[502] By acquiescing to these demands, of course, Walker came into office without the clout he otherwise would have had.

The appointment of Walker caught most people by surprise, although local officials were quick to praise him. In a story in the *Fort Lauderdale News*, Fort Lauderdale Mayor Edmund R. Burry called Walker "a very fine young man," Hollywood Vice Mayor B.L. David said, "I'm sure he'll do a good job," and State Senator Ryan described him as having "the character and integrity"[503] necessary for the post. State Representative Emerson Allsworth (D-Fort Lauderdale), however, made it clear that Walker's chief asset was his lack of a political resume: "[T]he governor has insisted all along that this delicate appointment be approached on a non-partisan, non-political basis and that it not be treated as a matter of political patronage."[504]

Sheriff Thomas J. Walker (March 1966 to November 1966)

Thomas Joseph Walker was born on December 7, 1920, in Butte, Montana, but moved to New York City when he was four. His father was Frank C. Walker, a successful corporate lawyer, past member of the Montana legislature, future confidant of Franklin D. Roosevelt, and U.S. Postmaster General from 1940 to 1945.

Like his father, Walker attended the University of Notre Dame and received a B.A. in journalism in 1942 (making him the first Broward sheriff to be a college graduate). He then enlisted in the U.S. Navy and served through the end of World War II. After being discharged, he returned to New York City and went to work for the shipping company Grace Lines, Inc.

In 1957, Walker moved to Fort Lauderdale from Scranton, Pennsylvania, where he had been involved in various real estate and theatrical ventures with his father. Once in Fort Lauderdale, Walker set up his own insurance agency and became friendly with Robert H. Gore, the owner of the *Fort Lauderdale News*.

Upon being named sheriff, Walker listed reducing traffic accidents and improving response times in the unincorporated areas as his top priorities, promised to appoint a citizens advisory committee to give Broward "the highest type of law enforcement," and made it clear that he was "determined to do all in my power to combat illicit gambling and vice in the country. [I will] attack this problem with the utmost vigor."[505]

Walker also set about to rehabilitate the department's reputation. While he did not plan to fire anyone, the new lawman suggested that for those thinking of taking a leave of absence, "now is the time to do it."[506]

Walker also ordered every deputy to submit to a lie detector test. Insisting that Michell's indictment had placed the entire department under a cloud,

Walker reasoned that the tests would restore public confidence by allowing him to determine if anyone had taken payoffs or hindered efforts to clamp down on gambling and other vice crimes. Predictably, several deputies refused to take the tests, causing Walker to accuse them of leading a conspiracy against him and threatening to fire them. When pressed about the matter, Walker claimed to "have a pretty good idea who these individuals are."[507]

At the time of Walker's appointment, the Sheriff's Office employed 205 people, including 130 deputies. Forty officers were assigned to the road patrol, twenty to the detective division, twelve to the civil division, seven served warrants, and the rest manned the booking desk and the jail. Recognizing that their paltry salaries made them more likely to take bribes, Walker announced that securing pay raises would be one of the main goals of his administration.

Despite having agreed to a limited tenure, Walker acted like a man who intended to stay for a long time. His many changes included: 1) switching candidate training sites (in the future, applicants would remain in Broward for their schooling); 2) naming Sam George as the first African-American member of the homicide and robbery division (a well-deserved assignment, given George's success in breaking up several burglary rings, including the River Rats); 3) ending (as of Sunday, May 1, 1966) the policy of paying black officers (of whom there were now eight) less than their white counterparts (according to Walker, "[t]he Negro deputies do just the same job as other employees, and are called upon at times to risk their lives, just like their white fellow officers"[508]); and, 4) quadrupling the size of the vice squad and ordering it to conduct a massive bolita crackdown (interestingly enough, the two men who had constituted the squad under Michell both left when Walker began his offensive).

In the meantime, Allen Michell had been arraigned and was free on $500 bond. In May, Judge Lambeth dismissed the charges against him because they were too vague, and on Monday, June 6th, the County Solicitor's Office announced that it was dropping the matter. As a result, Michell was reinstated as sheriff.

On Thursday, June 9th, however, Michell was indicted by a new grand jury, and once again Governor Burns named Walker interim sheriff. Because Walker was unable to be sworn in until Monday, June 13th, Captain George W. Dunson, the department's senior officer, received a telegram from Burns asking him to step in. This led the press to dub Dunson the "Weekend Sheriff" (a nickname he would have a hard time shaking) and telling readers, with obvious sarcasm, that "[a] 'weekend sheriff' has been appointed to watch over Broward County."[509]

Not willing to take any chances given recent events, the county commission convened an emergency session and approved new surety bonds for the entire department. In addition to needing new bonds, the officers also had to take new oaths. In fact, by the time the year was over, many deputies had sworn to do their jobs four times—once when Walker was appointed, a second time when Michell was reinstated, a third time when Walker returned, and a fourth time when Michell regained his job for good. It is likely that no group of police officers in America had ever been administered so many oaths of office over such a short period of time.

Walker's second stint as sheriff lasted five months. During it, Lawrence E. "Larry" Lang—who would later run for sheriff himself—served as Walker's chief deputy. In November, Michell's case went to trial. Over the course of seven days, Assistant County Solicitor Robert J. Fogan called forty-one witnesses, but Judge Lambeth refused to hear from most of them because they were not bolita experts. When the government rested, Lambeth ordered Michell acquitted on all charges and sent the jury home. This outcome so infuriated Hank Messick, a reporter for the *Miami Herald*, that he publicly called the trial a "whitewash."[510] Earlier, Messick had linked Lambeth and Michell by saying, "The bolita sheriff is before the bolita judge."[511] Although Lambeth threatened Messick with contempt for his remarks, he agreed to take no action after Messick offered an apology.

Sheriff Allen B. Michell (1966–69)

When Allen Michell again became sheriff on Wednesday, November 23, 1966, the first thing he did was remove most of the top brass that had served under Tom Walker. He also added a special squad to handle narcotics and morals crimes, an intelligence unit that would keep him informed of "everything that's going on in town,"[512] and an internal security division to check on the backgrounds and activities of the department's employees. Michell also disputed reports that he had reduced the number of men working on the vice squad, claiming that he had actually assigned *more* men to the unit but could not name them for tactical reasons. "I'm not going to tell anyone who these men are,"[513] the sheriff stated. "There's no sense in letting the opposition know what we're up to, is there?"[514]

During Michell's last two years in office, the Broward Sheriff's Office found itself in the middle of three sensational murder cases. The first involved an escaped Massachusetts mental patient named Stanley Everett Rice. Apprehended after being stopped for speeding, Rice admitted killing Nelson Williams, an 11-year-old boy who had been fishing at a Fort Lauderdale rock pit. After further questioning, Rice also confessed to a string of murders in Ohio and Canada.

Soon, however, newspapers were writing stories about a second child murderer, who they nicknamed the "Catch Me Killer" due to the fact that after a 12-year-old girl's body was discovered, a deputy had received a call from the man. Saying he had just murdered three people, he begged to be caught.

Freddie L. Pitts (center) and Wilbert Lee being led from
court after their second murder trial (1972)

Suspicion eventually settled on former Hollywood police officer Robert J. Erler, who by now was living at his sister's house in Phoenix. When a warrant for his arrest was issued, Erler threatened to commit suicide but was talked out of the idea by his brother. After briefly resisting extradition, Erler was returned to Florida by two of Michell's men. (Concerned that the stocky suspect might pose a security risk aboard a commercial flight, the deputies began the journey back to Broward by car but eventually gave up and purchased airplane tickets.)

While the Rice and Erler cases attracted considerable attention, they ended up being overshadowed by the saga of Freddie L. Pitts and Wilbert Lee, two African-Americans who in 1963 were accused of killing a pair of white gas station attendants in Port St. Joe, Florida. In 1966, however, a Broward County inmate named Curtis "Bo" Adams, Jr. claimed responsibility for the slayings while undergoing a polygraph test. Already doing time for the murder of a Broward gas station attendant, Adams's story seemed credible and Pitts and Lee, who had been sentenced to death,[515] moved to have their convictions set aside.[516]

Almost immediately, Adams recanted his confession, insisting that it was coerced and that other inmates, acting on orders from the jail's supervisor,

Curtis "Bo" Adams, Jr. (in shirt sleeves) testifying before the
Select Committee on the Pitts-Lee Claims Bills of the Florida
House of Representatives (1979)

had beaten him using a pipe wrapped in a sheet. His claim was vigorously denied by the polygraph examiner, Sheriff Michell, and former Sheriff Walker
(who claimed that Adams had gotten his dates mixed up). In the meantime,
Pitts and Lee were given a new trial,[517] again found guilty,[518] but finally released after being pardoned by Governor Reubin O'D. Askew. In 1998, after years
of hearings, the Florida Legislature voted to pay the pair $500,000 each for
their suffering.

Meanwhile, stories like Adams's spurred a state inquiry into the operations of the Broward County Jail. After three months, Interim State Attorney Russell B. Clarke and Shelby Highsmith, a Miami attorney who had been
hired by Governor Claude R. Kirk, Jr., concluded that although Michell
"might be considered administratively responsible for the poor conditions ...
no evidence was found to hold him criminally responsible."[519] Nevertheless,
the two investigators admonished Michell for his lax oversight and urged
him to fire the jail's top two administrators (Lieutenant Ted Arendas and
Deputy Don Ihle).

Claude R. Kirk, Jr., governor of Florida (1967–71)

After carrying out the report's recommendations (and also suspending Chief James Knight, his top civil deputy, for drinking while on duty), Michell announced that the problems had been solved. As proof, he invited state investigators to conduct a surprise visit so that they could see the improvements for themselves.

Even as he worked to defuse one crisis, Michell found himself engulfed by others. In May 1967, several high-ranking deputies claimed that officer morale had hit bottom because of low wages and the lack of job security. In particular, they blamed the department's personnel director, who happened to be Michell's former executive secretary, and now new wife, Helen. According to one officer, "She should never come into contact with people."[520] Another explained, "[i]t's the way she deals with people — an attitude of if-you-don't-like-it-then-quit."[521]

Stung by these criticisms, Michell answered in kind. "These complaints are coming from a bunch of dissidents who spend more time complaining than they do working."[522] Michell also said that he knew who the troublemakers were (despite the fact that reporters had quoted them without attribution) and promised there would be consequences. "I don't have to account for everything I do to [my deputies]. If they don't like it here, they can quit.... I don't have to give anybody pay raises if I don't want to; in fact, I may reduce some salaries."[523]

Outraged by these new threats, many officers demanded to be placed under a civil service system. In an attempt to quell the growing firestorm, Michell agreed to draw one up. But the plan he submitted to the state legislature only led to more protests. It called for a five member board, which would be appointed by the sheriff and supervised by the personnel director, who was to be given life tenure. Moreover, the sheriff would retain the power to hire, promote, demote, and fire deputies without input from the board. Although it quickly became obvious that the plan had no chance of being approved, Michell refused to make any concessions.

In the meantime, Michell submitted his proposed 1967–68 budget, which called for a 5% raise for all employees and requested funding for twenty-four new positions. Although the usual haggling with the county commission ensued, when the dust settled the department's budget had topped $2 million for the first time in history.

In February 1968, the South Broward Mayors Conference, at the urging of Hollywood Mayor Maynard A. Abrams, asked Michell to begin paying a fee each time the Sheriff's Office received help from a municipality's police department. Claiming that his officers were being asked for such assistance twenty-five times a month, Davie Mayor Fred Resnick said his town had begun scrutinizing such requests carefully so as not to strain its finances.

The mayors' demand drew a heated response from the county commission. "I thought it was a mutual assistance program," growled Commissioner J.W. "Bill" Stevens, while Commission Chairman Earle Kraft demanded to know: "Are the South Broward mayors just singling the sheriff's department out or are they going to ask the state to pay for the help they give the Florida Highway Patrol and the federal government for the help they give the FBI?"[524] But Michell was unperturbed, saying simply, "I have no funds to pay them."[525]

In March 1968, Michell was embarrassed when the Fort Lauderdale Police Department's vice squad arrested Morris Lessne, a local bookie who had been operating out of a smoke shop directly across the street from BSO headquarters. In reporting on the story, a local newspaper wrote, tongue-in-cheek, that Lessne had been "under the protective eye of the Broward Sheriff's Office."[526] A short time later, Floyd Hall, Michell's administrative aide, resigned from the force. Just six months earlier, Michell had promoted him to chief and placed him in charge of the criminal warrants and technical sections, the detective bureau, and the patrol and traffic divisions.

Michell finally got some good news to crow about when his deputies broke up a husband-and-wife counterfeiting operation in Hollywood that had been producing high-quality birth certificates, checks, and draft cards. Although the pair had not been caught, Michell noted that without their very expensive equipment (which he calculated was worth $6,000) they no longer posed a threat.

Less than a month later, deputies again made news when they nabbed Angelo and Anthony Bartemio, two Chicago gangsters, at Gulfstream Racetrack. The brothers, described by the FBI as being among the country's top jewel thieves, had lengthy police records, and officials congratulated Michell on his department's excellent work. In truth, however, the men had been caught by chance, for Michell's deputies had gone to the track to arrest a Dania bookmaker named Albert G. Bourke.

It was during this time that the department's 270 employees received a 7.5% pay raise, the eighth such increase during Michell's tenure. According to Michell, "[t]his raise brings us in line with other counties."[527]

By now, Michell was a candidate for the 1968 Republican nomination for sheriff, and for a time it appeared that he would win easily despite his recent troubles. But when Pompano Beach Mayor Edward J. "Ed" Stack entered the fray, observers realized that the race suddenly had turned into a two-man showdown. As a result, the contest's four other candidates were largely ignored by both the press and the public.

Stack began his campaign by criticizing Michell, saying that "[t]he conduct of the office of sheriff in the past several years does not reflect credit on the incumbent,"[528] and subsequently repeated this charge wherever he went. A week before the primary, a group of local Republicans, convinced that Stack's candidacy was tearing the party apart, sent a telegram to Richard M. Nixon (who was seeking the Republican presidential nomination) demanding that he dump Stack as his Broward campaign manager.

Stack's alleged use of Nixon volunteers to stuff his own mailers was another bone of contention, as was the claim that Stack was using Nixon campaign contributions to fund his race. Some also said that Stack, like Nixon, was courting the extreme right, and as a result was drawing support from members of the John Birch Society and the Ku Klux Klan. Stack denied these charges and said that "[t]he people of this county know me better than that."[529]

Despite the contretemps, on primary day Stack rolled to an impressive victory, collecting more votes than the combined total of his five challengers and outpolling Allen Michell two-to-one. Michell took the loss badly and made it clear that until his successor was sworn in, the department would continue to function as before, adding "I'm still sheriff here."[530]

Richard M. Nixon delegates at the 1968 Republican
National Convention in Miami Beach

Democratic voters picked from an equally crowded field of contenders. Despite his earlier promise to Governor Burns, Tom Walker briefly flirted with the idea of running for sheriff but dropped out when he failed to attract sufficient support. Five other candidates did enter the race, including Richard Basinger, who had lost to Michell in the 1964 general election, and Larry Lang, Walker's former chief deputy, who now was making a living as a private investigator. The voters ultimately settled on Basinger, giving him almost as large a victory as the Republicans had given Stack.

One month after the primaries, Michell again found himself on the hot seat when his deputies failed to serve most of the subpoenas issued by the Florida Legislature's Select Committee to Investigate Organized Crime and Law Enforcement. This "Little Kefauver" panel wanted to speak to witnesses from five South Florida counties, but Michell's men were able to locate only two of the ten Broward residents whose names were on its list. In response, State Senator Robert L. "Bob" Shevin (D-Miami), the committee's chair, railed against the "total ineptness of the deputy sheriffs"[531] and called for legislation authorizing service to be made by the Florida Bureau of Law Enforcement. Michell countered that his department had done its best and pointed out that "we can't just break [into] the houses."[532]

Robert L. "Bob" Shevin, Florida state senator (1966–70)

In June 1968, a group of about two dozen West Hollywood businessmen stormed into Michell's office and demanded better police protection. Claiming that nearly every store in their area had been burglarized, they accused Michell of doing nothing to solve the problem. After listening to the group's complaints, the sheriff explained that his hands were tied—he had neither the men nor the equipment to do more than he already was doing.

A few days later, a much larger group—consisting of 150 West Hollywood merchants and residents—sent an appeal for assistance to Governor Claude Kirk. At the same time, they asked Michell to deputize six local businessmen to patrol the area, a request the sheriff rejected. Noting that the men had declined his offer to join the department as reserves and undergo training, Michell said, "We're not going to just put men out there with guns."[533]

Convinced that waiting for Michell's replacement was not an option ("we can lose everything in six months,"[534] George Balmer, the group's leader, told reporters), the protestors began nightly vigilante patrols. This step seemed to break the logjam, for the number of deputies in the area soon increased sharply. Michell insisted, however, that he had not given in, and that it only appeared that the area was getting more protection because he had switched from unmarked to marked vehicles. Senator Shevin, who had supported the group and ridden on its patrols, said that "[t]he important thing is that the cars are there now."[535]

In July 1968, Michell received some favorable press when it was reported that the county's bolita rackets were taking in less money than just a few years earlier. In other news, the expansion of the Broward County Jail was nearing completion, holding out the promise that the facility's perennial overcrowding was about to become a thing of the past.

In October 1968, the Broward County School Board (at the time still officially called the Board of Public Instruction) asked Michell to deputize four of its officers. Having recently expanded its security force (due to increasing thefts and vandalism, particularly at night), Interim Superintendent William T. McFatter said the board now was looking to put "more authority and the power of a law enforcement agency behind them. We'd like them to have the power of arrest and to be tied in with the sheriff's radio network."[536] Michell, however, declined, saying that he did not want to give such muscle to men for whom he would be responsible, but over whom he would have no supervisory control.

As the November general election approached, both Basinger and Stack campaigned hard to succeed Michell (despite the fact that the job's annual salary remained a relatively stingy $15,500). Although they agreed on some issues (such as the need to expand the road patrol and start a department crime lab), the two men clashed repeatedly over whether the office's current budget ($2.3 million) was sufficient. Basinger thought it was, and promised to triple the number of officers in cars and build a first-rate lab without any additional funds. Stack, on the other hand, said that more money definitely was needed and came out in favor of new taxes, "unless the county commission wishes to cut their budget elsewhere."[537]

On Election Day, Stack easily beat Basinger, 91,147 votes to 61,118 votes (a margin of 60%–40%). Of course, Stack had outspent Basinger by a staggering amount ($30,000 to $4,000), the largest sum ever paid to win a Broward County office. As for Allen Michell, after leaving the Sheriff's Office he ran unsuccessfully for mayor of Plantation and later retired to Zephyrhills, Florida. Following his death at the age of seventy-nine in a Dade City nursing home on March 5, 1983, his body was taken to Arlington National Cemetery and buried with full military honors.[538]

Tombstone of Sheriff Allen Michell (at the Arlington
National Cemetery in Virginia)

CHAPTER 7

THE STACK-BUTTERWORTH-BRESCHER YEARS (1969–85)

Although no one could have known it at the time, the election of Edward J. Stack marked the beginning of a golden era for the Broward Sheriff's Office. For the next sixteen years, three lawyers would be in charge, and while there would be problems, there would be no grand jury probes, indictments, or major scandals. In the meantime, the department would grow from a small, rural, and often brutal police force into a large, urban, and increasingly sophisticated administrative agency.

Sheriff Edward J. Stack (1969–78)

Edward John Stack was born in Bayonne, New Jersey, on April 29, 1910, and grew up in Brooklyn, New York, the son of an Irish immigrant father. At James Madison High School, Stack ran track, was captain of the tennis team, participated in student government, and was nominated for "Handsomest Boy in the Senior Class," an election he lost to David "Sonny" Werblin, the future owner of the New York Jets football team.

Following high school, Stack received a B.A. from Lehigh University in 1931 and a law degree from the University of Pennsylvania in 1934. He then moved to New York City and began practicing law, using his spare time to teach economics at Hunter College and earn an M.A. in public law and government from Columbia University in 1938.

In 1942, Stack enlisted in the U.S. Coast Guard and saw duty aboard the PUEBLO, a weather-monitoring frigate stationed in San Francisco Bay. By the time he mustered out in 1946, he had been promoted to lieutenant.

After returning to New York City, Stack resumed his law practice, started a construction company, invested in real estate, and became a banker. In 1954, he moved to Pompano Beach, where he became the owner of the famed Sil-

Edward J. "Ed" Stack, sheriff of Broward County (1969–78)

ver Thatch Inn tennis resort (which he opened to the public for daily and Sunday masses) and served on the city's charter revision board.

In 1965, following a disagreement with Pompano Beach City Commissioner Harold Hart over sewer assessment fees, Stack decided to run for office and ended up unseating Hart by a three-to-one margin. Named mayor in 1967, Stack was re-elected to the city commission in 1968, just months before becoming sheriff.

During Stack's tenure as Broward's top lawman, he both modernized the Sheriff's Office and turned it into a potent electoral machine. For the latter, he offered no apologies, explaining, "Politics is the art of government. It is the lubricant for social progress."[539]

Even before taking office, Stack was determined to improve the department, and within a week of being elected he asked for an additional $2.3 million to beef up the road patrol. When the county commission balked at this request, Stack threatened to quit to "focus attention on the problem."[540] In response, Jack Wheeler, the county auditor, suggested that the sheriff-elect spend the money he had been allocated before deciding that more was needed.

The Silver Thatch Inn tennis resort in Pompano Beach (1965)

Undeterred, Stack set about looking for other sources of revenue and soon discovered that outgoing Sheriff Allen Michell had recently returned nearly $178,000 to the county's general fund. Calling this decision "incredible,"[541] Stack noted that the amount was enough to pay for six squad cars. As for Michell's claim that the road patrol was undermanned because he could not find enough good men, Stack insisted, "I know where the men are. There are men in departments that would love to come here."[542]

As his swearing-in date (Tuesday, January 7, 1969) approached, Stack busied himself making personnel changes. Among those he would let go was Chief Deputy Larry Lang. Although Lang had been a candidate for sheriff in the Democratic primary, he recently had been working with one of Stack's aides and had been led to believe that he would be allowed to keep his job. When asked about the matter, Stack said, "I had not stated publicly that Mr. Lang would be chief deputy so I [did not] think it appropriate to say publicly he would not be."[543]

Another early casualty was Chief James Knight, the head of the civil division and the Broward County Jail. With rumors swirling that Stack was getting ready to fire him, Knight announced in December that he would be resigning. A short time later, however, he changed his mind and said how long he remained would be "entirely up to the new sheriff."[544]

On the day after he took office, Stack brought in Robert Danner and Bernard Lenahan as his two top administrators. Both men were retired New York City Police Department detectives, and their appointment led more than one wag to refer to the new management team as the "NYPD Squad."

Stack soon announced a number of other changes, including: 1) the job of chief of operations was abolished (the incumbent was reassigned to a position focusing on the county's growing drug problem); 2) department heads now would report directly to the sheriff; 3) an additional rank—major—was created (the commanders of the detective bureau and the road patrol were both promoted to it); 4) seven more road patrol deputies were hired (by the end of the month, a total of twenty-two officers would join the agency); and, 5) the department's complaint desk was reorganized and for the first time staffed by gun-toting deputies. When asked why, Stack replied, "I don't think it is very good practice to have an unarmed man at the entrance to the sheriff's office."[545]

The most far-reaching move, however, was the institution of a mandatory training program for all deputies. Led by a full-time administrator, this educational initiative would include both in-house instruction and, for selected officers, off-site college courses. In addition, all new recruits would be required to start their careers by spending thirteen weeks working at the county jail, and up to a dozen deputies would be sent to the police academy every three months to build up the road patrol.

During his second month in office, Stack created a war room to track crimes. Using maps and colored push pins, the sheriff explained that "[t]his will show the incidence of crime. If we can find a pattern ... then we can send in a large force of men"[546] to the right place at the right time. The press likened the idea to a "wolf pack."[547]

In yet another step designed to make the department more efficient, Stack decided to consolidate the detective division. First to go was the vice squad, with its commander being demoted from captain to lieutenant and reassigned to the road patrol (his salary, however, stayed the same). The intelligence and special units soon met the same fate.

Stack also sought to make good on his campaign promise to build a modern crime lab. For years, the county's police chiefs had been calling for such a facility, and in October 1968 a Broward grand jury had agreed, pointing out that help had to be sought "from the Dade County Crime Laboratory for even the simplest lab work."[548] (Upon its release, Sheriff Michell criticized the report, claiming it was short on specifics and had overlooked the fact that Broward already had a lab, albeit a make-shift one, located on the seventh floor of the courthouse.)

As it happened, Stack did not have a moment to lose, for shortly after he took office the Dade crime lab announced that due to a lack of personnel, it had decided to stop accepting outside assignments. As a result, more than sixty pending prosecutions suddenly faced dismissal and Broward County Solicitor James W. Geiger threatened to turn away future drug cases (even as the sheriff told reporters that the department had just nabbed the greatest number of sellers ever). Calling the situation "sticky,"[549] Stack turned to the county commission, which voted to give him $60,000 in emergency funds.

On the following day, Stack announced that the department was going to start going after drug *users*, including those who imbibed in soft drugs (such as marijuana). This signaled an unprecedented change in direction, for in the past deputies always had focused on the *sellers* of hard drugs (such as heroin). Stack's plan drew substantial criticism from the public and even some police officers, who claimed that it would "only succeed in filling the jail with children."[550]

After a week of negative publicity, Stack did an about-face and decided that marijuana use among juveniles was not out of control. He also urged lawmakers to downgrade possession of the drug by teenagers from a felony to a misdemeanor to make convictions easier to obtain. And in a final switch, Stack indicated that he had worked out a way to continue using the Dade crime lab because "[i]t is a going concern and it would take a large outlay to duplicate."[551]

By now, the millionaire sheriff also was seeking a raise from the state legislature, asking it to increase his salary from $15,500 to $24,000 (the same as a circuit court judge). After explaining that he did not need more money and would not accept any, Stack told listeners that a boost was required because the maximum a sheriff could pay his assistants was $500 less than what he was making.[552] And at $15,000-a-year, Stack said, he was having trouble recruiting highly qualified candidates.

About six months into Stack's term, deputies arrested Linda Pierce, a former go-go dancer, for procuring prostitution (*i.e.*, working as a madam). As she was being booked, Pierce told deputies that the mob was out to get her and already had killed another prostitute and left her body in a refrigerator truck somewhere in the county. Before detectives could question her further, Pierce disappeared.

When the story leaked out, reporters demanded to know whether deputies had been sent to look for the truck. "Oh heavens no," the bemused sheriff replied, adding that the story obviously was a "smokescreen"[553] meant to intimidate Pierce's staff and keep them from testifying against her.

As he began work on his 1969–70 budget, one of Stack's main priorities was to increase the base pay of deputies, which currently stood at $6,100 but which he felt should be $7,000. The county commission finally agreed to this request, and one year later Stack was back, now looking to raise their salaries to $8,000 while adding twenty-four more officers. Asked how he could justify such large, back-to-back hikes, Stack explained that by reorganizing the department and adjusting its spending priorities, he had been able to increase the number of uniformed officers from sixty to eighty, purchase a patrol car for every deputy (thereby improving morale and leading to more off-duty arrests), and cut the felony crime rate in the county's unincorporated areas by 21% (compared to an 11% jump in the national crime rate). "I don't know of another police department that can point to the record we have here,"[554] the sheriff proudly exclaimed. Impressed by these figures, the commissioners approved their top lawman's funding requests.

In May 1971, Stack announced a crackdown on adult bookstores, a move meant to complement the State Attorney's Office's campaign against adult theaters, and soon deputies were arresting both the stores' owners and clerks. The sheriff also reported that his effort to push the Outlaws motorcycle gang out of Broward had succeeded, with most of the group having left for New Orleans. Although three of its members had stayed behind, Stack claimed that these men "have never been of the violent type."[555] (Three other Outlaws were in the county jail, waiting to be tried for murder, and jurors eventually found two of them guilty.)

In a further bit of news, Stack revealed that heroin was now his number two priority (just behind juvenile delinquency) and deputies were moving against all those involved in its sale and distribution. Stack then boldly predicted that "[w]ithin 90 days we will break up the current system. I don't say we are going to eliminate heroin but we are going to prove to the pushers [that Broward] is not a healthy area for them to operate in."[556]

For 1971–72, Stack proposed a $4.7 million budget, a 20% increase over the previous year. Once again, he asked for twenty-four new slots (four of which would go to the detective division while the rest would be used to bring the road patrol up to 100 officers), as well as an 11.25% pay increase for current deputies and more money for future hires. When Stack explained that as things currently stood BSO rookies were making $100 less than their counterparts in the Pompano Beach Police Department, County Commissioner Bill Stevens warned the nattily-dressed lawman, "They're going to make their police chief wear a uniform, and we wouldn't want that to happen to you, Sheriff."[557]

In April 1972, Stack reported that after seven months of work, deputies had arrested Fred Chapman, a key figure in the bolita rackets, and broken up a $1.5 million lottery operation.[558] One month later, he announced a major crackdown on drunk driving while chastising the courts for their gentle treatment of offenders, complaining that "cases involving drunk driving are equated in Broward County with spitting on the sidewalk."[559]

As matters turned out, 1972 was a very good year for Stack. First, a report issued by the Florida Department of Law Enforcement found that of all the major police departments in Broward County, the Sheriff's Office had the highest clearance rate for major crimes. (Stack told reporters that he was particularly pleased with these results because his department had only 1.2 officers per 100 residents, while Pompano Beach had 2.4 and Fort Lauderdale had 2.5.) Second, Stack's proposed 1972–73 budget, totaling almost $5.4 million, sailed through the county commission.

Still, not everything went right. Although he had preached frequently about the evils of marijuana use and had lamented the small number of convictions, in May 1972 Stack was forced to admit that his maid had found marijuana in his son's room. When asked if he planned to arrest the boy, Stack said "no" because the youngster had insisted that the stash belonged to a friend. As such, the lawman explained, there was no legal proof as to who owned the drugs. Moreover, the amount involved was "a very small quantity."[560]

In the September 1972 primary elections, Stack easily defeated his three Republican challengers (Hollywood police lieutenant Robert Milligan and former BSO deputies Donald O. Schultz and Ted Zeuch), collecting more than three times their combined vote total. On the Democratic side, Larry Lang, who had reopened his private detective agency after being fired by Stack, prevailed over Coconut Creek police sergeant F.R. "Bill" Kyle by a slightly less impressive count.

In the campaign between Lang and Stack, drug use at concerts at the Hollywood Sportatorium became a key issue. Opened in September 1970, the Sportatorium was a large (15,500 seats), crudely-constructed arena that lacked air conditioning and had terrible acoustics (frustrated by the building's echoes, Billy Joel later welcomed an audience to its replacement, the Miami Arena, by saying, "[This] sure beats the [expletive] out of the Hollywood Sporatorium!"[561]). Nevertheless, this structure had quickly made a name for itself by playing host to such bands as Led Zeppelin (September 1971), the Allman Brothers (January 1972), and Pink Floyd (April 1972).

Although BSO undercover agents had reported that drug use was rampant at the Hollywood site, Stack had declined to make any arrests. When Lang accused Stack of doing nothing, the sheriff explained that he was suing to close the "Sporthole" (as locals called the cement-and-sheet-metal facility) but worried that if officers were sent in during a concert their presence would cause a riot and result in innocent people getting hurt.

Nevertheless, on the following weekend Stack attended a concert (featuring country duo Delbert and Glen, English bluesman John Mayall, and the rock band Poco) to see for himself what was going on. Although there was very little drug use in evidence, Stack credited his deputies with heading off po-

Concert at the Hollywood Sportatorium in Pembroke Pines (c. 1975)

tential problems by confiscating three 55-gallon drums filled with liquor. According to the sheriff, "If that alcohol had gotten in, it could have been an entirely different scene."[562]

Stack's decision to supply each deputy with a patrol car also found its way into the race. To acquire the sixty vehicles he needed, Stack had taken out a personal bank loan. When government auditors decided that this constituted a technical breach of the state's bookkeeping procedures, Lang sought to make an issue out of it. Oddly enough, Florida Attorney General Bob Shevin, a Democrat, came to Stack's defense and commended him "for the selfless position he has voluntarily agreed to take so that his office may fulfill its responsibilities even at the cost of whatever personal fortune might be his."[563]

Yet another controversy involved the campaign itself. After a number of "Larry Lang for Sheriff" posters were found plastered over Fort Lauderdale traffic signs, Lang's manager accused Stack's supporters of trying to embarrass Lang by labeling him a lawbreaker. Stack responded by saying, "I'm not going to get into a gutter fight with this character. He has put up signs illegally in Fort Lauderdale before. But it is typical. I choose to ignore Lang at this point."[564]

Just before the election, Stack grabbed headlines with two major gambling raids. In the first, twenty-six people were arrested at a Dania casino, while in the second twelve individuals were taken into custody for running a bolita operation. As matters turned out, Stack did not need the publicity, for on Election Day he beat Lang easily, 157,219 votes to 85,052 votes (a 65%–35% margin).

Stack's second term began on Tuesday, January 2, 1973, and a short time later the county commission awarded the Sheriff's Office a contract to provide additional security at the Fort Lauderdale-Hollywood International Airport. The extra manpower was needed because, in an effort to combat hijackings, the federal government had decided that a certified police officer would have to be present every time a flight took off. Stack agreed to provide this service for $213,000 a year, explaining that he planned to hire eighteen additional deputies. Lee E. Wagener, the county's aviation director, had bid against Stack, offering to expand the airport's own police force by twenty-eight officers at a cost of $230,000 a year.

In the spring of 1973, the Florida Legislature overhauled the system used to determine the salaries of county officers. As a result, from now on they

> would receive as salary [a] base salary ... based on the county's population with compensation made for population increments over the minimum for each population group, which would be determined by multiplying the population in excess of the group minimum times the group rate. In addition ... [there would be] an additional adjustment ... based on the U.S. Department of Labor's Consumer Price Index, which would be multiplied by the applicable adjusted salary rate.[565]

During the next three decades, as Broward's population grew from 620,100 in 1970 to 1,623,018 in 2000, this new formula would make the county's sheriff very well paid indeed.

In the spring of 1974, Stack submitted his budget for the upcoming year and asked for a 56% boost ($6.25 million to $9.76 million), the largest annual increase in the department's history. In defending this proposal, Stack pointed to the rising cost of fuel (the recent Arab oil embargo had caused the price of gasoline to jump from twenty-three cents to forty-five cents a gallon), the need to hire forty-five new employees to work in the communications center (the department was about to start handling emergency calls for thirteen cities), and the fact that wages had to go up if they were to keep pace with inflation (Stack proposed a 15% pay hike for road deputies and a boost in the starting salaries of new deputies to $10,888). In addition, Stack wanted to buy a second helicopter for the department (upon purchasing the first a year earlier, he had told reporters that the acquisition had added a proven crime-fighting weapon to the department's arsenal).

Not surprisingly, the county commission refused to go along with Stack, insisting that he trim his request by $1.2 million. When it became clear that the two sides were stalemated, Stack headed to Tallahassee to plead his case to Governor Reubin Askew and the Cabinet.[566] Although County Commission Chairman Jack L. Moss also appeared at the hearing, the Cabinet quickly sided with Stack and restored $1 million in cuts. Years later, Moss admitted to being outfoxed by Stack and observed, "It's much better to control your own destiny than have two or three people in Tallahassee do so."[567]

In the spring of 1976, Stack began his third run for sheriff. A short time earlier, he had switched parties and become a Democrat, citing both a falling out with local Republican leaders and his close friendship with several top Democrats. Asked if he expected the change to affect his electoral chances, Stack replied, "I don't think it will make any difference if I run as a Republican or a Democrat."[568]

Stack's decision to drop out of the Republican primary opened the door for Robert Danner (Stack's one-time administrator). Danner had changed his affiliation to avoid having to face Stack in the primaries, but with Stack gone Danner now returned to being a Republican and easily won that party's nomination. In the 1976 general election, however, Stack had little trouble fending Danner off, beating him 199,685 votes to 122,600 votes (a margin of 62%–38%).

As in 1972, Stack again made headlines just before the election by cracking down on gambling. After deputies caught Robert "Pop" Jackson, a bolita operator, he offered to give the sheriff a piece of his action in exchange for his freedom. Hoping that Jackson would lead them to his bosses, the officers played along, and for months he regularly dropped off $1,500 at the department's booking desk. When it became clear that no further information was being developed, a surprised Jackson was arrested. Although the plan had failed (and allowed a criminal to keep working), the press saw it as a coup and congratulated Stack with headlines such as "Sheriff Traps Suspect in Gambling Set-Up."

Stack's third term as sheriff commenced on Tuesday, January 4, 1977, with the lawman determined to do something about the county's seedy sexual image. In May, seventeen people were arrested during raids on three nude dance studios located just west of Fort Lauderdale, for which the sheriff received favorable media coverage. Several weeks later, however, Circuit Judge Arthur J. Franza dismissed his case against a group of local convenience stores. Deputy Thomas McMillan had been sent to the shops with instructions to purchase adult magazines. He returned with two, but later testified that he could have bought more but had been given only $18 by his superiors. Upon hearing this, Franza

Kids "inspecting" a BSO helicopter (1974)

BSO helicopter in the air (1973)

Florida Governor Reubin O'D. Askew (center) and the Cabinet (1975)

*In the 1976 presidential election, Sheriff Ed Stack (seen here in a
Hollywood Sun-Tattler cartoon) was aggressively courted by Republicans
but urged voters to support Democrat Jimmy Carter*

flew into a rage and told Dohn Williams, the assistant state attorney, "[i]f you're going to conduct a pornographic war you should spend more than $18. Be serious about it and don't waste our time."[569]

Undeterred, Stack now started a new operation against the county's adult bookstores. For the next four months, deputies, often assisted by Fort Lauderdale police officers, harassed employees and patrons by asking for identification, taking down license plate numbers, suggesting that customers not enter (or quickly leave) the premises, and parking their patrol cars in front of the stores (often with their flashers left on). When the owners sued, U.S. District Judge Sidney M. Aronovitz took Stack to task for "becom[ing] a law unto himself" and ordered him to stop his "zone saturation."[570]

In the meantime, an effort had begun to unionize the department's employees. Stack said he was on the fence when it came to the agency's civilian employees and would neither support nor oppose the effort. Deputies, however, were a different story, and Stack made it clear that he "would resist and avail myself of whatever rights we have to stop such a movement."[571] Stack then added, "Remember, I'm not entirely anti-union. I was endorsed by the Broward County Federation of Labor in the last election."[572]

As the year wore on, the extent to which the mob was operating locally became a hotly-debated issue. Believing that organized crime was endemic, the City of Margate asked the county commission to request an investigation by the U.S. Senate's Judiciary Committee. Stack immediately voiced his objection to such a probe, which he thought was unnecessary, and the petition was rejected. Notwithstanding this vote, Commissioner Anne Kolb announced that she planned to contact the committee to see if it would be willing to come to Broward because, "It used to be a community would get aroused when a body turned up in a canal, but now people take a ho-hum attitude."[573] Upon hearing this, Stack reversed himself and said that he would welcome an inquiry lest "anyone … think that Ed Stack favors organized crime in Broward County."[574]

Stack also faced more mundane problems during this period. First, performance statistics showed that Broward deputies were taking longer to respond to calls than their Dade counterparts. Terming the issue serious, Stack promised things would get better and asked the county commission for permission to hire fifty additional road patrol deputies at a cost of $1 million. The sheriff explained that he was not asking for an increase in his budget, but instead would find the money by reducing spending in other areas.

Second, the department's much heralded Cooperative Dispatch Center was riddled with glitches. Not only was the countywide patrol channel dropping calls, but the computer used by deputies to check auto tags, criminal records, and

Broward deputies observing a moment of silence (1976)

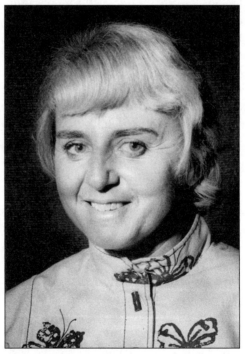

Anne Kolb, commissioner of Broward County (1975–81)

Dispatcher Susan Warshaw answering a call at the
Broward Sheriff's Cooperative Dispatch Center (1975)

drivers' licenses from their cars was prone to frequent crashes due to over-loading. Asked about the situation, one dispatcher said:

> We had one case where a deputy nearly got killed because the radios work so bad. He answered a domestic disturbance call, and when he opened the door he found the husband pointing a rifle at him. The deputy was yelling 10-24 (trouble, send help) into his radio, but we never received the call.
>
> Fortunately, he was able to talk the guy into giving up the gun.[575]

Others in the department voiced similar complaints, pointing out that nine crashes had occurred in a single 15-minute period, a budget survey was being conducted by hand "because the supervisors won't trust the computer any more," and most officers believed that nothing would be done "until a deputy gets killed because of the communications system."[576] Stack, however, insisted that "[o]ur system is working beautifully. I think we have one of the best communications systems in the state."[577] As for the kinks, Michael Levine, a supervisor, explained that the agency had plans to hire an additional technician within the next six months.

In June 1978, the sheriff announced that deputies had charged four members of the Outlaws motorcycle club with the long-unsolved murders of three rival Hell's Angels. The 1974 slayings had been ordered by club president James T. "Big Jim" Nolan and had been particularly gruesome, with the bodies turning up in a west Broward rock pit.

Unfortunately for the department, the news about these arrests was overshadowed by a rather Kafkaesque incident. Jury selection had begun for seven men accused of raping a fellow prisoner (Richard Harris) in the Broward County Jail, but it was becoming clear that counsel would soon exhaust the pool of potential jurors. As a result, fifteen deputies were dispatched by Circuit Judge Stanton S. Kaplan with directions to bring back 100 citizens. With additional instructions from their supervisor not to stray too far from the courthouse, the officers ordered every pedestrian they encountered to report for duty that afternoon.

When it learned what was taking place, the press lambasted both Kaplan and the deputies, quoting a bystander who compared the event to the impressment gangs of the British navy and noting that eight potential jurors had to be excused when they said their anger over the incident had made it impossible for them to be fair. After Kaplan apologized, Stack issued a statement disclaiming any knowledge of the orders and referring to them as "an anachronism."[578] And while he said his officers had done nothing wrong, he took pains to point out that "I don't want to suggest that it was appropriate either."[579]

By now, Stack was busy running for a seat in Congress. In May 1978, Representative J. Herbert Burke (R-Fort Lauderdale) had made himself vulnerable by getting arrested in the parking lot of a Dania strip club (after some negotiation, he agreed to plead guilty to disorderly conduct, public drunkenness, and witness tampering, for which he received three months on probation and a $150 fine). Stack had sought Burke's seat twice before—in 1966 and 1970—losing by 220 votes the first time and getting thrashed the second time.[580] Now, however, Stack had greater name recognition and a juicy scandal to talk about, and in November 1978 he beat Burke 104,653 votes to 64,793 votes (a margin of 62%–38%). In the postmortems, observers praised Stack for aggressively courting the county's condominium communities, the first politician to recognize (and harness) their emerging clout.

Stack's victory, however, came at a price. During the primaries he was accused of using deputies as campaign workers (including having them do political tasks while they were on duty at the courthouse), and in the general election he was labeled an alcoholic. Stack denied the former charge despite telling employees, "You have a chance to free your boss. If you can hang on for one more week, you can get rid of the old man and send him to Washington."[581]

Members of the Outlaws motorcycle gang getting ready to ride (1979)

J. Herbert Burke, U.S. Representative from Florida (1967–79)

Sheriff Ed Stack making a point during his campaign for Congress (1978)

As for the second accusation, he deftly turned it back against his Republican opponent. Freely admitting to being a recovering alcoholic, the sheriff said that he had not had a drink in ten years and rhetorically asked if Burke could say the same thing. Stack's age (sixty-eight) also became an issue, although Burke, being sixty-five, was unable to capitalize on it (or the fact that Stack had suffered a stroke in the 1970s and now wore a pacemaker).

As he prepared to move to Washington, Stack was asked to name his most significant accomplishments as sheriff. He responded by citing the creation of the county's 911 system,[582] the establishment of the BSO crime lab, and the formation of a local drug rehabilitation program. Had he chosen to, however, he could have added two more achievements:

> 1) Expanding the department. Under Stack's leadership, the Sheriff's Office had grown to 765 employees and the budget had risen to $16.6 million. The number of deputies had increased from sixty-eight to 229, while the number of patrol cars had jumped from fifteen to seventy-two. In addition to hiring the department's first female patrol officers and putting bailiffs at the courthouse, Stack had imposed tougher hiring standards for deputies (including psychological testing), improved their pay and benefits, and replaced their outdated green-and-gray uniforms and brimmed hats with snappy green-and-white outfits that were topped with Stetsons.[583]

> 2) Instituting the contract cities program. Shortly after winning the airport's expanded security contract in 1975, Stack began offering to take over municipal police functions, saying that cities would benefit by getting better protection at a lower cost. When Lauderdale Lakes became the first "contract city" in 1977, the Broward Police Chiefs Association railed against the consolidation of local police departments under an elected official. Stack responded by saying, "I think they are confusing the contractual relationship ... with a centralized police force."[584]

Dubbed the "High Sheriff" by his congressional colleagues, Stack's stay in Washington proved extremely short, for in October 1980 he was upset in the Democratic primary by Alan S. Becker (who in turned was defeated by Fort Lauderdale Mayor E. Clay Shaw). After returning home, Stack passed the Florida bar exam in 1981 (getting 90% of the questions right), sought the chairmanship of the Broward County Democratic Party (losing to Sunrise Mayor John Lomelo, Jr.), ran for Congress again (this time losing to Shaw), and eventually became the head of the Broward County Commission on Alcoholism.

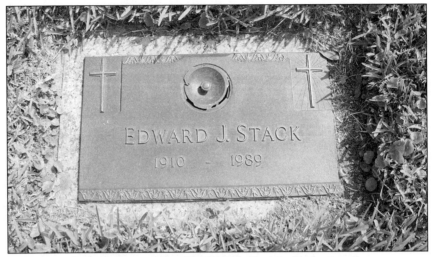

*Tombstone of Sheriff Ed Stack (Our Lady Queen of
Heaven Cemetery, North Lauderdale)*

Following his death on November 3, 1989, at the Imperial Point Medical
Center in Fort Lauderdale at the age of seventy-nine, there was a small service for the fallen lawman.[585] While some observers criticized his tenure as sheriff, saying it had been costly and inconsistent, ignored the needs of the
African-American and Seminole communities, and turned the department
into a political machine that Stack had exploited for his own benefit, others praised
him. When asked for his thoughts, future sheriff Kenneth C. Jenne II replied,
"I think Ed Stack will be remembered as a very progressive political figure. I
think he made as sheriff some of the greatest strides in the areas of mental
health and drug dependency than anyone in the history of this county. He
served Broward County very, very well."[586]

Sheriff Robert A. Butterworth, Jr. (1978–82)

The election of Ed Stack to Congress in November 1978 meant that someone was going to have to finish his term as sheriff, and on Thursday, December 21, 1978, Governor Reubin Askew chose Robert Alfred "Bob"
Butterworth, Jr. Like the man he was replacing, the new sheriff was a lawyer
who lacked a law enforcement background but was a gifted politician. And
like his predecessor, he would end up leaving the department when a greater
opportunity presented itself.

Robert A. "Bob" Butterworth, Jr., sheriff of Broward County (1978–82)

Bob Butterworth was born in Passaic, New Jersey, on August 20, 1942, and was only a child when his family moved to Hollywood, where his father ran a TV repair store. After earning a B.S. in business administration at the University of Florida in 1965, he enrolled in the University of Miami and received a law degree in 1969. For the next four years, he worked as an assistant state attorney, first in Dade County and then in Broward County, where he teamed up with another young prosecutor named Ken Jenne. Together the pair became known as "Batman and Robin" for their spirited crusades against corrupt public officials. In November 1974, Butterworth was elected to the Broward County Court, and in January 1978, eleventh months before being named sheriff, Governor Askew appointed him to the circuit bench.

Having inherited a department with no major problems, and facing an election in less than two years, Butterworth focused on some relatively small and non-controversial changes. At the urging of Captain Elihu Phares, he placed Breath Alcohol Testing vans (dubbed "BATmobiles") on the road to crack down on drunk drivers. He also added a second municipality to the contract cities program (Pembroke Park in 1980) and used his political skills to obtain approval

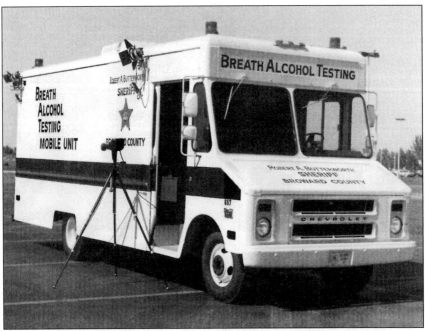

A BATmobile with the words "Robert A. Butterworth Sheriff
Broward County" on its hood and side panels (c. 1980)

for a new jail and win more funding for the department (resulting in 100 additional patrol deputies, increased salaries and qualifications for corrections officers, and an upgraded communications system).

In December 1979, however, Butterworth found himself enmeshed in controversy when he tried to block the Seminoles from opening a high-stakes bingo hall on their reservation near Hollywood. Claiming that such gambling was illegal, Butterworth had padlocked the $900,000 building, but the federal courts quickly reversed this decision and allowed the facility to open.[587] The tribe's victory now is recognized as giving birth to the $26 billion-a-year national Indian gambling industry.

Despite losing his showdown with the Seminoles, Butterworth faced only token opposition in the September 1980 Democratic primary and in November easily beat Republican challenger Earl Oltersdorf 262,168 votes to 118,231 votes (a margin of 69%–31%) to remain sheriff. Yet after being sworn in for a full four-year term on Tuesday, January 6, 1981, Butterworth declined to make use of his mandate. Instead, he continued to pursue small changes, adding Lauderhill to the contract cities program; starting an anonymous hotline that encouraged the public to call in tips in exchange for re-

A Broward deputy with his patrol car (1980)

wards (known as Crime Stoppers, the program proved to be a big hit); re-
designing the department's logo from a star with round points and the words

*Since 2004, the luxurious Seminole Hard Rock Hotel and Casino
has stood next door to the tribe's original bingo hall*

Broward deputies placing a suspect under arrest (c. 1980)

"Broward County Sheriff's Department" to a star with fine points and the words "Broward County Sheriff's Office";[588] and in July 1982 securing the largest budget in the department's history—$49.2 million, nearly double the 1980–81 allotment. In the meantime, Butterworth was able to report a substantial drop in criminal activity in the county's unincorporated sections and the department's three contract cities.

In September 1982, Governor D. Robert "Bob" Graham reached out to Butterworth and named him director of the Florida Department of Highway Safety and Motor Vehicles. For some time, the state's largest law enforcement agency (consisting of 4,400 employees and a $125 million budget) had been plagued by charges of corruption and mismanagement, and Butterworth's reputation as a straight shooter and honest public servant made him the obvious choice to turn things around. The job also came with a significant boost in pay. While sheriff, Butterworth's annual salary had reached $47,000, but as director he would be making $55,000. As for the Broward Sheriff's Office, its 1,200 employees were about to get their third boss in five years.

Sheriff George A. Brescher (1982–85)

On Saturday, October 16, 1982, Governor Bob Graham chose George A. Brescher, the chief judge of the Broward County Court, to complete the final two years of Bob Butterworth's term as sheriff. In discussing his pick, Graham noted that the county's new top lawman "has had hands-on experience at every level of the criminal justice system."[589] Unfortunately, what the incoming sheriff did not have were the political skills required to keep the job.

The choice of Brescher had been a compromise, and earlier it had appeared that the job would go to either State Senator Ken Jenne (D-Fort Lauderdale) or BSO Colonel Edward J. Werder. But when Jenne withdrew from consideration, Graham decided on Brescher. Asked about his successor, Butterworth said, "I recommended Brescher. Many, many people did. George was acceptable to everyone."[590] County Judge Larry S. Seidlin added, "George had no enemies. He was never ambitious enough to hurt people on the way up."[591] Asked for his assessment, Brescher replied, "There were a lot of names being bandied about. Different factions were pushing their different people. I didn't have any enemies at that point. In the end, it may very well have been a compromise."[592]

George Angen Brescher was born on March 24, 1943, in Elizabeth, New Jersey, and grew up in a tight-knit family, the son of a lawyer. After starting at Stetson University in DeLand, Florida, he returned home when his father became ill and finished his undergraduate studies at Monmouth College, re-

A member of the BSO bomb squad (1982)

ceiving a B.S. in business administration in 1966. He then moved back to Florida and earned a law degree at the University of Miami in 1969.

After graduation, Brescher served in the U.S. Army Judge Advocate General's Corps (1969–73) and then worked as a Broward County assistant state attorney (1973–77) and as a part-time prosecutor for the City of Plantation (1975–77). In October 1977, he was appointed to the Broward County Court by Governor Reubin Askew. Although he was re-elected twice without oppo-

George A. Brescher, sheriff of Broward County (1982–85)

sition, in 1982 he was rejected for a seat on the circuit court, an outcome that left him "utterly dejected."[593] Thus, when Graham called a short time later and asked him to become sheriff, Brescher welcomed the opportunity. "I was flattered, for sure. It's very flattering to hear you can do it, to hear no one but you can do it. People convinced me my career would involve new challenges. It was exciting."[594]

Within the department, however, many officers found Brescher's lack of law enforcement experience troubling and were only slightly mollified when, at his swearing in, he said: "On any given day and night, when someone in an emergency dials the 911 number and needs help—there has been a murder, a rape, a robbery—when they call that number, a sworn deputy sheriff is going to go out and meet that call—this is what it is all about."[595] But when two different oaths were then administered—one to the patrol deputies and another to the detention deputies—instead of both groups being sworn in at the same time, as had been done previously, a great deal of resentment was stirred up.

During his first few months in office, Brescher maintained a very low profile, although he did spend $200 to have his name painted over Butterworth's on the department's four BATmobiles. When questioned about this expense, spokeswoman Judi Maffei earnestly explained that the department had been able to save money because both Butterworth and Brescher had the same middle initial as well as last names that began with the letter "B." The press found this comment hilarious and accused Brescher of putting vanity ahead of the public's right to efficient government.

In most other instances, however, Brescher remained out of sight. When asked why, he noted that he was keeping his eyes open and his mouth shut while he learned the job, but his lack of visibility led to unfavorable comparisons with his predecessor, for whom hobnobbing had come easily. A frustrated Brescher exclaimed, "Look, I'm not a very good politician. Bob and I are different people. How visible I am doesn't have anything to do with what the [sheriff's office] is all about."[596] Somewhat peevishly, Brescher then added, "Sometimes I am frustrated by how often I have to do things solely for appearance's sake. You have to be seen. You have to do it. [But] I'm not going to allow this, or any job, to destroy my family life."[597]

Brescher's reluctance to get out and rub elbows soon led to whispers that he was planning to resign and return to the bench. When asked about this idea, he replied, "I won't say I wouldn't want to go back to being a judge. I really enjoyed the bench a great deal. But I'm not about to apply for a Circuit Court judgeship. Certainly not after just a few months at this job."[598]

Brescher claimed to be mystified by all the gossip, telling reporters, "It has me really intrigued. Is it coming from someone else who'd like to be Sheriff? I guess somebody wants to show that I have a lack of commitment or dedication to this job."[599] His top aides went further, claiming that Fort Lauderdale police chief Leo F. Callahan, Jr. was trying to discredit Brescher so that he could take over. When confronted, Callahan brushed off the accusations. "That's hysterical. I asked [Brescher] about the rumors when I heard them, so it certainly wasn't me. The sources of the rumor are Democratic Party people, so that seemed to lend some credence to it."[600]

A few months later, in an interview in the *Miami Herald*, Brescher admitted he was undecided about his future and declined to say whether he planned to run for sheriff in 1984. "I'll make those decisions after the summer and not before."[601] Then, following some more prodding, he confided, "I'll be frank. It's been tough, very tough. It's a very big change from what I'm used to doing. Every day there are totally new and different things being thrown at you. I enjoyed the judiciary very much. The trial and the excitement of the trial, just the human atmosphere of the courthouse.... I was very happy there."[602]

Brescher's ambivalence only led to more speculation, fanned by a report that Circuit Judge Melvin B. "Mel" Grossman was thinking about throwing his hat into the ring. "I'm considering it,"[603] Grossman acknowledged. "I enjoy immensely what I'm doing now, but you'd have to consider a position that's as important to Broward County as that."[604] In commenting on the situation, Joel V. Alesi, the second vice chairman of the Broward County Democratic Executive Committee, told reporters, "My gut feeling is if George is running, he'd better get about the business of running. He's not posturing himself to run now. As an appointed sheriff, he's got to come out early. There seems to be a rumor a week on this business."[605]

In the meantime, issues that had been contained under Butterworth were beginning to break loose. When asked why, Brescher responded, "I [am] the new kid on the block. I think some people [think] this [is] a good time to bring it to a head. I can't be intimidated by threats that they're going to drag me through the press and the media. I can't be intimidated."[606]

Still, there were those who were willing to try, including Brescher's own deputies, who were demanding better benefits, clearer training and promotion standards, increased pay, and job security. And although Florida state law made it illegal for deputy sheriffs to engage in collective bargaining,[607] 350 of the department's officers joined Lodge 32 of the Fraternal Order of Police to make their voices heard.

As the situation escalated, Brescher said, "I'll look at the issues but not at a contract,"[608] citing the state law. This clumsy statement infuriated the lodge members, who proceeded to impeach their recently-elected president, James Clark, for being too chummy with Brescher and for failing to work hard enough to get them a union contract. They then sought out the press, with spokesman Fred Postill warning, "The only recourse we have is public opinion. If public opinion doesn't force the Sheriff to bargain with us, a federal court will."[609]

Remarkably, Brescher reacted to the uproar by firing Clint Nye, the deputy who had spearheaded the effort to get rid of Clark. In addition, six other high-profile lodge members either were transferred or reassigned, with two being forced to get out of their patrol cars and walk a beat at the airport (which one reporter termed the department's "Siberia"[610]). As for Clark, he was promoted to investigator in the criminal division.

Not surprisingly, the lodge members cried foul, the press accused Brescher of union busting, Nye said the sheriff had "a vendetta"[611] against him, and Deputy Robert Deak claimed, "All the progress we made with former Sheriff Robert Butterworth is dead. At least he recognized we had grievances and listened to us. Brescher won't even do that."[612] Added Postill, "The place is polarized. Morale has never been lower."[613]

In a belated attempt to make peace, Brescher announced that starting on Wednesday, June 1, 1983, deputies would receive overtime pay (but at their regular hourly rate, not the time-and-a-half they had demanded). Brescher also claimed that his new organizational chart, which had eliminated the position of undersheriff and called for all department heads to once again report to him directly, would make him more accessible.

By now, the lodge had made good on its threat to take Brescher to federal court, and for nearly a year the parties sparred before U.S. District Judge Jose Gonzalez. In February 1984, however, he dismissed the lawsuit[614] due to a recent decision by the U.S. Court of Appeals for the Eleventh Circuit,[615] which had made it clear that deputies were not public employees and therefore had no right to unionize.

While the case dragged on, Brescher submitted his first budget, which sought $56.9 million for 1983–84. This figure was only slightly higher than Butterworth's last budget, and included no new programs, no new equipment, and no new personnel. And while it did propose to pay deputies overtime at time-and-a-half rates, the money to do so had been taken from a planned anti-mob intelligence unit. Upon hearing this, the county's police chiefs, who had pushed for the unit, were livid, but Brescher dismissed their outrage by saying that the unit was not needed. (In another move that drew the chiefs' ire, Brescher reduced the number of municipal deputies by 50% and limited participation to supervisors, even though the program's effectiveness depended on their subordinates.)

In yet another blunder, Brescher claimed that Charles H. Von Stein, a respected local businessman, was behind a prostitution ring that was operating out of a Fort Lauderdale storefront called the "Man's World Culture Center." In talking to reporters, the sheriff said:

> One of the big problems we think is getting to the right people. Traditionally, we've always just gone for the prostitute, but, behind every one you arrest is another to take their place so they go right back out on the street. Our feeling is [that if] we can get to the money behind them and put a hurt on them, that we can achieve some effective results.[616]

In fact, it had been Von Stein who had contacted the department to complain about the activities taking place at the center, and for more than a year he had been pushing deputies to arrest the proprietors. Claiming that the sheriff had sullied his reputation, Von Stein filed a federal lawsuit against Brescher and was awarded $550,000 in compensatory damages and $230,000 in punitive damages by the trial court, which chastised Brescher for "misuse of official power magnified greatly by publicity."[617] On appeal, however, the case was tossed out for failure to state a claim.[618]

Despite these missteps, Brescher was working hard to improve the department and within a relatively short time could point to a number of successes:

1) An annual 40-hour training program had been instituted for all deputies;
2) A crisis negotiating team had been formed;
3) New boats had been purchased for the marine patrol (leading to fewer accidents on the Intracoastal Waterway);
4) A gun range had been built, meaning that officers no longer had to use the one at Broward Community College (when the county commission had balked at the $1 million price tag, Brescher had gotten the range up and running for $30,000 using donated labor, land, and materials);
5) After a 13-year absence, the motorcycle unit had been restarted in an effort to reduce traffic fatalities (after a month of intensive training, each of the squad's six officers had received a new Harley-Davidson);
6) An increased effort had been made to curtail drunk driving;
7) Child abuse cases had been given a higher priority than under previous sheriffs;
8) All BSO employees had received a 5% pay increase;
9) The department had begun reimbursing officers for the cost of certain college courses;
10) A civil service-type program had been established to protect deputies from arbitrary firings;
11) Promotion lists were being adhered to and management-assessment exercises had been added to the process (with the head of the department's training division, Lieutenant Tony Halaska, explaining, "We're not looking for big, hulking dudes. We['re] look[ing] for people who know how to communicate."[619]); and,
12) The department's shoulder patch had been redesigned to have a more modern appearance.

In January 1984, Brescher announced that he would be running for sheriff, explaining that he made the decision to do so while on a European vacation with his wife Gretchen and daughter Heidi. Standing in front of 150 party leaders at the Marina Bay restaurant in Fort Lauderdale, the once-reluctant politician said, "I like this job. I've grown into it ... and accordingly, at this time, I announce to you I am a candidate for the retention of my job as sheriff of Broward County."[620] A beaming Bob Graham then praised Brescher as "a special Floridian ... who has made the decision to serve the people of Broward County," while an equally enthusiastic Bob Butterworth said, "I think George will be the first sheriff in the history of Broward County to be elected without opposition, either in the primary or the general election."[621] But for once,

Broward deputies at gun range (1985)

*Sheriff George Brescher testing out one of the
department's new motorcycles (1983)*

Butterworth's legendary political instincts had failed him.[622] Not only would Brescher face considerable competition, he would end up being turned out of office.

At first, however, things went well for Brescher. Overnight, his entire demeanor seemed to change. No longer shy and retiring, he suddenly was speaking with enthusiasm and urgency, using bold gestures to punctuate his words and wading into crowds to press the flesh. He also finally had realized the importance of getting the department to support him. Thus, when the county's Government Efficiency Study Committee released a report in April 1984 recommending that the road patrol be cut back (and eventually eliminated) as Broward's unincorporated areas shrank, Brescher sent out a department-wide memorandum promising to fight the proposal. "This ill-conceived plan has all of your jobs on the line. As sheriff, I cannot sit still while others attempt to disrupt years of hard work and dedication by each of you."[623] For its part, the committee accused Brescher of playing politics and distorting its words.

In a further attempt to mend internal fences, Brescher agreed to settle a wrongful termination lawsuit that Clint Nye had filed, paying the former officer $18,000. When the *Miami Herald* suggested that this decision had been made to win the backing of the members of Lodge 32, Phillip S. Shailer, Brescher's attorney, basically agreed. "The sheriff and his insurance carrier felt it was in the best interests of the department and the good relations the sheriff has developed with the FOP to get all this acrimony behind us."[624]

For the most part, however, the press painted a flattering picture of Brescher, even when he made mistakes. In March, after conducting a massive search to find Jonathan Marks, a two-year-old boy who had been abducted during a car hijacking at a West Hollywood auto repair shop, Brescher learned that the story was a hoax. Rather than criticize the sheriff for having sent thirty deputies on a wild goose chase, reporters praised him for suing the two men who had set off the massive manhunt and cost taxpayers $15,000.

Likewise, when deputies broke up a mob-run bookmaking and loan sharking operation and arrested thirteen people in May, the press congratulated Brescher even though the Broward State Attorney's Office, FBI, and Miami Strike Force on Organized Crime all claimed that the sheriff had jumped the gun to garner favorable headlines, thereby letting seventeen suspects escape. Denying that his actions had been politically-motivated, Brescher told reporters, "When knowledge of this investigation became widespread, if I didn't act, the individual [who was our informant, Joe Damiano, Sr.] and the lives of undercover agents could have been endangered. We would have preferred to wait another two weeks, but I didn't think it was wise."[625]

Insignia used by BSO posse members (1990)

The press even went so far as to publish pieces that, while hardly newsworthy, helped burnish Brescher's image. When he swore in a sheriff's posse of 251 citizens, explaining that they would be available to help out during hurricanes and other emergencies but would have no police powers, reporters commended Brescher while downplaying the fact that the previous posse, assembled by Bob Butterworth, had never once been activated. Similarly, when the *Miami Herald* discovered that the department was home to possibly the oldest active police officer in the country (Lieutenant Joe DeSantis, who at the age of seventy-nine was in charge of the agency's missing persons unit), it ran a story that quoted Brescher as saying, "Joe is an unbelievable guy. He does an outstanding job. You can't judge somebody by their age.... We're proud of Joe."[626]

Even the Broward County Commission seemed to be in the sheriff's corner. When he asked for $71 million for 1984–85, a 20% increase over the previous year's allotment, the commissioners readily said "yes." Among the various items tucked into the budget was an across-the-board raise for the department's 1,900 employees and an increase in the starting salaries of deputies (bringing their pay to a bit more than $20,000 a year).

Thus, when Nicholas G. "Nick" Navarro announced in January 1984 that he was entering the race for the Democratic nomination for sheriff (joining 24-

year-old Seminole policeman Daniel D. Goldberg), Brescher took the news in stride, especially because no one gave the former head of the department's organized crime division a chance. When reporters asked him about Navarro's bid, Democratic Party Chairman John Lomelo suggested, "He should save his money. I've said it all when I've said that."[627] Likewise, after ignoring Navarro for months, the *Miami Herald* in April printed the following humorous item about his campaign:

> During the St. Patrick's Day Parade in Fort Lauderdale, a couple of campaign workers were handing out literature for Nick Navarro. Navarro, who is running for Broward sheriff, was head of the Broward Sheriff's Organized Crime Division and one of the county's best-known cops. Then he and Sheriff George Brescher had a falling out, and Navarro resigned from the force.
>
> Campaign worker Susan Bryan said things were going well until she attempted to hand some literature and a bumper sticker to a young fellow who was watching the parade.
>
> "No way," the fellow said emphatically, "I'm not voting for that guy."
>
> Surprised, Bryan asked why.
>
> "Because he arrested me," the fellow responded.
>
> Navarro doesn't seem too dismayed by the loss.
>
> "OK," he said, "so I lose the criminal vote."[628]

In May, with his campaign struggling, Goldberg told reporters that he was contemplating running as an independent, but in June he changed his mind and became a Republican. When informed about the switch, Broward County Republican Executive Director William G. Glynn, Jr. said the move had been made without the party's knowledge or support.

In July, the Broward County Police Benevolent Association endorsed Brescher, and a few days later Brescher held a press conference in Fort Lauderdale to announce that he had lined up the support of former sheriffs Bob Butterworth, Ed Stack, and Tom Walker. Butterworth was particularly effusive, telling the audience that "the governor chose the right person to be sheriff [and we're] going to do everything we can to make sure Sheriff Brescher is going to be sheriff of Broward County for four more years."[629]

With Brescher now appearing to be a shoo-in, an angry Nick Navarro accused Butterworth of betrayal. Claiming that Butterworth had given him the idea of running against Brescher during a phone call in November 1983, Navarro insisted, "I have never heard so much double-talk in my life. When I talked to [Butterworth] he said, '[Brescher's] tearing down everything we've built up. I'm sorry I can't run against him myself. You do it.'"[630] Butterworth, however, demurred, saying that his decision to support Brescher should "not be a surprise to anyone. If this was an election of who should be arresting drug smugglers on the street, we should elect Nick Navarro. But this is an administrative job. You need someone who can work at all levels of law enforcement."[631] And then, to make it clear that Navarro had acted without his backing, Butterworth added, "I told [Navarro] 'Hold off, hold off. Don't operate out of emotion.' When he filed [to run for sheriff] I said, 'You've filed entirely too soon.'"[632]

A career law enforcement officer, Navarro had joined the Broward Sheriff's Office in 1971 to head up its newly-formed organized crime division. In November 1983, however, Brescher had reassigned him to the airport. Although he refused to say why, Brescher hinted that Navarro had given in to his position's temptations. When Navarro protested, Brescher apologized for the insinuation.

Refusing to accept the demotion, Navarro quit the force and announced his candidacy. Now, however, with no chance to win the Democratic primary, Navarro said he was going to run as a Republican, a decision that outraged Democrats and led Brescher to comment, "We have now found out who the real Nick Navarro is. The real Nick Navarro is Mr. Flip-Flop. Democrat today, Republican tomorrow. Who knows what the hell he'll be next month."[633] Navarro retorted, "I am not a chameleon, I'm a law enforcement officer."[634]

To stop Navarro, the Broward County Democratic Party moved to have his name struck from the ballot, citing a state law that barred candidates from switching affiliations within six months of a general election. But when the case came before Circuit Judge Joseph E. Price, he ruled that the party had waited too long to complain. Three weeks later, however, the Fourth District Court of Appeal reversed that decision.[635] Recognizing that this meant that the Republicans now had no candidate, the panel wrote, "Nothing in this opinion shall preclude the supervisor of elections from taking any lawful action to place a successor candidate on the ballot."[636]

In an editorial the next day with the headline "A Sorry Spectacle," the *Miami Herald* excoriated nearly everyone involved in the case:

> The Fourth District Court of Appeal's decision to drop Republican sheriff's candidate Nick Navarro from the Broward ballot Nov. 6 robs voters of the chance to choose between two men for one of the county's most powerful elective offices. Blame not the court for this travesty, however, but the Broward Democratic and Republican hierarchies.... When Mr. Navarro abruptly switched parties to run as a Republican last July, he did so at the urging of the Broward GOP lead-

ership. Republican leaders, eager to snatch the sheriff's office from longtime Democratic control, talked Mr. Navarro into dropping his Democratic candidacy against incumbent George Brescher and running as a Republican. Mr. Navarro's switch, which came one hour before the qualifying deadline, closely followed the endorsement of Mr. Brescher by three former sheriffs....

By any clear analysis, Mr. Navarro's eleventh-hour switch violated state election law, which prohibits candidates from changing parties within six months of the general election.... When he announced his switch, Mr. Navarro said that attorneys had thoroughly reviewed the move and found it defensible. Such a finding could have been based only on faulty legal analysis or outright disregard for the political process.

Broward Democratic leaders can claim no loftier accomplishment. Rather than challenge Mr. Navarro's switch immediately, they elected to keep quiet until it was too late for Republicans to select another candidate to face Mr. Brescher. Democratic leaders explain that they did not know that the party switch was illegal until recently, but several veteran party members admit that the matter was the talk of party headquarters immediately after it occurred.

Broward voters now face the prospect on Nov. 6 of electing a sheriff without opposition. Further aggravating the situation is the fact that Mr. Brescher, appointed sheriff two years ago by Gov. Bob Graham, will be able to serve for six years without ever facing the voters.... [637]

Later that day, U.S. District Judge Norman C. Roettger, Jr. took matters into his hands and ordered Navarro's name to be put back on the ballot. "I have considerable trouble with the definition of candidate,"[638] the jurist told a packed courtroom. "I would like to have the opportunity to hear the attorney general of Florida explain the statute. Granting a temporary injunction will not disserve the public interest. And I do not see where a judge should determine election results."[639] Stunned by this turn of events, the Democrats filed an emergency appeal.

In the meantime, Brescher and Navarro continued to do battle. The election had turned increasingly ugly after Navarro switched parties, with each side hurling unfounded charges at the other. While Navarro's supporters circulated rumors that Brescher's father-in-law was a Nazi war criminal and the sheriff was an anti-Semite, Brescher's supporters accused Navarro of being in league with the Ku Klux Klan. And when Brescher accused Navarro of having violated department rules regarding the disposal of contraband (referring to various pieces of marine equipment taken from the boats of drug smugglers),

Norman C. Roettger, Jr., U.S. District Judge for the
Southern District of Florida (1972–2003)

Navarro called Brescher "a wimp-and-a-half" and an "empty suit"[640] even as he told reporters, "I never thought that politics would get this dirty."[641] In the meantime, Brescher opened a new sub-station in the affluent western suburb of Bonaventure in an attempt (some said) to win its votes.

Not surprisingly, the campaign created deep divisions within the Sheriff's Office. Hoping to capitalize on his years of experience with the agency, Navarro said, "My qualifications are not only from sitting in a school room. My qualifications are coming from the trenches."[642] Meanwhile, officials from both camps were keeping track of which BSO employees were backing whom, with Navarro's supporters claiming they had been punished by their pro-Brescher superiors and knew of deputies who were tearing down Navarro's campaign signs and pressuring local businesses into putting up posters for Brescher.

Four days before the election, the *Miami Herald* gave Brescher its tepid endorsement. Noting that voters had been put in the position of having to "choose between two seriously flawed candidates who have been waging the dirtiest political campaign the county has seen in many years," the paper explained it had decided to support Brescher "with less than wholehearted enthusiasm."[643] It went on to say that:

To be sure, Mr. Brescher has not particularly distinguished himself in the two years since Gov. Bob Graham appointed him to fill the unexpired term of former Sheriff Robert Butterworth ... [and he] has often seemed unaware of major activities going on in his department, such as when a convicted drug dealer was allowed furloughs from the county jail in return for helping improve relations between inmates and guards.

A man of strong personal integrity, Mr. Brescher nonetheless has allowed the sheriff's office to continue to be used as a political vehicle for the Democratic Party ... [even though] Mr. Brescher has repeatedly described himself as nonpolitical.

If he wins a full four-year term, Mr. Brescher must gain a stronger grasp on his agency and overhaul his top administration to ensure that law-enforcement professionals—not political operatives—make the decisions.[644]

By Election Day, the question of Navarro's eligibility remained undecided, leading one reporter to call the race "the wildest sheriff's contest in county history" and one that seemed "to be directed by Mel Brooks."[645] To the surprise of many, when the ballots were counted, Navarro had won, edging Brescher 229,032 votes to 211,697 votes (a margin of 52%–48%). In the days that followed, analysts attributed Navarro's victory to the publicity he had received from the Democrats' efforts to have him removed from the ballot as well as Brescher's failure to run well among condominium voters.

As the results rolled in, a triumphant Navarro told a cheering crowd, "I'll be your sheriff for the next four years. And you can start looking for changes as soon as I take over."[646] Meanwhile, Brescher refused to face the press, finally emerging at 1:30 a.m. (long after most of his supporters had gone home) to say, "I gave it all I had. Elections are something. You never know what the voters are going to do."[647]

Even with Brescher's concession, Navarro's right to assume office remained uncertain, and for the next month just what was going to happen was anyone's guess. Dorothy W. Glisson, the deputy secretary of state in charge of elections, said that Governor Graham was prepared to appoint a temporary sheriff with a new election to follow in November 1986. Bruce S. Rogow, the Democrats' lead attorney, insisted that if Navarro was ruled ineligible, Brescher would be the automatic winner under Florida's complicated elections laws. And Linda A. Conahan, a lawyer for Navarro, predicted that the Florida Supreme Court ultimately would find that the election had been proper.

Finally, however, on Friday, December 7, 1984, Judge Roettger ruled in Navarro's favor, saying, "I don't know how the integrity of the election process is achieved by permitting voters a legitimate choice and then overturning it once it has been made."[648] Standing on the courthouse steps, an elated Navarro told his listeners, "It feels very good. I've got to get to work now. My transition period has been cut down by half."[649]

As he packed up his things, Brescher insisted he was proud of his record as sheriff, adding, "I have bittersweet feelings about leaving public service. Politics is funny, you're out there shaking hands but now I'm thinking it's time to move on to more substantial things."[650] When asked about his one-time boss and soon-to-be predecessor, an uncharacteristically circumspect Navarro replied, "I think George Brescher is a very good attorney and is going to be very successful in private practice."[651] George I. Platt III, the chairman of the Broward County Democrat Party, was more direct, saying, "George is not a good politician. We all recognized George's limitation."[652]

Despite having cost the Democrats the county's most powerful office, in July 1986 Governor Bob Graham reappointed Brescher to the Broward County Court. Four years later, Republican Governor Robert "Bob" Martinez, under pressure to cross party lines and name a Democrat, elevated Brescher to the Broward Circuit Court, where he continued to serve until his retirement in March 2006.

CHAPTER 8

THE NAVARRO YEARS (1985–93)

With Nick Navarro at the helm, the Broward Sheriff's Office returned to the media spotlight for the first time in decades. Colorful, controversial, and often accused of being corrupt, Navarro had a knack for getting the media's attention. Indeed, not since the days of Walter Clark had the county had such an outsized sheriff. But like Clark, Navarro, who had entered office as a political outsider and a man of the people, ultimately lost touch with his constituents and eventually was forced out by a public that had grown weary of his increasingly outrageous antics.

Sheriff Nicholas G. Navarro (1985–93)

Nicholas Gutierrez Navarro was born in Jaruco, Cuba, on November 11, 1929, and grew up being fascinated by American gangster movies. In 1950, following his sophomore year at the University of Havana, he decided to move to Pennsylvania to live with his older sister Delia and her husband Louis Hernandez. After being drafted into the U.S. Army and seeing combat in Korea, Navarro returned to Pennsylvania, became an American citizen, and went into the furniture business. Yearning for a more action-filled life, in 1959 he made his way to Miami and became a police officer. In 1963, he was hired as a special agent by the Federal Bureau of Narcotics (the forerunner of the U.S. Drug Enforcement Agency), but in 1968 accepted an invitation from Commissioner William L. Reed to join the new Florida Bureau of Law Enforcement. Within a year, he had been promoted to supervisor of the Orlando office.

By 1971, Navarro was ready to return to South Florida, and in October he was hired by Broward Sheriff Ed Stack to run the agency's new organized crime division. Navarro quickly fell in love with Stack's secretary, Sharron Watkins, and in 1972 the two wed. Although the couple asked Stack to perform the ceremony, the lawman declined, explaining that seven of the eight other couples he had married had ended up divorcing.

Nicholas G. "Nick" Navarro, sheriff of Broward County (1985–93)

In January 1977, Stack reassigned Navarro from the organized crime division to the internal affairs division, explaining that Navarro had become too well-known to remain in an undercover position. Soon, however, Navarro was transferred again, first to a liaison position with the State Attorney's Office and then to the department's airport security unit (a significant demotion). While Stack insisted that these moves were merely routine, Navarro was convinced that Stack was trying to bury him.

In January 1979, Sheriff Bob Butterworth gave Navarro back his old job as head of the organized crime division. In November 1983, however, Butterworth's successor, George Brescher, again relieved Navarro of his command and reassigned him to "administrative duties." In response, Navarro quit the department.

By now, Navarro's reputation for self-promotion, coupled with his willingness to bend the rules to make headlines, was well-established. In 1980, for example, he had sent an undercover operative to Colombia even though doing so was prohibited by American law. In 1981, he did so again, dispatching agents to Bimini to investigate the island's drug dealers. When this operation came to

*An interdicted drug courier's plane at North Perry Airport
in Pembroke Pines (1980)*

light, an outraged Bahamian government filed a protest with the U.S. Department of State, which in turn reprimanded Navarro (and for a time considered turning the matter over to the U.S. Department of Justice for criminal prosecution). Undaunted, Navarro replied, "I don't tell the State Department how to do their job and they better not tell me how to do mine. If they tell me where I can't go, I'll tell them where they can go!"[653]

In yet another such incident, Navarro in 1982 sought to fly BSO deputies to Antigua to kidnap Robert L. Vesco, the fugitive financier who had fled the United States in 1973 following the collapse of Investors Overseas Services Ltd., a mutual fund that had once managed $1.5 billion in assets (and from which Vesco was thought to have stolen at least $200 million). After being kicked out of Costa Rica in 1978, Vesco had gone to the Bahamas, but in 1981 he had moved to Antigua in his continuing quest to avoid arrest. Once in Antigua, Vesco began negotiating to buy half of the neighboring island of Barbuda, where he planned to start his own country (to be called New Aragon).

The opportunity to nab Vesco proved irresistible to Navarro. But when he presented his plan (which called for deputies to shoot Vesco with a tranquilizer gun and bring him back to Florida on a private jet) to his superiors, they quickly said "no." With a touch of understatement, Bob Butterworth noted, "a local sheriff's office is not in the business of going into foreign countries and kidnapping people…."[654]

These incidents had been all but forgotten by the time Navarro was sworn in as sheriff on Tuesday, January 8, 1985. But while speaking to reporters, he promised, "you guys in the press are going to get a lot of ink out of me in the next four years."[655] Within days, this comment began proving highly accurate.

Fugitive financier Robert L. Vesco being interviewed by reporter Margaret Osmer at his ranch in San Jose, Costa Rica (1974)

Throughout the recently-concluded campaign, Navarro had portrayed himself as a non-politician, a career law enforcement officer who was above the fray of petty politics. Indeed, he had reacted vehemently when, shortly after the election, Sheriff George Brescher had accused him of planning widespread firings and reassignments. "I told him I didn't want a bloodbath,"[656] Navarro said. "My God Almighty, why does this man do this?"[657] To emphasize the point, Navarro claimed, "[I] could care less who supported Brescher or was loyal to him."[658]

As soon as he took over, however, Navarro went back on his word and fired thirty of the department's 600 deputies. A stunned Ed Stack condemned these moves as a blatant political act, while Bob Butterworth called them "a massacre."[659] In a strongly-worded letter, Maynard Abrams, the president of the Broward County Crime Commission,[660] claimed that the dismissals were illegal. "Although you stated in the campaign that there would be no political reprisals," Abrams wrote, "many of these terminations appear to be just that."[661]

Not surprisingly, many of the axed officers went to court to get their jobs back, and in time a number of them were reinstated. Others, however, accepted settlements totaling $500,000. One of these was Captain Robert Broadhurst, who Sheriff Stack had described as an "ideal man for police work," Sheriff

Butterworth had labeled "a rising star," Sheriff Brescher had called a "star player,"[662] but who Navarro had decided lacked drive and initiative. When questioned by the press, a visibly angry Navarro responded, "I don't have to explain anything to you. I knew who these guys were and I didn't want them...."[663] Frank C. Kruppenbacher, the department's attorney, reacted with equal indignation, saying, "It was garbage that [Navarro] ever fired anyone for political reasons."[664]

In addition to handing out pink slips, Navarro demoted or reassigned dozens of employees, including James J. "Jim" Howard, the coordinator of Crime Stoppers, the department's highly successful telephone hotline. Under Howard's direction, tips from callers had resulted in the recovery of $10 million a month in stolen property, but after he resigned (following a demotion) the number fell to $2 million a month (an equally sharp drop in arrests also occurred). The decline did not go unnoticed by reporters, who pointed out that similar programs in Dade and Palm Beach counties were showing increased effectiveness. Further investigation by the press revealed that Howard's replacement was a Navarro crony who collected $2,000 a month in exchange for working just a few hours each week.

In June 1985, the Florida Legislature decided to give all county officers a hefty raise. As a result, Navarro's salary jumped from $56,212 to $68,058, a 21% increase. Asked for a comment, the lawman said, "That's a good raise. I thank them [the legislature] for it, very humbly."[665] In fact, this was to be the first of several pay boosts during Navarro's tenure, and by the time he left office in 1993 he was earning $97,171 a year.

In the meantime, the Police Benevolent Association had drafted a bill stripping Navarro of his right to hire and fire deputies. When the Broward legislative delegation threw its support behind the proposal, Navarro mobilized his fellow sheriffs, who worried that it might become a model for their departments. After a bruising floor fight, the Florida Senate passed the bill, only to watch it die in the House due to the parliamentary maneuvers of Speaker J. Harold Thompson (D-Gretna).

Navarro had little time, however, to savor his victory, for in June 1986 he was forced to settle a lawsuit (for $250,000) brought by Peter L. Foster. In April 1980, while working as an informant for Navarro, Foster had flown to Colombia to pick up $30,000 worth of marijuana from a drug ring. Intercepted by government agents, who accused him of violating Colombian airspace, he spent the next fifty-seven days in a jail in Baranquilla, where he was beaten daily (leaving him with a permanent limp). He finally was released after his parents paid a $25,000 fine.

Returning to the United States, Foster filed a federal lawsuit in 1982 claiming that Navarro had done nothing to help him out of his predicament. Upon

*J. Harold Thompson, Speaker of the Florida House
of Representatives (1985–86)*

learning of Foster's arrest, Navarro claimed that he had never met Foster, but a tape of a telephone conversation proved that Navarro had approached Foster and hired him to be an undercover operative.

When the settlement was announced, Navarro sought to pin responsibility for it on the department's underwriter. "I was ready to go to trial. [T]he insurance company opted to settle, [and] that is their decision."[666] Asked if the settlement proved that Foster had been telling the truth, Navarro replied, "That is Foster's opinion. We didn't do anything wrong."[667]

In an attempt to improve his image, Navarro announced that he was reactivating the municipal deputy program started by Ed Stack. As result, police departments throughout Broward County were invited to submit the names of detectives they wanted deputized; once approved, these officers would be able to make arrests anywhere in the county. A short time later, Navarro swore in the nominees with great fanfare and issued them deputy sheriff badges.

Navarro's enthusiasm for the program ebbed, however, after the county's police chiefs began signing Mutual Aid Agreements, which made it possible for their officers to work in reciprocating jurisdictions. Viewing these pacts as a threat to his own power, Navarro sent a letter to the mayor of every Broward city threatening to cancel the municipal sheriff arrangement.

Outraged by this turn of events, the chiefs accused Navarro of being a dictator and trying "to sabotage everything that [we] are working for."[668] To further make their point, at a meeting of the Broward County Police Chiefs Association they took the unprecedented step of publicly censuring the county's top lawman. Navarro brushed off their complaints by calling the group a "bunch of clucking hens."[669] By then, in what one chief referred to as "a snit,"[670] Navarro had fired all of the municipal deputies (a total of 120 officers) and ordered them to give back their badges. In the meantime, the Mutual Aid Agreement program continued to grow, and by June 1987 almost every city in the county had signed a contract.

The perennial problem of overcrowding at the county jail also was nipping at Navarro's heels. In June 1985, the sheriff had assured the county commission that prisoners would soon be transferred to the new main jail, thereby satisfying U.S. District Judge William M. Hoeveler (the jail's federal overseer) and avoiding a threatened showdown with the state's Department of Corrections. But when conditions continued to deteriorate, Hoeveler threatened to jail Navarro for defying a court order and housing seventy-three prisoners in a tent.

Navarro had particularly infuriated the judge by missing a hearing on the matter so that he could fly to Los Angeles to tape a television interview. Upon his return from California, Navarro appeared in court, apologized profusely, and explained that he had been unaware of the injunction prohibiting the use of tents, a claim one of the inmates' attorneys found "unbelievable."[671]

Although the problem of overcrowding at the jail had existed for years, Assistant U.S. Attorney Mark P. Schnapp charged that Navarro, in his quest for publicity, was making it worse by arresting scores of low-level drug dealers, thereby adding to the problem while failing to reduce the amount of crime in the county. Support for this assertion was not hard to find. In a series of drug raids dubbed "Operation Crackdown," Navarro and his deputies—in one instance accompanied by a BBC film crew—arrested 196 individuals. Although the effort drew flattering headlines, very few drugs were found and most of the suspects ended up being charged with loitering.

By August 1986, Hoeveler had had enough, and he ordered the county to pay a $1,000-a-day fine until the jail's population fell below his previously-set cap. By the time a solution finally was reached, Broward taxpayers had incurred $2.1 million in penalties, much of it the result of Navarro's numerous made-for-television raids.

William M. Hoeveler, U.S. District Judge for the
Southern District of Florida (since 1977)

In January 1986, Navarro caused a ruckus of a different sort when he decided to send three canine teams, two motorcycle units, and a patrol car into Tamarac after Councilman Sydney Stein expressed concern that the city's own department was too small to provide adequate protection and Police Chief Joseph McIntosh admitted he did not have enough officers to do the job. Accusing Navarro of overstepping his authority, both the Broward League of Cities and the Northwest Council of Mayors adopted resolutions demanding that the Sheriff's Office obtain explicit approval before sending deputies into any municipality. Asked to explain the resolutions, Dania Mayor John Bertino replied, "I think the general idea here is we want the Sheriff to stay the hell out of our cities."[672]

Despite his run-ins with the judiciary, other law enforcement agencies, and local officials throughout the county, Navarro's public image remained relatively untarnished during his first two years in office. But in August 1987, an editorial in the *Fort Lauderdale Sun-Sentinel* was headlined, "Navarro's Courthouse Performance Either Arrogant or Incompetent," and the accompanying piece described the sheriff as a "renegade law officer" who had "turned himself into a bad joke."[673]

The underlying events had been set in motion on Tuesday, July 28, 1987, when a highly publicized shootout in a Port St. Joe, Florida, courtroom left three people dead, including a judge and an attorney. On the following day, Broward Chief Circuit Judge Miette K. Burnstein ordered Navarro to post an additional thirty-five deputies at the main courthouse by the following Monday. Furious at being told what to do, Navarro declared that Burnstein had no authority over the Sheriff's Office, which led her to threaten to hold him in contempt. Navarro then grudgingly agreed to adhere to the order.

When Monday came, however, employees and visitors discovered that the sheriff had chosen to carry out Burnstein's mandate in an outrageous manner. Access to the 10-story building was restricted to a single door, and each person trying to pass through it was being checked by deputies equipped with hand-held metal detectors. This time-consuming process quickly resulted in a line of 1,000 people, who were forced to wait for up to three hours in the sweltering summer sun. Court administrators soon gave up and closed the building.

When he discovered what was taking place, Acting Chief Judge Arthur J. Franza ordered deputies to open an additional door to ease the congestion, which they promptly refused to do. Speaking to reporters later, Franza said, "I thought I was in another country. It was like a coup was taking place."[674]

The public also was angry, and it placed the blame squarely on the sheriff. Agreeing with this view, newspapers suggested that Navarro had either "bungled the job because it was too big for him or he threw a vindictive, heel-kicking tantrum that puts another gaping hole in his professional reputation."[675] The judges whose courtrooms had been disrupted expressed similar outrage. "It wasn't security officers that were blocking the doors, it was the Sheriff's ego," said Burnstein, while Franza exclaimed, "it's just like Disney World and we've got Mickey Mouse running the operation."[676]

For his part, Navarro was nonplussed, even after it was revealed that the shutdown had cost taxpayers $77,000 and imperiled at least five criminal prosecutions (due to the state's speedy trial laws). Determined to get to the bottom of things, Franza ordered Navarro to appear before him and explain his actions. When Navarro missed the hearing, an incensed Franza asked Governor Bob Martinez to arrest Navarro and ordered the Fort Lauderdale Police Department to immediately assume responsibility for the courthouse's security. Navarro responded by saying, "this is the biggest joke I have ever seen."[677]

The next day, however, a subdued Navarro appeared before Franza and apologized, explaining that the missed court appearance had been caused by "a moment of error"[678] and promising to have improved courthouse security in place by October. By now, Franza also had calmed down and withdrew his previous orders. Still, he made it a point to tell Navarro, "be a good Nick, not a *god*, Nick."[679]

One month later, Navarro was forced to back down again, this time reversing his earlier refusal to allow judges and police officers to carry weapons into the courthouse. "If you want bazookas, we'll allow bazookas,"[680] a petulant Navarro announced. "If you want tanks, we'll allow tanks."[681]

More bad publicity arrived two weeks later when the Fourth District Court of Appeal ruled that Navarro's policy of having deputies randomly search passengers at the county's bus and railroad stations was unconstitutional.[682] Carol Ann Kerwick had been a passenger in a car driven by Sean Brasky. While at an Amtrak parking lot in Fort Lauderdale, the pair had been approached by two deputies, who asked to see their identification and tickets. When it was explained that only Kerwick, who was from Connecticut and had been visiting friends in Margate, was traveling, the officers inspected her luggage, which was found to contain a kilogram of cocaine.

Following her arrest, Kerwick moved to suppress the drugs on the ground that the officers had lacked probable cause for their search. When Circuit Judge Robert L. Andrews agreed, Navarro appealed. At the Fourth District, Judge Harry L. Anstead upheld the order and repeated Andrews's observation that

[t]he spectre of American citizens being asked, by badge-wielding police, for identification, travel papers—in short a *raison d'être*—is foreign to *any* fair reading of the Constitution, and its guarantee of human liberties. This is not Hitler's Berlin, nor Stalin's Moscow, nor is it white supremacist South Africa. Yet in Broward County, Florida, these police officers approach every person on board buses and trains ("that

Robert "Bob" Martinez, governor of Florida (1987–91)

An Amtrak passenger train on its way to Fort Lauderdale (1982)

time permits") and check identification, tickets, ask to search luggage—all in the name of "voluntary cooperation" with law enforcement—to the shocking extent that just one officer, Damiano, admitted
that during the previous nine months, he, himself, had searched *in ex-
cess* of three thousand bags! In the Court's opinion, the founders of the
Republic would be thunderstruck.[683]

Predictably, Navarro reacted angrily. "We are working within the frame[work]
of the law, within the Constitution. Our officers are trying to do a good job."[684]
He then added that the ruling's comparison of the Broward Sheriff's Office to
Nazi Germany was causing some deputies "mental anguish because their parents or family members were victims of the Third Reich."[685]

In November 1987, Navarro again made headlines when three female judges,
citing reproductive health concerns, refused to walk through the metal detector at the county jail and asked to be exempted (a request Navarro denied).
This time the newspapers sided with the sheriff, with the *Fort Lauderdale Sun-
Sentinel* saying that the judges' refusal to be screened "delivers a remarkably
arrogant message to the public and to other county employees who are required to pass through the detectors: Your well-being ... is not as important
as ours."[686] The editorial went on to say that the fears expressed by the judges
had no scientific basis, and that if they are "bas[ing] their lifestyles on that
kind of information, none of them has eaten a meal or breathed the air since
at least 1975."[687]

*Harry L. Anstead, judge of the Florida Fourth
District Court of Appeal (1977–94)*

The tale grew even stranger a short time later, when one of the judges (June L. Johnson, who later would be removed from the bench for backdating traffic tickets) was quoted as saying that a second reason she could not go through the detector was that an eight-foot wide aura surrounded her body and would be damaged by the machine. Although Johnson subsequently denied making this comment, Chief Jailer Willis Roberts insisted she had, leading the *Miami Herald* to write, "So who's telling the truth here? We'll ask the psychics and let you know."[688]

By the beginning of 1988, Navarro had a lot of work to do if he was going to convince the public to give him four more years in office. In an attempt to restore some luster to his tarnished image, he decided to lead another televised drug raid. But the bust went awry—not only was the suspect not in the house, a woman who was present claimed to be in mourning for her late husband. Despite these bothersome details, Navarro proclaimed the operation a success.

Another pre-election event also ran into problems. After agreeing to participate in a community anti-drug march and help tear down a crack house, Navarro backed out when he spotted campaign signs for Democratic challenger Ralph A. Finno in the park where the procession was forming. When asked for a comment, Finno said: "The spotlight was no longer on Nick Navarro. He didn't want anybody to rain on his parade."[689] Navarro, however, had a different explanation for his decision to withdraw: "I did not anticipate I would walk into what appeared to be a political rally. This is not political. This was to be a service to the community."[690]

Despite these missteps, Navarro ended up easily winning a second term due to the lack of a credible challenger. After first beating Jim Howard (his former Crime Stoppers administrator) in the Republican primary by a tally of 28,620 votes to 13,943 votes (a margin of 67%–33%), he defeated Democrat James "Jim" Deckinger in the general election 281,675 votes to 169,535 votes (a margin of 62%–38%).

Deckinger, a former BSO deputy making his first run for political office, had been a dark horse candidate from the beginning, and actually had been beaten in the Democratic primary by Finno, a one-time Fort Lauderdale police captain. But with two other candidates in the race (former BSO deputy Walter Ramsdell and retired state corrections administrator Gil "Mr. G" Gesualdi), Finno had been unable to win a majority, thereby setting up a run-off with Deckinger. When Ramsdell and Gesualdi threw their support behind Deckinger, citing concerns about an on-going criminal investigation into Finno's past stemming from allegations of extortion and impersonating a police officer, Deckinger won the run-off in an upset, 25,138 votes to 22,440 votes (a margin of 53%–47%). But in the general election, Navarro's overwhelming financial advantage (he had raised $470,000 to Deckinger's $21,000) left little doubt about the outcome. While Deckinger complained that the sheriff was an "ineffective, publicity-hungry showboat," Navarro said, "I feel very good. The people have made the statement, not the media."[691]

Shortly before the election, the *Fort Lauderdale Sun-Sentinel*, deeming Deckinger too inexperienced to be sheriff, had reluctantly endorsed Navarro despite what it called his "autocratic manner and excessive desire for publicity and political power."[692] But it was Broward Republican Chairwoman Jo Smith, speaking a year earlier, who offered the most cogent explanation for Navarro's overwhelming victory: "I guess the main thing is that people forget. He has been in the headlines every day. People forget why. They only remember the name when they go to the polls."[693]

Navarro's second term began on Tuesday, January 3, 1989, and within just a few months a series of events would begin to unfold that would cast a shadow over the Sheriff's Office for years to come.

In March 1989, the U.S. Coast Guard stopped a 53-foot yacht on its way back from the Bahamas because its skipper, Jim Ramsey, had failed to hoist a mandatory yellow quarantine flag (Ramsey later would say that it had been too windy to do so). Upon boarding the LIBRA II, an officer noticed that the

Sheriff Nick Navarro (left) with Miami Dolphins coach Don Shula and sportscaster Howard Cosell at a charity fundraiser (1985)

hull identification number on the newly-renovated vessel's transom had been painted over. Because a 1986 Florida state law made it a felony to deface or remove such numbers, the officer had the boat brought to the Fort Lauderdale Coast Guard station.

When the Florida Marine Patrol and the U.S. Customs Service were contacted, neither was willing to get involved. Unsure what to do next, the Coast Guard decided to contact the Hollywood Police Department, but Ramsey asked that the Broward Sheriff's Office be called instead. In short order, officers from both agencies arrived and got into a protracted jurisdictional argument. Eventually, the Coast Guard decided to turn the boat over to the Sheriff's Office.

After taking control of the vessel, the deputies called for a drug-sniffing dog. Although the animal reacted excitedly, a search failed to turn up any illicit goods. And by now, an executive from Roscioli Yacht Sales Inc. had appeared with documents proving that it owned the boat. But rather than releasing the LIBRA II, the deputies impounded her so that a more thorough search for contraband could be undertaken.

Subsequently, the department advised Robert Roscioli that the boat would be returned to him if he made a $50,000 donation to the Sheriff's Office Law

Sergeant Jim Hansen, head of the BSO's K-9 squad (1986)

Enforcement Trust Fund. Although this amount soon was reduced to $25,000 and then to $15,000, Roscioli refused to pay. On his way to court, he explained, "They call it a reasonable offer. I call it legalized extortion."[694]

Tom McPherson, Florida state senator (1983–91)

In December 1989, Circuit Judge J. Cail Lee ordered the vessel released, but Navarro refused to do so. In the meantime, a *Fort Lauderdale Sun-Sentinel* investigation revealed that it was becoming routine for law enforcement officials to use forfeiture actions to extract large cash settlements from defendants.

Asked about these developments, State Senator Tom McPherson (D-Fort Lauderdale), the sponsor of the 1986 law that had ensnared the LIBRA II, observed, "With all the crime going on out on the water, if [the Sheriff's Office] has nothing better to do than take away someone's rightfully owned boat, that's a crime."[695] When he was told that Navarro's attorney, Bruce W. Jolly, was appealing Judge Lee's ruling while offering to settle the case for $15,000, McPherson exclaimed, "My God, that's crazy."[696]

Jim Ramsey, the skipper of the LIBRA II, pointed out that he had been a member of the committee that had helped draft the statute and fumed, "I can tell you firsthand that this is not what the law was intended to do."[697] Van Snider, the executive director of the Marine Industry Association, agreed and called Navarro's actions "scary."[698] And the *Fort Lauderdale Sun-Sentinel,* claiming that further litigation by the Sheriff's Office would be "perverse," accused Navarro of having "turned what should have been a valuable tool in the war on drugs and other criminal enterprises into a source of animosity, confusion and high-cost inconvenience."[699]

In October 1990, the Fourth District affirmed Judge Lee's ruling.[700] By now, the LIBRA II, which at one time had been worth $325,000, was in need of extensive repairs due to the department's poor stewardship. A fire had caused $65,000 in damages and squatters, who deputies had allowed to live on the boat, had stripped her of her parts and left her cabin in shambles. As a result, Roscioli ended up selling the vessel for less than half her pre-seizure value.

Jolly, Navarro's attorney, disputed these accounts. "The boat has not been trashed,"[701] he claimed, while insisting that the fire had not been BSO's fault. As a result, a new round of litigation began before Circuit Judge Patti E. Henning, who found that Roscioli was entitled to damages, attorneys' fees, costs, and interest amounting to more than $150,000. On appeal, the Fourth District reduced this amount after deciding that Roscioli could not recover either his attorneys' fees or the interest he had paid on the vessel's mortgage.[702] Even with these reductions, the total cost to the taxpayers of Broward County was more than $300,000.

As the LIBRA II saga dragged on, an untroubled Navarro continued to pursue his media career. In 1982, he had been asked to help Al Pacino get ready for his role as Cuban drug lord Tony Montana in the movie *Scarface.* Although it received only mixed reviews from the critics, the film quickly gained a cult following and Navarro was praised for his coaching.

Four years later, Navarro made it to prime-time national television on a segment of Geraldo Rivera's *American Vice: The Doping of a Nation.* Not only had the sheriff been interviewed, but a BSO drug raid had been aired live (the fact that three of the suspects were soon set free had been deemed immaterial). In order to improve the ratings, Navarro had allowed Rivera to tag along to a meeting at a Fort Lauderdale hotel room where deputies planned to buy cocaine. The deal had fallen apart, however, when one of the sellers recognized the famous newsman.

Navarro's next big break came in March 1989 when a FOX television series called *COPS* made its debut. The show was the brainchild of Malcolm Barbour and John Langley, the producers of Rivera's *American Vice* special, and had been given the green light when a writers' strike created a sudden need for unscripted programming. For their first season (fourteen episodes, each running thirty minutes), Barbour and Langley decided to focus on Navarro and the Broward Sheriff's Office.

Al Pacino as gangster Tony Montana in the 1983 movie "Scarface"

Broward Deputy Linda Canada in a scene from the TV show "COPS" (1989)

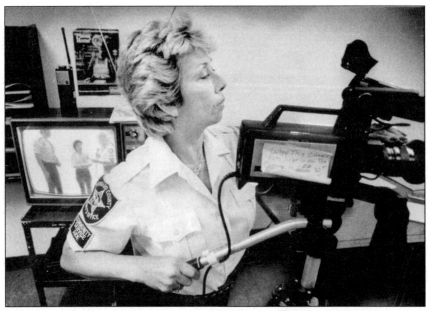

BSO Community Service Aide Nancy Thomas filming
an in-house television spot (1985)

Although the show took viewers to the seamiest parts of the county (much to the dismay of the local tourist industry) and often portrayed the department in a less-than-flattering light, Navarro was delighted by the attention. Yet in a remarkable bit of hypocrisy, he told his subordinates, "if you want to go to a life of stardom, turn in your badge and turn in your gun."[703] When this remark made its way into an issue of *TV Guide*, a local newspaper columnist wondered how "a sheriff who has logged more celluloid time than Bob Hope and Mr. Whipple combined"[704] expected anyone to take him seriously.

The final episode of the first season of *COPS* was a one-hour special filmed in the former Soviet Union, and when the second season began in September 1989 the show had moved on to Portland, Oregon. As a result, Navarro temporarily found himself out of the public eye. But in June 1990, the arrest of two members of the rap group *2 Live Crew* during a performance in Hollywood (coupled with the arrest of Charles Freeman, a store owner who had sold one of its albums) turned Navarro into a household name.

The band had been formed in 1985 by three members of the U.S. Air Force. From the beginning, its music featured sexually-explicit lyrics, and in 1986 the group's first album, *The 2 Live Crew Is What We Are*, went gold on the

*Record store owner Charles Freeman holding the 2 Live Crew
album "As Nasty As They Wanna Be" (1990)*

strength of such singles as "Throw the Dick" and "We Want Some Pussy." Its
second album, called *Move Something*, also went gold upon its release in 1988.

By now, the group was being run by Luther Campbell (who called himself
Luke Skyywalker until *Star Wars* creator George Lucas filed a lawsuit), and in
February 1989 it issued its most successful album, an 80-minute compilation
of eighteen songs called *As Nasty As They Wanna Be*. While all of the selec-
tions were filthy, the track "Me So Horny" particularly stood out and became
a massive hit after repeated airings on MTV.

Sensing an opportunity, in March 1990 Navarro went to state court and
convinced Judge Mel Grossman to declare the album obscene. Copies of the
order were then distributed to retail stores throughout the county, and within
days it became impossible to buy the album locally (resulting in the humorous tagline "Banned in Broward" being pasted across its cover in the rest of
the country). In response, the group sued Navarro in federal court.

In June 1990, Judge Jose Gonzalez ruled that the album was obscene but
found that Navarro's actions had amounted to an unconstitutional "prior re-
straint."[705] A short time later, he awarded the band nearly $22,000 to cover its
attorneys' fees and costs.[706] Refusing to concede, Navarro went to the U.S.
Court of Appeals for the Eleventh Circuit, which ended up dismissing the sher-

iff's entire case after deciding that the album had artistic value.[707] A further appeal to the U.S. Supreme Court proved equally fruitless.[708]

In the meantime, Navarro found himself on television, sitting in Geraldo Rivera's New York City studio debating the merits of the case with Luther Campbell. But back in South Florida, both the press and the public excoriated the sheriff for failing to go after real criminals. In an open letter to the lawman, one columnist asked, "The hysteria and publicity-grabbing just never stops, does it, King?"[709] The person who really upset Navarro, however, was a prankster who played snippets from the album over the department's radio frequency for thirty-five minutes. "Whoever is doing this better stop or we're going to find out who they are,"[710] the lawman sputtered.

By the time the dust finally settled, Navarro had become a national celebrity, appearing on ABC's *Nightline* and making the front page of the *New York Times* and *USA Today*; a Broward jury had acquitted the band of any wrongdoing; membership in the American Civil Liberties Union of Florida had soared; and sales of *As Nasty As They Wanna Be* had doubled. Bruce Rogow, the band's lawyer, gleefully told reporters, "The record was dead. It sold all it was ever going to sell. Now it's been resurrected. This record will go over 2.5 million. I'm talking Europe. I'm talking South America. This was front page news in Norway."[711] An equally excited Luther Campbell thanked the sheriff for the group's new-found fame and fortune, saying "Slick Nick did it!"[712] As for Navarro, he decided that the whole matter had been blown out of proportion and claimed to be a victim. "The jurors were unkind. Everyone is saying unkind things,"[713] he complained.

For the man who had once been the master of all media, Navarro suddenly seemed to be in trouble wherever he turned, including within his own agency. In November 1990, newspapers began to report a fall in department morale, which they attributed to rampant cronyism, and took special note of Navarro's "magic wand" promotions (under which individuals were allowed to bypass the department's competitive testing procedures). Among the lucky beneficiaries was Robert Freeman, a deputy who had been fired in 1983 for having sex with a 16-year-old babysitter and then lying about the affair. Attaching himself to Navarro's successful 1984 campaign, Freeman got himself rehired, was promoted to lieutenant, and became the head of an anti-gang unit, all while internal affairs reports about his behavior went missing.

Charges of financial improprieties also were beginning to surface, resulting in a further spate of bad press. In September 1990, Navarro had decided to switch the department's banking relationship from Florida National Bank to SunBank, just two months after being named a SunBank director. For SunBank, the change meant $130,000 a year in new fees (based on the depart-

*Attorney Bruce S. Rogow (in bow tie) looks on as his client
Luther Campbell addresses reporters (1990)*

Broward motorcycle deputies riding in formation (1990)

ment's $173 million budget and 3,000 employees), while Navarro was to receive annual director payments of at least $8,000.

When asked about the obvious conflict of interest, Navarro responded, "The board position allows me to see firsthand how the bank that handles Broward Sheriff's Office money operates. That's a benefit both to BSO employees and the taxpayers."[714] Left unsaid was the fact that in September 1985, Navarro had ordered the department to switch from SunBank to Florida National Bank (which had promptly named him a director) to punish the former for having backed George Brescher in the 1984 sheriff's race. In a particularly candid moment, SunBank chairman Daniel S. Goodrum told reporters, "We supported the fellow who ran against him. We have been attempting to get the business back over time."[715]

In October 1990, a headline in the Fort Lauderdale Sun-Sentinel declared, "Slew of Inquiries Test Navarro's Teflon Image," and the story that followed informed readers, "In recent weeks, the Sheriff's Office has been battered by allegations that include corruption, protection of drug dealers, questionable conduct by a top Navarro aide, gambling by deputies and suspect hiring practices."[716] When asked for a comment, the sheriff replied, "I take no offense to what they say. I could care less. I have been a target of a witch hunt. Now it is constant bad press."[717]

But it was not just reporters who were asking questions, for federal law enforcement officials also were wondering about Navarro's trustworthiness. In November 1990, it was revealed that the U.S. Attorney's Office was keeping the Sheriff's Office out of a corruption investigation at Port Everglades. In explaining why, one agent said, "The potential for compromising the integrity of the case is far too great. The exclusion is based on the Sheriff himself. It's not BSO. It's Nick."[718]

In June 1991, the Fort Lauderdale Sun-Sentinel reported that "a massive federal investigation is under way into allegations that the Broward Sheriff's Office is wracked by corruption—from deputies protecting drug dealers to case-fixing to Sheriff Nick Navarro handing out sweetheart contracts to his friends and political allies."[719] Four federal prosecutors were assigned to the matter, and subpoenas arriving at the Sheriff's Office demanded thousands of documents, including bank books, internal affairs reports, and personnel records. According to the instructions, all of this information was to be delivered to a federal grand jury in Fort Lauderdale.

During the following month, the public's attention briefly turned from the sheriff to one of his deputies. In 1982, Jeff Willets had joined the Tamarac Police Department, which in 1989 was absorbed by the BSO. While on patrol in 1985, Jeff had stopped a woman named Kathy Fede and given her a traffic

*Sheriff Nick Navarro displaying weapons confiscated during
a sting operation (1990)*

ticket. By 1986, the two had married. The pair bought a house in Tamarac and for a time appeared to be just another middle-class couple. But in July 1991, Kathy Willets was arrested for prostitution.

The story soon took several odd turns. According to attorney Ellis S. Rubin, Kathy had been a normal housewife with a job at a stock brokerage firm until the prescription drug Prozac had turned her into a nymphomaniac. As a result, Kathy began seeing other men. To meet them, she used a personals ad that read:

> Frosted Blond. Great tan, hot body, very sexual, turquoise eyes, romantic and sensual, seeking generous, affluent executive male, for day/evening interludes. Fun loving & hot. Enclose business card.[720]

Rubin also revealed that deputies had seized a notebook that contained a detailed list of Kathy's customers, which caused the press to go to court to get the names. Not surprisingly, a group of "John Does" opposed this motion, but Broward Circuit Judge John A. Frusciante ruled that the media was entitled to the information, a decision later upheld by the Florida Supreme Court.[721] In the meantime, Fort Lauderdale Vice Mayor Doug Danziger (who had been leading a campaign to close down the city's strip clubs) resigned when it was discovered that his name was on the list.

In February 1992, just before she appeared in a *Playboy* photo spread, Kathy agreed to plead guilty and perform 400 hours of community service. Jeff proved less lucky—charged with living off the earnings of a prostitute, he was given 364 days in jail. After serving their sentences, the couple moved to Las Vegas, where Kathy, by now calling herself "America's Favorite Nymphomaniac," commanded $1,500-an-hour as a professional escort.

As the Willets saga began to slip off the front pages, the television show *60 Minutes* called and asked Navarro if he would be willing to appear on the program. Navarro immediately said "yes" and, obliging as always, led a film crew on a drug raid. But when the segment aired in April 1992, the portrait that emerged was decidedly negative (in stark contrast to the accolades that had been heaped on Navarro by both Rivera and the producers of *COPS*). According to a review in the *Fort Lauderdale Sun-Sentinel*:

> Broward Sheriff Nick Navarro played to his biggest audience yet on Sunday night, being the subject of a *60 Minutes* story that painted him as a media-hungry politician enmeshed in controversy.
>
> The story, by reporter Steve Kroft, … detailed nearly two years' worth of negative newspaper stories that began with the arrest of two members of the rap group 2 Live Crew in summer 1990. The story touched on cronyism within Navarro's department, including his purchase of a

*Attorney Ellis S. Rubin (standing) with his clients
Jeff and Kathy Willets (1991)*

used car from car dealer Jim Moran, a friend and campaign supporter; the Sheriff's Office making crack cocaine for drug stings; Navarro's advisory council, businessmen who pay $5,000 each to socialize and conduct charity fund-raisers with Navarro; [and] the ongoing federal investigation into alleged corruption within the Sheriff's Office.[722]

When asked about the show, Navarro said "I thought it was a good story" but added, "I think there were a few things I told him that were omitted."[723]

As Kroft had pointed out, the Sheriff's Office under Navarro had become a hotbed of sweetheart contracts. More than $1.5 million in consulting and legal work had been doled out to friends and political supporters without competitive bids. Used cars were purchased at new car prices. Office space was rented from a major campaign donor for $761,000, even though other developers insisted they could provide equivalent quarters for less money. (Navarro answered them by saying that his employees were "hard-working guys"[724] who deserved expensive offices.)

Favored contractors were not the only ones sharing in the sheriff's largesse. In June 1991, for example, the *Fort Lauderdale Sun-Sentinel* described "the latest caper at Club Nick," which consisted of "190 management employees ... getting from $150 to $500 a year for expenses like new clothing,"[725] resulting in a total outlay of $52,000. In defending the program, the sheriff claimed it was a way to encourage employees to seek positions in upper management. When asked what he planned to do with his allowance, BSO finance director Michael Woodruff replied, "I'll probably spend it on clothes for me and my wife."[726]

The press soon had another boondoggle to write about—a four-day conference on narcotics control that Navarro had decided to hold aboard the EMERALD SEAS, a cruise ship whose itinerary included stops in the Bahamas and at a private island. Balking at the cost and questioning the need for a meeting at sea, most of the county's police chiefs refused to allow their officers to attend. "You know and I know what cruises are for—to have fun. I'm sure the participants would learn a great deal more here, in a classroom,"[727] said Lighthouse Point Police Chief Paul Mannino, president of the Broward Police Chiefs Association. "With the budget crunch we've got, we should be trying to save money everywhere we can, not taking cruises at taxpayer expense."[728] Navarro responded by accusing his critics of professional jealousy and small-mindedness and claimed that by spending time in the Bahamas, registrants would gain a better understanding of the role that country was playing in Florida's drug trade.

In addition to financial irregularities, the department was engaged in a number of other activities of dubious legality, including the operation of its own crack cocaine lab (John Pennie, the lab's director, said concocting the drug

The EMERALD SEAS docked in the Bahamas (c. 1985)

was a lot like "making fudge"[729]). In January 1992, the Fourth District Court of Appeal ordered the lab shut down.[730] In an opinion laced with sarcasm, Judge Mark E. Polen wrote:

> We find that the Sheriff of Broward County acted illegally in manufacturing "crack" for use in the reverse sting operation which led to the arrest of the appellant. Even more disturbing is the fact that some of the "crack," which is made in batches of 1200 or more rocks, escapes into the community where the reverse sting operations are conducted. The police simply cannot account for all of the rocks which are made for the purpose of the reverse stings.
>
> Such police conduct cannot be condoned and rises to the level of a violation of the constitutional principles of due process of law.[731]

Subsequently, the Florida Supreme Court decided that the lab constituted such gross governmental misconduct that the only appropriate remedy was to throw out the convictions of all those who had been arrested because of its activities.[732] Navarro called this decision "crap."[733]

As it turned out, making crack was only one of the ways in which the Sheriff's Office was adding to the county's crime rate. In an attempt to gather evidence against a gang of car thieves, for example, deputies allowed the suspects (who were armed) to repeatedly steal vehicles.

The BSO crime lab (c. 1990)

Likewise, Navarro targeted the gay and lesbian community, and in May 1991 used drugs as a pretext for simultaneous raids on two bars (Club 21 in Hallandale and the Copa Cabaret in Fort Lauderdale). After searching, video-taping, and harshly questioning 350 patrons, the 100 deputies and fifteen state alcohol and tobacco agents made a total of five arrests. Through a spokesman, the sheriff said that the officers had acted with appropriate respect, a claim that was scoffed at by the Broward chapters of the American Civil Liberties Union and the National Organization for Women.

In a belated attempt to make peace, Navarro in July 1992 named Captain Ron Cacciatore to be his special liaison to the gay and lesbian community (critics pointed out that Cacciatore was an odd choice for the post, inasmuch as he was under federal investigation for financial improprieties). In November 1993, the department (under Navarro's successor) agreed to make a $10,000 dona-tion to Center One, an AIDS service organization, as a further means of apol-ogizing. By this time, all of the records from the raids had been destroyed. Asked why they had not been preserved, BSO attorney Charles T. Whitelock said, "we have no idea."734

When the mood struck him, Navarro could even turn on the press (despite all it had done to make him famous). In November 1988, the *Broward Review*, a legal daily, had printed an article on its front page headlined "Navarro Failed to Act on Corruption Warnings." When the story appeared, Navarro reacted by pulling the department's $35,000-a-year advertising account with that paper.

The newspaper responded by filing a federal lawsuit, claiming that its First Amendment rights were being violated, but Navarro insisted that the timing of his decision to end the parties' 20-year relationship was pure coincidence. Rejecting this contention, in December 1989 U.S. District Judge James W. Kehoe found that the lawman had engaged in a clear case of retaliation and awarded the paper $23,000 in damages. Refusing to accept this decision, Navarro turned to the U.S. Court of Appeals for the Eleventh Circuit, which in August 1991 refused to hear the case.[735] He then went to the U.S. Supreme Court, which in March 1992 declined to become involved.[736]

By now, the paper's damages (it had retained the noted—and very expensive—First Amendment lawyer Floyd Abrams) had risen to $372,000 (according to Abrams, only $50,000 would have been due if the case had settled prior to trial). The Sheriff's Office tendered this bill to its insurance company, but it went bankrupt after paying $277,000. Navarro then asked the county commission to foot the rest of the tab but it refused and threatened to go after him personally for the money. In June 1993, however, it abandoned the idea after its attorneys concluded that such a lawsuit was unlikely to succeed. Commented Navarro, "I am very grateful to the County Commission for this wonderful decision, but they didn't have a leg to stand on."[737]

The beginning of the end for Navarro came in September 1992, when the two-term sheriff was defeated by Jim Howard in the Republican primary by a count of 19,584 votes to 17,201 votes (a margin of 53%–47%). Howard, the one-time Crime Stoppers supervisor who had done so poorly against Navarro four years earlier, had been given no chance, raising a mere $10,000 to Navarro's $500,000 and running his campaign out of a hangar at the Pompano Air Park (where he was working as a helicopter pilot). But as the results came in, it was clear that the public had had enough off the incumbent sheriff and wanted to see him go. In his concession speech, Navarro said, "Tonight we happened to have lost an election, but let me tell you what we have gained: We have gained love. We have gained friends. Sure, we have lost an election, but I feel like a winner and I love Broward County very much ... [and] I am still sheriff of this county until January of next year."[738]

Within hours, however, Navarro began looking for scapegoats and decided that his loss had been caused by a hostile media ("You guys did it,"[739] he told

First Amendment lawyer Floyd Abrams (1986)

Satellite image showing Hurricane Andrew crossing
the Florida peninsula (1992)

reporters) and low voter turnout (just 17% of the county's Republicans had gone to the polls). While the former had been expected, the latter had come as a last-minute surprise. Just before the primary, South Florida had been pummeled by Hurricane Andrew, a monster weather system that had ravaged southern Dade County. Although damage had been light in Broward County, the storm made campaigning difficult and media coverage non-existent.

In an editorial, the *Fort Lauderdale Sun-Sentinel* rejected Navarro's explanations and said the sheriff was solely to blame for his defeat:

> It wasn't the "media" that brought Navarro down, as he claims. And it wasn't voter confusion or apathy or anti-incumbent fever or new voting precincts or even the distraction of Hurricane Andrew, although they certainly were factors in every race on the ballot. It wasn't even victorious GOP opponent Jim Howard or Republican primary voters.... To find [the cause], Navarro need only look in the mirror.[740]

Unwilling to give up, Navarro announced that he was considering running in the general election as a write-in candidate, even though the deadline for doing so had long since passed. "We are looking at the statutes,"[741] Navarro explained.

"I'm tending to go [the write-in] route, if it can be done. If I decide to, it has to be done quickly. Time is of the essence. I have calls from community leaders saying, 'We want you to do it.' "[742]

In the meantime, a sense of disbelief, coupled with apprehension, settled over the department. Deputy Kevin Maccagli noted that "the general consensus ... was shock," while Sergeant Brett Sagenkahn said, "Some people are truly saddened. Some are very surprised. Some are just wondering what our future holds. We pretty much felt it would be a race between Cochran and Navarro."[743] And indeed, Ronald A. "Ron" Cochran, a former Fort Lauderdale police chief, had triumphed in the Democrat primary, easily beating his five challengers.

Whether Cochran would be facing just Howard, or both Howard and Navarro, became even more uncertain when Navarro announced that he was dropping his write-in bid and had hired Jacksonville lawyer Richard G. Rumrell to force the county to hold a new primary on Thursday, October 1st. According to Navarro's wife Sharron, such a step needed to be taken because "we've just been bombarded with calls from people who said they didn't know there was an election."[744]

When asked about a possible do-over, Howard responded, "If he wants to embarrass himself twice, I don't have any problem with that."[745] Cochran was equally blunt, saying, "It's patently ridiculous. He's not a very gracious loser."[746] Twenty-four hours later, the Broward County Canvassing Board certified the election results. Asked if this decision cleared the way for Navarro to go to court, the board's chairwoman, Circuit Judge Kathleen A. Kearney, replied, "Oh yes. That's where it's going."[747]

Much to everyone's surprise, however, four days later Navarro threw in the towel and conceded during a press conference in his Oakland Park campaign headquarters. Although Rumrell had insisted he could win a court challenge based on public confusion, Navarro told reporters, "This is it. The voters have spoken. Why bring it back again? Sharron and I realize that there is life after all of this."[748]

With Navarro out of the way, Cochran and Howard now began to square off. Ironically, Cochran had worked on Howard's 1988 campaign, ringing doorbells and handing out flyers, a fact Howard sought to use against Cochran. "I'm going to hold him to it," Howard said. "Why not? He went out there and sweated like all of us."[749] When asked about his previous endorsement, Cochran replied, "He is basically a good guy. I have no axes to grind."[750]

In early October, Howard announced that if he was elected, he would keep Ed Werder, Navarro's chief of staff, as his second in command, and promised that there would be no mass firings. "I want to make sure everybody will feel comfortable during the transition."[751] Asked about his plans, Cochran replied, "I have not selected anybody. That would be presumptuous. I have not promised anyone a job."[752]

In the meantime, Navarro continued to provide regular fodder for the press:

- The U.S. Attorney's Office announced that, notwithstanding the primary results, it planned to continue its corruption investigation. (In November 1995, when it finally closed the case without bringing any charges, it issued a letter saying, "This change in status is not intended to exonerate Mr. Navarro and reflects only that the current evidence would not support a reasonable likelihood of conviction at trial."753)
- The Youth and Victim Witness Program Inc., a non-profit organization Navarro had set up (and planned to keep running after he left office) was found to be engaged in massive fraud. When he had first unveiled the idea, Navarro had said that the group was going to build gyms in three neglected neighborhoods to give kids a place to go, using a combination of public funds (which would come from the pay phones at the county jail) and private donations. Now, however, it seemed that Navarro was using the organization to give jobs to his friends and steer lucrative contracts to his political supporters (including a contractor named Pasquale Luca, who had been paid $182,500 but had done no work). Making matters worse, two of the facilities (in Carver Ranches and Fort Lauderdale) had yet to break ground, while the third (in Lauderhill) was riddled with construction defects. (In December 1992, the Boys and Girls Club of Broward County agreed to take over the troubled program.)
- The December 1991 decision shifting the department's travel contract from Universal/Carlson Travel Network (with which the Sheriff's Office had been doing business for ten years) to Tivoli Travel Service was discovered to have been made after Tivoli promised to rebate part of its commissions to Navarro's youth program. While Universal/Carlson and the other companies that had bid on the contract also had been prepared to give up part of their fees (with some offering to pay more than Tivoli), they had insisted on making their contributions to the Sheriff's Office.
- In October 1992, Navarro asked companies to submit proposals to provide inmate health care, even though the current contract with Prison Health Services Inc. was not set to expire until September 1993. Following an acrimonious court hearing, Circuit Judge J. Leonard Fleet ruled that Navarro had no authority to award a new contract.
- Despite being a lame duck, in December 1992 Navarro signed a $900,000 contract with a New Jersey businessman named Theodore M. Sabarese. Under the agreement, Digital Products Corporation would supply the Sheriff's Office with 100 electronic prisoner bracelets and monitor them for three years, while Navarro would receive $2,000 a month for mar-

keting services. (When the first bill arrived, the department refused to pay it and sent back the unused bracelets, causing Digital Products to file a lawsuit. The case was settled in June 1995 for $84,000.)

With Navarro still dominating the headlines, it was easy to forget about the campaign between Cochran and Howard. And in truth, it was not much of a contest. On Election Day, the low-key Cochran easily beat Howard, 336,815 votes to 158,146 votes (a margin of 68%–32%), as the public voted along strict party lines. At a downtown victory celebration, Cochran told 400 cheering supporters, "You did this. You got us to this position. What you tell me is you very definitely want to see things change in the way we operate the Broward Sheriff's Office."[754] A bitter Howard accused Cochran of stealing the election. Noting that Cochran had been a lifelong Republican but had re-registered as a Democrat in August 1991, Howard said, "He's a Republican. He didn't have the guts to run as one."[755]

As he prepared to step down, Navarro told listeners that he and Sharron were happy. "We have each other. We're both healthy. We have a comfortable income, even without my new business."[756] Navarro then added, "My next title won't be mayor or governor. It'll be millionaire,"[757] explaining that he had decided to start a security consulting firm called Navarro Group Ltd. Inc. When asked what the company would do, he replied, "Whatever makes money, so long as it's legal. No more politics."[758]

After leaving office, Navarro fell out of public view. However, in May 1999, he resurfaced when newspapers reported that he had won $1 million in a weekend slot machine tournament at the MGM Grand Hotel in Las Vegas. When asked about his good fortune, he told the press, "They almost needed to revive me. The only time I've ever seen that kind of money is when we used to grab the dope dealers. I never thought that kind of money would be mine."[759]

Eighteen months later, Navarro again was in the news when he was sued in federal court for including the lyrics of four *2 Live Crew* songs (including "Me So Horny") in *The Cuban Cop*, his 1998 autobiography. Attorneys for the record label Lil' Joe accused Navarro of copyright infringement, insisting he had reprinted the words to boost his sales. Although the former sheriff denied he had done anything wrong and invoked the "fair use" defense, in November 2001 he settled the case.

CHAPTER 9

THE COCHRAN-MCCAMPBELL
YEARS (1993–98)

After eight tumultuous years of the arrogant, brash, and press-hungry Nick Navarro, the people of Broward County were ready for a change. What they now wanted was a quiet, seasoned, and unassuming sheriff, and in Ron Cochran they found exactly what they were looking for. A career law enforcement officer, Cochran had earned a reputation as a self-effacing leader who got things done. His critics, however, complained that he was too low key, called him an "Ivory Tower Cop"[760] for his bookish ways, and took delight in noting that when he was injured in the line of duty in 1979, it was because he had absent-mindedly walked into a door. Upon being named Fort Lauderdale Police Department chief in 1983, the *Miami Herald* described him as "a dreamer, a thinker, not a quick-draw Dick Tracy."[761]

Unruffled by these complaints (which he viewed as something of a compliment), the cerebral Cochran set out to restore the community's faith in the Sheriff's Office by depoliticizing the agency, ending its many questionable practices, and getting deputies to go out and meet the citizens who were paying their salaries. But for all the good he accomplished, in the end he would leave the department in shambles and, in the process, pave the way for even bigger scandals.

Sheriff Ronald A. Cochran (1993–97)

Ronald Alva Cochran was born on September 23, 1936, in Lancaster, Pennsylvania, and grew up in the nearby company town of Holtwood, a small enclave in the Appalachian foothills. At the urging of his father, who wanted him to become a dentist, he enrolled in Pennsylvania State University but dropped out after his freshman year to join the U.S. Navy. When his two-year tour ended in 1957, he moved to Florida and got a job as a ticket agent for Eastern Air Lines. In April 1958, he switched careers and became a Fort Lauderdale cop.

Ronald A. "Ron" Cochran, sheriff of Broward County (1993–97)

Over the next twenty-five years, Cochran rose steadily through the ranks, logging time in the detective division, marine patrol, and traffic enforcement unit. Along the way, he earned an A.S. from Broward Community College (1969) and a B.A. in public administration from Biscayne College (1979). In April 1983, he was named chief, and for the next four years he worked to soften the department's brutal image by allowing officers to grow beards and mustaches, ordering them to get out of their patrol cars and meet the public face-to-face, prohibiting them from working off-duty at strip clubs or bars featuring wet T-shirt contests, and requiring them to take sensitivity training classes (initiatives referred to as "community policing"[762]). An avid bike rider, in September 1984 he started a department bicycle unit as a practical, low-cost way to patrol downtown.

When he resigned from the Fort Lauderdale Police Department in May 1987, Cochran told reporters that having recently turned fifty, and with a $64,000-a-year pension, he was looking forward to doing something different with his life and planned to start by bicycling through Ireland with his wife Carol. After that, he joked, he might become a saloonkeeper. "It would just be a lot of fun to open a little Irish bar along the [New River], run a water taxi from a dock in back, put a bunch of tables on the sidewalk and have good friends coming in."[763] When questioned about his interest in being sheriff, he replied, "People have asked me if I'm running for sheriff, and some have asked me and others have pleaded with me. My response is that I've been in law enforcement for nearly 30 years and if I'm going to stay in, I'm going to stay with the finest department in Florida, and that's where I'm at right now."[764]

After taking two years off, Cochran returned to police work in June 1989 when he was named chief of the Broward Schools' special investigative unit (a position that had attracted fifteen other candidates). Asked why he wanted the post, Cochran said, "It's where I live, and it looks like an interesting job."[765] And while he promised to shake things up (telling reporters that as "a person who loves change, you can count on it"[766]), he did so in his usual modest way. "I'm going in humbled. The parallels to law enforcement are quite different. I have a lot to learn about the school system and what the needs are or the problems are, if there are any."[767]

When he finally decided to run for sheriff in August 1991, Cochran admitted, "I feel at this point a little out of my element. But I'm meeting a lot of nice people and I hope at some point there's some fun connected with it."[768] A year later, the *Fort Lauderdale Sun-Sentinel* endorsed him in an editorial in which it was noted:

> In his own quiet way, Ron Cochran exudes the kind of competence, intelligence, professionalism and leadership that every good sheriff should provide. He is the strongest candidate to challenge the incumbent Broward County sheriff in November, and deserves enthusiastic support in the Sept. 1 Democratic primary election.
>
> Cochran, who retired as Fort Lauderdale police chief in 1987, is a good police officer and a good law enforcement administrator ... but a lousy politician. His professorial speeches can be dreary. He's not comfortable hustling for campaign donations or backslapping condo commandos to win votes.
>
> Cochran has been called a "thinking person's cop," and indeed he is. A man of ideas, and ideals, he is the personification of integrity. He vows not to solicit or accept contributions from BSO employees or their family members, and to limit all contributions to $250 apiece....
>
> His top priority, if elected, is to return professional law enforcement management and leadership to the office of sheriff. He wants to institute fiscal restraint and accountability, by requiring standard business management practices such as competitive bidding instead of sweetheart deals for favored friends.

He supports setting up uniform standards for personnel decisions and development of a career service system, instead of promotions going to cronies and political supporters.

He vows to reduce the influence of politics on the BSO and cut back spending on overpriced cars, offices and overdone personal public relations efforts. He favors improved cooperation with municipal police departments, not fighting over turf.[769]

At his swearing-in ceremony on Tuesday, January 5, 1993, Cochran wasted no time making it clear that the Navarro era was over, saying that he intended to preside over a "BSO without an 'E' on the end. It was becoming the Biggest Show On Earth."[770] Cochran also advised the audience "not to look for the Broward Sheriff's Office on television, because it will be a smaller, less-conspicuous organization in the future."[771] And then, in a direct jab at his predecessor, he said, "I [have] made a promise never to appear on the Geraldo show."[772]

Despite these words, the new sheriff found himself inundated by reporters who wanted to know why, just before taking office, he had fired seventy employees, including top-level managers, rank-and-file deputies, and long-serving secretaries. Although he had indicated during the campaign that he would avoid mass layoffs, Cochran replied that the changes were necessary to make the agency efficient (Charles Whitelock, his attorney, put matters more bluntly, calling the department "bloated beyond belief"[773]). Claiming to have taken no pleasure in the firings, Cochran insisted that the cuts had been made "without political consideration [and] totally without vindictiveness."[774] Instead, they were simply the only way to quickly roll back the excesses of the previous administration. "You cannot create a lesser thing and not have lesser people involved in that organization,"[775] he explained, undoubtedly meaning to use the words "smaller" and "fewer."

Reaction to the firings proved swift. Nick Navarro called them a "massacre,"[776] while attorney Bruce Rogow, a one-time Cochran supporter, said, "I thought I was out of this sue-the-sheriff business, but it looks to me like this one is starting up just like the old sheriff. It looks like Cochran is destroying family values here. He is wiping out entire families. Not an ounce of grace went into this."[777] Those fired vowed to go to court to get their jobs backs. "He's definitely violated our civil rights. He's simply a Nazi,"[778] Fred Bellis, a former community involvement unit member, told reporters. Fort Lauderdale lawyer Wilton L. Strickland agreed, saying, "I do believe these people were denied procedural due process in their discharges. Most of these people were given no reason at all."[779] Asked about his pink slip, Lieutenant Robert Deak replied, "Never in my wildest dreams did I think I would be fired. After 18 years, I've done everything in this department you can do."[780] In a remarkable bit of understatement, the new sheriff observed, "We're going to be in a period of confusion and some disorder for quite a while until it all smooths out."[781]

Nor were matters helped by the impending opening of the department's new headquarters. Having long ago outgrown its ramshackle building in south Fort Lauderdale, the agency was renting temporary space at a dozen different locations scattered throughout the county at a cost of nearly $600,000 a year. To remedy this situation, in 1986 voters had approved a $32 million bond offering to build a new facility, which was expected to be ready by 1991. But the project had proved troubled from the start, and as design changes, cost overruns, and construction snags piled up the schedule fell farther and farther behind while the price tag ballooned to $66 million. As a result, Navarro's plans to include a hurricane-proof emergency command center, helicopter landing pad, and gun range were scrapped, although his palatial office (which critics regularly complained about) remained untouched.

Finally, in March 1993, the building was deemed ready despite a host of unresolved problems that ranged from the comical (no ovens in the cafeteria) to the inconvenient (parking spaces for only half the occupants) to the dangerous (a non-working 911 system). In addition, the location—on Northwest 27th Avenue and Broward Boulevard—presented its own challenges. The surrounding area, consisting primarily of pawn shops, strip clubs, and warehouses, was bleak and depressing. Moreover, the site sat just beyond Fort Lauderdale's western border, making it technically illegal because a state law required the sheriff's office to be located within the county seat.[782] To get around this problem, the county commission quietly voted to change the county seat from Fort Lauderdale to all of Broward County (a decision that remains little-advertised to this day). Asked about the wisdom of doing so, Commissioner Nicki E. Grossman replied, "There is some jealousy about Fort Lauderdale being the county seat. This is an opportunity to let all the county share that designation."[783]

Nevertheless, most employees applauded their new home, and an article in the *Fort Lauderdale Sun-Sentinel* noted that even with all of the cost cutting, "The building still has plenty of amenities, [including] private bathrooms with showers for first-year Sheriff Ron Cochran and two top aides; two video studios; aerobics and combat training rooms, done in glass block; a five-story lobby and atrium done in dark brown marble, with a monument to slain police officers; [and a] press briefing room [which Cochran has decided to turn] into a community meeting room, available for civic groups to use."[784]

It would take more than three months to get all of the employees and their belongings into the building. When he found out how much professional movers wanted for the job, Cochran decided to use inmates from the jail, sav-

One of the temporary offices rented by BSO (1983)

Artist rendering of the proposed BSO headquarters (c. 1985)

Nicki E. Grossman, commissioner of Broward County (1983–92)

ing the county $100,000 while giving prisoners more opportunities to leave their cells and earn money.

Money became a particularly sore issue for Cochran in April 1993 when he unveiled his first budget. Although he had run against his predecessor's financial excesses, Cochran found himself asking for $199.6 million, a $1.2 million increase over Navarro's final budget of $198.4 million. When several county commissioners balked, Cochran defended himself by saying, "After adding in inflation and automatic pay increases, last year's budget would come in at $203 million this year. We're holding the line on the budget. My orders were a no-growth budget."[785]

And, in fact, the sheriff was trying to hold the line. Rather than spend $40,000 to print new business cards, for example, he suggested that employees "just draw a line through"[786] Navarro's name. When he discovered that the department was paying $13,000 for a woman to clip articles about the Sheriff's Office from local newspapers (in addition to its three full-time public information officers), he cancelled the service. A songwriter, who had collected $75,000 for writing public service lyrics (including one ditty that included the lines, "Swimming is lots of fun. Swimming is lots of fun. Sing it again!"[787]) was shown the door. But in some instances, it was too late to do anything. New manuals summarizing state law had been purchased for $70,000 from a company headed by a BSO employee, even though the previous supplier had offered to do the job for $19,000. Adding insult to injury, the text now filled two volumes, making it less user-friendly than the previous one-volume format.

These problems, however, were just the tip of the iceberg. During an audit of the department's books, it was discovered that $2 million in cash had been deposited in secret accounts; $6.4 million had been shifted from the jail to other programs without the required approval of the county commission; uncashed checks (including one for $168,000) had been stuffed into manila file folders and promptly forgotten; $500,000 had been funneled to the Community Involvement Program, which generally was regarded as nothing more than a way for Navarro to boost his image; and nearly $1.3 million was sitting in a cash bond account even though the money belonged to the county and various municipalities.

The auditors also found other irregularities. For almost two years, the department had been paying dockage fees (amounting to more than $17,000) for an 81-foot wooden sailboat. The vessel had been seized by the U.S. Customs Service in 1990 and traded to the Sheriff's Office in 1991 for $31,000 in new gym equipment (although the Customs Service belatedly insisted that the boat had been a donation and the gym equipment merely a loan). While being piloted from Port Canaveral to Port Everglades, the boat had broken down, resulting in $60,000 in towing and repair charges. Upon learning these details, Cochran ordered the boat sold and later fired the department's accounting firm.

Cochran also worked to clean up other inherited messes. He disbanded the organized crime division (which had been the apple of Navarro's eye and had played such a key role during the first season of the television show *COPS*), transferring its eighty-three employees to other units. (Asked about this decision, spokesman Ott Cefkin replied, "The problem is not [the] Mafia going around sticking people up. The neighborhoods are getting it. There are people in the street committing burglaries. We're putting resources where they are needed."[788]) Cochran also had to deal with the fallout from the closing of the department's crack lab and the Club 21-Copa Cabaret raids. And he put an end to the use of reverse sting operations in the African-American community.

At the same time, Cochran projected a personal image that was far different from that of his flamboyant predecessor. Soft-spoken, shy, and modest al-

Newly-arrived BSO boot campers taking mattresses to their bunks (2000)

most to a fault, Cochran lived up to his billing as an idea man who hated politics and was not comfortable at either glad-handing or deal-making.

One of the major initiatives that Cochran introduced as sheriff was community policing, a carry-over from his days as Fort Lauderdale's police chief. Believing that society had to get "off the idea that you can solve all of the world's problems by tossing people in jail,"[789] Cochran pushed for prevention over incarceration, preached rehabilitation over punishment, and pleaded with deputies to become more involved in their communities and try new ways to solve old problems. As part of this effort, the sheriff encouraged the creation of citizen neighborhood patrols, sought to have drug users sent to treatment programs rather than jail, established a multi-million dollar boot camp in southwest Broward to help juvenile offenders turn their lives around, and changed the name of the Department of Detention to the Department of Corrections and Rehabilitation (a decision that resulted in new badges and new titles for the agency's 900 detention deputies).

Many of the department's officers found these changes quite unsettling and wondered about the sheriff's priorities. Outsiders expressed similar doubts and there were accusations that the county's top lawman was soft on crime. Although acknowledging that some of his deputies "just want to get into gun battles rather than get out of the car and ask people what the problem is and try to solve it," Cochran insisted that with time the department would "become more than a law-enforcement agency that locks people up and throws away the key."[790] Nevertheless, in May 1994 he was forced to start a newsletter called *Rumor Central* to address the department's sagging morale. Still, aides maintained that Cochran was on the right path. "We're talking about a totally different type of philosophy,"[791] Ott Cefkin said. "We're not in the business of kicking ass and taking names anymore. Some deputies don't like that. Ron calls them warriors. We're not going to stop arresting people but we're trying to make things better, work on crime prevention. Maybe some of these warriors should go elsewhere."[792]

Given his shyness and disdain for politics (which, depending on the circumstances, could come across as aloofness, indifference, or haughtiness), it is not surprising that Cochran often found himself mired in difficult situations. In late 1993, for example, the City of Lauderhill, which in 1981 had disbanded its police department and hired the Sheriff's Office (thereby becoming a contract city), began studying the idea of restarting its police force. While this plan was developed largely as a negotiating ploy designed to wangle certain concessions out of the department in the upcoming negotiations over a new contract, Cochran refused to play ball with the city's leaders. As a result, in April 1994 Mayor Ilene M. Lieberman announced that she had hired Michael S. Scott, a special assistant to St. Louis's police chief, to be the city's new police chief (the other finalist had been Robert S. Warshaw, the police chief of Statesville, North Carolina). Ironically, Scott was an ardent supporter of community policing.

The loss of the Lauderhill contract, coupled with the break-up of the organized crime division and several other units, led Cochran's critics to claim that, in addition to being soft on crime, he was intent on dismantling the department. Although his spokesman issued a press release refuting the charge, the truth was that Cochran did not harbor expansionist thoughts and, as a result, ended up adding no new contract cities during his tenure.

One thing that Cochran did want to do was have city police officers handle more of the workload. Thus, in October 1993, he procured an opinion from Attorney General Bob Butterworth stating that he could "delegate the authority to execute and serve civil and criminal process of the courts to municipal police officers by appointing these officers as special deputies to serve process."[793]

A short time later, a local bill was introduced in the Florida Legislature giving the department's 800 deputies the job security they had been seeking since the days of Sheriff Allen Michell. Cochran came out in favor of the plan, saying that it would prevent him and future sheriffs "from laying people off for political reasons"[794] and later added, "I think employees of this agency deserve

Lauderhill Mayor Ilene M. Lieberman (with Sheriff Nick Navarro)
dedicating a BSO youth clubhouse (1991)

the rights and protections that municipal agencies have."[795] With this backing the proposal passed easily, making Broward the first county in the state with a unionized sheriff's office.

As the 1996 general election neared, Cochran largely had accomplished his goal of bringing the department out of Nick Navarro's shadow. But whether this would be enough to earn him a second term was unclear, particularly given his inability to forcefully communicate his vision and his still-awkward campaign style. And, of course, he first would have to win the Democratic primary.

The most serious challenger was retired Long Island police commander Gary Steinberg, who had run against Cochran in 1992 and come in second in that year's primary. Joining him was former Drug Enforcement Agency supervisor Lionel G. Stewart and Plantation criminal defense attorney (and one-time county judge) Lawrence C. "Chris" Roberts.

With few substantive differences among them, Roberts, Steinberg, and Stewart spent most of their time hammering away at Cochran, accusing him of weak leadership, calling him soft on crime, and questioning his emphasis on community policing over traditional law enforcement techniques.

As usual, Cochran took the complaints in stride. When asked what he had done right during his first term, he replied, "Just about everything. I say that humbly, but sincerely."[796] When questioned about his philosophy, he said, "Have we properly conveyed what community policing is? I think we have, and yet I would not disagree that we could have worked harder at that.... It's something evolutionary. It takes some time for people to understand."[797] In speaking about his accomplishments, he noted, "Crime is down across the board. If you look at the record, it's better enforcement than we've had in a long, long time—more sensible and well-directed arrests. The jail is overflowing."[798] Reflecting on his campaign style, he observed, "I'm as political as I need to be, and I'm as high-profile as I need to be."[799] And when a reporter wondered why voters should re-elect him, he responded, "I have made a tremendous degree of reform in the way the Broward Sheriff's Office is run in every regard."[800]

In the meantime, the press was busy pointing out various problems with the campaigns of his challengers. Roberts had lost his seat on the county court in 1981 because of repeated drunk driving incidents (including one in which he pulled a gun on another motorist), but said that now he was sober and had a great desire to be sheriff. When asked about his lack of a police background, he dismissed this hole in his resume by pointing to his experience as a probation officer, prosecutor, and judge. These issues soon became moot, however, when Roberts's penchant for dirty tricks caused his campaign manager to quit, the State Attorney's Office to publicly rebuke him, and The Florida Bar to issue a reprimand.

Steinberg, who said he was not courting the Jewish vote even as he included a Star of David on some of his campaign literature, regularly mentioned his twenty-two years in law enforcement. Calling himself the "Crime Crusher," he claimed to be a highly-decorated anti-terrorist specialist who had commanded 1,500 officers while working for the Nassau County Police Department. But when his former colleagues were contacted to verify his exploits, none could. Confronted by a reporter, Steinberg said there are "things I can't talk about, undercover things. All this was confidential."[801] In fact, Steinberg had spent his entire career in Freeport, New York, a small suburban town with just 90,000 residents, primarily working in a K-9 unit.

The strangest candidate by far was Stewart, an African-American who convinced Jane Carroll, the Supervisor of Elections, to list him on the ballot as "Dark Horse" even though doing so violated state law. Stewart had entered the race late and insisted that the nickname referred to his electoral chances rather than to his race. Nevertheless, he heavily courted the county's black community.

In addition to their individual weaknesses, the three challengers shared two common problems: a lack of money and a lack of endorsements. While Cochran had raised $161,000 and won the backing of the Broward County Council of Professional Fire Fighters, the Broward County Police Benevolent Association, and the League of Hispanic Voters, Roberts ($90,000), Steinberg ($38,000), and Stewart ($18,000) were operating with far less funding and no official support. And it came as little surprise when both the *Fort Lauderdale Sun-Sentinel* and the *Miami Herald* came out for Cochran. In particular, the *Sun-Sentinel* pointed to Cochran's achievements, which it summarized as follows:

> Develop[ing] various programs targeted at turning young people away from a life of crime, including a "boot camp" called Operation Boot Strap.
>
> Work[ing] to hire and promote deputies based on professional credentials and performance, not cronyism or patronage.
>
> Deputiz[ing] city police officers to give them countywide powers to make arrests and fight crime.
>
> Developing community crime-fighting partnerships with businesses, religious groups and civic organizations.[802]

As voters went to the polls on primary day, most observers expected the crowded Democratic field to produce a run-off. But in a remarkable repeat of 1992, Cochran again came in first with 59% (41,980 votes), followed by Steinberg with 16% (11,512 votes). Stewart polled just 14% (9,752 votes), while Roberts finished last with 11% (7,863 votes). As he celebrated with 200 supporters at his headquarters in Lauderdale Lakes, Cochran claimed not to be surprised by the outcome. "I was pretty confident," he said, and then added, "I think what I've heard tonight is an endorsement of what I've been doing. My faith is reinforced."[803]

Asked for a comment, Roberts replied, "I'm surprised, and we're a little disappointed that the voter turnout wasn't higher. The [Democratic] machine carried Cochran in."[804] Jack Curtiss, Stewart's campaign manager, said that he had pinned his hopes on a large African-American turnout, but "[i]t didn't materialize."[805] As for Steinberg, he told reporters that he was looking forward to stopping Cochran in November. "I'm a lifelong Democrat, but I'm supporting Chief Wagner. It's not a question of the party. It's a question of the man."[806]

In voting for Kenneth R. Wagner over Frank Hill, the Republicans had chosen a man with a superb law enforcement resume but shaky political credentials. A native of Louisiana, Wagner had earned a bachelor's degree in law

enforcement from Southeastern Louisiana University and a master's degree in
criminal justice from Northeast Louisiana University and for a time had been
an assistant professor of criminal justice. After retiring from the Louisiana state
police as a troop commander, he had joined the Hallandale police department
in 1985 as assistant chief and been named chief in 1991.

Despite being a Democrat, Wagner had switched parties just before entering the Republican primary, where he easily beat BSO deputy Frank Hill, 17,704
votes to 8,523 votes (a margin of 68%–32%). With Wagner outspending him
3-to-1, Hill had sought to portray himself as the tougher candidate, advocat-
ing chain gangs for habitual offenders, calling for a countywide teen curfew,
and claiming that Cochran's real reason for wanting to be sheriff was so that
he could promote the agenda of his gay and lesbian supporters.

In many ways, the contest between Cochran, the Republican-turned-De-
mocrat, and Wagner, the Democrat-turned-Republican, was a repeat of the
Democratic primary, with Wagner taking aim at Cochran's community policing initiatives, accusing him of being soft on crime, and stressing the need
for personal responsibility rather than the social programs called for by the
sheriff. Once again, Cochran responded that his programs were working,
citing statistics showing that violent crime had fallen 23% and drug traf-
ficking arrests were up 82%. "Crime is down across the board,"[807] Cochran
emphasized repeatedly. "If you look at the record, its better enforcement
than we've had in a long, long time—more sensible and well-directed arrests."[808]

On Election Day, the public showed its support for Cochran's ideas 311,334
votes to 173,036 votes (a margin of 64%–36%). Calling the outcome a "convincing victory," Cochran said he hoped that "those people who have been trying to sabotage what we've been doing will get on board."[809] Wagner, on the other
hand, said that time was running out for Cochran. "I don't believe the general
public really heard what Mr. Cochran's philosophy was, so they didn't really
know what it is. Four more years of his philosophy and Broward County will be
ripe for a change."[810]

In fact, time *was* running out for Cochran, but for an entirely different reason. Shortly after being sworn in for his second term on Tuesday, January 7,
1997, Cochran, a three-pack-a-day smoker, began to experience headaches,
backaches, and flu-like symptoms, and in February doctors at Hollywood Memorial Regional Hospital removed a walnut-sized tumor from the right side of
his brain while discovering a spot on his lung, which turned out to be cancerous.

As Cochran recuperated at home, Henry L. Templeton, his chief of staff,
was left to run the department. Immediately, however, rumors began to cir-

culate that Cochran was not going to be able to return and that a new sheriff would be needed. Calling this talk "undignified speculation," the *Fort Lauderdale Sun-Sentinel* wrote in an editorial:

> The county will be well-served if in the future Cochran returns full-time to his duties. The sheriff is a respected law-enforcement officer, an honest, effective and dedicated public servant, and a first-rate human being.
>
> Even working at reduced speed as he recovers, Cochran would do an excellent job leading the department.
>
> Best wishes, sheriff. May your recovery be speedy and complete.[811]

Within days, Cochran was up and around, saying hello to friends at The Floridian Diner in Fort Lauderdale (where he was a long-time regular), stopping by the police academy, presiding over a promotion ceremony for sixteen deputies that had been delayed so that he could be present, and, as an accomplished artist, drawing comical pictures of himself in an MRI machine. But in March, he was back in the hospital for more surgery, and in April it was announced that his lungs did not appear to be healing properly. Nevertheless, Cochran continued to conduct bedside meetings with his aides as his condition permitted.

In May, Cochran admitted that it could be weeks, or possibly even months, before he would be back on the job. "I do need to be seen. I know that. But I've got to get all this cancer stuff behind me."[812] Nevertheless, in June he appeared at another promotion ceremony and told reporters that except for his hair loss, he was feeling fine.

By August, however, it was clear that his doctors' initial predictions of a full recovery had been erroneous, and the longstanding whispers over who might take over the $118,337-a-year post reached a new pitch. Most observers predicted it would be either State Senator Ken Jenne or County Commissioner Lori N. Parrish, even though neither of them had any law enforcement experience. Within the department, however, many thought the job would go to Templeton. In the meantime, everyone wondered whether Cochran would resign in order to facilitate a smooth transition.

Cochran, however, wanted to remain sheriff—Bob Butterworth later would say that the career lawman had decided to "die with his boots on."[813] At 3:30 a.m. on Friday, September 5, 1997, Cochran passed away at his Fort Lauderdale home surrounded by his wife Carol, son Michael, and daughters Kimberly and Michelle.[814] Five hours later, Susan W. McCampbell, the department's director of corrections and rehabilitation, was sworn in as acting sheriff after having been called to Cochran's residence.

Lori N. Parrish, commissioner of Broward County (1989–2005)

Acting Sheriff Susan W. McCampbell (1997–98)

Susan Waite McCampbell had been with the department since August 1994, and like Cochran strongly believed that inmates should be helped rather than punished. She also was a fellow Pennsylvanian, having been born on May 23, 1949, in the same hospital as Cochran and growing up in Lancaster, a mere twenty miles from where her future boss lived.

After receiving a B.A. in political science from American University in 1971, McCampbell had spent a year at the Brookings Institute developing evaluation criteria for programs funded by the U.S. Department of Justice's Law Enforcement Assistance Administration. She then joined the Northern Virginia Planning District Commission as director of public safety, where she helped twelve police departments and five sheriff's offices obtain grants and prepare proposed legislation. In 1975, she earned a master's degree in city and regional planning from Catholic University.

In October 1981, McCampbell became a program director at the Police Executive Research Forum in Washington, D.C., working on national accredita-

Susan W. McCampbell, acting sheriff of Broward County (1997–98)

tion standards for local law enforcement agencies. In May 1983, she was named assistant sheriff of Alexandria, Virginia, and placed in charge of the city's jail. Soon, she was appearing regularly on radio and television as the office's principal media spokeswoman.

While attending a law enforcement conference in the spring of 1994, McCampbell met Henry Templeton and subsequently agreed to join the Broward Sheriff's Office. In December 1994, she was promoted to director of corrections when Templeton, who had held the job since February 1993, became Cochran's chief of staff.

Cochran's decision to elevate McCampbell to the position of acting sheriff had been made in secret, with only his secretary being told. On Monday, September 1st, realizing that the end was near, Cochran had written a letter stating that he wanted McCampbell to be the next sheriff. It was on the basis of this document that Chief Circuit Judge Dale Ross had administered the oath of office to McCampbell.

When she arrived at Cochran's house, McCampbell knew that the sheriff had died but was stunned when she was told that he had left her in charge.

Dale Ross, chief judge of Broward County (1991–2007)

Speaking to reporters, she said, "It all happened so fast,"[815] and noted that the last time the pair had met was in late August, just before Cochran had gone on a Gulf Coast vacation. Cochran's longtime aide, Ott Cefkin, later filled in some of the details. "There came a point when he realized if he is unable to continue, life has to go on. His choice was Susan. He felt she had the entire package—marvelous administrative skills, great vision, accessibility and the same philosophies."[816]

Asked for an appraisal of the county's new acting sheriff, Chief Assistant Public Defender Howard L. Finkelstein credited McCampbell with improving jail conditions, seeking treatment for mentally ill inmates, and helping form the county's innovative mental health court. "I have come to know Susan personally over the past four years [and] have become overwhelmingly impressed with her knowledge, sincerity, integrity and ability. She is a winner by anybody's standards."[817]

Although Broward had never had a female sheriff, there had been thirteen women sheriffs in Florida history, beginning with Eugenia H. Simmons in Okeechobee County in 1938. However, the most recent female sheriff—Walton County's Ethyl C.M. Anderson—had held office for just a few months in 1970. And only one woman had ever been elected to the job (Sumter County's Marguerite P. Baldree, who succeeded her late husband in 1946).

As McCampbell mulled her next step, allies of Jenne and Parrish began intensive lobbying efforts to have their candidates appointed sheriff. Meanwhile, a number of other names were thrown into the hat, including Ken Wagner, who had lost to Cochran while running as a Republican in the 1996 general election but now was again a Democrat; Lionel Stewart, who had lost to Cochran in the 1996 Democratic primary; and Circuit Judge Stanton Kaplan, who had briefly considered running for sheriff in 1996.

On Wednesday, September 10, 1997, a memorial service was held for Cochran at Fort Lauderdale's Parker Playhouse. In a 10-minute eulogy that marked her first official chance to impress the county's political elite, McCampbell promised to carry on Cochran's work. "Change. Inspiring others to change. How people fear change, yet Ron Cochran caused us all to change.... Our legacy, our agenda for the coming years, is our commitment to continue to change our community by the power of our own actions."[818]

The next day, newspapers carried glowing accounts of McCampbell's performance, with the *Miami Herald* calling it "heartfelt, inspiring and memorable."[819] Broward County Commission Chairman Scott I. Cowan told the press that the speech had been "very good,"[820] while Public Defender Alan H. Schreiber used the word "terrific" to describe McCampbell.[821] The *Fort Lauderdale Sun-Sentinel* claimed that opposition to McCampbell was "melting" and added, "Among those no longer actively seeking the job are state Sen. Ken Jenne, D-Fort Lauderdale; Henry Templeton, the sheriff's department chief of staff; and Joe Gerwens, the department's inspector general."[822] Broward Democratic Party Chairman Mitchell Ceasar, however, insisted that many candidates were waiting in the wings to challenge McCampbell.

On Friday, September 12th, McCampbell submitted her formal application to become sheriff to Governor Lawton M. Chiles, Jr. In a story in the *Miami Herald*, the paper predicted that her opponents now would begin a full-court press:

> A tough question follows McCampbell: Can she hold the office next year in an election against what's sure to be a politically well-organized opponent? Jittery Democrats worry about a replay of 1984, when George Brescher, who had been appointed to replace the departed Bob Butterworth, lost to Republican Nick Navarro. The last thing Democrats want is to relive that episode.
>
> Who would want to undermine McCampbell? Almost anybody who wants to get the appointment. The stakes are just too high in an agency

Lawton M. Chiles, Jr., governor of Florida (1991–98)

Cochran once described as "a 3,000-member political action committee with badges and guns."[823]

As rumors swirled over what Chiles might do, the *Fort Lauderdale Sun-Sentinel* backed McCampbell and argued that Parrish, who by now was regarded as her main challenger (despite the fact that six other candidates had submitted applications to the governor), was unqualified for the job:

> Chiles should endorse Cochran's confidence in McCampbell by naming her sheriff until the term ends November 1998. Then, if she wants to keep the job, she can take her case—and her track record—to the voters.
>
> Parrish can take her case to the voters at the same time. She can tout her longtime residency in Broward County, cite her administrative experience at the Fort Lauderdale Swap Shop and drop the names of Broward County's political elite from one end of the campaign trail to the other.
>
> Then the voters of Broward County can make their choice. But they deserve better than having their decision preempted now by the

On September 18, 1997, readers of the editorial page of the Fort Lauderdale
Sun-Sentinel *were greeted by this Chan Lowe cartoon*

appointment of a highly-connected politician with no law enforcement experience as head of the sheriff's office.

At the same time, McCampbell deserves the chance to demonstrate
her commitment to Cochran's goals and ideals, which she has said
time and again that she shares, as well as her ability to carry them
out....

As for the power grab by Parrish, the less said the better. Friends
in high places aren't what it takes to run a professional law enforcement agency with 3,500 employees and an annual budget of $248
million.[824]

On the following day, however, the *Miami Herald* began asking pointed
questions about McCampbell's ascension:

Ron Cochran's final decision as sheriff of Broward County remains
shrouded in mystery two weeks after his death.

Days before he died, Cochran asked that Susan McCampbell follow
in his footsteps as acting sheriff. He put it in writing. But the letter, a

public record, cannot be found—and none of the people present at the somber succession ceremony knows where the letter is, though all say they saw it.

McCampbell said she doesn't have it. The sheriff's top lawyer, Charles Whitelock, said he doesn't have it. Neither does Attorney General Bob Butterworth, an aide said. Nor does Chief Circuit Judge Dale Ross, who swore in McCampbell on the morning of Sept. 5, hours after Cochran died.

"I guess somebody lost it," Ross said. "I sure hope it wasn't me."

If it ever turns up, the one-page typewritten letter would have emotional and political significance: It reflects Cochran's dying wish to see someone he trusted carry on his legacy of community-based crime prevention.

Moments before Ross swore in McCampbell as acting sheriff, the judge held what he described as a "brief evidentiary hearing" to verify the authenticity of the letter. It is the only documentation that proves McCampbell was Cochran's first choice.

To further complicate matters, no transcript of the hearing was made because it was held in front of Cochran's house in Fort Lauderdale's Tarpon River neighborhood.

"Judge Ross held a hearing, he took the folder, and that's the last I saw of it," said Whitelock, who testified. "He took it into evidence at that time."

"I know what Charlie Whitelock said, but I have no idea where that darn thing is," Ross said.

At about 8:30 a.m. Sept. 5, Ross appointed McCampbell acting sheriff of Broward's largest law enforcement agency. His one-paragraph order is on file in the courthouse, but there is no sign of the letter on which it is based.

Cochran's widow, Carol, recalled seeing the letter, but at the moment the scene was chaotic because of family members and friends coming and going.

"I handed it to Susan," she said Thursday. "There was just so much going on that day."

McCampbell said she gave the letter to Ross.

Whitelock said the letter was the result of a series of conversations between Cochran and Butterworth. Four letters were drawn up, each designating a different top aide as Cochran's chief deputy or preferred successor. Cochran ultimately decided on McCampbell over Tom Carney, Joe Gerwens and Henry Templeton.

The decision has been the subject of political speculation because McCampbell, hired three years ago from Virginia and most recently director of the jail system, was not seen as a Cochran confidante.[825]

Nor was the question of whether she had gained office legitimately McCampbell's only problem. Several recent incidents also had cast doubt on her organizational skills. In July 1997, convicted killer Lloyd Duest had managed to escape from a maximum security cell at the Broward County Jail after cutting his way through a window made out of bulletproof plastic and steel. Although the work was noisy and had taken several days, none of the guards on duty had noticed what he was doing. While Duest failed to get very far after sliding down the side of the building using a rope that had been left behind by construction workers, the incident had shocked the public and led guards to complain they were short-staffed and the facility was drifting as a result of Cochran's illness. McCampbell denied the charges, saying that the coverage had been adequate and that the problem appeared to be with the officers who had been on duty. "My concern is whether staff is doing their job. If you had 20 people up [on the eighth floor, where the most dangerous criminals were housed] and they're not doing their job, it wouldn't make a difference."[826]

One month later, a second escape occurred when bank robber Andrew Rodriguez walked out of the jail by pretending to be another inmate, who was scheduled to be released after making bail. Although the two men did not resemble each other, deputies had accepted Rodriguez's claim that he was Gino Beltran. Once again, McCampbell was forced to defend herself, and this time she blamed the incident on an outdated computer system. "There are 80,000 people getting booked in every year using 1970s software. It's obviously something we're concerned about."[827]

At the end of September, the Broward County Commission voted to name the department's headquarters in honor of Cochran. McCampbell said that the former sheriff would have been aghast at the decision to do so, having told her that he did not want any memorials—"not even a parking space."[828] "He was a very humble man, that was part of his charm,"[829] McCampbell reminded reporters. "That's why it took the County Commission about 30 seconds to rename the building after him."[830]

In November, a dedication ceremony was held. During the festivities, Commissioner Scott Cowan, who often had feuded with the late sheriff, was asked about Cochran's legacy. After offering warm praise, Cowan summed up his thoughts by saying that Cochran had exhibited "an authority we had not seen for some time in the Sheriff's Office."[831] Echoing this view, the *Fort Lauderdale*

*The Ronald A. Cochran Public Safety Complex in Fort Lauderdale,
home of the Broward Sheriff's Office (2001)*

Sun-Sentinel ran a headline praising Cochran as the "Architect of the Modern Sheriff's Office."

In the meantime, there remained the question of who would be named as his successor. And while the list of applicants had grown to sixteen, Chiles had given no indication who he was leaning towards, or even if he was leaning. When reporters asked his office for an update shortly before Christmas 1997, spokeswoman April Herrle said, "The governor feels there is not a pressing need to do something quickly."[832] Three weeks later, however, Chiles did name a new sheriff for Broward County.

CHAPTER 10

THE EARLY JENNE YEARS (1998–2000)

As the 20th century drew to a close, the people of Broward apprehensively welcomed their fourteenth sheriff, a career politician with no law enforcement experience. The appointment of Ken Jenne raised eyebrows inside and outside the department, and some commentators called it a step backwards for a man who once seemed destined to be governor. Others, however, saw it as a shrewd way to rebuild his hometown base after having been away in Tallahassee for nearly two decades. According to these observers, Jenne's time as sheriff would be short, for soon he would be moving on to bigger things.

In the end, Jenne surprised nearly everyone by serving as sheriff for almost ten years, during which time he won three elections by overwhelming margins. But when he finally did leave, it was not by choice and it was not to assume higher office. Instead, for the first time in history, a Broward sheriff was going to prison.

Sheriff Kenneth C. Jenne II (1998–2007)

On Friday, January 9, 1998, Governor Lawton Chiles named Kenneth Clarence Jenne II the new sheriff of Broward County, praising his "excellent wealth of knowledge, experience and integrity."[833] A short time earlier, the *Fort Lauderdale Sun-Sentinel* had thrown its support squarely behind Jenne, saying he "would be able to build the coalitions and win the public support needed to continue [Ron] Cochran's work of turning the sheriff's department into one of the nation's top police agencies."[834] Of course, not everyone agreed, and for months County Commissioner Lori Parrish had sought the job for herself. Even after she dropped out (citing her friendship with Jenne), others remained opposed to Jenne's nomination, including, most notably, members of Fort Lauderdale's gay and lesbian community, who still had not forgiven him for going back on his 1990 senate campaign promise to back a gay rights bill.[835]

Chiles's decision also spelled the end for Susan McCampbell. Although she had been running the department since Cochran's death in September 1997, she had fallen out of consideration by failing to answer the questions surrounding her elevation. At the press conference introducing Jenne, Chiles thanked McCampbell for her service and told reporters, "Susan took the reins during an extremely difficult time. She handled this job with tremendous skill and grace."[836] Despite saying she was looking forward to working with the new sheriff ("I'm thrilled to have Sen. Jenne as part of this family"[837]), in October 1998 McCampbell resigned, explaining in a press release, "I'm seeking new opportunities and challenges. It's been a wonderful experience working for the Broward Sheriff's Office. I'm looking forward to enjoying more time with my family and friends."[838]

Born in New Haven, Connecticut, on December 1, 1946, Jenne had grown up in Lake Worth, Florida, where his father worked for the local utility company and his mother was employed by the Palm Beach County Clerk of Courts. After earning an A.A. from Palm Beach Junior College in 1966 and a B.A. in political science from Florida Atlantic University in 1968, Jenne had gone to Florida State University and emerged with a law degree in 1972.

Upon his return to South Florida, Jenne became an assistant state attorney and quickly struck up a friendship with fellow prosecutor Bob Butterworth. Nicknamed "Batman and Robin" by their colleagues, the two men displayed uncommon zeal in going after corrupt politicians and managed to stand out in an office that prided itself on its hard-charging ways.

In 1974, as a result of his interest in good government, Jenne was named executive director of the commission that had been formed to draft Broward County's first charter, which brought "home rule" to the county. Aided by this experience, in 1975 Jenne was elected to the Broward County Commission. Within a year, he had been made its chairman.

Looking for bigger challenges, in 1978 Jenne won a seat in the Florida Senate. Representing District 29 (Fort Lauderdale-Hollywood), Jenne became a leading advocate for education and health care reform and was recognized as one of the Democratic Party's rising stars.

In 1982, Jenne was viewed as a potential successor when Bob Butterworth resigned as Broward sheriff. But claiming he could do more good by staying where he was, Jenne took himself out of the running and the position went to Judge George Brescher. Although some people speculated that Jenne had withdrawn because he planned to run for attorney general in 1986, it was Butterworth who ended up getting that job. Instead, Jenne sought the senate presidency and for a time appeared likely to get it. At the last minute, however, a group of conservative Democrats threw their support behind John W. Vogt of Cocoa

Kenneth C. "Ken" Jenne II (third from left) attending a ribbon cutting cere-
mony while serving on the Broward County Commission (1975)

Beach as a way to punish Jenne, who by now had made numerous enemies
due to his mercurial nature and vindictive personality.

In 1988, Jenne decided to give up his senate seat in a bid to become state insurance commissioner. After a bitter battle, he was defeated by Republican
Tom Gallagher, a former state representative from Dade County who was now
the secretary of the Florida Department of Professional Regulation. Despite
this loss, Jenne's political star remained bright, and many people felt he was a
future candidate for governor or even U.S. senator.

Following two years practicing law, Jenne returned to the Florida Senate in
1990 when he won District 30 (Cooper City-Davie), beating veteran legislator
Tom McPherson in the Democratic primary and Republican John Rodstrom
in the general election. Because he did not live in the district, Jenne rented an
apartment in Davie for $450 a month, giving up the homestead exemption on
his long-time house in Hollywood Hills.

In the spring of 1992, the Florida Legislature reapportioned the state, and
that fall Jenne ran unopposed in Senate District 29, whose boundaries now

Ken Jenne caucusing with fellow state legislators (1985)

stretched from Hallandale on the east coast to Everglades City on the west coast and ran as far north as Clewiston, just south of Lake Okeechobee. Asked what he knew about this enormous area, Jenne quipped, "I plan to take a tour."[839]

Also on the ballot that fall was a proposal to limit state legislators to eight years in office. Its easy passage meant that Jenne would have to leave the senate by November 2000, when he would be just fifty-three years old. And so, even as he served as chairman of the Broward County Legislative Delegation (1992), was named Democratic senate leader (1994), and was re-elected without opposition (1996), Jenne began searching for another public office.

For a time, it appeared he might return to local government, especially if an effort to rewrite the Broward charter succeeded in making the county mayor a true chief executive with broad powers. But when this proposal ran into trouble, opposed by a coalition of groups who offered their own, watered-down plan, Jenne was forced to look elsewhere. And the sheriff's job—which by now paid $124,556-a-year, oversaw 3,300 employees, and had an annual budget of $248 million—was an attractive possibility. As Jenne later explained, "I look at a sheriff as the only person in my community where you can reach out to the entire community and affect everything—one way or the other. When you're the executive, you can put the ball in play, and you can be the visionary. You can have a greater sense of accomplishment."[840]

When Chiles called and asked him to become Broward's next sheriff, Jenne could claim no previous law enforcement experience. Jenne's supporters sought to overcome this fact by pointing out that during his time in the Florida Senate, Jenne had chaired the Criminal Justice Committee; helped rewrite the state's DUI, felony murder, and juvenile justice laws; served on the Governor's Task Force on Organized Crime; and played a leading role in the revision of the state's sentencing guidelines. But in a letter to the editor of the *Fort Lauderdale Sun-Sentinel*, political activist Frederick W. Guardabassi scoffed at these credentials:

> Why does Broward County need a sheriff anyway? The most qualified candidate, acting Sheriff Susan McCampbell, was not appointed by Gov. Chiles because she didn't have the right political background, and what has that got to do with being a good sheriff? Sen. Ken Jenne's law enforcement background is as thin as that of some of his predecessors, namely Ed Stack and George Brescher. If law enforcement experience is not important, then what is the point in having a sheriff at all?[841]

In the meantime, the employees in the Sheriff's Office took a wait-and-see approach, unsure what to expect. At his induction at the Broward Center for the Performing Arts (which Public Information Officer Ott Cefkin first described as an "inauguration" and then a "coronation" before finally correcting himself and calling it a "swearing in"[842]), Jenne told the overflow audience that he was committed to keeping kids in school and off drugs, promised to stand up for the victims of child abuse, domestic abuse, and elder abuse, and said that the time had come "to put the 'service' back into public service."[843] But the loudest applause was heard when the new sheriff announced his opposition to privatizing the county's correctional facilities, an option being considered by the county commission. In the weeks that followed, Jenne further endeared himself by eschewing the mass firings that had become a hallmark of sheriff changes. In fact, Jenne left the entire department intact.

Ken Jenne being sworn in as sheriff by his wife Caroline as
their children Evan and Sarah look on (1998)

Deputies receiving their oaths from newly-installed Sheriff Ken Jenne (1998)

Sheriff Ken Jenne (third from left) at his swearing in with three of his
predecessors: George Brescher, Bob Butterworth, and Tom Walker (1998)

Lacking a law enforcement background, and with voting just a few months away (for Chiles's appointment was effective only until the next general election in November 1998), Jenne immediately set out to burnish his image by observing roll calls, riding in patrol cars, and reviewing operations at the county's detention centers. At the same time, he waged a highly public, and ultimately successful, fight to keep the Sheriff's Office in charge of the county's jail system. And to make sure everyone knew there was a new sheriff in town, he hired Presser Gray, Inc., a Miami graphic design firm, to redesign the department's wagon-wheel logo so that it included the words "Ken Jenne." Soon, the new emblem could be found on department buildings, coffee cups, flags, Frisbees, magnets, office equipment, pencils, pins, rugs, stationery, and t-shirts. Oddly, however, no change was made to the department's patrol cars.

For their part, the rank-and-file were happy. In an interview with a reporter, Commander Jim Layman, the head of the Port Everglades sub-station, summed up matters by saying, "Initially we were concerned that a politician was being put in. Us guys [sic] who have been cops all of our lives, we're leery of someone who is not a cop coming in.... However, this guy is not a normal politician. He has the best interests of Broward County and the Sheriff's Office at heart."[844]

Sheriff Ken Jenne's redesigned department logo (1998)

Jenne's frequent visits to the jail earned him special praise from the department's correctional officers, who were used to being treated as second-class citizens. In a letter of appreciation, they wrote, "We have seen more of you the first couple of months than any other sheriff in recent memory. From the upgrading of the food served to your employees, to the war you have waged for us against privatization, we can't thank you enough."[845]

In September 1998, a contest was held to pick the Democratic nominee for sheriff. Because no one had filed on the Republican side, the winner of the Democratic primary would automatically be elected to fill out the last two years of Ron Cochran's term. Faced with only token opposition from George Albo, a former Miami-Dade detention deputy, Jenne rolled to a big victory— 49,040 votes to 7,341 votes (a margin of 87%–13%)—in a race that attracted only 10% of the eligible voters, the lowest turnout in county history. Nevertheless, Jenne took the campaign seriously, collecting $274,000 in contributions, printing brochures that touted his anti-crime plans and mentioned his purchase of a bloodhound to track missing children, promising to crack down on juvenile crime (an issue that polls revealed was high on the list of voter concerns), and shaking hands everywhere he went.

On election night, Jenne reveled in the size of his win and claimed that it erased any question about his fitness for office. "I'm very encouraged by it. Our campaign was based on what we were doing in the sheriff's office and not on anything negative. I consider this margin a real mandate but a huge responsibility."[846] He then added, "There is no higher honor than earning the confidence of the people of this county to do a job that is so close to all of our hearts. To protect our families, our children, our neighborhoods."[847]

With the election behind him, Jenne now turned his attention to the future. Whereas his predecessor Ron Cochran had envisioned a time in which all patrol duties would be performed by local police agencies, Jenne preferred that cities give up their own departments and turn all law enforcement responsibilities over to the Sheriff's Office. Such "regional policing," Jenne argued, could provide the same service at a fraction of the cost because of favorable economies of scale. Jenne also claimed citizens would benefit because statistics showed that the Sheriff's Office was twice as successful at solving crimes as the average local police department. By 2000, Jenne had added Oakland Park, Pompano Beach, and Southwest Ranches to his agency's list of contract cities.

In the meantime, Jenne looked for other ways to enlarge the department and expand its reach. In April 1999, for example, the department's web site (www.sheriff.org) was unveiled. In addition to "information on services and specialty units at the BSO," the site contained "[a profile of] Jenne, safety tips, news releases, composite sketches and mug shots of suspects ... [as well as] crime statistics and job openings."[848]

In July, the Sheriff's Office took over local child abuse investigations from the Florida Department of Children and Families. In September, it absorbed the county's Department of Community Control. In October, it assumed responsibility for the Broward Drug Court's treatment program. And by now, its School Resource Program was the largest in the state.

Jenne described these changes as representing more than increased size — to him, they offered proof that the Sheriff's Office was providing citizens with better and more varied services. But to his detractors, they were merely evidence that the sheriff was engaged in kingdom building to satisfy his personal ego.

Ignoring these criticisms, Jenne forged ahead with his plans to remake the Sheriff's Office. To help identify and protect at-risk individuals, a special victims and family crimes section was formed. To provide promising officers with executive leadership training, a Center for Advanced Criminal Justice Studies was started in conjunction with Florida Atlantic University. And to ensure that the department was keeping up its standards, certification was sought (and received) from various organizations, including the Commission on Accreditation for Law Enforcement Agencies.

In September 2000, Jenne ran for re-election. Once again, the Republicans declined to nominate anyone. Opposing Jenne in the Democratic primary was Lionel Stewart, the former federal drug enforcement agent and retired U.S. Army criminal investigator who had lost to Ron Cochran in 1996.

For the second time in two years, Jenne scored an impressive triumph, beating Stewart 68,134 votes to 34,792 votes (a margin of 66%–34%). At a party at the Riverside Hotel in Fort Lauderdale, Jenne told reporters, "I think our victory is a comment about the job the men and women at BSO have done over the past three years. We've come a long way but we're not contented. We want to continue to see the crime rate fall and our crime clearance rate climb."[849]

Postscript

In September 2004, Jenne again won the Democratic nomination for sheriff, easily beating Karl Tozzi, a retired BSO sergeant, by a tally of 133,707 votes to 39,022 votes (a margin of 77%–23%). Once more lacking a Republican challenger, Jenne automatically received a second four-year term. As in 2000, Jenne watched the election returns at the Riverside Hotel, and later attributed his success to the trust he had built up over the years. "Whenever you've been a long-term incumbent, people get to know you, get a feel for what you're about. I feel we've really reached out into the community, into every community, and it makes me feel good."[850]

To overcome Jenne's enormous financial advantage ($440,000 to $33,000), Tozzi had tried to make an issue out of "PowerTrac," Jenne's method of evaluating personnel based on their crime clearance rates. For some time, questions had been raised about the validity of the department's increasingly favorable statistics, and in February 2004 the State Attorney's Office had begun investigating two deputies suspected of falsifying case reports. Tozzi, a 34-year veteran of the department, claimed that Jenne's demand for ever-better numbers had led many deputies to misclassify crimes (turning serious felonies into routine misdemeanors), prematurely close cases, and even arrest individuals they knew were innocent.

Although this issue had failed to resonate with the voters, the press kept hammering away at it as more and more abuses came to light. Finally, in May 2005, Jenne announced that the system would be overhauled.

By now, however, the sheriff had a bigger problem—federal investigators were looking into his personal finances. In December 2002, Jenne and two of his senior officers (Undersheriff Tom Carney and Lieutenant Colonel Tom

Brennan) had formed their own consulting firm (called Havloc, LLC) and there were accusations that they were moonlighting for that company while on the job. Claiming that what he did on his own time was his own business, Jenne stonewalled. But the more he refused to cooperate, the more damaging information the investigation seemed to turn up. And as calls for Jenne to quit became louder and louder, the department was left to twist in the wind.

On Tuesday, September 4, 2007, just as he was about to be indicted, Jenne agreed to resign and plead guilty to three counts of tax evasion and one count of conspiracy to commit mail fraud. In an e-mail announcing his decision, Jenne wrote: "Today, I'm retiring from public service. I need to turn my attention to myself and my family."[851]

The press had a field day, reporting at length how Jenne had enriched himself by entering into improper business arrangements with department contractors and then failing to report the payments (totaling more than $150,000) on his tax returns. Although many of the details were convoluted, there was at least one transaction that the public had no trouble understanding: a $20,000 loan given to Jenne by a local real estate developer named Philip Procacci, from whom the department had leased several properties, had been disguised to look like it was a loan to Marian Yoka, one of Jenne's secretaries.

While most observers attributed Jenne's actions to the sharp difference between his yearly earnings as a lawyer in private practice (nearly $900,000) and his salary as sheriff ($169,841), former Sheriff Bob Butterworth (having returned to public life as secretary of the Florida Department of Children and Families) offered a different explanation: "[H]e might have stayed too long on the job."[852]

In November 2007, U.S. District Judge William P. Dimitrouleas reluctantly sentenced the former lawman to a year and a day in prison (the extra day being added to make Jenne eligible for early parole). "I think at one time that Mr. Jenne could have become governor of this state,"[853] the judge sighed. "But I don't think the book is closed on Mr. Jenne. I think we'll see Mr. Jenne come back and continue his good work."[854] Following the court proceedings, Jenne was assigned federal inmate number 77434-004 and sent to the U.S. Penitentiary in Jonesville, Virginia (a Florida lockup was felt to be too dangerous). There, he raised vegetables in the prison garden. In addition to his prison term, Jenne agreed to give up his law license for five years and was stripped of his state pension.

On Friday, October 26, 2007, Governor Charles J. "Charlie" Crist, Jr. tapped BSO Major Alfred T. "Al" Lamberti to fill out the remainder of Jenne's term. Calling Lamberti a "great man," Crist said that the appointment was "the best thing for the people"[855] of Broward. But to some observers, it was a calculated political move. As a Republican, Crist found himself under heavy pressure to name a Republican, even though Jenne, like most of the county's residents,

*Sheriff Ken Jenne (bottom right) leaving the federal courthouse in
Fort Lauderdale after pleading guilty to mail and tax fraud (2007)*

Alfred T. "Al" Lamberti, sheriff of Broward County (since 2007)

was a Democrat. Hoping to defuse matters, Lamberti (who claimed to be only a nominal Republican while steadfastly refusing to change his registration) quickly promised to be everyone's sheriff. "I only know one way to do this job, and it has nothing to do with party affiliation. You call 911, we're coming. We don't ask you what your party affiliation is."[856]

Alfred Thomas Lamberti was born in New York City on April 14, 1954, and grew up in nearby Westchester County. After graduating from Yonkers High School in 1972, where he had been a first-rate baseball player, he enrolled in Florida State University with plans to pursue an athletic career. Following his sophomore year, however, he moved to South Florida and began taking criminal justice classes. After receiving an A.S. in Law Enforcement from Palm Beach Junior College in 1977, he joined the Broward Sheriff's Office as a detention deputy.

During the next thirty years, Lamberti finished college (earning a B.A. in Criminal Justice at Florida Atlantic University in 1981) and steadily worked his way up the ranks. By the time of his appointment as sheriff, Lamberti was serving as the regional director of the Patrol Services Bureau.

Sheriff Al Lamberti announcing the BSO's new motto
"Pride in Service with Integrity" (2007)

Four days after Jenne's sentencing, Lamberti sought to put the department's troubles behind it by announcing that the agency now had an official motto (the first in its history). Under a large banner depicting four officers and the new slogan ("Pride in Service With Integrity"), the county's top lawman sketched out his vision for the future.

In January 2008, Lamberti started to campaign for his own four-year term, with gun violence at the top of his list (in part because of the recent on-the-job killings of Deputies Paul Rein and Christopher Reyka). But with no opposition in the Republican primary, he was largely able to watch from the sidelines as the Democrats engaged in a particularly bruising fight to pick a nominee. After considerable mudslinging, Scott J. Israel, the police chief of tiny North Bay Village (and until recently a Republican himself), emerged victorious from the five-man field, garnering 22,927 votes (32%) and narrowly avoiding a run-off with Richard Lemack, a Hollywood assistant city manager, who got 22,285 votes (31%).

Although not a typical Democratic candidate, Israel relied heavily on the party's traditional constituencies (particularly Jewish voters) and its two-to-one advantage in registered voters across the county. In the end, however, Lamberti's enormous war chest ($1 million, nearly twice Israel's $600,000), greater name recognition, and solid record—coupled with endorsements from both the *Miami Herald* (which praised his "calm demeanor"[857]) and the *South Florida Sun-Sentinel* (which congratulated him for getting the department "back on an even keel"[858])—convinced enough Democrats to cross party lines despite the electrifying presidential campaign of Senator Barack H. Obama (D-Ill.). Thus, when the results finally were certified (a process that was held up by an unprecedented number of overseas ballots), Lamberti had beaten Israel 348,420 votes to 333,045 votes (a margin of 51%–49%). Asked about his impressive victory, Lamberti said that he was grateful "that the people approve of what I've been doing for the past year."[859]

CHAPTER 11

THE BROWARD COUNTY JAIL
(1915–2000)

Florida law anticipates that every sheriff will maintain a county jail,[860] and the Broward Sheriff's Office fulfills this expectation through its Department of Detention. With 1,800 employees, 5,700 beds, and a $220 million budget, the Broward County Jail is the twelfth largest local jail in the United States (Los Angeles County has the largest such jail, with an average daily population of nearly 20,000 inmates).

The Broward County Jail actually consists of five separate lockups. Run in accordance with the state's Model Jail Standards, these facilities collectively are approved by the National Commission on Correctional Health Care (since 1995), American Correctional Association (1996), and Florida Corrections Accreditation Commission (2000).

Inmates awaiting bail, trial, or sentencing normally are housed in either the maximum security Main Jail in Fort Lauderdale (opened in 1985) or the medium security Joseph V. Conte Facility in Pompano Beach (1999).[861] After sentencing, they may be transferred to the medium security Stockade Facility in Fort Lauderdale (1951)[862] or the maximum security Paul Rein Detention Facility in Pompano Beach (2004).[863] Special needs inmates are sent to the medium security North Broward Bureau in Pompano Beach (1979). To accommodate future growth, a new jail is scheduled to open in Pompano Beach by 2012. This medium security facility is expected to cost $65 million and have room for 1,000 inmates.

For much of its existence, however, the Broward County Jail was a fairly modest operation. Indeed, until 1976, when inmates filed a class action lawsuit against Sheriff Ed Stack, the jail usually ranked at or near the bottom of the agency's concerns.

The Paul Rein Detention Facility in Pompano Beach (2008)

Early Years (1915–50)

In October 1915, the newly-appointed Broward County Commission agreed to purchase the old Fort Lauderdale school house for $12,000 and turn it into the county courthouse. Plans also were drawn up for a six-cell "center corridor" jail and the Southern Structural Steel Company in Birmingham, Alabama, was contacted and advised that the county was "in the market for some jail cells."[864]

One month later, the commission appointed Raiford Priest to the post of superintendent of public roads at a salary of $60 per month. From then on, Sheriff Aden Turner was authorized to deliver prisoners to Priest, who would set them to work. The county road gang soon became a Broward fixture, much as it was in other southern towns.

The upkeep of the county jail was one of Turner's most important duties (as it would be for all of his successors), and in April 1918 the state jail inspector paid a visit to the facility. At the end of his tour, he "pronounced it to be in as good condition as any in the state."[865]

By this time, the jail was housed in a three-story concrete building that was described as fully fireproof. The bottom floor was occupied by the chief jailer while the second floor, divided into three sections, housed the actual cells. There were a total of ten cells, with six in one compartment and two in each of the others. Each cell had a pair of cots, a toilet, a sink, and a bit of furni-

A group of early Broward leaders (from left to right): County Engineer Herbert C. Davis, County Commissioners Charles E. Ingalls, Alexander B. Lowe, and J.J. Joyce, and County Attorney Wilfred I. Evans (1915)

Broward County's first courthouse (1915)

*A Broward County chain gang cleaning up hurricane damage
in downtown Fort Lauderdale (1926)*

ture (typically a chair and a small writing table). The third floor contained a laundry room and a recreation room. According to the state inspector, the jail was large enough to meet the county's current needs. Moreover, if the area's crime rate continued to fall, the planned addition of more cells to the third floor would not be necessary.

Despite this glowing report, in November 1919 two prisoners—Joe Bratton and Lawrence Lindberg—complained of mistreatment. The men had been arrested for "beating their way on a train" (*i.e.*, riding without tickets), and in their affidavits they claimed they had been abused while in custody. According to the *Fort Lauderdale Herald*, which published their allegations, the pair had been denied needed medical attention, given inadequate food, and served contaminated water, which had forced them to sell their clothes to buy drinkable water.

Turner responded to these charges by inviting the press to investigate his office. He also offered reporters two rebuttal affidavits. The first, from George Lowry, a veteran of the 138th Aero Squadron who had served in France during World War I, stated that he had been confined to the jail at the same time as Bratton and Lindberg. In contrast to their story, Lowry insisted there had been no problems with either the food or the water, and that to the best of his knowledge no prisoner had been mistreated. The second affidavit was signed by Dr. T.S. Kennedy, who said he had personally cared for Bratton and Lindberg. As a result, the matter was dropped.

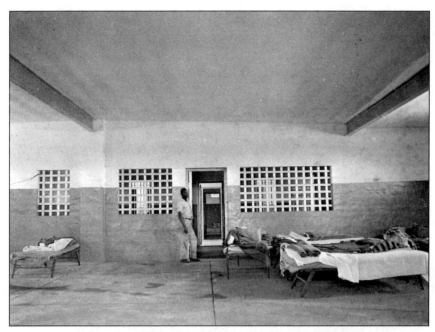

Dormitory at the Broward County convict camp (1935)

A few months later, the *Fort Lauderdale Sentinel* announced that because Turner was concentrating on prevention rather than punishment, the Broward County Jail was empty. When asked about this remarkable state of affairs, Turner credited Prohibition, saying, "No booze, no men in jail."[866] Of course, this statement completely ignored the fact that many prisoners were doing hard labor at the county's convict camp, where they were made to work on the chain gang.

In fact, the county budget depended on prison labor. Not only were inmates used to build roads and leased out to private firms (a practice sanctioned by state law until 1923),[867] they helped maintain the county's property. In July 1918, for example, the county commission fired J.K. Gordon, the courthouse's janitor, and ordered Turner to use convicts to keep the building clean.

In May 1921, the county recorded its first jail break. Under a headline that read, "Prisoners Escape from County Jail but are Captured," the *Fort Lauderdale Herald* reported that Deputy Priest had forgotten to lock the cell doors following a meal. After noticing this mistake, three inmates—robbers Anderson Carter and E.L. Henson and land swindler J. Mitchell—managed to slip out of the building and steal a car, $20 in cash, and a Colt revolver. Within a day, however, they had been captured by the city marshal in Eustis, Florida, and Deputy A.H. Walker was sent to retrieve them.

Inmate cards of Roy Matthews (top) and Hanford Mobley (bottom) (1923)

In March 1922, Paul Bryan took over as Sheriff and Fred M. Powell, a former Palm Beach deputy, was named chief deputy and jailer. Powell, who recently had moved to Fort Lauderdale from Hobe Sound, took up residence in the jail.

In November 1922, Roy Matthews and Hanford Mobley, two members of the notorious Ashley gang, were delivered into Bryan's custody. They had been captured while robbing the Bank of Stuart and had been placed in the Palm Beach County Jail, but repairs to that facility required that they be moved. Eventually assigned to a cell on the top floor of the Broward County Jail, the pair spied a trap door in the ceiling and used it to gain access to the roof. From there, they lowered themselves down the side of the building using blankets and sheets they had tied together.[868]

When the break was discovered, a sheriff's posse set off in pursuit of the escapees and telegrams were sent to authorities up and down the coast, even though most observers felt the pair had headed to the Everglades, where the Ashley gang normally hid out.

In May 1927, the foundation of the new Broward County Courthouse was poured, and one year later a dedication ceremony was held. In this facility, the county jail occupied the upper floors. The $375,000 building had been designed by John M. Peterman, who in the 1920s was one of Broward's leading

The second Broward County courthouse (c. 1950)

architects. Favoring the "Mediterranean Revival" style, Peterman's other local commissions included the Colored School (later renamed Dillard High School), the First Baptist Church, and Fort Lauderdale's city hall. While working on the courthouse, Peterman consulted regularly with Sheriff Bryan, as evidenced by a 1926 letter in which he asked the lawman to "kindly drop in my office sometime during Monday, January 17, [so] that we may go over the plans for the new Court House and Jail."[869]

In August 1927, the U.S. Coast Guard patrol boat CG-249 captured a pair of rum runners in the waters between Florida and the Bahamas. Although the two smugglers—James H. Alderman and Robert E. Weech—were patted down for weapons, they were neither bound nor confined, and a short time later, when his captors were occupied with other duties, Alderman managed to get hold of a gun and kill boatswain Sidney C. Sanderlin. He then fatally wounded machinist Victor A. Lamby and seized control of the vessel.

After toying with the idea of making the rest of the crew walk the plank, Alderman decided to set them adrift in a burning boat. Before he could carry out his plan, however, several of the captives ran towards him. In the resulting melee, U.S. Secret Service agent Robert E. Webster lost his life[870] and sea-

Architect John M. Peterman (c. 1925)

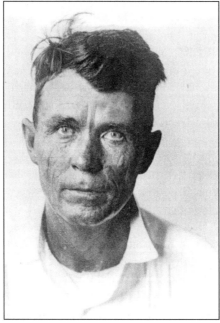

Pirate James H. Alderman (1883–1929)

man Jodie Hollingsworth was seriously injured, but Alderman and Weech were recaptured.

Upon the ship's return to Fort Lauderdale, the two men were taken into federal custody, brought to Miami, and placed on trial before Judge Halsted Ritter. In January 1928, Alderman, who by now had been dubbed the "Gulf Stream Pirate" by the press, was found guilty of piracy and sentenced to death by hanging, with the execution to be carried out in May 1928 in Fort Lauderdale.[871] A series of appeals,[872] as well as an unsuccessful plea for leniency to President Herbert C. Hoover, pushed the date back to August 1929.

As the fateful day (Saturday, August 17th) drew near, the public's thirst for details became insatiable. In an attempt to keep a lid on matters, Judge Ritter wrote to Sheriff Turner in July and asked him to withhold from the press all information regarding the case. "Whatever the newspaper reporters may be able to obtain from sources outside of the United States Marshal and his assistants, you and your deputies and employees, I probably cannot control," Ritter admitted, "but I am determined that the sources which I can control shall not feed to the public anything concerning this execution."[873]

In the meantime, two sites had been proposed for the execution—the old county jail and the new county jail. Although Turner made it clear that he preferred the former location because its courtyard afforded considerable privacy, it eventually was decided that Alderman would be hung on the roof of the new jail (which really was the roof of the new county courthouse). To obstruct the public's view, it was agreed that a wall would be erected around the scaffold. With these matters settled, Deputy W.F. Fox from the U.S. Marshal's Office in Miami drove up to Fort Lauderdale "to arrange for bids for the erection of the scaffold."[874]

As these plans moved forward, the Broward County Commission, with a fair amount of justification, balked. Worried that the proceedings might damage the roof and, in the process, nullify its warranty, the commissioners demanded that the federal government post a bond to cover the cost of any repairs. Meanwhile, a citizens' petition had been drawn up and now was circulating throughout Fort Lauderdale, calling for the location of the execution to be changed to a more inconspicuous spot.

Five days before the hanging, Judge Ritter relented and ordered Alderman to be executed at the Fort Lauderdale Coast Guard base. As a result, a set of gallows were hastily erected in a giant metal seaplane hangar and three U.S. deputy marshals were told that they would be drawing straws to see which one of them would pull the trapdoor's lever.

On the evening before his execution, Alderman was moved from Miami to the Broward County Jail. As he arrived, David H. Crooks, a reporter with the

United States Coast Guard Base in Fort Lauderdale (c. 1935)

Miami Herald, attempted to take a picture but was stopped by U.S. Chief Deputy Marshal Leo M. Mack and two other federal officers (U.S. Deputy Marshal O.H. Mathews and U.S. Border Patrol Officer Walter E. Bedenbaugh). Mack then brought Crooks to Turner's office, where he was released only after he promised not to publish an account of the incident.

As soon as he was free, however, Crooks spoke to both the Associated Press and the *Fort Lauderdale Daily News*. When the story subsequently appeared, the public was outraged over how Crooks (who was a veteran and a respected member of the local chapter of the American Legion) had been treated. As a result, arrest warrants (listing a host of charges, including assault and battery) were issued for all three officers, which required them to post bonds in order to be able to leave the city.[875]

In the meantime, Alderman had been placed in a back room to wait for the county's chief jailer, Deputy Dad Howell, who had been instructed to take him to a specially-prepared cell. When Howell finally arrived, Alderman jumped up from his chair and warmly greeted the officer, shaking his hand and saying, "I am Horace Alderman, your new prisoner. I have seen your picture in [the] newspapers several times and that is how I know you. I have also heard many pleasant things about you and the kindness you show to prisoners under your care."[876] According to reporters, the genial Howell responded by promising to take good care of Alderman.

On the following day, Alderman arose early, ordered breakfast, and ate heartily. A short time later, after being handcuffed, he was led down the stairs to a waiting Lincoln patrol wagon (which had been furnished by the Fort Lauderdale Police Department). On the ten-minute journey to the Coast Guard base, Alderman was accompanied by five guards and his vehicle was escorted by six cars filled with federal officers as well as deputies from Broward, Dade, and Palm Beach.

Coast Guardsmen carrying service rifles were doing picket duty around the hangar where the execution was to take place, while others were patrolling the base's perimeter. When the motorcade pulled up to the entrance, Alderman was rushed inside. Although he remained calm during the events that followed, an improperly-tied knot resulted in a long and painful death, permanently haunting everyone who witnessed it.[877]

In 1931, Turner, a strict Prohibitionist, was badly embarrassed when Jack French, a federal prisoner being held in the Broward County Jail, got drunk. But when Sanford Bates, the director of the U.S. Bureau of Prisons, wrote to complain about the incident, Turner insisted that he was blameless and suggested that the alcohol had been provided by either French's lawyer or the federal guard that had transported him to Fort Lauderdale. The irritated lawman then sarcastically added, "I have always treated Federal prisoners the same as our own County prisoners and that is not by serving them with liquor."[878]

As the Great Depression gripped the nation, Turner found himself with an even more vexing problem. For many years, most of the department's money had come from feeding the jail's inmates. While the county paid the Sheriff's Office sixty-five cents a day for each prisoner, the meals provided actually cost considerably less. Now, however, the county was behind in its payments, causing Turner to threaten to close the jail and set all of the inmates free. After much jawboning, the county commission finally gave in and paid most of what it owed, thereby acknowledging what Turner had known all along: in the hands of a determined official, the jail could be a very powerful bargaining chip.

In January 1933, Walter Clark was sworn in as Broward's third sheriff, a post he would hold (with only slight interruption) until July 1950. Although Clark quickly appointed his brother Bob as chief deputy, he rehired most of the department's officers, including chief jailer Arden Marshall. When Dad Howell left the Sheriff's Office in 1929, Marshall had succeeded him and by all accounts had done a good job. Nevertheless, when Clark was suspended in July 1942, his replacement, Sheriff Eddie Lee, fired Marshall and tapped Ed Hansen, the former supervisor of county roads, prisoners, and shops, to be the new warden. When Clark was reinstated in June 1943, Marshall again became chief jailer.

Broward County Jailer Arden Marshall (c. 1935)

Inmates at the Broward County Jail (1940)

In July 1935, an inmate named James Wilkinson climbed to the courthouse's roof, tied together several lengths of fire hose, and slid down to the ground. When a reporter inquired about the escape, Marshall replied that he "was too busy to check the prisoners to see if [Wilkinson was] still in [the] jail."[879] A short time later, Sheriff Clark confirmed that Wilkinson was gone.

Later Years (1951–2000)

In April 1951, two Fort Lauderdale police officers were summoned to the city bus station, where a Miss Cronin was acting in a bizarre fashion. After trying to talk to her, the officers concluded that she was delusional and therefore brought her to the Broward County Jail. For the next twelve days, the highly agitated woman was confined to a cell, where she "scream[ed], yell[ed] and kick[ed] and act[ed] in an ungovernable manner."[880]

After her release, Cronin filed a lawsuit claiming that she had been mistreated at the jail. According to her complaint, she had been denied proper clothing, had had her foot stomped on by Deputy James Welch, and had not been taken before a magistrate for a competency determination, as required by state law.

Following a directed verdict in favor of Sheriff Amos Hall (who argued that he had been unaware of Cronin's confinement) and a jury verdict in favor of Welch (who insisted that Cronin had been given clothes but had refused to wear them, had banged her foot against a door during a psychotic episode, and had not been denied a hearing), Cronin appealed to the Florida Supreme Court. Although it upheld the dismissals, it took pains to point out that as sheriff, Hall was responsible for the jail and everything that occurred there.[881]

In December 1956, Sheriff-elect Quill Lloyd decided to take a tour of the jail to acquaint himself with the facility. According to one reporter, what he found was chaos caused by "lamentable bedding conditions, dirty bath facilities, [and] prisoner unrest."[882] Despite this fact, neither Lloyd nor his successors took any significant action to ameliorate these problems.

Finally, in February 1976, three prisoners filed a federal class action lawsuit against Sheriff Stack.[883] According to the plaintiffs, 1,200 inmates were now packed into cells designed to hold 275, forcing them to sleep in hallways that were littered with garbage. Unable to deny these allegations, Deputy County Attorney Alexander Cocalis later admitted: "I can't describe how filthy, crowded, rusty, just horrid that place was.... You could go the dog pound and the dogs were in better shape than those detainees."[884] Appalled by these conditions, Judge William Hoeveler ordered the county to take action.

The centerpiece of the government's response was the construction of a new main jail, which rose on a five-acre site along the New River adjacent to the Broward County Courthouse. Built at a cost of $48 million, the eight-story tower, containing 840 beds, opened in August 1985. The first 158 inmates to occupy the facility were walked across the parking lot from the old county jail, while an additional twenty-eight prisoners were transferred from the Hollywood annex, which was then closed.

It did not take long for the new building's security to be tested. In September 1985, an unidentified inmate on the sixth floor fabricated a makeshift rope out of a bed sheet and a blanket as part of a plan to shatter a reinforced window and climb down a wall. A surprise inspection, however, foiled his plans.

Although there have since been many other escape attempts, some remain particularly notable: in February 1986, Richard Balliet, a 73-year-old prisoner, arranged to have his son spring him using a forged legal writ, but was ratted out by a drug dealer who had been invited to participate in exchange for $700,000; in October 1989, Willie Willis Jr., a detainee on the eighth floor, inexplicably sought to tunnel his way out; in March 1990, inmate Roberson Torchon had just about made it out of the building when he forgot to turn in his fake ID at the last checkpoint, thereby rousing suspicion; in March 1995, serial rapist John Fogelman was killed when the bedsheets he had tied together to make a 74-foot-long rope snapped, plunging him fifty feet to his death (in the aftermath, two jail supervisors were fired, another was demoted, and a fourth was given a five-day suspension); and in July 1997, convicted killer Lloyd Duest spent days painstakingly sawing through steel and bulletproof glass only to be apprehended after just two hours on the run (most of which he had spent trapped on a construction scaffold).

Typically, however, escapes have involved prisoners switching identities with inmates about to be released. With the jail processing more than 1,000 prisoners each week, such mix-ups had become embarrassingly common by 1997, when three such incidents took place in a two-month period. Chastened officials blamed the problem on an antiquated computer system.

Despite its cost, the new jail actually did little to relieve overcrowding. Due to the closing of the old jail and its annexes, the county now had just 150 additional beds, and by August 1986 prisoners once again were being forced to sleep on the floor.[885] With Judge Hoeveler having set a cap of 1,613 prisoners, BSO officials began making plans to release the least dangerous inmates. But when Miette Burnstein, Broward County's chief judge, rejected this solution, Hoeveler began fining the county $1,000 a day and threatened to post federal marshals at the jail to restrict new admissions.

The new Broward County Jail under construction (1983)

Aerial view of the Broward County Jail (2001)

Caught between a rock and a hard place, Sheriff Nick Navarro ordered the old jail reopened while 568 cells in the new jail were converted from single occupancy to double occupancy (a fix known as "double-bunking"). The Florida Department of Corrections refused to go along with this idea, however, unless the county first made $1 million in safety improvements to the old jail. When it refused to do so, the state took the county to court, and in July 1987 the old jail was closed for a second time.

By September 1987, the situation had become desperate. Although the county had room for 1,920 prisoners, it had 2,280 inmates under confinement, and the charges imposed by Judge Hoeveler now stood at $421,000. With no end in sight to the impasse, the county commission agreed to dip into its emergency reserve fund and withdrew $90,000 to pay for three more months of levies.

Again forced to find a way out of the problem, in July 1988 Navarro pushed to house inmates in a canvas tent at the North Broward Detention Complex. But this move drew a sharp rebuke from both the prisoners' attorney and the county attorney, who, like his counterpart, accused the sheriff of exacerbating the crisis by engaging in unnecessary drug sweeps designed solely to garner headlines and burnish his re-election chances. Agreeing with this assessment, Hoeveler issued an order enjoining the tent and threatened to quadruple the county's daily fine to $4,000. By now, the county had paid $700,000 in penalties.

Nevertheless, in January 1989, Navarro—who two months earlier had been re-elected by a wide margin—decided to flout Hoeveler's order. In addition to enraging the judge, Navarro's decision did not sit well with the City of Pompano Beach, which had granted him a building permit only after being assured that the tent would be used solely as a processing center. At a press conference, Navarro admitted that he had violated his agreement with the city but claimed that as an elected county official he had done nothing wrong. Will Willis, a city building inspector, responded to this argument by telling the press, "When people are mandated to uphold the law, or enforce the law, I would like to believe they have an equal responsibility to obey it."[886]

Navarro's actions earned him a stern rebuke from the *Fort Lauderdale Sun-Sentinel*, leading a spokesman to insist that the sheriff had lacked alternatives. Subsequently, however, Navarro claimed that he had not had a chance to read the order and therefore "had no indication whatsoever that I was prohibited from using that tent."[887] Remarkably, Judge Hoeveler accepted this explanation and did not hold Navarro in contempt, even after Navarro missed a hearing on the matter because he had been in Los Angeles filming a television show. Many observers later claimed that Hoeveler had been pressured to overlook Navarro's insouciance because of a public relations campaign orchestrated by the sheriff's political supporters.

In March 1989, with the class action lawsuit in its thirteenth year, Hoeveler warned that he would begin releasing inmates in ninety days if the county continued to drag its feet. In November 1985, he had made the same threat, and now he mused that "perhaps that would have been the best way to go, whether the citizens of Broward County liked it or not."[888] As before, however, he took no action.

Finally, in November 1993, a settlement was reached between the inmates and the county (due, in no small part, to the efforts of Sheriff Ron Cochran). According to the terms of the agreement, the county would maintain a cap of 3,656 inmates (at the time the system's maximum occupancy), except during major emergencies. Moreover, once occupancy reached 88% of capacity, early release and other programs would be utilized to reduce the prisoner population so that, in the words of Peter Corwin, an assistant to the county administrator, "everyone has a bed."[889] The county also promised to develop a comprehensive inmate grievance procedure and comply with state and national prisoner health care standards. In January 1995, Judge Hoeveler formally rescinded his daily fine.

Despite the settlement, overcrowding remained a persistent problem. As a result, Cochran rented 150 cells in Key West (at a cost of $1.7 million), looked into sending prisoners to jails in Louisiana and Texas, got permission to house inmates in the courthouse's holding cells, and inquired about using courtrooms as overnight prisons (an idea that received a chilly reception from the judiciary). In addition, Broward County Chief Judge Dale Ross reassigned five judges to help move along 300 non-jury cases and promised a second blitz for jury trials.

Despite these efforts, Cochran soon found himself being sued by prisoner advocates for allowing matters to remain out of control. Insisting that he had done nothing wrong, the lawman blamed the other members of the Public Safety Coordinating Council, the body charged with keeping the inmate population below the cap, and claimed that their lack of cooperation had brought matters to a standstill. Accepting this explanation, Judge Hoeveler sharply rebuked the PSCC and gave Cochran the power to release inmates whenever capacity reached 96%.

The winding down of the overcrowding lawsuit should have brought some much-needed peace, but by now an even more contentious issue had arisen. In 1991, Sam Fields, a lobbyist for the Tennessee-based Corrections Corporation of America, proposed having that firm run the county's jails instead of the Broward Sheriff's Office. By 1992, this idea had begun to gain traction with the county commission (which was looking for ways to save money), but in March 1993 it agreed, by a 6–1 vote, to give Cochran a year to prove that he could run the jails more economically than his predecessor Nick Navarro.

In June 1994, CCA's proposal again came up for a vote, with Fields claiming that the company could save taxpayers $12 million a year (down from his earlier figure of $20 million). By now, Cochran was on record as favoring limited privatization, having endorsed a plan during the previous month to have an outside firm build and operate a work release facility for up to 600 non-violent offenders. Nevertheless, he once again opposed CCA's plan. Meanwhile, BSO detention deputies, worried about a possible cut in wages and benefits, set up a picket line outside the county commission's chambers and told the press that turning the jails over to CCA would compromise public safety. Fields responded to this claim by saying, "they don't know what they're talking about.... I [am] appalled by their ignorance [of our company]."[890] Unwilling to take a firm stand, the county commission unanimously voted to refer the matter to the PSCC for further study.

Not surprisingly, this decision satisfied no one, and the issue continued at a steady boil until March 1995, when Cochran and the county commission agreed to a new plan: while the department would continue to run the county's existing jails, including the planned Joseph V. Conte men's prison in Pompano Beach, all future facilities would be put up for bid.

And so matters stood until January 1998, when Ken Jenne was sworn in as Broward's fourteenth sheriff. Wasting no time, Jenne used his swearing-in ceremony as an opportunity to launch a full-blown attack on Cochran's compromise, telling his audience (which included all of the county's commissioners), "We're going to run our jail, not boost a business. I guarantee our professional corrections team will get the job done, efficiently and effectively."[891]

Jenne did not have to wait long for a fight, because by March 1998 the commission was getting ready to decide who would run the county's newest jail, a 750-bed women's facility in Pompano Beach. Facing intense competition from the Wackenhut Corrections Corporation, a Palm Beach Gardens company with impressive political connections, Jenne finally agreed to let it build the $25 million jail in exchange for BSO having the right to run it. In a press conference announcing the deal, Jenne crowed, "We're giving the people of Broward County the best of both worlds. They are the construction experts and we are the corrections experts. Good things come from partnerships like this."[892]

In the meantime, the new Conte men's prison had slipped seriously behind schedule. Even worse, sloppy work by Church & Tower, Inc., the general contractor, had resulted in numerous problems, including faulty lightning rods, inoperative doors and elevators, malfunctioning air conditioning and electri-

The Joseph V. Conte Facility in Pompano Beach (2001)

cal systems, and poor drainage. The delay also meant that overcrowding at the
main jail was again a problem, and a federal special master reported that conditions now were worse than they had been in 1976.

In October 1998, Church & Tower failed for the tenth time to meet its deadline, leading Jenne to threaten court action. Five months later, matters reached
a new low when the company revealed that it had lost the jail's master key
(meaning that more than 400 locks would have to be replaced). Upon learning of this latest fiasco, the county commission, with Jenne's support, finally
threw Church & Tower off the job and hired the Centex Rooney Construction
Company to complete the building. Several months later, in May 1999, a now
ebullient Jenne led reporters on a tour and proclaimed, "This is one of the
most cost-effective jails in the state of Florida. We've corrected the problems
and believe the facility is ready."[893]

Appendix A

The Sheriffs of
Broward County

No.	Name Place of Birth Date of Birth Place of Death Date of Death Interment	College Military Service Prior Work Experience Spouse Children Religion Political Party	Tenure
1.	Aden Waterman Turner Jacksonville, Florida September 14, 1865 Fort Lauderdale, Florida December 13, 1940 Evergreen Cemetery, Fort Lauderdale (section 9, row 8)	None None Farmer and road contractor Mary Agnes, Benjamin, C. Joseph, David, Edmund, Grace, Mary, Ralph, Reden, and Rudolph Methodist Democrat	Appointed October 1915 by Governor Park Trammell (after non-binding primary in June 1915) Elected 1916 Re-elected 1920 Suspended February 1922 by Governor Cary A. Hardee Removed May 1923 by Florida Senate Lost 1924 in Democratic primary Re-elected 1928 Lost 1932 in Democratic primary

2.	Paul Calhoun Bryan
	Crescent City, Florida
	January 13, 1891
	Bay Pines, Florida
	July 16, 1942
	Evergreen Cemetery, Fort
	    Lauderdale (section 9,
	    row 9)
		Attended Rollins College,
		    1908–10
		United States Army
		    (World War I)
		Assistant postmaster
		Jessie (known as Maude)
		Betty, Daniel, and Paul, Jr.
		Baptist
		Democrat
			Appointed March 1922
			    by Governor Cary A.
			    Hardee
			Elected 1924
			Lost 1928 in Democratic
			    primary

3.	Walter Reid Clark
	Fort Lauderdale, Florida
	December 11, 1904
	Baltimore, Maryland
	April 26, 1951
	Evergreen Cemetery, Fort
	    Lauderdale (section 5,
	    row 1)
		None
		None
		Butcher
		Avis (1st) and Odelle (2d)
		Curtis
		Presbyterian
		Democrat
			Elected 1932
			Re-elected 1936
			Re-elected 1940
			Suspended July 1942 by
			    Governor Spessard L.
			    Holland
			Re-instated June 1943 by
			    Florida Senate
			Re-elected 1944
			Re-elected 1948
			Suspended July 1950 by
			    Governor Fuller Warren
			Removed April 1951 by
			    Florida Senate

4.	Edward Tullis Lee
	Brooklet, Georgia
	December 31, 1910
	South Miami, Florida
	February 17, 1969
	Evergreen Cemetery, Fort
	    Lauderdale (section 6,
	    row 8)
		None
		United States Coast Guard
		Minor league baseball
		    player and Florida Power
		    and Light dispatcher
		Genevieve
		Edwina and Ronald
		Baptist
		Democrat
			Appointed July 1942 by
			    Governor Spessard L.
			    Holland
			Appointment expired June
			    1943

5.	Amos Harris Hall Morganfield, Kentucky November 14, 1914 Plantation, Florida September 2, 1966 Lauderdale Memorial Park Cemetery, Fort Lauderdale (block 23, row 6)	Attended Duke University, 1933–34 United States Army Air Force (World War II) Insurance executive and real estate developer Gladys (1st), Dorothy (2d), and Betty (3d) Kathy and Leslie Presbyterian Democrat	Appointed July 1950 by Governor Fuller Warren Elected 1952 Did not seek re-election 1956
6.	Justice Acquilla Lloyd Unincorporated Spencer County, Indiana November 26, 1894 Pembroke Pines, Florida May 11, 1978 Lauderdale Memorial Gardens Cemetery, Fort Lauderdale (St. Luke garden)	None United States Army (World War I) Car salesman, farmer, police officer, and firefighter Erma Alva and Jean Protestant (Disciples of Christ) Democrat (to 1956), Republican (1956–60), and Democrat (after 1960)	Elected 1956 Lost 1960 in Republican primary Lost 1960 in general election as write-in candidate
7.	Allen Brandt Michell Charleston, South Carolina April 18, 1903 Dade City, Florida March 5, 1983 Arlington National Cemetery, Arlington, Virginia (section 69, grave 527)	None United States Army (World War II) Career Philadelphia police officer Florence (1st) and Helen (2d) Michael and Terry Presbyterian Republican	Elected 1960 Re-elected 1964 Suspended March 1966 by Governor W. Haydon Burns Suspension lifted June 1966 Re-suspended June 1966 by Burns Second suspension lifted November 1966 Lost 1968 in Republican primary

8.	Thomas Joseph Walker Butte, Montana December 7, 1920 Still living	B.A., University of Notre Dame, 1942 United States Navy (World War II) Insurance executive Ruth Barbara, Frank, Hallie, Shelley, and Thomas, Jr. Catholic Democrat	(a) Appointed March 1966 by Governor W. Haydon Burns Appointment expired June 1966 (b) Re-appointed June 1966 by Governor Burns Re-appointment expired November 1966 *** (a) Until Walker could be sworn in, Civil Division Chief James W. Knight, Sr. (1917–87) served as Acting Sheriff (March 8–14, 1966) (b) Until Walker could be re-sworn in, Captain George W. Dunson (1906–74) served as Acting Sheriff (June 10–13, 1966)
9.	Edward John Stack Bayonne, New Jersey April 29, 1910 Fort Lauderdale, Florida November 3, 1989 Our Lady Queen of Heaven Cemetery, North Lauderdale (section C, grave F991)	B.A., Lehigh University, 1931 LL.B., University of Pennsylvania, 1934 M.A., Columbia University, 1938 United States Coast Guard (World War II) Attorney and politician Jean Kathleen and William Catholic Republican (to 1975) and Democrat (1975 on)	Elected 1968 Re-elected 1972 Re-elected 1976 Resigned December 1978 after being elected to the United States House of Representatives

10.	Robert Alfred Butterworth, Jr. Passaic, New Jersey August 20, 1942 Still living	B.S., University of Florida, 1965 J.D., University of Miami, 1969 None Attorney and judge Saundra (1st) and Marta (2d) Brandon, BreAnne, and Robert III Catholic Democrat	Appointed December 1978 by Governor Reubin O'D. Askew Elected 1980 Resigned October 1982 to become Director of the Florida Department of Highway Safety and Motor Vehicles
11.	George Angen Brescher Elizabeth, New Jersey March 24, 1943 Still living	B.S., Monmouth College, 1966 J.D., University of Miami, 1969 United States Army (Viet Nam War) Attorney and judge Gretchen Heidi Catholic Democrat	Appointed October 1982 by Governor D. Robert Graham Lost 1984 in general election
12.	Nicholas Gutierrez Navarro Jaruco, Cuba November 11, 1929 Still living	Attended University of Havana, 1948–50 United States Army (Korean War) Career Florida law enforcement officer Joan (1st) and Sharron (2d) Cynthia, Diana, John, and Nicholas Catholic Democrat (to 1984) and Republican (1984 on)	Elected 1984 Re-elected 1988 Lost 1992 in Republican primary

13.	Ronald Alva Cochran Lancaster, Pennsylvania September 23, 1936 Fort Lauderdale, Florida September 5, 1997 Cremated	A.S., Broward Community College, 1969 B.A., Biscayne College, 1979 United States Navy Career Fort Lauderdale police officer Jane (1st) and Carol (2d) Kimberly, Michael, and Michele Protestant Republican (to 1991) and Democrat (1991 on)	Elected 1992 Re-elected 1996 Died in office September 1997 *** Until Cochran's successor could be sworn in, Corrections and Rehabilitation Director Susan W. McCampbell (b. 1949) served as Acting Sheriff (September 5, 1997–January 9, 1998)
14.	Kenneth Clarence Jenne II New Haven, Connecticut December 1, 1946 Still living	A.A., Palm Beach Junior College, 1966 B.A., Florida Atlantic University, 1968 J.D., Florida State University, 1972 United States Army Reserve Attorney and politician Caroline Evan and Sarah Episcopalian Democrat	Appointed January 1998 by Governor Lawton M. Chiles, Jr. Elected 1998 Re-elected 2000 Re-elected 2004 Resigned September 2007
15.	Alfred Thomas Lamberti Bronx, New York April 14, 1954 Still living	A.S., Palm Beach Junior College, 1977 B.A., Florida Atlantic University, 1981 United States Coast Guard Reserve Career BSO deputy Holly (1st) and Holly (2d) Jaime, Joey, and Nicholas Catholic Republican	Appointed October 2007 by Governor Charles J. Crist, Jr. Elected 2008

Appendix B

Broward County Sheriff Election Results

Year	Democratic Primary (* = incumbent)	Republican Primary (* = incumbent)	General Election (* = incumbent)
1915	*Saturday, June 12* L.M. Bryan 61 (12%) Lucian Craig 92 (18%) J.A. Saxon 61 (12%) Aden W. Turner 295 (58%)	*Saturday, June 12* No candidates	None Aden W. Turner (D) (appointed automatically by Governor Park Trammell)
1916	*Tuesday, June 6* C.L. Harper 181 (29%) Aden W. Turner* 440 (71%)	*Tuesday, June 6* No candidates	*Tuesday, November 7* Aden W. Turner (D)* (elected automatically) *Note: Socialist candidate E.B. Steele's petition to be listed as a candidate was rejected by the courts*
1920	*Tuesday, June 8* Henry H. Marshall 153 (30%) Aden W. Turner* 359 (70%)	*Tuesday, June 8* No candidates	*Tuesday, November 2* Quinten M. Gornto (Socialist) 116 (15%) Aden W. Turner (D)* 661 (85%)
1924	*Tuesday, June 3* Paul C. Bryan* Won—vote total unknown Aden W. Turner Lost—vote total unknown *Note: All records for this election were destroyed in the 1926 Hurricane*	*Tuesday, June 3* No candidates	*Tuesday, November 4* Paul C. Bryan (D)* (automatically elected)

1928	*Tuesday, June 5* Paul C. Bryan* 1,415 (29%) W.M. "Bill" Johnson 885 (18%) J.F. Karnatz 555 (11%) E.L. Sessions 483 (10%) Aden W. Turner 1,538 (32%)	*Tuesday, June 5* Fred M. Wertz (unopposed)	*Tuesday, November 6* Aden W. Turner (D) 2,402 (55%) Fred M. Wertz (R) 1,986 (45%)
1932	*Tuesday, June 7* Jerome R. Barnes 1,003 (24%) William "Bill" Budd 237 (6%) Brack Cantrell 606 (14%) Walter R. Clark 861 (20%) Lucian Craig 215 (5%) W.M. "Bill" Johnson 448 (11%) C.M. "Buck" Moseley 191 (5%) Aden W. Turner* 668 (16%) *Run-Off* *Tuesday, June 28* Jerome R. Barnes 1,633 (40%) Walter R. Clark 2,408 (60%)	*Tuesday, June 7* Joseph P. Moe (unopposed)	*Tuesday, November 8* Walter R. Clark (D) 3,065 (60%) Joseph P. Moe (R) 2,077 (40%)
1936	*Tuesday, June 2* Brack Cantrell 1,634 (32%) Walter R. Clark* 3,486 (68%)	*Tuesday, June 2* Joseph P. Moe (unopposed)	*Tuesday, November 3* Walter R. Clark (D)* 4,862 (78%) Joseph P. Moe (R) 1,367 (22%)

1940	*Tuesday, May 7* Brack Cantrell 2,312 (26%) Walter R. Clark* 5,141 (58%) R.B. McDonald 1,364 (15%)	*Tuesday, May 7* No candidates	*Tuesday, November 5* Walter R. Clark (D)* (elected automatically)
1944	*Tuesday, May 2* Walter R. Clark* (unopposed)	*Tuesday, May 2* No candidates	*Tuesday, November 7* Walter R. Clark (D)* (elected automatically)
1948	*Tuesday, May 4* Walter R. Clark* 8,897 (53%) Joseph C. Mackey 3,395 (20%) Frank Tuppen 4,446 (27%)	*Tuesday, May 4* George J. Burckel (unopposed)	*Tuesday, November 2* George J. Burckel (R) 5,594 (34%) Walter R. Clark (D)* 11,100 (66%)
1952	*Tuesday, May 6* Robert L. "Bob" Clark 7,570 (32%) Amos H. Hall* 11,637 (49%) Justice A. Lloyd 2,271 (10%) Tony Salvino 2,378 (10%) *Run-Off* *Tuesday, May 27* Robert L. "Bob" Clark No votes (withdrew) Amos H. Hall* 13,182 (100%)	*Tuesday, May 6* Andy Phillips (unopposed)	*Tuesday, November 4* Amos H. Hall (D)* 18,055 (57%) Andy Phillips (R) 13,623 (43%)

1956	*Tuesday, May 8* Vance M. "Buzz" Currin 567 (2%) Roland R. Kelley 9,149 (31%) Tony Salvino 5,288 (18%) Claude A. Tindall 8,226 (28%) Frank Tuppen 6,418 (22%) *Run-Off* *Tuesday, May 29* Roland R. Kelley 10,988 (44%) Claude A. Tindall 14,162 (56%)	*Tuesday, May 8* Justice A. Lloyd 2,490 (54%) Ernest C. Murray 2,113 (46%)	*Tuesday, November 6* Justice A. Lloyd (R) 28,172 (50.1%) Claude A. Tindall (D) 28,078 (49.9%)
1960	*Tuesday, May 3* Claude H. Anderson, Sr. 3,752 (11%) Paul J. Grosso 1,255 (4%) W.J. "Jack" Mathis, Jr. 2,543 (7%) Tony Salvino 9,673 (27%) Lou Slone 1,943 (5%) Claude A. Tindall 16,487 (46%) *Run-Off* *Tuesday, May 24* Tony Salvino 15,687 (39%) Claude A. Tindall 25,003 (61%)	*Tuesday, May 3* Justice A. Lloyd* 5,794 (47%) Allen B. Michell 6,480 (53%)	*Tuesday, November 8* Justice A. Lloyd* (write-in) Negligible (0%) Allen B. Michell (R) 54,414 (53%) Claude A. Tindall (D) 48,361 (47%)

1964	*Tuesday, May 5* Richard A. Basinger 14,531 (33%) Percy K. Hempstead 6,978 (16%) Justice A. Lloyd 12,414 (28%) Tony Salvino 10,299 (23%) *Run-Off* *Tuesday, May 26* Richard A. Basinger 27,314 (57%) Justice A. Lloyd 20,403 (43%)	*Tuesday, May 5* William N. Horgan 3,593 (24%) Allen B. Michell* 11,412 (76%)	*Tuesday, November 3* Richard A. Basinger (D) 63,165 (49%) Allen B. Michell (R)* 66,716 (51%)
1968	*Tuesday, May 7* Richard A. Basinger 12,128 (51%) Marvin C. Bennett, Jr. 2,362 (10%) Lester Berger 1,742 (7%) George W. Dunson 1,786 (8%) Lawrence E. "Larry" Lang 5,701 (24%)	*Tuesday, May 7* John R. Hovey 2,023 (7%) John G. Lang 1,309 (5%) Allen B. Michell* 7,571 (27%) Albert R. Molina 680 (2%) Frank R. Pinter 910 (3%) Edward J. Stack 15,209 (55%)	*Tuesday, November 5* Richard A. Basinger (D) 61,118 (40%) Edward J. Stack (R) 91,147 (60%)
1972	*Tuesday, September 12* F.R. "Bill" Kyle 10,140 (39%) Lawrence E. "Larry" Lang 16,109 (61%)	*Tuesday, September 12* Robert Milligan 2,937 (8%) Donald O. Schultz 3,645 (10%) Edward J. Stack* 28,743 (77%) Ted F. Zeuch 1,904 (5%)	*Tuesday, November 7* Lawrence E. "Larry" Lang (D) 85,052 (35%) Edward J. Stack (R)* 157,219 (65%)

1976	*Tuesday, September 7* Jack E. Brown 19,233 (31%) Edward J. Stack* 43,223 (69%)	*Tuesday, September 7* Robert A. Danner 11,432 (36%) Robert L. Lane 4,586 (14%) Earl Oltersdorf 4,988 (16%) Donald O. Schultz 11,027 (34%) *Run-Off* *Tuesday, September 28* Robert A. Danner 9,718 (60%) Donald O. Schultz 6,540 (40%)	*Tuesday, November 2* Robert A. Danner (R) 122,600 (38%) Edward J. Stack (D)* 199,685 (62%)
1980	*Tuesday, September 9* Robert A. Butterworth, Jr.* 62,007 (79%) Donald O. "Orsi" Schultz 16,059 (21%)	*Tuesday, September 9* Earl Oltersdorf 21,669 (62%) N. Edward Roehling 13,059 (38%)	*Tuesday, November 4* Robert A. Butterworth, Jr. (D)* 262,168 (69%) Earl Oltersdorf (R) 118,231 (31%)
1984	*Tuesday, September 4* George A. Brescher* (unopposed)	*Tuesday, September 4* Nicholas G. Navarro (unopposed)	*Tuesday, November 6* George A. Brescher (D)* 211,697 (48%) Nicholas G. Navarro (R) 229,032 (52%)
1988	*Tuesday, September 6* James "Jim" Deckinger 18,696 (29%) Ralph A. Finno 28,045 (43%) Gil "Mr. G" Gesualdi 4,089 (6%) Walter E. Ramsdell 14,261 (22%) *Run-Off* *Tuesday, October 4* James "Jim" Deckinger 25,138 (53%) Ralph A. Finno 22,440 (47%)	*Tuesday, September 6* James J. "Jim" Howard 13,943 (33%) Nicholas G. Navarro* 28,620 (67%)	*Tuesday, November 8* James "Jim" Deckinger (D) 169,535 (38%) Nicholas G. Navarro (R)* 281,675 (62%)

1992	*Tuesday, September 1* Ronald A. Cochran 53,345 (59%) Craig S. Glasser 13,020 (14%) Elwood E. "Woody" King 2,617 (3%) Louis J. "Lou" Lupino 5,346 (6%) Walter E. Ramsdell 2,322 (3%) Gary Steinberg 14,483 (16%)	*Tuesday, September 1* James J. "Jim" Howard 19,584 (53%) Nicholas G. Navarro* 17,201 (47%)	*Tuesday, November 3* Ronald A. Cochran (D) 336,815 (68%) James J. "Jim" Howard (R) 158,146 (32%)
1996	*Tuesday, September 3* Ronald A. Cochran* 41,980 (59%) Lawrence C. "Chris" Roberts 7,863 (11%) Gary Steinberg 11,512 (16%) Lionel G. "Dark Horse" Stewart 9,752 (14%)	*Tuesday, September 3* Frank Hill 8,523 (32%) Kenneth R. "Ken" Wagner 17,704 (68%)	*Tuesday, November 5* Ronald A. Cochran (D) 311,334 (64%)* Kenneth R. "Ken" Wagner (R) 173,036 (36%)
1998	*Tuesday, September 1* George Albo 7,341 (13%) Kenneth C. Jenne II* 49,040 (87%)	*Tuesday, November 3* No candidates	*Tuesday, November 3* Kenneth C. Jenne II (D)* (elected automatically)
2000	*Tuesday, September 5* Kenneth C. Jenne II* 68,134 (66%) Lionel G. Stewart 34,792 (34%)	*Tuesday, September 5* No candidates	*Tuesday, November 7* Kenneth C. Jenne II (D)* (elected automatically)

2004	*Tuesday, August 31*
	Kenneth C. Jenne II
	  133,707 (77%)*
	Karl Tozzi 39,022 (23%)
		Tuesday, August 31
		No candidates
			Tuesday, November 2
			Kenneth C. Jenne II (D)*
			  (elected automatically)

2008	*Tuesday, August 26*
	Shahrukh "Shak" Dhanji
	  4,101 (6%)
	Scott J. Israel 22,927 (32%)
	Richard "Rick" Lemack
	  22,285 (31%)
	Wiley Thompson 15,258
	  (21%)
	Bruce L. Udolf 7,730
	  (11%)
		Tuesday, August 26
		Alfred T. "Al" Lamberti*
		  (unopposed)
			Tuesday, November 4
			Scott J. Israel (D) 333,045
			  (49%)
			Alfred T. "Al" Lamberti
			  (R)* 348,420 (51%)

Note: Percentages may not add up to 100% due to rounding. Names appear as shown on the ballot.

NOTES

Notes to Preface

1. *See further* William Alfred Morris, *The Medieval English Sheriff to 1300* (London: Manchester University Press, 1927), and Richard Gorski, *The Fourteenth-Century Sheriff: English Local Administration in the Late Middle Ages* (Rochester, NY: Boydell Press, 2003). *See also Sweat v. Waldon*, 123 Fla. 478, 167 So. 363, 364 (1936) (Div. B) ("The office of sheriff is one of ancient origin. Its creation goes back to the time of King Alfred of England, and maybe further.")

2. See Article VIII, § 1(d) of the Florida Constitution (2008). The state's first constitution (1838) made no mention of sheriffs, while the second (1861) partially set out their duties (Article IV, § 27) but failed to specify a selection method. The third (1865) required sheriffs to be elected (Article XVII, § 5), but the fourth (1868) directed the governor to appoint a sheriff in each county for a term of four years (Article VI, § 19). The state's fifth constitution (1885) once again made the office elective (Article VIII, § 6) beginning in November 1888 (Article XVIII, § 10), and this provision was carried over when the constitution underwent a wholesale revision in 1968.

In 1957, Miami-Dade County, using its recently-expanded home rule powers, replaced its elected sheriff with an appointed police chief. To date, it remains the only Florida county to have taken this step. See Jack R. Greene ed., *The Encyclopedia of Police Science* 787–88 (New York: Routledge, 3d ed. 2006). In 2002, Palm Beach County opted to have future sheriff candidates run in non-partisan elections. No other Florida county has followed suit, although it has been suggested that Broward consider doing so. *See* Fred Grimm, *Nonpartisan Sheriff for Broward? Let Voters Decide*, Miami Herald, Feb. 8, 2009, at B1.

3. A sheriff's duties are now set out in detail in § 30.15 of the Florida Statutes (2008), which reads as follows:

(1) Sheriffs, in their respective counties, in person or by deputy, shall:

(a) Execute all process of the Supreme Court, circuit courts, county courts, and boards of county commissioners of this state, to be executed in their counties.

(b) Execute such other writs, processes, warrants, and other papers directed to them, as may come to their hands to be executed in their counties.

(c) Attend all terms of the circuit court and county court held in their counties.

(d) Execute all orders of the boards of county commissioners of their counties, for which services they shall receive such compensation, out of the county treasury, as said boards may deem proper.

(e) Be conservators of the peace in their counties.

(f) Suppress tumults, riots, and unlawful assemblies in their counties with force and strong hand when necessary.

(g) Apprehend, without warrant, any person disturbing the peace, and carry that person before the proper judicial officer, that further proceedings may be had against him or her according to law.

(h) Have authority to raise the power of the county and command any person to assist them, when necessary, in the execution of the duties of their office; and, whoever, not being physically incompetent, refuses or neglects to render such assistance, shall be punished by imprisonment in jail not exceeding 1 year, or by fine not exceeding $500.

(i) Be, ex officio, timber agents for their counties.

(j) Perform such other duties as may be imposed upon them by law.

(2) Sheriffs, in their respective counties, in person or by deputy, shall, at the will of the board of county commissioners, attend, in person or by deputy, all meetings of the boards of county commissioners of their counties, for which services they shall receive such compensation, out of the county treasury, as said boards may deem proper.

(3) On or before January 1, 2002, every sheriff shall incorporate an antiracial or other antidiscriminatory profiling policy into the sheriff's policies and practices, utilizing the Florida Police Chiefs Association Model Policy as a guide. Antiprofiling policies shall include the elements of definitions, traffic stop procedures, community education and awareness efforts, and policies for the handling of complaints from the public.

4. *See* Walter H. Anderson, *A Treatise on the Law of Sheriffs, Coroners and Constables, with Forms* (Buffalo: Dennis & Company, 1941).

5. *See* Harry C. Buffardi, *The History of the Office of Sheriff*, available at http://www.correctionhistory.org/html/chronicl/sheriff/toc.htm.

6. *See* William Warren Rogers and James M. Denham, *Florida Sheriffs: A History 1821–1945* (Tallahassee: Sentry Press, 2001), and Victor R. Silvestri, *Encyclopedia of Florida Sheriffs 1821–2008* (Clanton, AL: Heritage Publishing Consultants, Inc., 2009).

Notes to Chapter 1

7. *See* Robert P. Porter et al., "Progress of the Nation 1790 to 1890," *in* I Department of the Interior, *Report on Population of the United States at the Eleventh Census: 1890*, at xxxiv (Washington, DC: U.S. Government Printing Office, 1895) ("Up to and including 1880 the country had a frontier of settlement, but at present the unsettled area has been so broken into by isolated bodies of settlement that there can hardly be said to be a frontier line.").

8. Stuart B. McIver, *Dreamers, Schemers and Scalawags: The Florida Chronicles (Vol. 1)*, at 149 (Sarasota: Pineapple Press, Inc., 1994).

9. Known as the Warren Act, the law now appears at Fla. Stat. §§ 588.12–588.26 (2008). Its constitutionality was upheld in *Lynch v. Durrance*, 77 So. 2d 458 (Fla. 1955) (Div. A).

10. Frederic Remington, *Cracker Cowboys of Florida*, 91 Harper's New Monthly Magazine, Aug. 1895, at 339, 339.

11. Doug Sarubbi ed., *Orange County Sheriff's Office, Orlando, Florida—150th Anniversary History Book* 29 (Paducah, KY: Turner Publishing Company, 1994).

12. Jim Bob Tinsely, *Florida Cow Hunter: The Life and Times of Bone Mizell* 19 (Orlando: University of Central Florida Press, 1990).

13. *Id.* at ix.

14. Remington, *supra* note 10, at 342.

15. *See infra* note 103 and accompanying text.

16. *BSO Earns Coveted Triple Crown Award*, Miami Herald, July 5, 2000, at 2B (explaining that the department had been accredited by the American Correctional Association, American Society of Crime Laboratory Directors, Commission on Accreditation for Law Enforcement Agencies, Government Finance Officers Association, and National Commission on Correctional Health Care).

Notes to Chapter 2

17. *See Lasseter v. Bryan*, 67 Fla. 478, 65 So. 590 (1914).

18. *Editorial*, Fort Lauderdale Sentinel, Apr. 30, 1915, at 4.

19. *White Star Line Makes First Trip*, Fort Lauderdale Sentinel, July 2, 1915, at 1.

20. *Automobiles Arrive on Time*, Fort Lauderdale Sentinel, Oct. 29, 1915, at 1.

21. *Broward Officials Nominated Saturday*, Fort Lauderdale Sentinel, June 18, 1915, at 1.

22. Wendy Shaffer, *Out of the Rough*, Miami Herald, Sept. 30, 1990, at 12 (Neighbors).

23. Wesley W. Stout, *Our Jail a Box-Car*, Fort Lauderdale Daily News, Mar. 16, 1954, at 6A.

24. *See* Glyndon G. Van Deusen, *William Henry Seward* 153 (New York: Oxford University Press, 1967). Although the circumstances surrounding this remark are unknown, most historians believe that Seward uttered it in 1860 as a rebuke to U.S. Senator Stephen A. Douglas (D-Ill.), who frequently used the N-word.

25. *Coast Guard Chief Warns Miami Klan*, Fort Lauderdale Daily News, May 6, 1938, at 1.

26. *Editorial*, Fort Lauderdale Sentinel, Oct. 8, 1915, at 4.

27. *See infra* notes 167–73 and accompanying text.

28. *Tar and Feather White Pastor of Negro Church*, Miami Herald, July 18, 1921, at 1.

29. *Marshal Bryan Kills a Coon*, Fort Lauderdale Sentinel, Apr. 11, 1913, at 1.

30. *Ft. Lauderdale's Shame*, Fort Lauderdale Sentinel, Sept. 17, 1915, at 4.

31. *Id.*

Notes to Chapter 3

32. This chapter originally was published as William P. Cahill, *The First Sheriffs of Broward County, Florida: 1915–1933*, 24 Broward Legacy 3 (2003–2004). It is reprinted here (as revised) with the kind permission of the Broward County Historical Commission.

33. *Editorial*, Fort Lauderdale Sentinel, June 18, 1915, at 4.

34. *Broward County Celebration*, Fort Lauderdale Sentinel, Oct. 8, 1915, at 1.

35. This was the day that all of the county's new officers were sworn in, *see id.*, and marks the official start of Broward County. *See* Broward County Historical Commission, *Broward Milestones*, at http://www.broward.org/history/timeline.htm.

36. *Brutal Murder at Pompano*, Fort Lauderdale Sentinel, Nov. 19, 1915, at 1.

37. *See Will Write Candidates Names on Tickets*, Fort Lauderdale Sentinel, Oct. 27, 1916, at 1 (reporting on Circuit Judge H. Pierre Branning's refusal to put the party on the ballot

"because their petitions were not in the form required by the statute."). Had Steele been allowed to run, he would have been a formidable candidate, for in 1916 the Socialists were at the height of their popularity (the party fractured the following year over the question of whether to support or oppose America's entry into World War I). For a further discussion, *see* Ray F. Robbins II, *The Socialist Party in Florida: 1900–1916* (1971) (unpublished M.A. dissertation, Samford University).

In deciding that the Socialists' petition was defective, Judge Branning adopted the argument of County Attorney Wilfred I. Evans. In a letter dated October 18, 1916, he had written:

> There are three methods provided by law by which a party may become a candidate for county office in a general election, to-wit:
>
> 1. By nomination in a regularly conducted primary.
> 2. By petition of any caucus, convention or mass meeting.
> 3. By petition addressed to the candidate himself and signed by twenty-five [individuals] qualified to vote for said office.
>
> The petition of the Socialist party cannot be considered because it is not addressed to the elector or electors themselves, requesting them to become candidates but is addressed to the clerk of the circuit court or board of county Commissioners.
>
> I therefore advise that you do not consider said petition.

Socialist Candidates Not on Ticket, Fort Lauderdale Sentinel, Oct. 20, 1916, at 1. Few people, however, were taken in by this explanation, and instead understood that: "When it comes to local offices, 'vote her democratic' is the ruling of the 'powers that be.'" *Id.*

38. *Bootlegger Gets Six Months and $100*, Fort Lauderdale Sentinel, May 25, 1917, at 1.

39. *Sheriff Captured Three More Stills*, Fort Lauderdale Sentinel, Aug. 29, 1919, at 1.

40. *Moonshine Liquor User in Trouble*, Fort Lauderdale Sentinel, Aug. 6, 1920, at 1.

41. *Tar and Feathers for Davie Slacker*, Fort Lauderdale Sentinel, Apr. 26, 1918, at 5.

42. *German Sympathizer Meets His Waterloo*, Fort Lauderdale Sentinel, May 10, 1918, at 1.

43. *Id.*

44. *Id.*

45. *Id.*

46. *Id.*

47. *Id.*

48. *Sheriff Says Good Bye to N. C. Pike*, Fort Lauderdale Sentinel, May 18, 1917, at 1.

49. *Pompano School Teacher in Trouble*, Fort Lauderdale Herald, Sept. 26, 1919, at 1.

50. *White Star Auto Held Up by Bandits on Dixie Highway*, Fort Lauderdale Herald, Oct. 3, 1919, at 1.

51. *Id.*

52. *Sheriff Turner Attacked by a Negro Desperado*, Fort Lauderdale Sentinel, Jan. 16, 1920, at 1.

53. *Id.*

54. *Id.*

55. *Id.*

56. *Id.*

57. *Sheriff Turner Narrowly Escapes Death at Hands of Desperate Negro*, Fort Lauderdale Herald, Jan. 16, 1920, at 1.

58. *Id.*

59. *Thirteen Wiretappers Caught Here—Raid Made by Governor's Agent Assisted by Local Sheriff's Office*, Fort Lauderdale Herald, Feb. 3, 1922, at 1.

60. *"Con" Mens' Bonds Are $110,000*, Fort Lauderdale Herald, Feb. 10, 1922, at 1.

61. *Alleged Wiretappers Show Up for Trial in Circuit Court*, Fort Lauderdale Herald, Mar. 17, 1922, at 1.

62. *Wiretappers Plead Guilty in Circuit Court and are Given a Fine of $20,000.00*, Fort Lauderdale Herald, Mar. 31, 1922, at 1.

63. *Sheriff is Suspended*, Fort Lauderdale Herald, Mar. 3, 1922, at 1.

64. *Id.* As has been pointed out elsewhere, exactly why Hardee picked Bryan is unclear:

> Little is known of the personal history of Sheriff Paul C. Bryan ... but, if this editor were given the task of writing an obituary for him, it would behoove him to ask why Bryan was appointed in the first place? Given the facts of his tender age and lack of political acumen and dearth of previous law enforcement experience, the selection of Paul C. Bryan to be sheriff of this large county at a significant time in its history remains a mystery. It is almost as if Paul C. Bryan enjoyed a special relationship with the governor or with the Democratic party— but there is no indication of that either.... One can only assume that Paul C. Bryan was a compelling personality, a glib talker, and a salesman of quality who wasted his talents in the menial job of sheriff of this county....

Silvestri, *supra* note 6, at 105.

65. *See* Genealogical Society of Broward County Florida (GSBC), *Notable Persons of Broward County Florida*, at http://www.rootsweb.ancestry.com/~flgsbc/resources/biographies.html ("Susie Bryan was the Fort Lauderdale Postmistress for 15 years and reportedly the first white woman to be settle[d] in Broward Co., FL in 1898.)."

66. *Rollins Alumnus New Sheriff of Broward County*, Rollins Sandspur, Mar. 14, 1922, at 1.

67. *Id.*

68. By this time, the sport had become a local passion:

> One activity embraced by all of Fort Lauderdale's "communities" was baseball. Since 1909 Fort Lauderdale had fielded a town team, playing like teams from neighboring areas. "Beat Miami!" was the usual rallying cry.... Games were played at Stranahan Field, on land located at the southwest corner of Federal Highway and Broward Boulevard that was donated by the Stranahans....
>
> By the 1920s the town team had turned semi-pro and town shops would close so all locals could attend the game. In 1924 the Fort Lauderdale team—now named the Tarpons—won the East Coast League pennant. In 1925, at the height of the [land] boom, a new ballpark was created on West Broward Boulevard at the site of the present Fort Lauderdale police headquarters.

Susan Gillis, *Fort Lauderdale: The Venice of America* 33–34 (Charleston, SC: Arcadia Publishing, 2004).

69. *Commissioner Dan Johnson Shot to Death*, Fort Lauderdale Herald, Feb. 16, 1923, at 1.

70. *Miami Man Taken in Custody Here on Grave Charge*, Fort Lauderdale Herald, Apr. 14, 1922, at 1.

71. *Young Men Accused of Rape*, Fort Lauderdale Sentinel, Dec. 22, 1922, at 1.

72. Letter from Cary A. Hardee, Governor of Florida, to Paul C. Bryan, Sheriff of Broward County, dated Dec. 27, 1923.

73. Letter from Paul C. Bryan, Sheriff of Broward County, to O.W. Brady, dated July 23, 1926.

74. Letter from D.E. Richer, Inspector—American Express Company, to Paul C. Bryan, Sheriff of Broward County, dated June 9, 1925.

75. Letter from Paul C. Bryan, Sheriff of Broward County, to D.E. Richer, Inspector—American Express Company, dated June 12, 1925.

76. Letter from Cary A. Hardee, Governor of Florida, to Paul C. Bryan, Sheriff of Broward County, dated May 24, 1923.

77. *Id.*

78. Letter from John W. Tidball, President—Fort Lauderdale Chamber of Commerce, to Paul C. Bryan, Sheriff of Broward County, dated May 5, 1925.

79. *23 Aliens Picked Up by Sheriff at Deerfield on Sun.*, Fort Lauderdale Herald, Apr. 20, 1923, at 1.

80. Letter from Cary A. Hardee, Governor of Florida, to Paul C. Bryan, Sheriff of Broward County, dated Sept. 16, 1924.

81. *Governor's Action is Sustained in the Removal of A. W. Turner*, Fort Lauderdale Herald, May 11, 1923, at 1.

82. *While Away Hours in Writing Book*, Fort Lauderdale Sentinel, June 18, 1915, at 2.

83. Hardee 9/16/24 Letter, *supra* note 80.

84. *Former Chief Deputy Hicks Elected J.P.*, Fort Lauderdale Daily News, Nov. 3, 1926, at 1.

85. Letter from P.F. Hambsch, Prohibition Administrator, to Paul C. Bryan, Sheriff of Broward County, dated Apr. 15, 1926.

86. *Id.*

87. Letter from Paul C. Bryan, Sheriff of Broward County, to P.F. Hambsch, Prohibition Administrator, dated Apr. 17, 1926.

88. *Id.*

89. Hambsch 4/15/26 Letter, *supra* note 85.

90. *Florida Dry Raiders Arrest 32*, St. Petersburg Evening Independent, Jan. 27, 1927, at 1.

91. *Sheriff Bryan, Deputies and 7 Police Held on Liquor Charges*, Fort Lauderdale Daily News, Jan. 27, 1927, at 1.

92. *Florida Dry Raiders*, *supra* note 90.

93. *See further* Donald D. Spencer, *History of Gambling in Florida* 105 (Ormond Beach, FL: Camelot Publishing Co., 2007).

94. *See Pompano Horse Club, Inc. v. State ex rel. Bryan*, 93 Fla. 415, 111 So. 801 (1927) (en banc). In two other cases decided on the same day, it was held that dog tracks also could not sell certificates, *see Reinmiller v. State*, 93 Fla. 462, 111 So. 633 (1927) (Div. B), and giving investors the right to seek refunds did not make the scheme lawful. *See Tampa Jockey Club v. State*, 93 Fla. 459, 111 So. 816 (1927) (en banc).

95. Telegram from Paul C. Bryan, Sheriff of Broward County, to John W. Martin, Governor of Florida, dated Mar. 12, 1927.

96. Walter St. Denis, *Pompano Track Closed When Governor Speaks*, Miami Herald, Mar. 13, 1927, at 25.

97. *Governor Would Send Guard Here to Enforce Laws*, Fort Lauderdale Daily News, Jan. 6, 1928, at 1.

98. Telegram from Paul C. Bryan, Sheriff of Broward County, to John W. Martin, Governor of Florida, dated Jan. 5, 1928.

99. Donald G. Lester, *Justice of the Peace W.A. Hicks*, 15 Broward Legacy 2, at 10 (Winter/Spring 1992).

100. *See Hicks v. State*, 97 Fla. 199, 120 So. 330 (1929) (Div. A).

101. *W. Hicks Trial Enters Fourth Day*, Fort Lauderdale Daily News, Apr. 17, 1930, at 1.

102. *See Paul Bryan Dies 36 Hours Following Sister's Death Here*, Fort Lauderdale Daily News, July 16, 1942, at 1.

103. Lester, *supra* note 99, at 20 n.45.

104. Letter from Aden W. Turner, Sheriff of Broward County, to J.A. Johnson, Sheriff of Polk County, dated Jan. 13, 1931.

105. Letter from Aden W. Turner, Sheriff of Broward County, to Frank Karel, Sheriff of Orange County, dated Jan. 21, 1931.

106. Letter from Aden W. Turner, Sheriff of Broward County, to Richard W. Thomas, Sheriff of Oneida County (N.Y.), dated Mar. 5, 1931.

107. Telegram from Aden W. Turner, Sheriff of Broward County, to Richard W. Thomas, Sheriff of Oneida County (N.Y.), dated Dec. 24, 1931.

108. Letter from Aden W. Turner, Sheriff of Broward County, to the H. & W.B. Drew Company—Jacksonville, dated Oct. 17, 1930. Today, Florida law is quite specific when it comes to how badges are to look: "For purposes of uniformity and in aid of the recognition of their official identity by the public, a badge in the shape of a five-pointed star with a replica of the great seal of Florida with the map of Florida superimposed thereon inscribed in the center is designated as the official badge to be worn by the sheriffs and deputy sheriffs of all counties of the state." *See* Fla. Stat. §30.46(2) (2008).

109. *Legion Post Resents Sheriff's Action*, Fort Lauderdale Daily News, Aug. 9, 1929, at 1.

110. *Deputy Campbell Resigns Office*, Fort Lauderdale Daily News, Sept. 14, 1929, at 1.

111. *Resigned Deputy Explains Position*, Fort Lauderdale Daily News, Sept. 19, 1929, at 1.

112. *WCTU Deplores City Lawlessness*, Fort Lauderdale Daily News, Mar. 19, 1930, at 1.

113. Letter from Aden W. Turner, Sheriff of Broward County, to Doyle E. Carlton, Governor of Florida, dated Aug. 6, 1930.

114. For their part, the defendants argued that because of the vagaries of Florida's Gulf Stream, they had been fishing in international waters and therefore could not be tried in a state court. *See Just Where Is This Famed Florida Gulf Stream? What Is Your Guess*, Fort Lauderdale Daily News, Apr. 21, 1932, at 1 (noting that this contention caught prosecutor Louis F. Maire off guard and led him to ask for a postponement of the trial "until authoritative data on the subject of the location of the Gulf Stream could be introduced."). As has been pointed out elsewhere, this question continues to bedevil Florida's courts. *See* Robert M. Jarvis, *Case Note: Territorial Waters*, 34 Journal of Maritime Law and Commerce 351 (Apr. 2003).

115. *Governor Asked for Aid and Protection*, Fort Lauderdale Daily News, Oct. 25, 1929, at 1.

116. *Id.*

117. *Id.*

118. *Sheriff Wars on Robbers*, Fort Lauderdale Daily News, July 26, 1932, at 1.

119. *Booze Burglars Loot Liquor in a Brazen Break-In*, Fort Lauderdale Daily News, June 6, 1930, at 1.

120. *First Civil Indian Wedding Held in County Ends Groom Jail Term*, Fort Lauderdale Daily News, Apr. 29, 1929, at 1.

121. *"Voodoo" Doctor Lands in Prison*, Fort Lauderdale Daily News, Mar. 27, 1930, at 2.

122. *Al Capone Not Wanted Here*, Fort Lauderdale Daily News, Mar. 19, 1930, at 1.

123. *Al Capone is in Miami for a Rest*, Fort Lauderdale Daily News, Apr. 21, 1930, at 1.

124. *Dade Grand Jury Denounces Capone*, Fort Lauderdale Daily News, Apr. 25, 1930, at 1.

125. *One Florida City Welcomes Capone*, Miami Herald, Mar. 21, 1930, at 1.

126. *Sheriff Receives Written Threat*, Fort Lauderdale Daily News, Mar. 20, 1930, at 1.

127. *Id.*

128. *Gangland Note is En Route to A. W. Turner*, Fort Lauderdale Daily News, Mar. 21, 1930, at 1.

129. *Id.*

130. *Written Threat, supra* note 126.

131. Letter from B.A. Tolbert, Dean of Students—University of Florida, to Aden W. Turner, Sheriff of Broward County, dated Nov. 18, 1931.

132. Letter from Aden W. Turner, Sheriff of Broward County, to J.C. Sheffield, Chief of the U.S. Immigration Service—West Palm Beach Office, dated Apr. 4, 1929.

133. *Id.*

134. Letter from Aden W. Turner, Sheriff of Broward County, to Doyle E. Carlton, Governor of Florida, dated Mar. 8, 1929.

135. *"Hobo Special" Makes One-Way Trip to Line*, Fort Lauderdale Daily News, Nov. 5, 1930, at 1.

136. Letter from L.M. Hatton, Jr., Sheriff of Hillsborough County, to Aden W. Turner, Sheriff of Broward County, dated Feb. 1, 1929.

137. *Id.*

138. Letter from Cary D. Landis, Attorney General of Florida, to Aden W. Turner, Sheriff of Broward County, dated May 17, 1932.

139. Letter from Norman MacKay, Advertising Director—Miami Broadcasting Company, to Aden W. Turner, Sheriff of Broward County, dated May 13, 1932. Included with the letter was the following sample announcement, which the station offered to air for two weeks during the day for $32.50 or at night for $65:

> Broward County voters attention: A.W. Turner, your sheriff, has a message for you. Mr. Turner says: "My aim has been to serve the citizens of Broward county to the fullest extent of my ability, honestly, without fear or favor. If you feel I have accomplished this in the past I shall appreciate your votes on June 7th."

140. As usual, Turner came right to the point. In full, his message read: "This is to authorize you to release to Mrs. W. M. Mears, the twenty one chickens that you are holding subject to the Sheriff's orders." Letter from Aden W. Turner, Sheriff of Broward County, to William Gregory, dated Feb. 13, 1930.

141. Letter from Aden W. Turner, Sheriff of Broward County, to Ernest Amos, Comptroller of Florida, dated Jan. 15, 1930.

142. Letter from Aden W. Turner, Sheriff of Broward County, to U.S. Marshal's Office—Miami, dated May 16, 1932.

143. Letter from Aden W. Turner, Sheriff of Broward County, to Leo M. Mack, Chief Deputy, U.S. Marshal's Office—Jacksonville, dated July 27, 1932.

144. Report of Aden W. Turner, Sheriff of Broward County, to Ernest Amos, Comptroller of Florida, dated Dec. 31, 1931, at 1.

145. Letter from Aden W. Turner, Sheriff of Broward County, to Cary D. Landis, Attorney General of Florida, dated Feb. 3, 1932.

146. In campaigning for a fifth term, Turner ran on his record, which he described as including closing down the area's roadhouses, solving all but a handful of crimes, and fight-

ing a never-ending battle with the "professional criminals that try to harbor themselves in Broward county." *Turner Seeking Reelection on Past Record*, Fort Lauderdale Daily News, May 27, 1932, at 4. Turner also claimed his department was "the most efficient Sheriff's office in the state." *Id.*

147. *Closing of Jail Threatened by Unpaid Sheriff*, Miami Herald, July 10, 1932, at 1.

148. *No Pay, No Arrests is Sheriff's Policy*, Fort Lauderdale Daily News, Aug. 27, 1932, at 7.

149. *"Bloody Broward,"* Fort Lauderdale Daily News, Nov. 12, 1931, at 4.

150. Report of Aden W. Turner, Sheriff of Broward County, to Ernest Amos, Comptroller of Florida, dated June 30, 1930, at 1.

151. Letter from Aden W. Turner, Sheriff of Broward County, to F.O. Dickinson, dated Sept. 3, 1930.

152. *Id.*

153. *See Allen [sic] W. Turner, Broward's First Sheriff, is Dead*, Fort Lauderdale Daily News, Dec. 13, 1940, at 1.

Notes to Chapter 4

154. *Turner Campaign Ad*, Fort Lauderdale Daily News, June 8, 1932, at 2.

155. *Hand Severely Cut in Sausage Mill*, Fort Lauderdale Sentinel, Oct. 3, 1919, at 8.

156. *See Lasher v. State*, 80 Fla. 712, 86 So. 689 (1920).

157. *Clark Campaign Ad*, Fort Lauderdale Daily News, Nov. 7, 1932, at 2.

158. Letter from Walter R. Clark, Sheriff of Broward County, to Kenneth A. Marmon, Superintendent—Seminole Indian Agency, dated Mar. 30, 1948.

159. Bryan Brooks, *The Day They Lynched Reuben [sic] Stacey*, Fort Lauderdale Sun-Sentinel, July 17, 1988, at 10 (Sunshine Magazine).

160. *Mrs. Mollison Revamps Story of Arrest Here*, Fort Lauderdale Daily News, Jan. 31, 1934, at 1.

161. *Id.*

162. *Chambers v. State*, 136 Fla. 568, 187 So. 156, 157 (1939) (Div. A).

163. *Negroes Await Death in Chair*, Fort Lauderdale Daily News, July 11, 1933, at 1.

164. *Id.*

165. *See Chambers v. State*, 111 Fla. 707, 151 So. 499 (1933) (en banc), *petition granted*, 113 Fla. 786, 152 So. 437 (1934) (Div. B).

166. *See Chambers v. State of Florida*, 309 U.S. 227 (1940).

167. It now is known that what actually took place is this: "Stacey, a homeless tenant farmer, had gone to [Jones's] house to ask for food; [Jones] became frightened and screamed when she saw Stacey's face." Dora Apel, *Imagery of Lynching: Black Men, White Women, and the Mob* 40 (Piscataway, NJ: Rutgers University Press, 2004).

168. *Grand Jury Called to Probe Mob*, Fort Lauderdale Daily News, July 20, 1935, at 1.

169. *The Law Must Say*, Fort Lauderdale Daily News, July 20, 1935, at 1.

170. Brooks, *supra* note 159.

171. Tony Pugh, *Jim Crow Justice Delivered by Lynch Mob*, Miami Herald, Feb. 12, 1992, at 1 (Broward).

172. *Id.*

173. *Id.*

174. *Law Loses Prisoner to Death When Local Man Takes Poison*, Fort Lauderdale Daily News, Sept. 18, 1935, at 1.

175. Rogers and Denham, *supra* note 6, at 253.

176. When the matter reached the Florida Supreme Court, however, it found the legislation constitutional. *See Lee v. City of Miami*, 121 Fla. 93, 163 So. 486 (1935) (en banc).

177. *See 2 Slot Operators Pay License Fee in Broward Area*, Fort Lauderdale Daily News, Nov. 16, 1935, at 1 (quoting Clark as saying, "[I]f they operate here they will have to stay within the law. I will be guided by State Attorney Marie in the interpretation of the law governing operation of the machines.").

178. *Look Out for the Confidence Men*, Fort Lauderdale Daily News, Mar. 28, 1935, at 1.

179. *Id.*

180. After it became apparent that many local officials were planning to conduct raids as soon as the licenses expired, the Florida Supreme Court stepped in and held that the machine's owners had to be given a "reasonable" amount of time to remove their devices from the state. *See Bechtol v. Lee*, 129 Fla. 374, 176 So. 265 (1937).

181. *Florida Voters, in Grand Sweep, Place in Democrats and Cast Out Slot Devices*, Fort Lauderdale Daily News, Nov. 5, 1936, at 1.

182. *Broward's Shame is Exposed by Magazine in Sensational Article on Racketeering*, Fort Lauderdale Daily News, Mar. 4, 1937, at 1.

183. *Id.*

184. *Id.*

185. *Id.*

186. *Broward's Shame*, Fort Lauderdale Daily News, Mar. 3, 1937, at 1.

187. *Hollywood Police Raid Game Joints*, Fort Lauderdale Daily News, Mar. 4, 1937, at 1.

188. *Vice Affidavits Sent to Governor*, Fort Lauderdale Daily News, Mar. 6, 1937, at 1.

189. *Gambling is Given Whitewash Coat*, Fort Lauderdale Daily News, Mar. 10, 1937, at 1.

190. *No Gambling? Writer Tells of "Little Incident,"* Fort Lauderdale Daily News, Mar. 4, 1937, at 1.

191. *Id.*

192. *20 'Reds' Nabbed in Raid Here*, Fort Lauderdale Daily News, Apr. 29, 1938, at 1.

193. *Id.*

194. *Broward Becomes Battleground as Clark Stands Pat*, Fort Lauderdale Daily News, May 6, 1938, at 1.

195. *Id.*

196. *Id.*

197. *Judge Discharges Persons Arrested in Negro Section*, Fort Lauderdale Daily News, May 20, 1938, at 1.

198. *Gambling Flourished, FBI Avers*, Fort Lauderdale Daily News, May 25, 1943, at 1.

199. *Hoover Says Police Corrupt*, Fort Lauderdale Daily News, Feb. 6, 1940, at 1.

200. *Holland Postpones Appointment of New Sheriff—Delays Selection After Suspending Walter R. Clark*, Fort Lauderdale Daily News, July 21, 1942, at 1.

201. *Hunters Close in on Miami Killer*, Fort Lauderdale Daily News, July 23, 1942, at 1.

202. *Manhunt for Miami Slayer is Called Off*, Fort Lauderdale Daily News, July 25, 1942, at 1.

203. *Holland Postpones Appointment*, *supra* note 200.

204. *'Eddie' Lee Named as New Sheriff*, Fort Lauderdale Daily News, July 23, 1942, at 1.

205. J.K. Van Denburg, Jr., *Pass in Review*, Fort Lauderdale Daily News, July 24, 1942, at 1.

206. *Id.*

207. *'Eddie' Lee Named, supra* note 204.

208. *Hollywood Man Arrested on Bookie Charge*, Fort Lauderdale Daily News, Aug. 13, 1942, at 7.

209. *Sheriff Keeps Up Drive Against Vice in Broward County*, Fort Lauderdale Daily News, Aug. 26, 1942, at 2.

210. *Holland Raps Verdict on Clark*, Fort Lauderdale Daily News, June 2, 1943, at 1.

211. *Id.*

212. *See Former County Sheriff Edward Lee, 58, Dies*, Fort Lauderdale News, Feb. 18, 1969, at 2B.

213. *Gambler 'Charity' Probed*, Fort Lauderdale Daily News, June 6, 1950, at 1A.

214. *Bolita's Illegal Gambling*, Fort Lauderdale Daily News, Apr. 12, 1948, at 4.

215. *Id.*

216. *Id.*

217. *Threats Mar Campaign*, Fort Lauderdale Daily News, May 3, 1948, at 1.

218. *'What Mobs?' Asks Sheriff After Expose*, Fort Lauderdale Daily News, Feb. 20, 1948, at 1.

219. *Clark Re-Election Ad*, Fort Lauderdale Daily News, May 3, 1948, at 18.

220. *Broward Gambling Spots Close*, Fort Lauderdale Daily News, Feb. 23, 1950, at 1B.

221. Ironically, after this business was shut down, one of its fronts—a juke box enterprise known as the Broward Music Company—began making money honestly. In 1956, the Florida Supreme Court decided that Clark's widow Odelle was entitled to a share of its profits. *See Williams v. Clark*, 90 So. 2d 805 (Fla. 1956) (en banc).

222. *Sheriff Stands Revealed as Unfit for Office*, Fort Lauderdale Daily News, July 17, 1950, at 1A.

223. William H. Kramer, *Walter Reid Clark: Legendary Sheriff of Broward County* 83 (1993) (unpublished M.A. dissertation, Florida Atlantic University).

224. Henry Kinney, *Gov. Warren Suspends Clark*, Fort Lauderdale Daily News, July 21, 1950, at 1A.

225. *Id.*

226. *Humanitarian Gesture?*, Fort Lauderdale Daily News, Apr. 4, 1951, at 8A.

227. In *Sullivan v. Leatherman*, 48 So. 2d 836 (Fla. 1950) (en banc), the Florida Supreme Court had tossed out an indictment accusing Sullivan of corruption, thereby placing Warren's suspension order on shaky legal grounds:

On November 10, 1950, Thomas J. Kelly was appointed by the Governor 'to be Sheriff in and for Dade County pending the suspension of Jimmy Sullivan from the tenth day of November, A. D. 1950, until the end of the next session of the Senate unless an appointment be sooner made and confirmed by the Senate.'

This Court, by a decision rendered on November 21, 1950, held void the indictment upon which the suspension of Sullivan was based.

Thereafter on April 7, 1951, the Governor issued an executive order reinstating Sullivan, reciting that: 'The Supreme Court of the State of Florida, Sullivan v. Leatherman, 48 So.2d 836, on November 21, 1950 held that said indictment did not charge Jimmy Sullivan with any crime under the laws of the State of Florida, or that he wilfully failed to perform any duty imposed on him by law, or that he acted corruptly in the performance of any duty imposed on him, and said indictment was void; and * * * the official transcript of the evidence presented to the Grand Jury which returned the indictment has been examined and does not show the violation of any law of the State of Florida by Jimmy Sullivan, nor does it show that he wilfully failed to perform any duty imposed on him by law, or that he acted corruptly in the performance of any duty imposed upon him by law.'

State ex rel. Kelly v. Sullivan, 52 So. 2d 422, 423–24 (Fla. 1951) (en banc).

228. *Fuller Warren Heads the List of Florida's Sorriest Governors*, Fort Lauderdale Daily News, Apr. 10, 1951, at 6A.

229. *Id.*

230. *See Funeral Services for Walter Clark Set for Monday: Long Illness Fatal to Former Sheriff of Broward County*, Fort Lauderdale Daily News, Apr. 27, 1951, at 1A.

Notes to Chapter 5

231. An elisor is a substitute designated by a court when the sheriff is disqualified or otherwise unavailable. *See* Paul Coltoff et al., *Sheriffs and Constables*, *in* 80 Corpus Juris Secundum: A Contemporary Statement of American Law as Derived from Reported Cases and Legislation §48, at 151 (St. Paul, MN: West Group, 2000) ("Where neither sheriff nor coroner can act in the performance of functions of the sheriff's office, the emergency may in a proper case be met by appointment of a special officer called an 'elisor,' to perform the required duties.").

232. *New Broward Sheriff Pledges War on Gambling*, Fort Lauderdale Daily News, July 25, 1950, at 1A.

233. *Hall to Sell Fronton Stock: Renews Pledge to Halt Gambling*, Panama City News Herald, July 27, 1950, at 1.

234. *Deputies Must Enforce Law to Keep Jobs, Sheriff Says*, Fort Lauderdale Daily News, July 26, 1950, at 1A.

235. *Sheriff's Edict Rough on Bingo*, Fort Lauderdale Daily News, Aug. 15, 1950, at 1A.

236. John Hopkins, *Sheriff Bans Bingo, Free Game Pinballs*, Fort Lauderdale Daily News, Aug. 25, 1950, at 1B.

237. *Sheriffs, Constables Warned*, Fort Lauderdale Daily News, Aug. 26, 1950, at 1B.

238. *Hunt for Records in Gambling Probe Proves Fruitless*, Fort Lauderdale Daily News, Aug. 11, 1950, at 1A.

239. John C. Hopkins, *Broward, Dade to Team Against Gamblers*, Fort Lauderdale Daily News, Nov. 11, 1950, at 1B.

240. *Deputies Raid $1,000 Whiskey Still*, Fort Lauderdale Daily News, Nov. 7, 1952, at 1B.

241. *The People Speak in Broward County*, Fort Lauderdale Daily News, May 7, 1952, at 1A.

242. *Deputies Get Six-Day Week; Sheriff Denies Discord Exists*, Fort Lauderdale Daily News, Nov. 10, 1952, at 1B.

243. Frank Hogan, *Arrest by Negro Protested*, Fort Lauderdale Daily News, Sept. 16, 1957, at 8A.

244. *Id.*

245. Douglas McQuarrie, *Negro Deputy Attacked, Felled by Four Bullets*, Fort Lauderdale Daily News, Dec. 10, 1953, at 1B.

246. Don Brickner, *1st Deputy Recalls All of Broward*, Hollywood Sun-Tattler, June 8, 1981, at 1A.

247. *See* Letter from Paul C. Bryan, Sheriff of Broward County, to David Sholtz, President—Florida State Chamber of Commerce, dated Nov. 21, 1927 ("I have always found it very hard to employ a county motorcycle man without a great deal of criticism. For this reason I don't employ them at all.").

248. *Hall Won't Run; Tindall, Salvino to Vie*, Fort Lauderdale Daily News, Aug. 3, 1955, at 1A.

249. Jack W. Gore, *Broward County Republicans Face a Big Test When They Take Over*, Fort Lauderdale Daily News, Jan. 6, 1957, at 6A.

250. *Hall Won't Run, supra* note 248.

251. Al Rockefeller, *Kelley Enters Sheriff's Race; Holt Steps Up*, Fort Lauderdale Daily News, Mar. 19, 1956, at 1A.

252. Douglas McQuarrie, *This State of Affairs*, Fort Lauderdale Sunday News, May 6, 1956, at 1B.

253. Jack W. Gore, *Discussion on Political Candidates Seeking Certain County Offices*, Fort Lauderdale Sunday News, May 6, 1956, at 6A.

254. *5/6/56 State of Affairs, supra* note 252.

255. Frank Hogan, *Court House Comment*, Fort Lauderdale Sunday News, Apr. 15, 1956, at 6B.

256. Douglas McQuarrie, *Tuppen Aid to Kelley*, Fort Lauderdale Daily News, May 28, 1956, at 1A.

257. *Tuppen Stand: He Is and Isn't Kelley Backer*, Fort Lauderdale Daily News, May 29, 1956, at 1A.

258. *Id.*

259. Fred Pettijohn, *His Definition of Endorsement Fails to Jibe*, Fort Lauderdale Daily News, May 29, 1956, at 1B.

260. Douglas McQuarrie, *Tindall Beats Kelley*, Fort Lauderdale Daily News, May 30, 1956, at 1A.

261. Douglas McQuarrie, *Jury to Intensify Probe of Gambling—Sheriff's Officers Cleared*, Fort Lauderdale Daily News, Sept. 6, 1956, at 1B.

262. *Id.*

263. *Hall Files for Divorce Citing Wife's 'Jealousy,'* Fort Lauderdale Daily News, Sept. 5, 1956, at 1A.

264. *Id.*

265. A Lloyd campaign ad, for example, advised readers:

As sheriff it shall be my purpose to provide rigid enforcement of all Florida laws which come under the jurisdiction of my office.

This enforcement will be without prejudice and without favoritism.

Honesty and efficiency for Broward County; equal rights for all, special privileges for none.

Lloyd Campaign Ad, Fort Lauderdale Sunday News, Nov. 4, 1956, at 10B.

266. *Tindall Charges Debate Planned to 'Smear' Him*, Fort Lauderdale Sunday News, Nov. 4, 1956, at 1B.

267. *Tindall Campaign Ad*, Fort Lauderdale Daily News, Nov. 3, 1956, at 12A.

268. John Hopkins, *Sheriff Recount Sought*, Fort Lauderdale Daily News, Nov. 8, 1956, at 1A.

269. *See* Paul Meighan, *Ex-Sheriff Amos Hall Dies: Ruled Suicide by Examiner*, Fort Lauderdale News, Sept. 4, 1966, at 1A.

270. Immediately after the election, the *Fort Lauderdale Daily News* had suggested that Lloyd also was the first Republican sheriff in state history, but this claim was erroneous, for nearly all of the sheriffs appointed in Florida during Reconstruction were Republicans. *See further* Silvestri, *supra* note 6.

271. Douglas McQuarrie, *Ax to Fall on Brass, Lloyd Vows*, Fort Lauderdale Daily News, Nov. 8, 1956, at 1A.

272. *Hall Blasts Lloyd for Statements*, Fort Lauderdale Daily News, Nov. 9, 1956, at 1B.

273. *Ax to Fall, supra* note 271.

274. Douglas McQuarrie, *This State of Affairs*, Fort Lauderdale Sunday News, Dec. 16, 1956, at 1B.

275. Douglas McQuarrie, *This State of Affairs*, Fort Lauderdale Sunday News, Dec. 2, 1956, at 1B.

276. John Hopkins, *Sheriff Drops Veil About News Reports*, Fort Lauderdale Sunday News, Jan. 8, 1957, at 1B.

277. *Id.*

278. *'Don't Talk to Press,' Sheriff Tells Men*, Fort Lauderdale News, Mar. 13, 1959, at 1A.

279. *County Crime Unit Plan Picks Up Steam Tonight*, Fort Lauderdale Sunday News, Jan. 31, 1957, at 1B.

280. *Id.*

281. Douglas McQuarrie, *6 'Top Bookies' Seized in Raids*, Fort Lauderdale Sunday News, Feb. 3, 1957, at 1A.

282. *Id.*

283. *Id.*

284. Douglas McQuarrie, *Jury Aides Accused of 'Lousing Up' Raid*, Fort Lauderdale Daily News, Feb. 5, 1957, at 1B.

285. *Grand Jurors Back Up Grant and Vitale*, Fort Lauderdale Daily News, Feb. 6, 1957, at 1B.

286. *Id.*

287. *Id.*

288. *Jury Aides Accused, supra* note 284.

289. *Sheriff's Men Cleared of 'Rough' Tactics*, Fort Lauderdale Daily News, Feb. 9, 1957, at 1B.

290. John Hopkins, *Lloyd Charges Long 'Out to Get Him,'* Fort Lauderdale Daily News, Feb. 8, 1957, at 1B.

291. *Id.*

292. *Id.*

293. Douglas McQuarrie, *Public Apathy Kills County Crime Unity*, Fort Lauderdale Daily News, Feb. 25, 1957, at 1B.

294. Douglas McQuarrie, *This State of Affairs*, Fort Lauderdale Sunday News, Apr. 21, 1957, at 1B.

295. Frank Hogan, *2 Deputies Nab Bolita Ring King*, Fort Lauderdale Daily News, Apr. 27, 1957, at 1C.

296. *Id.*

297. *Bolita Charges Filed Against 'Ham' Morris*, Fort Lauderdale Daily News, May 17, 1957, at 1B.

298. Ed Magill, *Lloyd 'Foggy' on Raid Fix; 'Can't Recall,'* Fort Lauderdale Sunday News, July 28, 1957, at 1A.

299. Douglas McQuarrie, *This State of Affairs*, Fort Lauderdale Sunday News, July 28, 1957, at 1B.

300. *55 Persons Are Arrested in 'Hectic' Friday Night*, Fort Lauderdale Daily News, Aug. 17, 1957, at 1C.

301. Broward Sheriff's Office, *Deputy Arthur Fillebrown*, http://sheriff.org/about_bso/other/memoriam/fillebrown/index.cfm.

302. Frank Hogan, *14 Seized in Sweeping Bolita Raids*, Fort Lauderdale Sunday News, Sept. 8, 1957, at 1B.

303. Frank Hogan, *Three Guilty Verdicts Returned Against Six*, Fort Lauderdale News, Feb. 22, 1958, at 1B.

304. *Id.*

305. *Hallandale Cop Denies Taking Money*, Fort Lauderdale Daily News, Nov. 1, 1957, at 1B.

306. *Id.*

307. *No Reply on Charge*, Fort Lauderdale Daily News, Oct. 11, 1957, at 1B.

308. *Sheriff's Agents Nab City Negroes*, Fort Lauderdale Daily News, Oct. 12, 1957, at 1B.

309. *Id.*

310. *Id.*

311. *Sheriffs Get Word: Grab Bolita Chiefs*, Fort Lauderdale News, June 26, 1958, at 10A.

312. Douglas McQuarrie, *Bolita Witness Claims Police Pressured Him*, Fort Lauderdale News, May 13, 1958, at 1B.

313. Douglas McQuarrie and Richard Milne, *Sheriff, Solicitor Targets of Favor-Taking Charge*, Fort Lauderdale Daily News, June 1, 1957, at 1A.

314. *Id.*

315. *Id.*

316. Douglas McQuarrie, *Deputy is Accused*, Fort Lauderdale Sunday News, June 2, 1957, at 1A.

317. *Id.*

318. John Hopkins, *Bondsman Vows to Blow Lid Off Court House*, Fort Lauderdale Daily News, June 29, 1957, at 1B.

319. *Id.*

320. *Id.*

321. Frank Hogan, *Lost 'Court' Papers Found*, Fort Lauderdale Daily News, July 6, 1957, at 1C.

322. Frank Hogan, *Sheriff Blasted by Anderson*, Fort Lauderdale Daily News, July 7, 1957, at 1B.

323. *Id.*

324. *Id.*

325. *Id.*

326. Joe Rukenbrod, *Sweeping Bond Probe Due for Broward Courts*, Fort Lauderdale Daily News, Aug. 24, 1957, at 1B.

327. John Hopkins, *Grand Jury Omits Sheriff in Report*, Fort Lauderdale Daily News, Sept. 7, 1957, at 1C.

328. *Lloyd Target of Ouster Suit by Anderson*, Fort Lauderdale Daily News, Sept. 10, 1957, at 1B.

329. Frank Hogan, *State Hits Lloyd Election Spending*, Fort Lauderdale News, Feb. 17, 1958, at 1B.

330. *Dinner Set for Sheriff*, Fort Lauderdale News, Jan. 23, 1958, at 1B.

331. *Lloyd Removal Hearing Set*, Fort Lauderdale News, Mar. 8, 1958, at 1B.

332. Douglas McQuarrie and Frank Hogan, *Deputies Raise Fund to Aid Sheriff*, Fort Lauderdale News, Mar. 11, 1958, at 1B.

333. Douglas McQuarrie, *Sheriff Lloyd Sued for $750,000*, Fort Lauderdale News, June 10, 1958, at 1A.

334. Frank Hogan, *Judge Mulls Fate of Sheriff Lloyd*, Fort Lauderdale News, July 3, 1958, at 1B.

335. *Id.*

336. *Bondsman to Seek Rehearing on Dismissal of Court Suit*, Fort Lauderdale News, Oct. 14, 1958, at 7B.

337. Frank Hogan, *Anderson Drops Lloyd Lawsuits*, Fort Lauderdale News, Apr. 19, 1959, at 1B.

338. Frank Hogan, *Sheriff's Raiders Destroy Huge Still*, Fort Lauderdale Daily News, June 6, 1957, at 1B.

339. *Lloyd Orders Curb on Beanfield Piracy*, Fort Lauderdale News, Nov. 27, 1958, at 1B.

340. Bud Honey, *Lloyd Nips 'Vigilantes'; Grabs Deputy Cards*, Fort Lauderdale News, Feb. 11, 1958, at 1B.

341. *Id.*

342. *Id.*

343. *Id.*

344. *Housewife, Deputy in Conflict on Profanity Incident Stories*, Fort Lauderdale Daily News, July 27, 1957, at 1C.

345. *Dad Seeks Probe in Youth's Arrest*, Fort Lauderdale News, June 21, 1958, at 1B.

346. Frank Hogan, *Ex-Partner of Sheriff Awaits Trial*, Fort Lauderdale Daily News, Apr. 20, 1957, at 1B.

347. *Sheriff 'Sorry' About Fracas Over Dance*, Fort Lauderdale News, July 14, 1959, at 1B.

348. *Initiation Prank by 40 and 8 Boomerangs*, Fort Lauderdale Daily News, Sept. 7, 1957, at 1C.

349. *7/28/57 State of Affairs*, supra note 299.

350. Douglas McQuarrie, *This State of Affairs*, Fort Lauderdale Sunday News, Aug. 11, 1957, at 1B.

351. Douglas McQuarrie, *This State of Affairs*, Fort Lauderdale News, July 6, 1958, at 1B.

352. Frank Hogan, *More Deputies to Get Boot*, Fort Lauderdale Daily News, July 16, 1957, at 1B.

353. *Id.*

354. Anne Kolb, *Sheriff's 'Cab Service' Popular*, Fort Lauderdale News, Mar. 18, 1958, at 8A.

355. John Hopkins, *Sheriff Takes Over Big Crime Probes*, Fort Lauderdale News, Nov. 18, 1958, at 1B.

356. *Id.*

357. *Lloyd Plans Roadblocks*, Fort Lauderdale News, Sept. 19, 1959, at 1B.

358. *Arrest May End Robberies*, Fort Lauderdale News, Apr. 4, 1960, at 1C.

359. *Sheriff Lloyd Happy Over Legislature Action*, Fort Lauderdale Daily News, May 22, 1957, at 1B.

360. Under the new law, sheriff salaries were tied to county populations, with the amounts ranging from as little as $6,000 to as much as $15,000. Due to a technicality, this system was struck down in *Shelton v. Reeder*, 121 So. 2d 145 (Fla. 1960), but was reinstituted upon passage of a properly-enacted statute. *See* Fla. Stat. § 145.071 (2008) (dividing the state into six "population groups" and providing for additional pay in certain circumstances).

361. *See supra* note 141 and accompanying text.

362. *County Sorry: Can't Foot Bill*, Fort Lauderdale Daily News, May 30, 1957, at 1A.

363. *Lloyd Refutes Data on Office Expenses*, Fort Lauderdale News, Apr. 20, 1959, at 2B.

364. *Id.*

365. *Indigent Mental Cities' Problem?*, Fort Lauderdale News, Sept. 18, 1959, at 1B.

366. *Id.*

367. *6 Road Patrol Cars Bear Lloyd's Name*, Fort Lauderdale News, Jan. 24, 1960, at 1B.

368. *Id.*

369. *Deputies on Trial*, Fort Lauderdale News, Apr. 4, 1960, at 1C.

370. *Stripper's Sentence Withheld*, Fort Lauderdale Daily News, Apr. 16, 1957, at 1B.

371. *Coker Starts Stag Show Probe*, Fort Lauderdale News, Jan. 14, 1960, at 1C.

372. Ed Hensley, *Deputies Nab 5 in Bolita Raid*, Fort Lauderdale News, Feb. 13, 1960, at 1B.

373. *Bolita Raids Put 4 Negroes Behind Bars*, Fort Lauderdale News, Mar. 27, 1960, at 1B.

374. *Paddy Wagon Seeks Votes*, Fort Lauderdale News, Mar. 21, 1960, at 1C.

375. *Id.*

376. *Collins Raps Lloyd for 'Misconduct,'* Fort Lauderdale News, Mar. 24, 1960, at 1C.

377. Ed Hensley, *'Paddy Wagon' Politics Blasted*, Fort Lauderdale News, Mar. 22, 1960, at 1C.

378. *Political 'Order' Denied by Lloyd*, Fort Lauderdale News, Mar. 24, 1960, at 1C.

379. *Id.*

380. *Id.*

381. *Ex-MP Colonel in Sheriff Race*, Fort Lauderdale News, Mar. 14, 1960, at 1C.

382. *Tindall Joins Sheriff Race*, Fort Lauderdale News, Feb. 15, 1960, at 1C.

383. *Anderson Campaign Ad*, Fort Lauderdale News, Apr. 14, 1960, at 2C.

384. *Id.*

385. Ed Hensley, *Sizzling Book Raps Tindall*, Fort Lauderdale News, Apr. 11, 1960, at 1C.

386. *'Quill' Aides Pondering Fate at Meet Tonight*, Fort Lauderdale News, June 1, 1960, at 1C.

387. *Id.*

388. Ed Hensley, *Sheriff Blames News for Election Defeat*, Fort Lauderdale News, June 2, 1960, at 1A.

389. Ed Hensley, *Collins May Investigate Lloyd*, Fort Lauderdale News, June 2, 1960, at 1A.

390. *Sheriff Blames News*, *supra* note 388.

391. *Id.*

392. *Id.*

393. *Id.*

394. *Collins May Investigate*, *supra* note 389.

395. Ed Hensley, *Lloyd's Bid Wins Scorn*, Fort Lauderdale News, June 3, 1960, at 1A.

396. Ed Hensley, *Collins Probe of Lloyd Sought*, Fort Lauderdale News, June 10, 1960, at 1B.

397. Ed Hensley, *Lloyd Free to Fire 'Disloyal' Deputies*, Fort Lauderdale News, June 17, 1960, at 1B.

398. Alan MacLeese, *Sheriff is Accused*, Fort Lauderdale News, June 24, 1960, at 1A.

399. *Id.*

400. *Id.*

401. *Id.*

402. *Judge Quashes Lloyd Warrant*, Fort Lauderdale News, June 29, 1960, at 1C.

403. *Lloyd Suit vs. Castle Thrown Out*, Fort Lauderdale News, July 6, 1960, at 1B.

404. *Sheriff is Accused*, *supra* note 398.

405. Alan MacLeese, *Sheriff Lends Radio to Dade TV Man*, Fort Lauderdale News, July 29, 1960, at 1C.

406. *Id.*

407. *Id.*

408. *Id.*

409. Alan MacLeese, *Cold Trail Hinders Sheriff Probe*, Fort Lauderdale News, Aug. 10, 1960, at 1C.

410. *Id.*

411. *Id.*

412. Alan MacLeese, *Charges of Theft Unproved*, Fort Lauderdale News, Aug. 12, 1960, at 1B.

413. *Cold Trail*, *supra* note 409.

414. *Harried Deputy … A Weird Tale*, Fort Lauderdale News, Aug. 10, 1960, at 2C.

415. *Id.*

416. *Claim Osborne 'Asked' Arrest*, Fort Lauderdale News, Aug. 28, 1960, at 1B.

417. *Id.*

418. *Sheriff Hires New Aides; One is Son*, Fort Lauderdale News, Aug. 11, 1960, at 1B.

419. Tom Vinciguerra, *Lloyd Admits Custody Row Slip-Up*, Fort Lauderdale News, Aug. 18, 1960, at 1A.

420. *Id.*

421. Doris Fortune, *Lloyd's Write-In Campaign May Mean Ouster from GOP*, Fort Lauderdale News, Aug. 21, 1960, at 1B.

422. *Id.*

423. *Why Did Sheriff Make Picture?*, Fort Lauderdale News, Aug. 22, 1960, at 1B.

424. *Id.*

425. *Sheriff Expands Road Patrol Work*, Fort Lauderdale News, Oct. 24, 1960, at 1B.

426. *Id.*

427. *Id.*

428. Tom Vinciguerra, *Sheriff Race Marred by 'Report,'* Fort Lauderdale News, Nov. 2, 1960, at 2C.

429. *Lloyd Fires Aide, Demotes Prober*, Fort Lauderdale News, Nov. 11, 1960, at 2C.

430. Tom Vinciguerra, *Ex-Sheriff Overspent Budget, Says Auditor*, Fort Lauderdale News, Sept. 22, 1961, at 1A.

431. *Lloyd to Seek Bill Payment from County*, Fort Lauderdale News, Sept. 23, 1961, at 1B.

432. *Id.*

433. *See Former County Sheriff, J.A. Lloyd, Dies at 83*, Fort Lauderdale News, May 11, 1978, at 3B.

Notes to Chapter 6

434. *10 Deputies Get 'Notice' as Michell Trims Ranks*, Fort Lauderdale News, Dec. 31, 1960, at 1B.

435. Tom Vinciguerra, *Michell 'Taps' Bud Mehl*, Fort Lauderdale News, Dec. 29, 1960, at 1C.

436. *Michell Takes Sheriff's Reins*, Fort Lauderdale News, Jan. 3, 1961, at 1C.

437. Tom Vinciguerra, *Michell Names Top Assistants*, Fort Lauderdale News, Dec. 29, 1960, at 1C.

438. *Id.*

439. *Id.*

440. *More Deputies May Feel Sheriff's Ax*, Fort Lauderdale News, Jan. 4, 1961, at 1B.

441. *Sheriff Selects Ex-Chief*, Fort Lauderdale News, Feb. 1, 1961, at 1C.

442. *Id.*

443. *'Line Busy,' to Bettors*, Fort Lauderdale News, Jan. 31, 1961, at 1C.

444. Ed Hensley, *15,000 Riot at Beach*, Fort Lauderdale News, Mar. 27, 1961, at 1A.

445. *Id.*

446. *Gambling Lid Held Tight Here*, Fort Lauderdale News, Apr. 30, 1961, at 1B.

447. *Id.*

448. *Id.*

449. *Id.*

450. *Sheriff Warns of Fund Dangers*, Fort Lauderdale News, May 24, 1961, at 1B.

451. *Id.*

452. *Sheriff Lists His Needs*, Fort Lauderdale News, May 6, 1961, at 1B.

453. *Sheriff Warns, supra* note 450.
When the question of providing county residents with around-the-clock service refused to go away, a sharp rebuttal appeared in print:

> They crop up at regular intervals, these "demands" of residents of unincorporated areas that they be given increased "protection" by the sheriff's department. Usually they want regular and frequent patrols by uniformed deputy sheriffs, something of the nature of [a] regular police force.
>
> It is not the duty of the sheriff, nor are residents of unincorporated areas entitled to such service. The sheriff, in reality, is an officer of the court, not the head of a police force.
>
> We have frequently heard people of the unincorporated areas declare they are "taxpayers" and as such are "entitled" to such police type patrols. Rubbish!
>
> The taxes they pay to the county entitles them to county government, which they receive. By no stretch of the imagination does it entitle them to municipal type services.

John C. Gerard, *Drop City Police; Let Sheriff Do It?*, Fort Lauderdale News, Apr. 27, 1962, at 9A.

454. Dave Hinton, *Sheriff Shakes Up Top Echelon*, Fort Lauderdale News, June 15, 1961, at 1D.

455. Tom Vinciguerra, *'Rackets? Sure—Just a Way of Life!,'* Fort Lauderdale News, Oct. 7, 1961, at 1A.

456. Milton Kelly, *State Investigates Sheriff*, Fort Lauderdale News, Sept. 14, 1961, at 1A.

457. Tom Vinciguerra, *Bryant Announces Probe of Sheriff*, Fort Lauderdale News, Sept. 15, 1961, at 1A.

458. Tom Vinciguerra, *Jury Will Investigate Sheriff*, Fort Lauderdale News, Sept. 19, 1961, at 1A.

459. Jack W. Gore, *Investigation of Sheriff's Office is Warranted by Rush of Ugly Rumors*, Fort Lauderdale News, Sept. 15, 1961, at 8A.

460. *Id.*

461. *Bryant Announces Probe, supra* note 457.

462. *Id.*

463. *Id.*

464. John Smolko, *Sheriff Offers Help, Denies He'll Resign*, Fort Lauderdale News, Oct. 10, 1961, at 1C.

465. *Id.*

466. *State Investigates Sheriff, supra* note 456.

467. *Gator Bites But Duty Calls*, Fort Lauderdale News, June 18, 1962, at 1C.

468. Jim Guier, *Escaped Convict on Way to Prison*, Fort Lauderdale News, Sept. 7, 1962, at 1A.

469. Fred Burrall, *County Bolita Wide Open*, Fort Lauderdale News, Sept. 17, 1962, at 1A.

470. Jack W. Gore, *Sheriff Should Know Vice Cannot Flourish When Law Enforcement is Strong*, Fort Lauderdale News, Sept. 19, 1962, at 8A.

471. Fred Burrall, *Deputy Sheriffs Tied to Bolita Loot*, Fort Lauderdale News, Sept. 18, 1962, at 1A.

472. *Id.*

473. John Smolko, *Gambling Minimized by Michell*, Fort Lauderdale News, Sept. 19, 1962, at 1A.

474. Tom Vinciguerra, *Obtain Own Bolita Data, Sheriff Told*, Fort Lauderdale News, Sept. 19, 1962, at 1A.

475. *Id.*

476. *Id.*

477. *County Approves Sheriff Center*, Fort Lauderdale News, Dec. 12, 1962, at 2BN.

478. *Sheriff Puts Men on New Pay Plan*, Fort Lauderdale News, Jan. 3, 1963, at 2C.

479. *Id.*

480. *Id.*

481. *Id.*

482. *Id.*

483. Doris Fortune, *Sheriff's 'Late' Bonds Up for Jury Airing*, Fort Lauderdale News, Jan. 17, 1964, at 1C.

484. *See* Fla. Stat. §30.09(1)(a) (2008) ("Each deputy sheriff who is appointed shall give bond as required by the board of county commissioners. The amount of the bond and the bond must be approved by the board of county commissioners. The bond must be filed with the clerk of the circuit court and be conditioned upon the faithful performance of the duties of his or her office. A deputy sheriff may not perform any services as deputy until he or she subscribes to the oath prescribed for sheriffs.").

485. Doris Fortune, *Jury Finds No Violation Intent*, Fort Lauderdale News, Jan. 24, 1964, at 1C.

486. *See* Fla. Att'y Gen. Op. 64-180 (Dec. 18, 1964).

487. Jim Guier, *Sheriff Indicates Bolita at Low Ebb*, Fort Lauderdale News, Mar. 18, 1964, at 1A.

488. *Id.*

489. *Id.*

490. Fred Burrall, *Bolita Wide Open in County*, Fort Lauderdale News, Mar. 18, 1964, at 1A.

491. *Id.*

492. *Five Fall Into Bolita Net*, Fort Lauderdale News, Mar. 21, 1964, at 1A.

493. Jim Guier, *Gambling Faces Sweeping Probe*, Fort Lauderdale News, Mar. 25, 1964, at 1A.

494. *Basinger's Margin Over Lloyd is 7,000*, Fort Lauderdale News, May 27, 1964, at 1A.

495. Tom Ensign, *Campaign Hits Snag*, Fort Lauderdale News, Oct. 1, 1964, at 1B.

496. *Deputies Find Bolita 'Elusive,'* Fort Lauderdale News, May 19, 1967, at 2C.

497. Tom Vinciguerra, *Michell Suspended as Sheriff Following Indictment by Jury*, Fort Lauderdale News, Mar. 8, 1966, at 1A.

498. *Deputy Named to Take Over for Sheriff*, St. Petersburg Times, Mar. 11, 1966, at 2B.

499. *Michell Suspended*, supra note 497.

500. *Insurance Man Appointed Acting Broward Sheriff*, St. Petersburg Times, Mar. 12, 1966, at 7B.

501. Tom Vinciguerra, *Insurance Official is Interim Sheriff: Burns Names Walker*, Fort Lauderdale News, Mar. 11, 1966, at 1A.

502. *Michell Suspended*, supra note 497.

503. Sylvia Maltzman, *Tom Walker? 'He'll Do a Good Job,'* Fort Lauderdale News, Mar. 11, 1966, at 1B.

504. *Id.*

505. *Insurance Official*, supra note 501.

506. Gene Janas, *Let's Get Job Done is Motto*, Fort Lauderdale News, Mar. 28, 1966, at 1B.

507. Gene Janas, *Sheriff Warns 'Conspirators Will Be Fired,'* Fort Lauderdale News, Mar. 26, 1966, at 1A.

508. Jim Savage, *Sheriff Changes Discriminatory Pay Schedules*, Miami Herald, May 9, 1966, at 1B.

509. *Dunson Appointed 'Weekend Sheriff,'* Fort Lauderdale News, Mar. 11, 1966, at 1A.

510. Harry S. Rape, *Lambeth May Cite Messick*, Miami Herald, Nov. 23, 1966, at 1A.

511. *Id.*

512. George Waas, *Michell Open to Possible Civil Service*, Fort Lauderdale News, Nov. 25, 1966, at 1B.

513. *Id.*

514. *Id.*

515. *See Lee v. State*, 166 So. 2d 131 (Fla. 1964), *cert. denied*, 380 U.S. 917 (1965).

516. *See Lee v. State*, 188 So. 2d 872 (Fla. 1st Dist. Ct. App. 1966), *cert. denied*, 386 U.S. 983 (1967).

517. *See State v. Pitts*, 241 So. 2d 379 (Fla. 1st Dist. Ct. App. 1970), *opinion vacated*, 247 So. 2d 53 (Fla.), *and new trial ordered*, 249 So. 2d 47 (Fla. 1st Dist. Ct. App. 1971).

518. *See Pitts v. State*, 307 So. 2d 473 (Fla. 1st Dist. Ct. App.), *cert. dismissed*, 423 U.S. 918 (1975).

519. Maureen Collins, *Jail Inquiry Raps Laxity of Michell*, Fort Lauderdale News, Jan. 6, 1968, at 1A.

520. George Waas, *Low Morale is Charged by Deputies*, Fort Lauderdale News, May 17, 1967, at 1B.

521. *Id.*

522. *Id.*

523. *Id.*

524. Marilyn Springer and Bill Martinez, *Pay for Aid from Police, County Asked*, Fort Lauderdale News, Feb. 13, 1968, at 1B.

525. *Id.*

526. *Bookie Charge Faces Sheriff's 'Neighbor,'* Fort Lauderdale News, Mar. 8, 1968, at 1B.

527. *All Sheriffs Employees Get Pay Hikes*, Fort Lauderdale News, Mar. 28, 1968, at 1B.

528. *Stack to File for Sheriff Job*, Fort Lauderdale News, Mar. 29, 1968, at 2B.

529. *Replace Stack, Nixon is Asked*, Fort Lauderdale News, May 2, 1968, at 1B.

530. Roland Scott, *Stack Winner Over Michell*, Fort Lauderdale News, May 8, 1968, at 1A.

531. Irene Stuber, *Snubbed Probers Blast Deputies*, Fort Lauderdale News, June 6, 1968, at 1B.

532. *Id.*

533. Marilyn Springer, *BSO Offered 5-Point Plan*, Fort Lauderdale News, June 27, 1968, at 2B.

534. *Id.*

535. *Patrols Up, Rides Cut*, Fort Lauderdale News, Aug. 9, 1968, at 2B.

536. *Schools to Seek Arresting Power*, Fort Lauderdale News, Oct. 11, 1968, at 2C.

537. *Patrol Needs are Stressed*, Fort Lauderdale News, May 20, 1968, at 1B.

538. *See Brigadier General Allen Brandt Michell*, Fort Lauderdale Sun-Sentinel, Mar. 8, 1983, at 6B.

Notes to Chapter 7

539. Ray Lynch and Stephen d'Oliveira, *Political Force Ed Stack Dies*, Fort Lauderdale Sun-Sentinel, Nov. 4, 1989, at 1A.

540. Roland Scott, *Stack Urges More Funds*, Fort Lauderdale News, Nov. 13, 1968, at 1B.

541. *Stack Eager to Get 'Leftovers,'* Fort Lauderdale News, Jan. 3, 1969, at 1C.

542. *Id.*

543. *Lang Claims Stack 'Boot,'* Fort Lauderdale News, Dec. 9, 1968, at 2B.

544. *Division Chief to Stay on Job*, Fort Lauderdale News, Jan. 6, 1969, at 1B.

545. Richard Matthews, *Road Patrolmen Hired by Sheriff*, Fort Lauderdale News, Jan. 17, 1969, at 2B.

546. Jed Drews, *'Wolf Pack' Patrols Aim of BSO Shifts by Stack*, Fort Lauderdale News, Feb. 21, 1969, at 1B.

547. *Id.*

548. *Crime Lab Idea Gets Praise, Questions*, Fort Lauderdale News, Oct. 8, 1968, at 1B.

549. Jed Drews, *Dope Cases Blocked by Lab Snafu*, Fort Lauderdale News, May 2, 1969, at 1B.

550. Jed Drews, *Stack Eyes Mass Narcotics Arrests*, Fort Lauderdale News, May 6, 1969, at 1BN.

551. *Stack Says Youths' Use of Dope 'Exaggerated,'* Fort Lauderdale News, May 13, 1969, at 3B.

552. *Stack Asks Salary Hike [So] He Can Pay Aides More*, Fort Lauderdale News, Mar. 7, 1969, at 1B (observing that "many other state and county officials [also] cannot pay assistants more than they get.").

553. *Go-Go-Gal's Murder Yarn a Fairy Tale?*, Fort Lauderdale News, May 3, 1969, at 1B.

554. *Crime Down, Fund Needs Up—Stack*, Fort Lauderdale News, May 7, 1970, at 2BN.

555. Scott Heimer, *Outlaws Change Cities But Keep Old Habits*, Fort Lauderdale News, May 29, 1971, at 13A.

556. *Heroin Crackdown Nets Three Arrests*, Fort Lauderdale News, May 29, 1971, at 1B.

557. *Sheriff Presents Budget*, Fort Lauderdale News, May 8, 1971, at 1B.

558. In announcing the capture, Stack called Chapman "very likely the number-one-bolita-operator active in Broward County." *See* Gene Janas, *Stack: Raid Broke $1.5 Million Lottery*, Fort Lauderdale News, Apr. 6, 1972, at 1A.

559. *DWI Crackdown Urged by Sheriff*, Fort Lauderdale News, May 26, 1972, at 1C.

560. Scott Heimer, *'Pot Found in my Home': Stack*, Fort Lauderdale News, May 16, 1972, at 1B.

561. Ron Ishoy, *Mara or Sal: Hey, Tammy, Tell Us True*, Miami Herald, Mar. 19, 1990, at 1C.

562. Mark Miller, *Lawmen Listen and Look, Make Few Busts on Drugs*, Fort Lauderdale News, Oct. 30, 1972, at 1C.

563. Peggy Poor, *Patrol Car Deal Rapped*, Fort Lauderdale News, Oct. 5, 1972, at 3B.

564. *Sheriff Candidate's Signs are Violation, City Warns*, Fort Lauderdale News, Oct. 31, 1972, at 2B.

565. Florida Legislative Committee on Intergovernmental Relations, *Finalized Salaries of Elected County Constitutional Officers and Elected School District Officials for Fiscal Year 2009*, at 19 (Aug. 2008), available at http://www.floridalcir.gov/UserContent/docs/File/reports/finsal09.pdf.

566. *See Broward County v. Administration Commission*, 321 So. 2d 604 (Fla. 1st Dist. Ct. App. 1975), and *Broward County v. Administration Commission*, 321 So. 2d 605 (Fla. 1st Dist. Ct. App. 1975).

567. Scott Wyman, *Al Lamberti and Politics*, Broward Politics, May 12, 2008, at http://weblogs.sun-sentinel.com/news/politics/broward/blog/2008/05/al_lamberti_and_history_1.html.

568. Margaret Croxton, *Stack May Switch Parties*, Fort Lauderdale News, May 28, 1975, at 1A.

569. Michael A. Lednovich, *Judge Brands $18 Porn War Waste of Time*, Fort Lauderdale News, May 14, 1977, at 1B.

570. *P.A.B., Inc. v. Stack*, 440 F. Supp. 937, 939, 942 (S.D. Fla. 1977).

571. James I. Helm, *Stack: I Won't Block Union*, Fort Lauderdale News, May 13, 1977, at 2C.

572. *Id.*

573. Paul Carson, *Stack Now Backs Crime Probe*, Fort Lauderdale News, May 21, 1977, at 1B.

574. *Id.*

575. Dave Casey, *County's Police Communications System Bugged by Shortcomings*, Fort Lauderdale News, May 31, 1977, at 1B.

576. *Id.*

577. *Id.*

578. Chuck Crumbo and George McEvoy, *Judge Sorry for Jury Collaring*, Fort Lauderdale News, May 4, 1978, at 1B.

579. *Id.*

580. Running against Burke in 1970 had required Stack to go to court and have the state's "resign-to-run" law declared inapplicable to races for federal offices. *See Stack v. Adams*, 315 F. Supp. 1295 (N.D. Fla. 1970).

581. Vicky Billington, *Ed Stack: Old Pro's 12-Year Goal a Week Away; But at 68, It Could be His Last Hurrah*, Fort Lauderdale News, Oct. 31, 1978, at 3A.

582. In 1957, the National Association of Fire Chiefs had proposed creating a single national number that could be used to report fires. Ten years later, the President's Commission on Law Enforcement and Administration of Justice embraced the idea but expanded it to include all emergencies. Subsequently, after consulting with the Federal Communications Commission, AT&T designated 911 for this purpose and began encouraging local communities to adopt it. Stack immediately took to the idea and became one of its biggest boosters.

583. Since 1957, Florida has required the "color combination of forest green and white ... on the motor vehicles and motorcycles used by the various sheriffs of Florida and their deputies." *See* Fla. Stat. §30.46(1). Although no similar law exists regarding uniforms, the same colors now are used for them by sheriff departments throughout the state.

584. Frank Rinella, *County Chiefs Oppose Police Merger*, Fort Lauderdale News, May 25, 1977, at 10B.

585. *See* Lynch and d'Oliveira, *supra* note 539.

586. *Id.*

587. *See Seminole Tribe of Florida v. Butterworth*, 491 F. Supp. 1015 (S.D. Fla. 1980), *aff'd*, 658 F.2d 310 (5th Cir. 1981) (Unit B), *cert. denied*, 455 U.S. 1020 (1982).

588. R.E. Hawkins, *Deputies to Shoulder New Patch*, Miami Herald, Sept. 3, 1982, at 2BR.

589. Paul Anderson, *Judge is Named Broward Sheriff*, Miami Herald, Oct. 17, 1982, at 7B.

590. Suzanne Spring, *Brescher: New Sheriff, New Style*, Miami Herald, May 15, 1983, at 1 (Broward).

591. *Id.*

592. *Id.*

593. *Id.*

594. *Id.*

595. Ann Frank, *Heidi Steals New Sheriff's Show*, Fort Lauderdale News, Oct. 27, 1982, at 1B.

596. *New Sheriff*, *supra* note 590.

597. *Id.*

598. Dan Ray and Marc Fischer, *Sheriff Wrestles Rumors of Return to the Bench*, Miami Herald, Feb. 6, 1983, at 10 (Broward).

599. *Id.*

600. *Id.*

601. *New Sheriff*, *supra* note 590.

602. *Id.*

603. Dan Ray and Marc Fischer, *Judge Could Run, But Won't if Brescher's in Sheriff's Race*, Miami Herald, May 1, 1983, at 7 (Broward).

604. *Id.*

605. *Id.*

606. *New Sheriff*, *supra* note 590.

607. *See Murphy v. Mack*, 358 So. 2d 822 (Fla. 1978), *receded from in Coastal Florida Police Benevolent Ass'n, Inc. v. Williams*, 838 So. 2d 543 (Fla. 2003).

608. Geraldine Baum, *Deputies Demand a Contract*, Miami Herald, Mar. 23, 1983, at 1 (Broward).

609. *Id.*

610. John Wolin, *The Sheriff is Cracking Down—on the FOP*, Miami Herald, Apr. 23, 1983, at 1 (Broward).

611. Brian Duffy, *Union Official Loses His Badge Despite Favorable Job Review*, Miami Herald, Apr. 16, 1983, at 2 (Broward).

612. Suzanne Spring, *Deputies Sue to Get Pact Talks: Kill State Law, FOP Asks Court*, Miami Herald, Apr. 28, 1983, at 1 (Broward).

613. *Id.*

614. *See Fraternal Order of Police, Sheriff's Lodge No. 32 v. Brescher*, 579 F. Supp. 1517 (S.D. Fla. 1984).

615. *See Sikes v. Boone*, 562 F. Supp. 74 (N.D. Fla.), *aff'd*, 723 F.2d 918 (11th Cir. 1983), *cert. denied*, 466 U.S. 959 (1984).

616. Avram Goldstein, *Developer Sues Over TV Arrest: Manager Didn't Aid Prostitutes*, Miami Herald, Dec. 14, 1983, at 1 (Broward).

617. *See Von Stein v. Brescher*, 696 F. Supp. 606, 616 (S.D. Fla. 1988).

618. *See Von Stein v. Brescher*, 904 F.2d 572, 573–74 (11th Cir. 1990) ("As misleading as Defendant Brescher's media statement may have been ... we find that Defendant Brescher's statement did not extinguish or significantly alter any right guaranteed to Plaintiff by the United States Constitution or by Florida law.").

619. Jennifer L. Schenker, *Soft Touches*, Miami Herald, Mar. 6, 1984, at 2 (Broward).

620. Dan Ray, *Brescher Charges Full Speed Ahead*, Miami Herald, Jan. 14, 1984, at 1 (Broward).

621. *Id.*

622. Butterworth also had gotten his local history wrong, for in 1944 Walter Clark had been re-elected sheriff without either a primary or general election opponent. *See supra* text following note 212.

623. Brian Duffy, *Brescher Challenges Proposal*, Miami Herald, Apr. 15, 1984, at 1 (Broward).

624. Doug Delp, *A Question of Extremely Good Timing*, Miami Herald, Apr. 18, 1984, at 1B.

625. Jennifer L. Schenker, *Broward Investigation of Mob Leads to Arrest of 13 Suspects*, Miami Herald, May 26, 1984, at 1A.

626. Jennifer L. Schenker, *Cop's Career Spans Half a Century*, Miami Herald, Sept. 23, 1984, at 1 (Broward).

627. Jennifer L. Schenker, *Former Organized-Crime Chief Plans to Oppose Ex-Boss in Bid for Sheriff*, Miami Herald, Jan. 13, 1984, at 1 (Broward).

628. Doug Delp, *Gee, Seems as if the Judge Never Even Left*, Miami Herald, Apr. 2, 1984, at 1C.

629. Mike Sante, *Sheriff's Endorsement Seen as 'Betrayal,'* Miami Herald, July 20, 1984, at 1 (Broward).

630. *Id.*

631. *Id.*

632. *Id.*

633. Justin Gillis, *Navarro Switches Parties—Bitter Words for Ex-Boss*, Miami Herald, July 21, 1984, at 1 (Broward).

634. *Id.*

635. *See Polly v. Navarro*, 457 So. 2d 1140 (Fla. 4th Dist. Ct. App. 1984).

636. *Id.* at 1144.

637. *A Sorry Spectacle*, Miami Herald, Oct. 24, 1984, at 22A.

638. Stephen J. Hedges, *Navarro Back on Broward Ballot: U.S. Judge Reinstates Sheriff Candidate*, Miami Herald, Oct. 25, 1984, at 1A.

639. *Id.*

640. Brian Duffy, *Navarro Leads Brescher in Sheriff's Race*, Miami Herald, Nov. 7, 1984, at 1A.

641. Jennifer L. Schenker, *Sheriff's Race Divides Deputies*, Miami Herald, Oct. 21, 1984, at 1 (Broward).

642. Christine Evans, *Candidates' Final Push Covers Potpourri of Issues*, Miami Herald, Aug. 31, 1984, at 3 (Broward).

643. *For County Sheriff*, Miami Herald, Nov. 2, 1984, at 22A.

644. *Id.*

645. Bill Braucher, *Tough Tactics Could Backfire on Democrats*, Miami Herald, Oct. 26, 1984, at 1 (Broward).

646. Brian Duffy, *Navarro Exults After Win, But Legal Hurdles Remain*, Miami Herald, Nov. 8, 1984, at 1A.

647. *Id.*

648. Stephen J. Hedges, *Judge Says Navarro Can Take Office*, Miami Herald, Dec. 8, 1984, at 2B.

649. *Id.*

650. Helen Rojas, *Brescher Prepares to Leave Office*, Fort Lauderdale Sun-Sentinel, Jan. 7, 1985, at 1B.

651. *Id.*

652. *Id.*

Notes to Chapter 8

653. Jennifer L. Schenker, *Navarro Made Headlines, Waves Too*, Miami Herald, Dec. 4, 1983, at 2D.

654. Larry Keller, *Navarro Proposed Vesco Kidnap Plan: Idea to Bring Fugitive to U.S. Got Killed*, Fort Lauderdale Sun-Sentinel, Oct. 17, 1992, at 1A.

655. Jonathon King, *The Law According to Nick*, Fort Lauderdale Sun-Sentinel, Jan. 3, 1993, at 6 (Sunshine Magazine).

656. Stephen J. Hedges, *Brescher Blasts Talk of BSO Firings, Transfers*, Miami Herald, Nov. 15, 1984, at 1 (Broward).

657. *Id.*

658. *Id.*

659. Patricia Elich, *Deputies Say Dismissals Mark Them 'Untouchable,'* Fort Lauderdale Sun-Sentinel, May 27, 1986, at 1B.

660. In 1976, nearly two decades after Sheriff Quill Lloyd's ill-fated Citizens Committee on Law Enforcement, retired BSO Deputy Frank Pinter, who had run for sheriff in 1968

but had lost to Ed Stack in the Republican primary, founded the BCCC as "a non-profit, non-partisan, non-political, tax-exempt fact finding body." *See Statement of Founder Frank R. Pinter*, Broward County Crime Commission, at http://www.browardcrime.com. According to Pinter, the BCCC would "not sit in judgment of community morals, act as [a] vigilante group, [or] have any authority other than the weight of public opinion, nor have any extra-legal rights," but would work on "behalf of law-abiding citizens generally and the community at large in the fight against crime and corruption." *Id*

In 1982, William Milmoe and six other Broward businessmen formed a competing organization known as the Citizens Crime Commission of Broward County, Inc. to "quietly wor[k] for realistic changes." Jennifer L. Schenker, *Powerbrokers Push for Change in Justice System*, Miami Herald, Dec. 27, 1984, at 4 (Broward). By 1986, however, the group was defunct.

661. Michele Cohen, *Crime Commission Attacks Navarro*, Fort Lauderdale Sun-Sentinel, Jan. 26, 1985, at 3B.

662. Larry Keller, *Taxpayers Foot Bill for Lawsuits: Navarro's Firings, Demotions of Employees Prompted Court Battles*, Fort Lauderdale Sun-Sentinel, Aug. 14, 1988, at 1B.

663. *Id.*

664. Mike Sante, *Two Deputies Drop Suits, Rehired: Sheriff's Legal Woes Aren't Over*, Miami Herald, Dec. 15, 1985, at 1 (Broward).

665. Dan Ray, *Broward County Officials Win Big Raises; Legislators Went Beyond Usual Formula This Year*, Miami Herald, July 3, 1985, at 1 (Broward).

666. Patricia Elich, *Pilot Gets $250,000 in Colombian Incident*, Fort Lauderdale Sun-Sentinel, June 19, 1986, at 1B.

667. *Id.*

668. David Uhler, *Chiefs Angered by Letter: Sheriff's Threat Upsets Police*, Fort Lauderdale Sun-Sentinel, Dec. 12, 1986, at 3B.

669. David Uhler, *Censured Sheriff Says Group's Vote Keyed by Politics*, Fort Lauderdale Sun-Sentinel, Jan. 10, 1987, at 4B.

670. David Uhler, *Chiefs Group Censure Navarro*, Fort Lauderdale Sun-Sentinel, Jan. 9, 1987, at 1B.

671. Jon Marcus, *Judge Forgives Navarro: Broward Sheriff Apologizes for Housing Inmates in Tent*, Fort Lauderdale Sun-Sentinel, Feb. 8, 1989, at 1B.

672. David Jackson, *League Backs Move to Restrict Navarro's Deputies*, Fort Lauderdale Sun-Sentinel, Mar. 7, 1986, at 5B.

673. *Navarro's Courthouse Performance Either Arrogant or Incompetent*, Fort Lauderdale Sun-Sentinel, Aug. 4, 1987, at 6A.

674. *Id.*

675. *Id.*

676. Michelle Ruess and David Uhler, *Disorder in the Court: Measures Bring Broward Courthouse Chaos*, Fort Lauderdale Sun-Sentinel, Aug. 4, 1987, at 1A.

677. Michelle Ruess and Larry Keller, *Judge: Arrest Sheriff; Martinez Asked to Take Action*, Fort Lauderdale Sun-Sentinel, Aug. 5, 1987, at 1A.

678. Michelle Ruess, *Courthouse Quiet as Navarro, Judges Patch Feud*, Fort Lauderdale Sun-Sentinel, Aug. 6, 1987, at 1A.

679. *Id.*

680. Michelle Ruess, *Sheriff Yields Ground on Security Measures*, Fort Lauderdale Sun-Sentinel, Sept. 2, 1987, at 3B.

681. *Id.*

682. *See State v. Kerwick*, 512 So. 2d 347 (Fla. 4th Dist. Ct. App. 1987).

683. *Id.* at 348–49.

684. Jay Carney, *Sheriff's Searches Ruled Unconstitutional*, Miami Herald, Sept. 19, 1987, at 3 (Broward).

685. Renee Krause, *Navarro Disputes Comparison to Fascist State*, Fort Lauderdale Sun-Sentinel, Sept. 19, 1987, at 3B.

686. *Judges Off Base with Their Protests of BSO Security Measures at Jail*, Fort Lauderdale Sun-Sentinel, Nov. 18, 1987, at 18A.

687. *Id.*

688. Ron Ishoy, *Judge, Is There Really an Aura in the Court?*, Miami Herald, Nov. 23, 1987, at 1C.

689. Beverly Stracher, *Opponent's Signs at Drug Rally Anger Navarro*, Fort Lauderdale Sun-Sentinel, Oct. 2, 1988, at 3B.

690. *Id.*

691. Casey Frank, *Broward Re-Elects Navarro*, Miami Herald, Nov. 9, 1988, at 2B.

692. *Re-Elect Navarro to Sheriff's Post*, Fort Lauderdale Sun-Sentinel, Oct. 26, 1988, at 18A.

693. Marilyn Weeks, *Navarro Took His Lumps in Latest Fray*, Fort Lauderdale Sun-Sentinel, Aug. 9, 1987, at 1B.

694. Tom Lassiter and Mike Billington, *Sheriff's Office Keeps Yacht: Officials Demanding $15,000 for Its Release, Owner Says*, Fort Lauderdale Sun-Sentinel, Apr. 9, 1990, at 1B.

695. *Id.*

696. Tom Lassiter and Mike Billington, *Senator Says Office 'Misjudged Statute,'* Fort Lauderdale Sun-Sentinel, Apr. 9, 1990, at 4B.

697. *Id.*

698. *Id.*

699. *Change Contraband Seizure Law to Prevent Law Enforcement Abuses*, Fort Lauderdale Sun-Sentinel, Apr. 10, 1990, at 10A.

700. *See In re Forfeiture of One 1980 53 Foot Hatteras Vessel*, 568 So. 2d 443 (Fla. 4th Dist. Ct. App. 1990).

701. Tom Lassiter and Mike Billington, *Owner: Boat Seizure Comedy of Errors*, Fort Lauderdale Sun-Sentinel, Apr. 9, 1990, at 4B.

702. *See In re Forfeiture of One 1980 53 Foot Hatteras Vessel*, 642 So. 2d 1106 (Fla. 4th Dist. Ct. App. 1994).

703. Steve Weller, *Is 'TV Guide' Talking About Our Sheriff Nick or Some Other Cinema Star?*, Fort Lauderdale Sun-Sentinel, June 20, 1989, at 10A.

704. *Id.*

705. *See Skyywalker Records, Inc. v. Navarro*, 739 F. Supp. 578 (S.D. Fla. 1990).

706. *See Skyywalker Records, Inc. v. Navarro*, 742 F. Supp. 638 (S.D. Fla. 1990).

707. *See Luke Records, Inc. v. Navarro*, 960 F.2d 134 (11th Cir. 1992).

708. *See Navarro v. Luke Records*, 506 U.S. 1022 (1992).

709. Gary Stein, *Public Won't Take Rap for This Show; Memo to: King-for-Life Navarro Re: How the Public Feels*, Fort Lauderdale Sun-Sentinel, June 13, 1990, at 1 (Local).

710. Barbara Walsh, *Navarro Raps Radio Prankster: 2 Live Crew Played on Police Channel*, Fort Lauderdale Sun-Sentinel, June 13, 1990, at 1B.

711. Scott Higham and Don Van Natta, Jr., *Navarro, Crew Share PR Coup*, Miami Herald, June 12, 1990, at 1A.

712. *Id.*

713. Ardy Friedberg, *Sheriff Stung by Criticism Over Crew: Navarro Exasperated Over Media, 'Unkind' Jurors*, Fort Lauderdale Sun-Sentinel, Oct. 25, 1990, at 1B.

714. Andrew Martin and Dana Banker, *Sheriff: Appointment Not Linked to Money*, Fort Lauderdale Sun-Sentinel, Nov. 21, 1990, at 5B.

715. Tom DuBocq, *Navarro a Paid SunBank Director*, Miami Herald, Nov. 20, 1990, at 2 (Broward).

716. Larry Keller, *Slew of Inquiries Test Navarro's Teflon Image*, Fort Lauderdale Sun-Sentinel, Oct. 27, 1990, at 1B.

717. *Id.*

718. Andrew Martin and Larry Keller, *Port Investigation Locks Out Navarro*, Fort Lauderdale Sun-Sentinel, Nov. 23, 1990, at 1B.

719. Andrew Martin and Tom Davidson, *Navarro Faces U.S. Inquiry: Thousands of Records Sought in Corruption Investigation*, Fort Lauderdale Sun-Sentinel, June 28, 1991, at 1A.

720. Ardy Friedberg, *Deputy Charged with Pimping for Wife*, Fort Lauderdale Sun-Sentinel, July 25, 1991, at 1A.

721. *See Post-Newsweek Stations, Florida Inc. v. Doe*, 612 So. 2d 549 (Fla. 1992).

722. Scott Higham, *60 Minutes Profiles Navarro*, Fort Lauderdale Sun-Sentinel, Apr. 13, 1992, at 6B.

723. *Id.*

724. John Grogan and Dunstan McNichol, *Navarro, Friend Make No-Bid Deal: Boca Raton Developer Contributed to Campaign*, Fort Lauderdale Sun-Sentinel, May 2, 1988, at 1A.

725. Gary Stein, *Nick's Fashion Sense Lacks Common Sense*, Fort Lauderdale Sun-Sentinel, June 14, 1991, at 1B.

726. *Id.*

727. Dana Banker, *Deputies to Take Learning Cruise: Some Police Chiefs Question How Much Officers Would Learn*, Fort Lauderdale Sun-Sentinel, July 24, 1991, at 3B.

728. *Id.*

729. Mike Williams, *Sheriff's Lab Makes Coke to Use in Stings*, Miami Herald, Apr. 19, 1989, at 1 (Broward).

730. *See Kelly v. State*, 593 So. 2d 1060 (Fla. 4th Dist. Ct. App. 1992).

731. *Id.* at 1062.

732. *See State v. Williams*, 623 So. 2d 462 (Fla. 1993).

733. John Kennedy, *Navarro Went Too Far by Making Cocaine, Court Rules*, Fort Lauderdale Sun-Sentinel, July 2, 1993, at 8A.

734. Buddy Nevins, *Sheriff to Donate $10,000 as Settlement for Club Raid*, Fort Lauderdale Sun-Sentinel, Nov. 17, 1993, at 5B.

735. *See Review Publications v. Navarro*, 943 F.2d 1318 (11th Cir. 1991).

736. *See Navarro v. Review Publications, Inc.*, 503 U.S. 938 (1992).

737. Jim Haner, *County Drops Bid to Get Legal Fees From Navarro*, Miami Herald, June 9, 1993, at 6 (Broward).

738. Steve Bousquet, *Sheriff Navarro Dumped*, Miami Herald, Sept. 2, 1992, at 1A.

739. Tom Davidson and Michael E. Young, *Navarro's Fall: National Fame to Bitter Defeat*, Fort Lauderdale Sun-Sentinel, Sept. 2, 1992, at 8A.

740. *Who Killed Sheriff Nick Navarro? It Was Really Suicide, Not Homicide*, Fort Lauderdale Sun-Sentinel, Sept. 3, 1992, at 26A.

741. Larry Keller, *Navarro Mulls Write-In Bid, Though Deadline Has Passed*, Fort Lauderdale Sun-Sentinel, Sept. 3, 1992, at 12A.

742. *Id.*

743. Kathleen Kernicky, *Loss Stuns Deputies Who Wonder Who Next Boss Will Be*, Fort Lauderdale Sun-Sentinel, Sept. 4, 1992, at 4B.

744. Larry Keller, *Navarro Drops Write-In Plan, Aims to Force New Primary*, Fort Lauderdale Sun-Sentinel, Sept. 4, 1992, at 4B.

745. Steve Bousquet and Ronnie Greene, *Navarro Backers Want Rematch with Howard*, Miami Herald, Sept. 4, 1992, at 1 (Broward).

746. *Id.*

747. Bob LaMendola, *Navarro's Objections Thrown Out: Vote-Certifying Board Turns Down Arguments*, Fort Lauderdale Sun-Sentinel, Sept. 5, 1992, at 3B.

748. Kathleen Kernicky, *'This Is It,' Defeated Navarro Says*, Fort Lauderdale Sun-Sentinel, Sept. 9, 1992, at 1B.

749. Rick Pierce, *Howard Plans to Use Fact that Cochran Once Endorsed Him*, Fort Lauderdale Sun-Sentinel, Sept. 13, 1992, at 4B.

750. *Id.*

751. Rick Pierce, *Sheriff's Candidate Picks Backup Month Before Election: GOP's Howard Names Second in Command*, Fort Lauderdale Sun-Sentinel, Oct. 7, 1992, at 5B.

752. *Id.*

753. Steve d'Oliveira, *Investigation of Ex-Sheriff Dropped: Lack of Evidence Cited in Dispute Over Consulting Contract for Navarro*, Fort Lauderdale Sun-Sentinel, Nov. 8, 1995, at 1B.

754. Steve Bousquet, *Cochran Captures Sheriff's Office*, Miami Herald, Nov. 4, 1992, at 1B.

755. Rick Pierce, *Cochran Takes Sheriff's Race: Former Lauderdale Police Chief Gains Easy Victory Over Howard*, Fort Lauderdale Sun-Sentinel, Nov. 4, 1992, at 1B.

756. Martha Gross, *Nick and Sharron Navarro: Sheriff of Naught*, Fort Lauderdale Sun-Sentinel, Nov. 3, 1992, at 1E.

757. *Id.*

758. *Id.*

759. Buddy Nevins, *Leaving Las Vegas a Rich Man*, Fort Lauderdale Sun-Sentinel, May 26, 1999, at 3B.

Notes to Chapter 9

760. Paul Saltzman, *Police Chief Cochran Resigns*, Miami Herald, Apr. 11, 1987, at 3 (Broward).

761. Jonathan Sacks and Suzanne Spring, *Cochran Would Bring New View to Police*, Miami Herald, Apr. 18, 1983, at 1 (Broward).

762. As has been pointed out elsewhere, the term "community policing" suggests different things to different people, but generally connotes a policy of involving citizens in local law enforcement activities. *See further* Nigel G. Fielding, *Community Policing* 1 (New York: Oxford University Press, 1995) (explaining that the phrase "has several meanings"), and Jeremy M. Wilson, *Community Policing in America* 8 (New York: Routledge, 2006) (concluding that the phrase has "no clear definition").

763. David Uhler, *Cochran to Retire as Chief*, Fort Lauderdale Sun-Sentinel, Apr. 10, 1987, at 1A.

764. *Id.*

765. Vicki McCash, *Cochran to Head School Security*, Fort Lauderdale Sun-Sentinel, June 23, 1989, at 7B.

766. *Id.*

767. Kimberly Crockett, *Top School Security Post Goes to Ex-Chief*, Miami Herald, June 22, 1989, at 1 (Broward).

768. *Navarro Gets Challenger*, Fort Lauderdale Sun-Sentinel, Nov. 11, 1991, at 3B.

769. *For Sheriff: Cochran Deserves Nomination, Support of Democrats*, Fort Lauderdale Sun-Sentinel, Aug. 23, 1992, at 4G.

770. Larry Keller, *Cochran Sworn in as Sheriff, Promises Greater Efficiency*, Fort Lauderdale Sun-Sentinel, Jan. 6, 1993, at 1B.

771. *Id.*

772. Ronnie Greene, *Cochran Defends Dismissals: Says Cuts are Not Vendettas*, Miami Herald, Jan. 6, 1993, at 1 (Broward).

773. Larry Keller, *Employees Tearful, Angry at Mass Firing*, Fort Lauderdale Sun-Sentinel, Jan. 5, 1993, at 1B.

774. *Cochran Defends Dismissals, supra* note 772.

775. *Id.*

776. *Employees Tearful, supra* note 773.

777. *Cochran Defends Dismissals, supra* note 772.

778. *Employees Tearful, supra* note 773.

779. Larry Keller, *Fired Sheriff's Aides Hire Lawyers: Former Employees Consider Lawsuits to Fight Their Dismissals*, Fort Lauderdale Sun-Sentinel, Jan. 7, 1993, at 4B.

780. *Employees Tearful, supra* note 773.

781. *Cochran Defends Dismissals, supra* note 772.

782. *See* Fla. Stat. §30.10 (2008) ("The place of office of every sheriff shall be at the county seat of the county.").

783. Patty Shillington, *Safety Facility Tests County-Seat Status*, Miami Herald, Nov. 6, 1986, at 6 (Broward).

784. Bob LaMendola, *New Complex Applauded, but Errors Surface*, Fort Lauderdale Sun-Sentinel, May 2, 1993, at 1B.

785. Larry Keller, *Sheriff's Request Rises: Cochran, Despite Criticism of Navarro, Seeks Increase*, Fort Lauderdale Sun-Sentinel, Apr. 30, 1993, at 1B.

786. Larry Keller, *Navarro's Name a Costly Legacy for New Sheriff*, Fort Lauderdale Sun-Sentinel, Jan. 4, 1993, at 1B.

787. Larry Keller, *Sheriff Fires Songwriter to Save Cash*, Fort Lauderdale Sun-Sentinel, Feb. 11, 1993, at 1B.

788. Bob LaMendola, *Sheriff Breaks Up Crime Unit: Navarro's Organized Crime Division Sent to Other Operations*, Fort Lauderdale Sun-Sentinel, May 1, 1994, at 1B.

789. *Cochran Sworn, supra* note 770.

790. Barbara Walsh and Buddy Nevins, *Low Morale Still Plagues Sheriff's Office*, Fort Lauderdale Sun-Sentinel, May 12, 1994, at 1B.

791. *Id.*

792. *Id.*

793. *See* Fla. Att'y Gen. Op. 93-69 (Oct. 8, 1993).

794. Cindy Elmore, *Sheriff's Deputies*, Fort Lauderdale Sun-Sentinel, July 13, 1994, at 1B.

795. Kevin Davis, *Sheriff's Deputies Get Contract*, Fort Lauderdale Sun-Sentinel, Sept. 13, 1994, at 3B.

796. Ron Ishoy, *Style Counts in Busy Race for Sheriff*, Miami Herald, Aug. 25, 1996, at 1 (Broward).

797. *Id.*

798. *Id.*

799. *Id.*

800. *Id.*

801. Buddy Nevins, *Campaign Claims of Sheriff Hopeful Don't Hold Up*, Fort Lauderdale Sun-Sentinel, Feb. 16, 1996, at 1B.

802. *In Vital Sheriff's Race, Best Choices are Nominees Cochran and Wagner*, Fort Lauderdale Sun-Sentinel, Aug. 25, 1996, at 6G.

803. Larry Keller, *Sheriff Cochran Conquers 3 Rivals: Democratic Race Easy for Incumbent*, Fort Lauderdale Sun-Sentinel, Sept. 4, 1996, at 1B.

804. Ron Ishoy and Annmarie Dodd, *Cochran vs. Wagner in November*, Miami Herald, Sept. 4, 1996, at 1B.

805. *Sheriff Cochran Conquers, supra* note 803.

806. Steve Bousquet, *Teaming Up Against Cochran*, Miami Herald, Sept. 7, 1996, at 1 (Broward).

807. Ron Ishoy, *Crime Stats Key in Race for Sheriff*, Miami Herald, Oct. 27, 1996, at 1 (Broward).

808. *Id.*

809. Ron Ishoy, *Big Win for Cochran: Says Victory Will Help Programs*, Miami Herald, Nov. 6, 1996, at 1B.

810. *Id.*

811. *Cochran Not Daunted by Challenges*, Fort Lauderdale Sun-Sentinel, Feb. 15, 1997, at 14A.

812. Steve Bousquet, *Ailing Sheriff Says He'll Still Hang in There*, Miami Herald, May 10, 1997, at 1 (Broward).

813. Buddy Nevins and Donna Pazdera, *Ron Cochran, Architect of Modern Sheriff's Office, Dies*, Fort Lauderdale Sun-Sentinel, Sept. 6, 1997, at 1A.

814. *Id.*

815. Donna Leinwand, *Next Sheriff: Pro or Politico?*, Miami Herald, Sept. 6, 1997, at 1 (Broward).

816. *Id.*

817. *Id.*

818. Buddy Nevins, *McCampbell's Eulogy Makes a Good Impression: Interim Chief Shows Vision, Officials Say*, Fort Lauderdale Sun-Sentinel, Sept. 11, 1997, at 6A.

819. Steve Bousquet, *McCampbell Better Prepare for Opposition*, Miami Herald, Sept. 13, 1997, at 1 (Broward).

820. *McCampbell's Eulogy, supra* note 818.

821. *Id.*

822. *Id.*

823. *McCampbell Better Prepare, supra* note 819.

824. *Opt for Professionalism in Sheriff with Cochran Choice of McCampbell*, Fort Lauderdale Sun-Sentinel, Sept. 18, 1997, at 26A.

825. Steve Bousquet, *Cochran's Succession Letter Can't Be Found*, Miami Herald, Sept. 19, 1997, at 1 (Broward).

826. Donna Pazdera, *Cutbacks at Jail Preceded Escape: Cell Inspections, Staffing Were Sporadic,* Fort Lauderdale Sun-Sentinel, Aug. 14, 1997, at 1A.

827. Donna Pazdera and Mary C. Williams, *Inmate Assumes Identity, Walks Out,* Fort Lauderdale Sun-Sentinel, Aug. 27, 1997, at 1A.

828. Lane Kelley, *County Dedicates Complex: Building Takes Cochran's Name,* Fort Lauderdale, Nov. 7, 1997, at 3B.

829. *Id.*

830. *Id.*

831. *Id.*

832. Buddy Nevins, *Governor Still Mum on Sheriff Selection: Politically Powerful Seek to Influence Pick,* Fort Lauderdale Sun-Sentinel, Dec. 21, 1997, at 1B.

Notes to Chapter 10

833. Steve Bousquet and Meg James, *It's Official: Jenne Gets Nod for Broward County Sheriff,* Miami Herald, Jan. 10, 1998, at 1A.

834. *Jenne Has What It Takes to be Sheriff; Gov. Chiles Should Offer Him the Job,* Fort Lauderdale Sun-Sentinel, Oct. 18, 1997, at 14A.

835. Reflecting his community's animosity towards Jenne, noted civil rights lawyer Allan Terl wrote a letter as he was dying from AIDS in which he begged Governor Chiles not to appoint Jenne, whom he called a "liar" and a "political opportunist of the highest magnitude." Buddy Nevins, *Gay-Rights Activist was Active to the End: Wrote Deathbed Slam of Sheriff Candidate,* Fort Lauderdale Sun-Sentinel, Dec. 4, 1997, at 8B.

836. Bousquet and James, *supra* note 833.

837. Buddy Nevins, *Ken Jenne, the New Broward County Sheriff, Reflects on His New Duties and Goals as well as on His Supporters and Detractors,* Fort Lauderdale Sun-Sentinel, Jan. 10, 1998, at 4A.

838. Julie Kay, *Two BSO Officials Who Aspired to be Sheriff Quit,* Miami Herald, Oct. 8, 1998, at 3B.

839. Steve Bousquet, *Twenty-Six Candidates Unopposed,* Miami Herald, July 18, 1992, at 1 (Broward).

840. Steve Bousquet, *Broward Sheriff Fulfills a Mighty Dream,* Miami Herald, Jan. 12, 1998, at 1A.

841. Frederick W. Guardabassi, *Sheriff Exists Only for Patronage Purposes,* Fort Lauderdale Sun-Sentinel, Jan. 18, 1998, at 4G.

842. Buddy Nevins, *Confusion, Jitters Greet Swearing-In of Jenne as Sheriff,* Fort Lauderdale Sun-Sentinel, Jan. 20, 1998, at 3B.

843. Ron Ishoy, *Sheriff: I'll Protect the People—Ken Jenne Takes Oath in Broward,* Miami Herald, Jan. 21, 1998, at 1A.

844. David Fleshler, *Challenger Faces Uphill Fight in Sheriff's Race,* Fort Lauderdale Sun-Sentinel, Aug. 18, 1998, at 1B.

845. Steve Bousquet, *Very Visible Jenne Impresses Skeptics,* Miami Herald, June 13, 1998, at 1 (Broward).

846. Sabrina L. Miller, *Jenne Wins 4-Year Term,* Miami Herald, Sept. 2, 1998, at 6B.

847. *Id.*

848. *BSO Announces Opening of Its Web Site,* Miami Herald, Apr. 28, 1999, at 2B.

849. Ardy Friedberg, *Jenne, Satz Sail to Victory and Re-Election*, Fort Lauderdale Sun-Sentinel, Sept. 6, 2000, at 5B.

850. Evan S. Benn, *Jenne Trounces His Opponent to Win Another 4-Year Term*, Miami Herald, Sept. 1, 2004, at 3B.

851. Paula McMahon, *'End of an Era in Broward Politics': Guilty Plea Could Draw Two Years in Prison for Jenne*, South Florida Sun-Sentinel, Sept. 5, 2007, at 10A.

852. Fred Grimm, *Longevity Built Jenne's Path to Fraud*, Miami Herald, Nov. 18, 2007, at B1.

853. Wanda J. DeMarzo et al., *Jenne Can Leave Prison in 10 Months*, Miami Herald, Nov. 17, 2007, at A1.

854. *Id.*

855. Wanda J. DeMarzo et al., *Governor Names Veteran Cop as Broward Sheriff*, Miami Herald, Oct. 27, 2007, at A1.

856. Michael Mayo, *Coffee Talk with Sheriff Al Lamberti*, Mayo on the Side, Nov. 1, 2007, at http://weblogs.sun-sentinel.com/news/columnists/mayo/blog/2007/11/coffee_talk_with_sheriff_al.html.

857. *The Miami Herald Recommends for Broward Sheriff*, Miami Herald, Oct. 17, 2008, at A18.

858. *Choose Al Lamberti for Broward County Sheriff*, South Florida Sun-Sentinel, Oct. 15, 2008, at 18A.

859. *It's Official, Lamberti Wins*, South Florida Sun-Sentinel, Nov. 17, 2008, at 6B.

Notes to Chapter 11

860. No law, however, requires a county to have a jail. *See further* Fla. Att'y Gen. Op. 91-25 (Apr. 18, 1991). *See also* Fla. Stat. §902.21 (2008) ("If a person is committed in a county where there is no jail, the committing trial judge shall direct the sheriff to deliver the accused to a jail in another county.") and §950.01 (2008) ("When it appears to the court at the time of passing sentence upon any prisoner who is to be punished by imprisonment in the county jail that there is no jail in the county suitable for the confinement of such prisoner, the court may order the sentence to be executed in any county in this state in which there may be a jail suited to that purpose, and the expense of supporting such prisoner shall be borne by the county in which the offense was committed.").

861. On Wednesday, July 11, 1979, three-year BSO Deputy Joseph V. Conte was killed while transporting inmate Gary R. Eaton from a dentist appointment back to the main jail. The attack had been planned by Eaton and Dawn A. Sobel, who enlisted her friend John A. Gombos to help carry out the ambush. All three were found guilty of murder and given long prison terms, although Sobel later was allowed to take a plea, thereby making her eligible for parole. *See further Eaton v. State*, 438 So. 2d 822 (Fla. 1983), and *Sobel v. State*, 564 So. 2d 1110 (Fla. 4th Dist. Ct. App. 1990), *review denied*, 576 So. 2d 291 (Fla. 1991).

862. The stockade's roots go back to November 1915, when it was established by the Broward County Commission as a convict camp, later evolving into a maximum security institution housing road gangs. In 1982, it was turned into a minimum security facility operated by the Broward County Social Service Division, but in February 1986 it was transferred to the Broward Sheriff's Office following charges that it was suffering from poor administration and lax oversight.

863. Originally known as the North Jail, the facility was renamed in September 2008 to honor Deputy Paul Rein, who had been shot to death in November 2007 while transporting a prisoner (Michael Mazza) to Fort Lauderdale to stand trial for bank robbery. After winning approval to change the name, Sheriff Al Lamberti told reporters, "It is a great tribute to a great man. It won't bring Paul back, but it will keep his legacy alive." *North Jail Will Be Named for Slain Deputy*, South Florida Sun-Sentinel, Apr. 30, 2008, at 3B.

Rein's death also led to an overhaul of the department's prisoner transport policies. *See* Sallie James and Sofia Santana, *Sheriff Changes Transport Policies*, South Florida Sun-Sentinel, Aug. 13, 2008, at 1B (explaining that "deputies transporting inmates will be heavily armed, with pepper foam canisters on inmate buses, Tasers, and soon, rifles—in addition to their service weapons. The Sheriff's Office transferred a dozen deputies to transport duty, so they can pair up for trips with unruly or violent inmates. The agency also is working with Broward Health (formerly the North Broward Hospital District) on plans for the county's first inmate ward.... Currently, hospitalized inmates are housed at different hospitals, each guarded by at least one armed deputy. A single ward would be 'more cost-effective and safe,' [Broward Health chief executive officer Frank] Nanske said.").

864. *Commissioners Report*, Fort Lauderdale Sentinel, Oct. 8, 1915, at 1.

865. *County Jail Kept in Best Condition*, Fort Lauderdale Sentinel, Apr. 5, 1918, at 1.

866. *No Prisoners in County Jail*, Fort Lauderdale Sentinel, May 7, 1920, at 1.

867. Today, Florida continues to prohibit counties from leasing prisoners to private interests, *see* Fla. Stat. §951.10 (2008), while allowing them to be used on public work projects. *See* Fla. Stat. §951.01 (2008).

868. *See Two Robbers Escape from Jail*, Fort Lauderdale Sentinel, Dec. 15, 1922, at 1. Not everyone, however, agrees with this account. According to some sources, the two men were brought to Fort Lauderdale after discovery of a plot against the Palm Beach jail and their subsequent escape was engineered by Broward Deputy William A. Hicks. *See* James Carlos Blake, *Red Grass River: A Legend* 267–75 (New York: Avon Books, Inc., 1998) (incorrectly identifying Hicks as "W.W. Hicks").

869. Letter from John M. Peterman, Architect—Broward County Courthouse, to Paul C. Bryan, Sheriff of Broward County, dated Jan. 14, 1926.

870. As has been explained elsewhere, the trip had been undertaken at Webster's behest:

Our mission was to take Mr. Webster to the island of Bimini in the Bahamas[.]

[I]t seems that two brothers had learned the art of making counterfeit money in France, one was caught in New Orleans and it was thought the other one was passing counterfeit money to the rum runners in the Miami area to buy liquor in the islands and I believe Mr. Webster was sent to check this out.

Frank Lehman, *Encounter with the Gulf Stream Pirate* 4 (s.l.: s.n., 1979).

871. Like everyone else, Judge Ritter believed that maritime law required pirates to be executed in the first port to which they had been brought following capture. As a result, he ordered Alderman to be hung in Fort Lauderdale. *See id.* at 47 ("Alderman was charged with murder and piracy on the high seas, the penalty for which is hanging at the nearest port to where the crime was committed.").

This conclusion, however, was erroneous. While it had long been clear that pirates had to be *tried* in such ports, *see, e.g.*, 1 U.S. Att'y Gen. Op. 185, 185 (Aug. 29, 1815) ("prosecutions [of] persons for alleged acts of piracy committed on the high seas, or in any place out of the jurisdiction of any particular State ... should take place in the district where the offender is apprehended, or into which he may first be brought"), no precedent required that they had to be *executed* there. *See further* 18 U.S.C. §3596 (2008) (making it clear that federal officials have broad discretion when it comes to determining the most suitable place for an execution).

872. *See Alderman v. United States*, 31 F.2d 499 (5th Cir.), *cert. denied*, 279 U.S. 869 (1929).

873. Letter from Halsted L. Ritter, U.S. District Judge—Southern District of Florida, to Aden W. Turner, Sheriff of Broward County, dated July 19, 1929.

874. *Alderman to be Hanged on Roof of Court House*, Fort Lauderdale Daily News, July 18, 1929, at 1. J.G. Johnson, a Miami contractor, won the bid.

875. *Warrant for Third Alderman Guard; Two Are Arrested*, Miami Herald, Aug. 17, 1929, at 1 (quoting Fred W. Pine, Crooks's lawyer, as saying, "The fact that these men were officers gave them no special privilege to attack or molest a newspaper man or any other individual.").

Because the bonds (which were set at $100 each for Mack and Mathews and $250 for Bedenbaugh) did not indicate when their case would be heard, Mack asked Turner to keep an eye on the court calendar and "advise me when we should be there to answer the charges against us." Letter from Leo M. Mack, Chief Deputy, U.S. Marshal's Office—Jacksonville, to Aden W. Turner, Sheriff of Broward County, dated Sept. 14, 1929.

876. *Tonight is to be Alderman's Last*, Fort Lauderdale Daily News, Aug. 16, 1929, at 1.

877. *See* "Hanging a Pirate," *in* Stuart B. McIver, *Murder in the Tropics: The Florida Chronicles (Vol. 2)*, at 130 (Sarasota: Pineapple Press, Inc., 1995). As McIver explains, the hanging was botched due to inexperience:

> Broward's problem was this. The county had never hanged anybody before and had no idea how to go about it. How do you build a gallows? Dade County pine or possibly oak? What kind of rope do you use and how strong should it be? How do you tie a hangman's knot? About the only thing the county felt comfortable about was serving the condemned man his last good meal to send him off into eternity....
>
> [T]he man picked to do the deed was Bob Baker, the one-legged sheriff from Palm Beach County. His credentials were the best Sheriff Turner could find. He was, in fact, the only one in the area who knew how to tie the hangman's knot, essential if the doomed man was to be rendered unconscious quickly. Otherwise, the result would be a slow, painful—some would say cruel—death.
>
> A wool sailor's cap did the job as a hood to cover Alderman's face. He was escorted up the nine steps to the fifteen-foot-high gallows platform. The pirate was humming, "Jesus, Here I'm Coming," as he stepped onto the trap door. Baker slipped the noose of the manila rope around his neck and pulled it tight. Finally, his legs were tied together [and] Baker said to him, "Then, goodbye and may God have mercy on your soul."
>
> The bolt shot back at 6:04 a.m. Alderman fell seven feet and hung there. He choked and kicked for a full twelve minutes before he was finally strangled to death. Despite his resume, Baker had not tied the knot properly.

Id. at 123–29.

In an interesting postscript, McIver points out that despite the government's extraordinary precautions, one newspaper reporter—Eddie Hay of the *Miami Herald*—managed to get inside the hangar and witnessed the execution. He was not, however, allowed to tell the public what he had seen:

> Back at the paper, Hay quickly wrote the only eyewitness account. Then came the word. The paper was not going to run the story.

Frank B. Shutts, owner and publisher of the *Herald*, had been a classmate of Judge Ritter's at Depauw University. At the last minute, Shutts, a lawyer himself, decided he would not defy the judge's edict. He told his news editor, John Pennekamp, to pull the story.

Id. at 130.

878. Letter from Aden W. Turner, Sheriff of Broward County, to Sanford Bates, Director—Federal Bureau of Prisons, dated Nov. 5, 1931.

879. *Prisoner Slides to Freedom from Court House Top*, Fort Lauderdale Daily News, July 19, 1935, at 1.

880. *Warren for Use and Benefit of Cronin v. Hall*, 66 So. 2d 230, 231 (Fla. 1953) (Spec. Div. A).

881. This warning, however, should not have been necessary, for Florida law had long made it clear that sheriffs were responsible for the acts of their deputies. *See* Fla. Stat. § 30.07 (2008) ("Sheriffs may appoint deputies to act under them who shall have the same power as the sheriff appointing them, and for the neglect and default of whom in the execution of their office the sheriff shall be responsible.").

882. *12/16/56 State of Affairs, supra* note 274.

883. When the case was re-filed in 1978 for technical reasons, three new prisoners—Ollie Carruthers, Gerald Tice, and William Zervos—were substituted due to the fact that the original plaintiffs—George Jonas, Marvin Williams, and Arthur Woiters—had been released. *Compare Jonas v. Stack*, 758 F.2d 567 (11th Cir. 1985) *with Carruthers v. Jenne*, 209 F. Supp. 2d 1294 (S.D. Fla. 2002).

884. Bob Knotts and Bob LaMendola, *Inmates Settle*, Fort Lauderdale Sun-Sentinel, Nov. 17, 1993, at 1B.

885. Ironically, it was during this time that the county began charging inmates two dollars a day for their room and board pursuant to a recently-passed state law. A class action lawsuit challenging this "subsistence fee" on due process grounds was rejected in *Solomos v. Jenne*, 776 So. 2d 953 (Fla. 4th Dist. Ct. App. 2000), *review granted*, 799 So. 219 (Fla. 2001), *and review dismissed*, 820 So. 2d 941 (Fla. 2002).

886. Sallie James, *Navarro Defies Judge: Sheriff Using Tent to House Prisoners*, Fort Lauderdale Sun-Sentinel, Jan. 29, 1989, at 1A.

887. Marcus, *supra* note 671.

888. Jon Marcus, *Judge Threatens to Free Inmates*, Fort Lauderdale Sun-Sentinel, Mar. 4, 1989, at 3B.

889. Knotts and LaMendola, *supra* note 884.

890. Barbara Walsh, *Deputies Picket Against Plan to Privatize County Jail System*, Fort Lauderdale Sun-Sentinel, June 21, 1994, at 3B.

891. Donna Pazdera and Buddy Nevins, *Captive Audience for New Sheriff: Jenne Assumes Command and Unveils His Priorities*, Fort Lauderdale Sun-Sentinel, Jan. 21, 1998, at 1B.

892. Julie Kay, *BSO, Wackenhut Agree on Jail Plan*, Miami Herald, Apr. 1, 1998, at 1 (Broward). Despite these warm remarks, WCC's reliability already was in serious question. In February 1998, the company had begun operating the new Broward County Work Release Center in Pompano Beach, which had been scaled back from the 600 beds that Sheriff Ron Cochran had proposed to a more modest 150 beds. Within weeks of its opening, the institution was rocked by reports that inmates were being abused, trading sex for preferential treatment, and walking away at rates double those of comparable facilities. Despite calls for reform, conditions failed to improve, and in August 1999 the county commission or-

dered Jenne to take charge of the situation, even though the operating agreement it had signed clearly prohibited him from doing so. Finally, in February 2006 the county and WCC agreed to terminate their relationship so that WCC (by now known as The Geo Group, Inc.) could run the building as a federal immigration detainee center.

893. Connie Piloto, *New Jail Finally Opens in Pompano*, Miami Herald, May 21, 1999, at 1B.

BIBLIOGRAPHY

Constitutions and Statutes

Florida Constitution Article IV, § 27 (1861)
Florida Constitution Article XVII, § 5 (1865)
Florida Constitution Article VI, § 19 (1868)
Florida Constitution Article VIII, § 6 and Article XVIII, § 10 (1885)
Florida Constitution Article VIII, § 1(d) (2008)
Florida Statutes §§ 30.07, 30.09, 30.10, 30.15, 30.46, 145.071, 588.12–588.26, 902.21, 950.01, 951.01, and 951.10 (2008)
United States Code title 18, § 3596 (2008)

Cases

Alderman v. United States, 31 F.2d 499 (5th Cir.), *cert. denied*, 279 U.S. 869 (1929)

Bechtol v. Lee, 129 Fla. 374, 176 So. 265 (1937)

Broward County v. Administration Commission, 321 So. 2d 604 (Fla. 1st Dist. Ct. App. 1975)

Broward County v. Administration Commission, 321 So. 2d 605 (Fla. 1st Dist. Ct. App. 1975)

Carruthers v. Jenne, 209 F. Supp. 2d 1294 (S.D. Fla. 2002)

Chambers v. State, 111 Fla. 707, 151 So. 499 (1933) (en banc), *petition granted*, 113 Fla. 786, 152 So. 437 (1934) (Div. B)

Chambers v. State, 136 Fla. 568, 187 So. 156 (1939) (Div. A)

Chambers v. State of Florida, 309 U.S. 227 (1940)

Eaton v. State, 438 So. 2d 822 (Fla. 1983)

Fraternal Order of Police, Sheriff's Lodge No. 32 v. Brescher, 579 F. Supp. 1517 (S.D. Fla. 1984)

Hicks v. State, 97 Fla. 199, 120 So. 330 (1929) (Div. A)

In re Forfeiture of One 1980 53 Foot Hatteras Vessel, 568 So. 2d 443 (Fla. 4th Dist. Ct. App. 1990)

In re Forfeiture of One 1980 53 Foot Hatteras Vessel, 642 So. 2d 1106 (Fla. 4th Dist. Ct. App. 1994)

Jonas v. Stack, 758 F.2d 567 (11th Cir. 1985)

Kelly v. State, 593 So. 2d 1060 (Fla. 4th Dist. Ct. App. 1992)

Lasher v. State, 80 Fla. 712, 86 So. 689 (1920)

Lasseter v. Bryan, 67 Fla. 478, 65 So. 590 (1914)

Lee v. City of Miami, 121 Fla. 93, 163 So. 486 (1935) (en banc)

Lee v. State, 166 So. 2d 131 (Fla. 1964), *cert. denied*, 380 U.S. 917 (1965)

Lee v. State, 188 So. 2d 872 (Fla. 1st Dist. Ct. App. 1966), *cert. denied*, 386 U.S. 983 (1967)

Luke Records, Inc. v. Navarro, 960 F.2d 134 (11th Cir. 1992)

Lynch v. Durrance, 77 So. 2d 458 (Fla. 1955) (Div. A)

Murphy v. Mack, 358 So. 2d 822 (Fla. 1978), *receded from in Coastal Florida Police Benevolent Ass'n, Inc. v. Williams*, 838 So. 2d 543 (Fla. 2003)

Navarro v. Luke Records, 506 U.S. 1022 (1992)

Navarro v. Review Publications, Inc., 503 U.S. 938 (1992)

P.A.B., Inc. v. Stack, 440 F. Supp. 937 (S.D. Fla. 1977)

Pitts v. State, 307 So. 2d 473 (Fla. 1st Dist. Ct. App.), *cert. dismissed*, 423 U.S. 918 (1975)

Polly v. Navarro, 457 So. 2d 1140 (Fla. 4th Dist. Ct. App. 1984)

Pompano Horse Club, Inc. v. State ex rel. Bryan, 93 Fla. 415, 111 So. 801 (1927) (en banc)

Post-Newsweek Stations, Florida Inc. v. Doe, 612 So. 2d 549 (Fla. 1992)

Reinmiller v. State, 93 Fla. 462, 111 So. 633 (1927) (Div. B)

Review Publications v. Navarro, 943 F.2d 1318 (11th Cir. 1991)

Seminole Tribe of Florida v. Butterworth, 491 F. Supp. 1015 (S.D. Fla. 1980), *aff'd*, 658 F.2d 310 (5th Cir. 1981) (Unit B), *cert. denied*, 455 U.S. 1020 (1982)

Shelton v. Reeder, 121 So. 2d 145 (Fla. 1960)

Sikes v. Boone, 562 F. Supp. 74 (N.D. Fla.), *aff'd*, 723 F.2d 918 (11th Cir. 1983), *cert. denied*, 466 U.S. 959 (1984)

Skyywalker Records, Inc. v. Navarro, 739 F. Supp. 578 (S.D. Fla. 1990)

Skyywalker Records, Inc. v. Navarro, 742 F. Supp. 638 (S.D. Fla. 1990)

Sobel v. State, 564 So. 2d 1110 (Fla. 4th Dist. Ct. App. 1990), *review denied*, 576 So. 2d 291 (Fla. 1991)

Solomos v. Jenne, 776 So. 2d 953 (Fla. 4th Dist. Ct. App. 2000), *review granted*, 799 So. 2d 219 (Fla. 2001), *and review dismissed*, 820 So. 2d 941 (Fla. 2002)

Stack v. Adams, 315 F. Supp. 1295 (N.D. Fla. 1970)

State v. Kerwick, 512 So. 2d 347 (Fla. 4th Dist. Ct. App. 1987)

State v. Pitts, 241 So. 2d 399 (Fla. 1st Dist. Ct. App. 1970), *opinion vacated*, 247 So. 2d 53 (Fla.), *and new trial ordered*, 249 So. 2d 47 (Fla. 1st Dist. Ct. App. 1971)

State v. Williams, 623 So. 2d 462 (Fla. 1993)

State ex rel. Kelly v. Sullivan, 52 So. 2d 422 (Fla. 1951) (en banc)

Sullivan v. Leatherman, 48 So. 2d 836 (Fla. 1950) (en banc)

Sweat v. Waldon, 123 Fla. 478, 167 So. 363 (1936) (Div. B)

Tampa Jockey Club v. State, 93 Fla. 459, 111 So. 816 (1927) (en banc)

Von Stein v. Brescher, 696 F. Supp. 606 (S.D. Fla. 1988)

Von Stein v. Brescher, 904 F.2d 572 (11th Cir. 1990)

Warren for Use and Benefit of Cronin v. Hall, 66 So. 2d 230 (Fla. 1953) (Spec. Div. A)

Williams v. Clark, 90 So. 2d 805 (Fla. 1956) (en banc)

Attorney General Opinions

Florida Attorney General Opinion 64-180 (Dec. 18, 1964)

Florida Attorney General Opinion 91-25 (Apr. 18, 1991)

Florida Attorney General Opinion 93-69 (Oct. 8, 1993)

1 United States Attorney General Opinion 185 (Aug. 29, 1815)

Books

Allen, Dale and Rick Capone, *Deerfield Beach* (Charleston, SC: Arcadia Publishing, 2000)

Anderson, Walter H., *A Treatise on the Law of Sheriffs, Coroners, and Constables, with Forms* (Buffalo: Dennis & Company, 1941)

Apel, Dora, *Imagery of Lynching: Black Men, White Women, and the Mob* (Piscataway, NJ: Rutgers University Press, 2004)

Barnes, Jay, *Florida's Hurricane History* (Chapel Hill: University of North Carolina Press, 2d ed. 2007)

Blake, James Carlos, *Red Grass River: A Legend* (New York: Avon Books, Inc., 1998)

Board, Prudy Taylor, *The History of Dania Beach, Florida: A Century of Pioneer Spirit* (Virginia Beach: Donning Company Publishers, 2004)

Bramson, Seth H., *Florida East Coast Railway* (Charleston, SC: Arcadia Publishing, 2006)

Brown, Jr., Canter, *Florida's Peace River Frontier* (Orlando: University of Central Florida Press, 1991)

Bucholz, Andy, *Police Equipment* (San Diego: Thunder Bay Press, 1999)

Burnett, Gene M., *Florida's Past: People and Events That Shaped the State—Volume 1* (Sarasota: Pineapple Press, Inc., 1986)

———, *Florida's Past: People and Events That Shaped the State—Volume 2* (Sarasota: Pineapple Press, Inc., 1988)

Burt, Al, *The Tropic of Cracker* (Gainesville: University of Florida Press, 1999)

Cahill, William P., *The Story of Margate, Florida, 1955–2005* (San Antonio: Historical Publishing Network, 2006)

Calhoun, Frederick S., *The Lawmen: United States Marshals and Their Deputies, 1789–1989* (Washington, DC: Smithsonian Institution Press, 1990)

Campbell, Luther and John R. Miller, *As Nasty As They Wanna Be: The Uncensored Story of Luther Campbell of the 2 Live Crew* (Fort Lee, NJ: Barricade Books, 1992)

Cavaioli, Frank J., *Lauderdale-by-the-Sea* (Charleston, SC: Arcadia Publishing, 2003)

Cuthbertson, Milbrey C., *Broward County: Gateway to the World* (Montgomery, AL: Community Communications, Inc., 1999)

Dinnerstein, Leonard, *The Leo Frank Case* (New York: Columbia University Press, 1968)

Ferrell, Robert H. ed., *FDR's Quiet Confidant: The Autobiography of Frank C. Walker* (Niwot, CO: University Press of Colorado, 1997)

Fielding, Nigel G., *Community Policing* (New York: Oxford University Press Inc., 1995)

Foner, Eric and John A. Garraty eds., *The Reader's Companion to American History* (New York: Houghton Mifflin Company, 1991)

George, Paul S., *Twentieth Century Journey: A History of the City of Oakland Park* (Fort Lauderdale: Historic Broward County Preservation Board, 1991)

Gillis, Susan, *Broward County: The Photography of Gene Hyde* (Charleston, SC: Arcadia Publishing, 2005)

———, *Fort Lauderdale: The Venice of America* (Charleston, SC: Arcadia Publishing, 2004)

——— and Daniel T. Hobby, *Fort Lauderdale* (Charleston, SC: Arcadia Publishing, 1999)

Gorski, Richard, *The Fourteenth-Century Sheriff: English Local Administration in the Late Middle Ages* (Rochester, NY: Boydell Press, 2003)

Greene, Jack R. ed., *The Encyclopedia of Police Science* (New York: Routledge, 3d ed. 2006)

Groneman, Carol, *Nymphomania: A History* (New York: W.W. Norton & Company, 2000)

Guthrie, Jr., John J., *Keepers of the Spirits: The Judicial Response to Prohibition Enforcement in Florida, 1885–1935* (Westport, CT: Greenwood Press, 1998)

Herzog, Arthur, *Vesco* (New York: Doubleday & Company, 1987)

Hobby, Daniel, *Broward County: A Contemporary Portrait* (Virginia Beach: Donning Company Publishers, 1992)

Howard, Walter T., *Lynchings: Extralegal Violence in Florida During the 1930s* (Selinsgrove, PA: Susquehanna University Press, 1995)

Huffstodt, James T., *Everglades Lawmen: True Stories of Game Wardens in the Glades* (Sarasota: Pineapple Press, Inc., 2000)

Kemper, Marlyn, *Dania in Perspective: A Comprehensive Documented History of the City of Dania* (Fort Lauderdale: Historic Broward County Preservation Board, 1983)

————, *Davie in Perspective: A Comprehensive Documented History of the Town of Davie* (Fort Lauderdale: Historic Broward County Preservation Board, 1987)

————, *Hallandale in Perspective: A Comprehensive Documented History of the City of Hallandale* (Fort Lauderdale: Historic Broward County Preservation Board, 1984)

————, *Hollywood in Perspective: A Comprehensive Documented History of the City of Hollywood* (Fort Lauderdale: Historic Broward County Preservation Board, 1982)

————, *Plantation in Perspective: A Comprehensive Documented History of the City of Plantation* (Fort Lauderdale: Historic Broward County Preservation Board, 1986)

————, *Pompano Beach in Perspective: A Comprehensive Documented History of the City of Pompano Beach* (Fort Lauderdale: Historic Broward County Preservation Board, 1982)

Kirk, Cooper, *William Lauderdale: General Andrew Jackson's Warrior* (Fort Lauderdale: Manatee Books, 1982)

Lehman, Frank, *Encounter with the Gulf Stream Pirate* (s.l.: s.n., 1979)

Ling, Sally J., *Run the Rum In: South Florida During Prohibition* (Charleston, SC: History Press, 2007)

Longley, Maximilian, *What Measure Ye Mete: The Life and Times of Judge Halsted Ritter* (Lincoln, NE: iUniverse, Inc., 2003)

Martin, Sidney Walter, *Florida's Flagler* (Athens: University of Georgia Press, 1949)

Maurer, David W., *The Big Con: The Story of the Confidence Man and the Confidence Game* (Indianapolis: The Bobbs Merrill Company, 1940)

McCarthy, Kevin M., *Baseball in Florida* (Sarasota: Pineapple Press, Inc., 1996)

McGoun, William E., *Southeast Florida Pioneers: The Palm and Treasure Coasts* (Sarasota: Pineapple Press, Inc., 1998)

McIver, Stuart, *Glimpses of South Florida History* (Miami: Florida Flair Books, 1988)

McIver, Stuart B., *Coral Springs: The First Twenty-Five Years* (Norfolk: Donning Company, 1988)

————, *Dreamers, Schemers and Scalawags: The Florida Chronicles (Vol. 1)* (Sarasota: Pineapple Press, Inc., 1994)

————, *Greater Fort Lauderdale and Broward County: The Venice of America* (Fort Lauderdale: Copperfield Publications, 1999)

————, *Fort Lauderdale and Broward County: An Illustrated History* (Woodlands Hills, CA: Windsor Publications, Inc., 1983)

————, *The Island City: The Story of Wilton Manors* (Wilton Manors, FL: City of Wilton Manors, 1997)

Messick, Hank, *Syndicate in the Sun* (New York: Macmillan, 1968)

Miller, Gene, *Invitation to a Lynching* (Garden City, NY: Doubleday & Company, 1975)

Miller, Nyle H. and Joseph W. Snell, *Why the West Was Wild: A Contemporary Look at the Antics of Some Highly Publicized Kansas Cowtown Personalities* (Norman: University of Oklahoma Press, 2003)

Missall, John and Mary Lou Missall, *The Seminole Wars: America's Longest Indian Conflict* (Gainesville: University Press of Florida, 2004)

Morris, Allen, *Florida Place Names: Alachua to Zolfo Springs* (Sarasota: Pineapple Press, Inc., 1995)

Morris, Peter F. and Catherine A. Perkins, *The Florida Reference Guide to Correctional Statutes, Standards and Institutions* (Flushing, NY: Looseleaf Law Publications, Inc., 2008)

Morris, William Alfred, *The Medieval English Sheriff to 1300* (London: Manchester University Press, 1927)

Mustaine, Beverly, *On Lake Worth* (Charleston, SC: Arcadia Publishing, 1999)

Navarro, Nick and Jeff Sadler, *The Cuban Cop* (Boca Raton: TransMedia Publishing, Inc., 1998)

Newton, Michael, *The Encyclopedia of American Law Enforcement* (New York: Facts on File, 2007)

Ostrom, Thomas P., *The United States Coast Guard: 1790 to the Present* (Oakland, OR: Red Anvil Press, rev. ed. 2006)

Proctor, Samuel, *Napoleon Bonaparte Broward: Florida's Fighting Democrat* (Gainesville: University of Florida Press, 1950)

Richard, Candice, *Seventy-Three Years by the Sea: Lauderdale-by-the-Sea, 1924–1997* (Lauderdale-by-the-Sea, FL: City of Lauderdale-by-the-Sea, 1997)

Roesch, Brian K., *Another Sixth Sense: The Fort Lauderdale Story* (Lincoln, NE: Writers Club Press, 2002)

Rogers, William Warren and James M. Denham, *Florida Sheriffs: A History, 1821–1945* (Tallahassee: Sentry Press, 2001)

Sarubbi, Doug ed., *Orange County Sheriff's Office, Orlando, Florida—150th Anniversary History Book* (Paducah, KY: Turner Publishing Co., 1994)

Sherwood, Frank P., *County Governments in Florida* (Lincoln, NE: iUniverse, 2008)

Silvestri, Victor R., *Encyclopedia of Florida Sheriffs 1821–2008* (Clanton, AL: Heritage Publishing Consultants, Inc., 2009)

Simmons, Glen and Laura Ogden, *Gladesmen: Gator Hunters, Moonshiners, and Skiffers* (Gainseville: University of Florida Press, 1998)

Simms, Louis M., *In Place of Pearls: A Brief History of Deerfield Beach* (Hamilton, New Zealand: RIMU, 1984)

Spencer, Donald D., *History of Gambling in Florida* (Ormond Beach, FL: Camelot Publishing Company, 2007)

Ste. Claire, Dana, *Cracker: The Cracker Culture in Florida History* (Gainesville: University Press of Florida, 1998)

Stevens, Dennis J., *An Introduction to American Policing* (Sudbury, MA: Jones and Bartlett Publishers, 2008)

Stuart, Hix C., *The Notorious Ashley Gang: A Saga of the King and Queen of the Everglades* (Stuart, FL: St. Lucie Printing Co., 1928)

Sullivan, Larry E. ed., *Encyclopedia of Law Enforcement* (Thousand Oaks, CA: Sage Publications, 2005)

Swanson, Charles R. et al. eds., *Police Administration: Structures, Processes, and Behavior* (Upper Saddle River, NJ: Pearson Prentice Hall, 7th ed. 2008)

Thuma, Cynthia, *Wilton Manors* (Charleston, SC: Arcadia Publishing, 2005)

Thuma, Cynthia A., *Sport Lauderdale: Big Names and Big Games* (Charleston, SC: History Press, 2007)

Tinsley, Jim Bob, *Florida Cow Hunter: The Life and Times of Bone Mizell* (Orlando: University of Central Florida Press, 1990)

Van Deusen, Glyndon G., *William Henry Seward* (New York: Oxford University Press, 1967)

Vestal, Stanley, *Dodge City: Queen of Cowtowns* (New York: Harper & Brothers, 1952)

Vogel, Ronald K., *Urban Political Economy: Broward County, Florida* (Gainesville: University of Florida Press, 1992)

Wagner, Victoria, *The History of Davie and Its Dilemma* (Fort Lauderdale: Nova/NYIT University Press, 1982)

Wagy, Tom R., *Governor LeRoy Collins of Florida: Spokesman of the New South* (University, AL: University of Alabama Press, 1985)

Wangberg, Wendy and Kevin Knutson, *Coral Springs* (Charleston, SC: Arcadia Publishing, 2003)

Warner, David T., *High-Sheriff Jim Turner: High Times of a Florida Lawman* (Montgomery, AL: Black Belt Press, 1998)

Weidling, Philip and August Burghard, *Checkered Sunshine: The Story of Fort Lauderdale, 1793–1955* (Gainesville: University of Florida Press, 1966)

Wilbanks, William, *Forgotten Heroes: Police Officers Killed in Early Florida, 1840–1925* (Paducah, KY: Turner Publishing Company, 1998)

Wilson, Jeremy M., *Community Policing in America* (New York: Routledge, 2006)

Wise, Dennis, *"Honor" Above All Else: Removing the Veil of Secrecy* (Bloomington, IN: AuthorHouse, 2006)

Yant, Martin, *Tin Star Tyrants: America's Crooked Sheriffs* (Buffalo: Prometheus Books, 1992)

Chapters

Coltoff, Paul et al., "Sheriffs and Constables," *in* 80 *Corpus Juris Secundum: A Contemporary Statement of American Law as Derived from Reported Cases and Legislation* (St. Paul, MN: West Group, 2000)

Gustafson, Jill and Barbara J. VanArsdale, "Police, Sheriffs, and Other Law Enforcement Officers," *in* 40 *Florida Jurisprudence 2d* (Eagan, MN: Thomson/West, 2008)

Porter, Robert P. et al., "Progress of the Nation 1790 to 1890," *in* I Department of the Interior, *Report on Population of the United States at the Eleventh Census: 1890* (Washington, DC: U.S. Government Printing Office, 1895)

"Hanging a Pirate," *in* McIver, Stuart B., *Murder in the Tropics: The Florida Chronicles (Vol. 2)* (Sarasota: Pineapple Press, Inc., 1995)

"Stop and Go," *in* McIver, Stuart B., *Touched by the Sun* (Sarasota: Pineapple Press, Inc., 2001)

"The Liquor Pirate, 1929," *in* McCarthy, Kevin M. and William L. Trotter, *Twenty Florida Pirates* (Sarasota: Pineapple Press, Inc., 1994)

"The Waco Kid," *in* Borchard, Edwin M., *Convicting the Innocent: Errors of Criminal Justice* (New Haven, CT: Yale University Press, 1932)

Articles

Anonymous, *The White Flag [of Osceola]*, 33 Florida Historical Quarterly 218 (January–April 1955)

Bousquet, Stephen C., *The Gangster in our Midst: Al Capone in South Florida, 1930–1947*, 76 Florida Historical Quarterly 297 (Winter 1998)

Boyd, Mark F., *The Seminole War: Its Background and Onset*, 30 Florida Historical Quarterly 3 (July 1951)

Brooks, Jr., James Thomas, *Napoleon Broward and the Great Land Debate*, 11 Broward Legacy 40 (Winter/Spring 1988)

Brown, Jr., Canter, *The Florida Crisis of 1826–1827 and the Second Seminole War*, 73 Florida Historical Quarterly 419 (April 1995)

Cahill, William P., *The First Sheriffs of Broward County, Florida: 1915–1933*, 24 Broward Legacy 3 (2003–2004)

Carter, III, James A., *Florida and Rumrunning During National Prohibition*, 48 Florida Historical Quarterly 47 (July 1969)

Chalmers, David, *The Ku Klux Klan in the Sunshine State: The 1920's*, 42 Florida Historical Quarterly 209 (January 1964)

Clark, James C., *Civil Rights Leader Harry T. Moore and the Klu Klux Klan in Florida*, 73 Florida Historical Quarterly 166 (October 1994)

Crawford, Jr., William G., *Broward County Courthouse History: The Forties*, 17 Broward Legacy 14 (Winter/Spring 1994)

———, *Capone Island—From Swampland to Broward County's Deerfield Island Park: 150 Years of Florida Land History*, 19 Broward Legacy 2 (Summer/Fall 1996)

———, *Judge Vincent C. Giblin: Broward's First Circuit Judge was Capone's Lawyer, Dade Judge in the '50s*, 18 Broward Legacy 2 (Summer/Fall 1995)

———, *The Long Hard Fight for Equal Rights: A History of Broward County's Colored Beach and the Fort Lauderdale Beach 'Wade-ins' of the Summer of 1961*, 67 Tequesta 19 (2007)

Cunningham, Denyse, *The Big Blow: Broward County and the 1926 Hurricane*, 28 Broward Legacy 2 (Summer 2008)

Davis, Jack E., *"Whitewash" in Florida: The Lynching of Jesse James Payne and Its Aftermath*, 68 Florida Historical Quarterly 277 (January 1990)

Dibble, Ernest F., *Giveaway Forts: Territorial Forts and the Settlement of Florida*, 78 Florida Historical Quarterly 207 (Fall 1999)

Dillon, Jr., Rodney E., *South Florida in 1860*, 60 Florida Historical Quarterly 440 (April 1982)

Dovell, J.E., *The Everglades Before Reclamation*, 26 Florida Historical Quarterly 1 (July 1947)

Flynt, Wayne, *Religion at the Polls: A Case Study of Twentieth-Century Politics and Religion in Florida*, 72 Florida Historical Quarterly 469 (April 1994)

———, *Sidney J. Catts: The Road to Power*, 49 Florida Historical Quarterly 107 (October 1970)

George, Paul S., *Flamboyant Floranada: Broward's Unique Boom-Era Development*, 15 Broward Legacy 2 (Summer/Fall 1992)

———, *Where the Boys Were*, 18 South Florida History Magazine 5 (Winter 1991)

Givonetti, L. Davis, *Fort Lauderdale's Shame: Nativism and the Julia Murphy Incident*, 18 Broward Legacy 21 (Summer/Fall 1995)

Guthrie, Jr., John J., *Rekindling the Spirits: From National Prohibition to Local Option in Florida, 1928–1935*, 74 Florida Historical Quarterly 23 (Summer 1995)

Hughes, Kenneth J., *Survey of Old Cars: The First Registered Motor Vehicles in Broward County, Florida: October 1915 to July 1916*, 21 Broward Legacy 18 (Summer/Fall 1998)

Jarvis, Robert M., *Case Note: Territorial Waters*, 34 Journal of Maritime Law and Commerce 351 (April 2003)

———, *The 2007 Seminole-Florida Gambling Compact*, 12 Gaming Law Review 13 (February 2008)

——— and Phyllis Coleman, *Early Baseball Law*, 45 American Journal of Legal History 117 (April 2001)

Kemper, Marilyn, *On Trial: William A. (Bill) Hicks*, 1 Broward Legacy 8 (January 1977)

King, Vivian R., *Anything Goes or Enough Already? Sexually Explicit Lyrics: Florida and Texas Prospectives—Skyywalker Records, Inc. v. Navarro*, 17 Thurgood Marshall Law Review 113 (Fall 1991) (student comment)

Kirk, Cooper, *Andrew Christian Frost: Founder of Dania*, 3 Broward Legacy 16 (Summer/Fall 1979)

———, *Foundations of Broward County Waterways*, 8 Broward Legacy 2 (Winter/Spring 1985)

———, *The Abortive Attempt to Create Broward County in 1913*, 12 Broward Legacy 2 (Winter/Spring 1989)

———, *The Vanished Communities of Broward County*, 14 Broward Legacy 20 (Summer/Fall 1991)

Knetsch, Joe, *Governor Broward and the Details of Dredging: 1908*, 14 Broward Legacy 38 (Winter/Spring 1991)

———, *Jesup's Strategy, the Founding of Fort Lauderdale and the Role of Lieutenant Colonel James Bankhead*, 19 Broward Legacy 19 (Winter/Spring 1996)

———, *The Impact of Drainage on the Development of Early Broward County*, 20 Broward Legacy 30 (Winter/Spring 1997)

——— and Laura Ethridge, *An Historical Overview of Broward County Agriculture, 1915–1940*, 15 Broward Legacy 21 (Winter/Spring 1992)

Knott, James R., *Napoleon B. Broward: Life and Times of a Florida Governor—Story of Broward County's Namesake*, 3 Broward Legacy 2 (Summer/Fall 1979)

Kramer, William H., *Walter Reid Clark—Broward County's Legendary Sheriff: The Formative Years*, 14 Broward Legacy 25 (Winter/Spring 1991)

Lester, Donald G., *Broward Politics 1928–1938: Political Influence in Depression Era Broward*, 13 Broward Legacy 2 (Summer/Fall 1990)

———, *Justice of the Peace W.A. Hicks*, 15 Broward Legacy 2 (Winter/Spring 1992)

———, *The Darsey Case: Little Scottsboro Revisited*, 11 Broward Legacy 2 (Winter/Spring 1988)

———, *The Fort Lauderdale Daily News and the Broward Sheriff's Office 1948–1951*, 20 Broward Legacy 2 (Winter/Spring 1997)

———, *The Pompano Race Track Confronts the Martin Administration*, 17 Broward Legacy 2 (Winter/Spring 1994)

Mahon, John K., *The First Seminole War, November 21, 1817–May 24, 1818*, 77 Florida Historical Quarterly 62 (Summer 1998)

Martin, Harold, *Real Baseball Provided by the East Coast League*, 5 Broward Legacy 2 (Winter/Spring 1982)

McGoun, Bill, *A History of Broward County*, 2 Broward Legacy 15 (September 1978)

McPherson, William, *Managing the Mental Health Population at the Broward Sheriff's Office*, 70 Corrections Today 62 (June 2008)

Megna, Ralph J. and Patrick R. Currie, *Draining the Everglades: Governor Broward's Plan Makes Possible the Development of South Florida*, 2 Broward Legacy 29 (September 1978)

Otto, John S., *Open-Range Cattle-Herding in Southern Florida*, 65 Florida Historical Quarterly 317 (January 1987)

Page, David P., *Bishop Michael J. Curley and Anti-Catholic Nativism in Florida*, 45 Florida Historical Quarterly 101 (October 1966)

Parsons, Marjorie Dickey, *The October 1947 "Hurricane": Disaster on Top of Disaster*, 14 Broward Legacy 31 (Summer/Fall 1991)

Pleasants, Julian M., *Frederic Remington in Florida*, 56 Florida Historical Quarterly 1 (July 1977)

Poleo, Barbara A., *Seminoles and Settlers: South Florida Perspectives 1890–1920*, 21 Broward Legacy 18 (Winter/Spring 1998)

Prior, Leon O., *German Espionage in Florida During World War II*, 39 Florida Historical Quarterly 374 (April 1961)

Remington, Frederic, *Cracker Cowboys of Florida*, 91 Harper's New Monthly Magazine 339 (August 1895)

Scott, Patrick S., *Early Broward County Airports*, 25 Broward Legacy 2 (2004–2005)

Silverstein, Judy, *The Gulfstream Pirate*, 6 Coast Guard Magazine 28 (2007)

Skidmore, Max J., *The Folk Culture of "The Travelers": Clans of Con Artists*, 20 Journal of American Culture 73 (Fall 1997)

Steele, W.S., *Last Command: The Dade Massacre*, 46 Tequesta 5 (1986)

Symposium, *The Complete Story of Osceola*, 33 Florida Historical Quarterly 161 (January–April 1955)

Symposium, *The Creation of Broward County*, 11 Broward Legacy 2 (Summer/Fall 1988)

Williams, Wilma, *Hollywood During the Depression*, 4 Broward Legacy 28 (Summer/Fall 1981)

Winsberg, Morton D., *The Advance of Florida's Frontier as Determined from Post Office Openings*, 72 Florida Historical Quarterly 189 (October 1993)

Youngs, Larry R., *The Sporting Set Winters in Florida: Fertile Ground for the Leisure Revolution, 1870–1930*, 84 Florida Historical Quarterly 57 (Summer 2005)

Theses

Carroll, John J., *Comparing Regulatory and Distributive Police Programs for Crime Reduction: An Evaluation of Effectiveness and Efficiency* (2003) (unpublished Ph.D. dissertation, Florida Atlantic University)

Johns, Claude J., *A Case Study on the Sheriff's Office in Three Florida Counties* (1953) (unpublished M.S. dissertation, Florida State University)

Kramer, William H., *Walter Reid Clark: Legendary Sheriff of Broward County* (1993) (unpublished M.A. dissertation, Florida Atlantic University)

Morin, Christopher S., *The Relationship Between a Sheriff's Educational Level and Incentives Offered by the Sheriff's Office to Obtain a College Education* (1995) (unpublished M.A. dissertation, University of South Florida)

Robbins II, Ray F., *The Socialist Party in Florida: 1900–1916* (1971) (unpublished M.A. dissertation, Samford University)

Surette, Raymond B., *Uncertainty and Organizational Reaction: The Special Case of Sheriff Elections and Arrests* (1979) (unpublished Ph.D. dissertation, Florida State University)

Swando, Matthew J., *An Analysis of the Effects of Officer Demographic Characteristics, Work Orientations, and Agency Readiness on Openness to Organizational Change: Community Policing in a Sheriff's Office* (2000) (unpublished M.A. dissertation, University of South Florida)

Walgren, Jennifer, *An Examination of the Effects of Sheriff's Deputies' Readiness to Implement Community-Oriented Policing on Job Satisfaction* (2000) (unpublished M.A. dissertation, University of South Florida)

Newspapers

Broward Daily Business Review
Fort Lauderdale Daily News

Fort Lauderdale Herald
Fort Lauderdale News
Fort Lauderdale Sentinel
Fort Lauderdale Sun-Sentinel
Fort Lauderdale Sunday News
Hollywood Sun-Tattler
Miami Herald
New York Times
Palm Beach Post
Panama City News Herald
Rollins Sandspur
South Florida Sun-Sentinel
St. Petersburg Evening Independent
St. Petersburg Times

Web Sites

Broward County Crime Commission, http://www.browardcrime.com
Broward County Historical Commission, http://www.broward.org/history
Broward Sheriff's Office, http://www.sheriff.org
———, *Setting the Record Straight*, http://browardsheriff.blogspot.com
Buffardi, Harry C., *The History of the Office of Sheriff*, http://www.correction
    history.org/html/chronicl/sheriff/toc.htm
Commission on Accreditation for Law Enforcement Agencies, http://www.calea.org
Crawford, William G., Jr., *Window Into Time: A History of the Broward County
    Courthouse*, http://www.browardbar.org/courthouse/index.htm
Crime Stoppers International, http://www.c-s-i.org
Duay, Debbie L., *Broward County Cemetery Records—Broward County, Florida*,
    http://www.learnwebskills.com/browardcem/index.htm
———, *Broward County Elected Officials and Their Families, 1915 to 1969*,
    http://www.learnwebskills.com/sar/browardofficials.htm
Florida Legislative Committee on Intergovernmental Relations, http://www.florida
    lcir.gov
Florida Peace Officers' Association, Inc., http://www.myfpoa.org
Florida Police Chiefs Association, http://www.fpca.com
Florida Sheriffs Association, http://www.flsheriffs.org
Genealogical Society of Broward County Florida (GSBC), http://www.rootsweb.
    ancestry.com/~flgsbc/
Harris, Jay, *Broward Sheriff's Office Insignia, Badge and Patch Collection*,
    http://www.patchmethru.com/broward.html

Heritage Microfilm, Inc., *NewspaperArchive.com*, http://www.newspaperarchive.com
National Sheriffs' Association, http://www.sheriffs.org
Ruby, Pat, *A History of the Fort Lauderdale Police Department*, http://www.flpd.org/
    index.aspx?page=41
The Generations Network, *Ancestry Library Edition*, http://www.ancestrylibrary.com
The Officer Down Memorial Page, Inc., *Broward County Sheriff's Office*,
    http://www.odmp.org/agency/428-broward-county-sheriffs-office-florida
Tipton, Jim, *Find a Grave*, http://www.findagrave.com

Correspondence (from the files of the Broward County Historical Commission)

Letter from Paul C. Bryan, Sheriff of Broward County, to O.W. Brady, dated
    July 23, 1926
Letter from Paul C. Bryan, Sheriff of Broward County, to P.F. Hambsch, Pro-
    hibition Administrator, dated Apr. 17, 1926
Letter from Paul C. Bryan, Sheriff of Broward County, to D.E. Richer, In-
    spector—American Express Company, dated June 12, 1925
Letter from Paul C. Bryan, Sheriff of Broward County, to David Sholtz, Pres-
    ident—Florida State Chamber of Commerce, dated Nov. 21, 1927
Letter from Walter R. Clark, Sheriff of Broward County, to Kenneth A. Mar-
    mon, Superintendent—Seminole Indian Agency, dated Mar. 30, 1948
Letter from P.F. Hambsch, Prohibition Administrator, to Paul C. Bryan, Sher-
    iff of Broward County, dated Apr. 15, 1926
Letter from Cary A. Hardee, Governor of Florida, to Paul C. Bryan, Sheriff of
    Broward County, dated May 24, 1923
Letter from Cary A. Hardee, Governor of Florida, to Paul C. Bryan, Sheriff of
    Broward County, dated Dec. 27, 1923
Letter from Cary A. Hardee, Governor of Florida, to Paul C. Bryan, Sheriff of
    Broward County, dated Sept. 16, 1924
Letter from L.M. Hatton, Jr., Sheriff of Hillsborough County, to Aden W.
    Turner, Sheriff of Broward County, dated Feb. 1, 1929
Letter from Cary D. Landis, Attorney General of Florida, to Aden W. Turner,
    Sheriff of Broward County, dated May 17, 1932
Letter from Leo M. Mack, Chief Deputy, U.S. Marshal's Office—Jacksonville,
    to Aden W. Turner, Sheriff of Broward County, dated Sept. 14, 1929
Letter from Norman MacKay, Advertising Director—Miami Broadcasting
    Company, to Aden W. Turner, Sheriff of Broward County, dated May 13, 1932
Letter from John M. Peterman, Architect—Broward County Courthouse, to
    Paul C. Bryan, Sheriff of Broward County, dated Jan. 14, 1926

Letter from D.E. Richer, Inspector—American Express Company, to Paul C. Bryan, Sheriff of Broward County, dated June 9, 1925

Letter from Halsted L. Ritter, U.S. District Judge—Southern District of Florida, to Aden W. Turner, Sheriff of Broward County, dated July 19, 1929

Letter from John W. Tidball, President—Fort Lauderdale Chamber of Commerce, to Paul C. Bryan, Sheriff of Broward County, dated May 5, 1925

Letter from B.A. Tolbert, Dean of Students—University of Florida, to Aden W. Turner, Sheriff of Broward County, dated Nov. 18, 1931

Letter from Aden W. Turner, Sheriff of Broward County, to Ernest Amos, Comptroller of Florida, dated Jan. 15, 1930

Letter from Aden W. Turner, Sheriff of Broward County, to Doyle E. Carlton, Governor of Florida, dated Mar. 8, 1929

Letter from Aden W. Turner, Sheriff of Broward County, to Doyle E. Carlton, Governor of Florida, dated Aug. 6, 1930

Letter from Aden W. Turner, Sheriff of Broward County, to F.O. Dickinson, dated Sept. 3, 1930

Letter from Aden W. Turner, Sheriff of Broward County, to the H. & W.B. Drew Company—Jacksonville, dated Oct. 17, 1930

Letter from Aden W. Turner, Sheriff of Broward County, to William Gregory, dated Feb. 13, 1930

Letter from Aden W. Turner, Sheriff of Broward County, to J.A. Johnson, Sheriff of Polk County, dated Jan. 13, 1931

Letter from Aden W. Turner, Sheriff of Broward County, to Frank Karel, Sheriff of Orange County, dated Jan. 21, 1931

Letter from Aden W. Turner, Sheriff of Broward County, to Cary D. Landis, Attorney General of Florida, dated Feb. 3, 1932

Letter from Aden W. Turner, Sheriff of Broward County, to Leo M. Mack, Chief Deputy, U.S. Marshal's Office—Jacksonville, dated July 27, 1932

Letter from Aden W. Turner, Sheriff of Broward County, to J.C. Sheffield, Chief of the U.S. Immigration Service—West Palm Beach Office, dated Apr. 4, 1929

Letter from Aden W. Turner, Sheriff of Broward County, to Richard W. Thomas, Sheriff of Oneida County (N.Y.), dated Mar. 5, 1931

Letter from Aden W. Turner, Sheriff of Broward County, to U.S. Marshal's Office—Miami, dated May 16, 1932

Report of Aden W. Turner, Sheriff of Broward County, to Ernest Amos, Comptroller of Florida, dated June 30, 1930, at 1

Report of Aden W. Turner, Sheriff of Broward County, to Ernest Amos, Comptroller of Florida, dated Dec. 31, 1931, at 1

Telegram from Paul C. Bryan, Sheriff of Broward County, to John W. Martin, Governor of Florida, dated Mar. 12, 1927

Telegram from Paul C. Bryan, Sheriff of Broward County, to John W. Martin, Governor of Florida, dated Jan. 5, 1928
Telegram from Aden W. Turner, Sheriff of Broward County, to Richard W. Thomas, Sheriff of Oneida County (N.Y.), dated Dec. 24, 1931

Death Certificates

Baltimore City Health Department, Certificate of Death for Walter Reed [sic] Clark, dated Apr. 27, 1951 (Registration No. 51-3847) (Dr. Marjorie F. Ellicott—Johns Hopkins Hospital)
Department of Health and Rehabilitative Services—Division of Health, Bureau of Vital Statistics, Certificate of Death (Florida) for Justice A. Lloyd, dated May 11, 1978 (State File No. 78-037062) (Dr. Jose Rozas—South Florida State Hospital)
Office of Vital Statistics, Certificate of Death (Florida) for Ronald Alva Cochran, dated Sept. 8, 1997 (State File No. 97-103459) (Dr. Frederick Wittlin)
Office of Vital Statistics, Amended Certificate of Death (Florida) for Allen Brandt Michell, dated Mar. 7, 1983 (State File No. 83-029159) (Dr. John L. Ingham—Royal Oaks Nursing Resort)
Office of Vital Statistics, Certificate of Death (Florida) for Edward John Stack, dated Nov. 8, 1989 (State File No. 89-110319) (Dr. Pierre Courchesne—Imperial Point Medical Center)
State Board of Health—Bureau of Vital Statistics, Certificate of Death (Florida) for Paul C. Bryan, dated July 16, 1942 (State File No. 14016, Registrar's No. 969) (Dr. William E. Kendall—Bay Pines Veterans Administration Facility)
State Board of Health—Bureau of Vital Statistics, Certificate of Death (Florida) for Amos Harris Hall, dated Sept. 4, 1966 (State File No. 66-042909) (Dr. Roger K. Haugen—Broward County Medical Examiner's Office)
State Board of Health—Bureau of Vital Statistics, Certificate of Death (Florida) for Edward Tullis Lee, dated Feb. 19, 1969 (State File No. 69-008894, Registrar's No. 1975) (Dr. Dimitri L. Contostavlos—Dade County Medical Examiner's Office)
State Board of Health—Bureau of Vital Statistics, Certificate of Death (Florida) for Aden Waterman Turner, dated Dec. 13, 1940 (State File No. 22294, Registrar's No. 655) (Dr. Curtis H. Sory)

About the Authors

William P. Cahill (CahillWilliamP@aol.com) holds a B.S. in Mathematics from St. John's University, an M.A. in Clinical Psychology from Fordham University, and an Ed.D. in Higher Education from Florida Atlantic University. At his retirement in 2005, he was a faculty member at Florida Atlantic University, having previously taught at Nova Southeastern University and the University of Maryland. He is the author of *The Story of Margate, Florida, 1955–2005* (San Antonio: Historical Publishing Network, 2006).

Robert M. Jarvis (jarvisb@nsu.law.nova.edu) holds a B.A. in Political Science from Northwestern University, a J.D. from the University of Pennsylvania, and an LL.M. from New York University. Since 1987, he has been a professor of law at Nova Southeastern University. This is his eighteenth book.

INDEX

Ghiotto, Frank, 167, 169–70, 178, 179
Giblin, Vincent C., 69, 72
Glisson, Dorothy W., 243
Glynn, Jr., William G., 239
Goldberg, Daniel D., 239
Gombos, John A., 388 n.861
Gonzalez, Jr., Jose A., 183, 234, 265
Goodbread, Kossie A., 20, 22, 27
Goodrich, C. "Dick," 86
Goodrum, Daniel S., 268
Gordon, J.K., 325
Gore, Alonzo P. "Lon," 36, 37
Gore, Jack W., 167
Gore, Sr., Robert H., 112, 114, 115, 193
Gornto, Quinten M., 37–38
Graham, D. Robert "Bob," 229, 231, 235, 241, 243, 244
Grant, Lionel, 140–42
Gray, Robert, 95
Gray, Steadman T., 59, 60
Green, William, 145
Griffin, Jeanine, 161
Griffin, William E., 161–62
Griffith, Andy, xxiv, xxv
Grigsby, Ben W., 138–39, 140–41, 142, 143, 146, 148, 151, 155, 161
Grimes, E.G., 53, 56
Grossman, Melvin B. "Mel," 232–33, 265
Grossman, Nicki E., 285, 287
Guardabassi, Frederick W., 309
Gunn, James, 147

Halaska, Tony, 235
Hall, Amos H.
    Biographical details, 121–23, 134, 135–36
    Criminal cases and investigations
        Alcohol, 125

Cattle rustling, 126
Gambling, 123–25, 134
Death, 135–36
Deputies
    Appointment of African-Americans, 126–28
    Controversy regarding location of, 126
    Expansion in number of, 128
    Motorcycle squad, creation of, 128–29
    Pay and benefits, 155, 159
    Praise for, 137–38
    Shakeup upon taking office, 123–24
    Shortening of work week, 128
    Traffic division, creation of, 128–29
Divorce, 134
Inter-agency relations, 125, 128–30
Jail operations, 333
Later life and legacy, 130–31, 135–36
Named sheriff of Broward County (1950), 121
Photographs of, 123, 129, 130
Sheriff elections
    1952 race (won), 126
    1956 race (declined to run), 130–31
Tombstone, 136
Hall, Betty, 135
Hall, Floyd, 199
Hall, Gladys, 134
Hambsch, Philip F., 55
Hankerson, Ozie, 127–28
Hansen, Ed, 102, 103, 107, 331
Hansen, Jim, 260
Hardee, Cary A., xxiv, 40, 42, 43, 45, 46, 47–49, 53, 56, 359 n.64
Hardie, Dan, 52